Amidst Cheers, They Marched to War

Hannah Spencer has spent most of her life in the villages of Preston on Stour and Wimpstone. She has been researching local history for several years and also writes for various local history and family history magazines. Find her at http://hannah-spencer-author.weebly.com or http://100daysofhistory.blogspot.co.uk

Also by the author:

Non-fiction

Preston on Stour: A Two Thousand Year History, 2016, Matador.

Fiction

The Story of Light, 2014, Moon Books.

The Wolf of Allendale, 2017, HarperLegend.

AMIDST CHEERS, THEY MARCHED TO WAR

Four Warwickshire Villages.
One Century of Conflict.

HANNAH SPENCER

Matador
9 Priory Business Park,
Wistow Road, Kibworth Beauchamp,
Leicestershire. LE8 0RX
Tel: 0116 279 2299
Email: books@troubador.co.uk
Web: www.troubador.co.uk/matador
Twitter: @matadorbooks

ISBN 978 1789014 594

British Library Cataloguing in Publication Data.
A catalogue record for this book is available from the British Library.

Printed and bound by CPI Group (UK) Ltd, Croydon, CR0 4YY
Typeset in 11pt AdobeGaramond Pro by Troubador Publishing Ltd, Leicester, UK

Matador is an imprint of Troubador Publishing Ltd

Acknowledgements

Firstly, my grateful thanks to everybody who has shared photographs, family stories and memories of the two world wars and brought this book to life.

Also thanks to Mick Jennings for advice on the manuscript. Pete Mumford, Pete Summerton, Matt Evans (www.aviationarchaeology.org.uk), Nick Pratley and the late Jack Pratley for their generous sharing of research and archive material. Robert Howe and Richard Parnham for sharing research and extensive local knowledge. Will Spencer for help and sharing research. Roger, David and Alison Hawkins for permission to explore Atherstone aerodrome. Dr Bob Shaw of Defford Airfield Heritage Group and the staff of Wellesbourne Military Museum for advice and expertise. The RAF Museum for the site plan of Atherstone airfield. www.aircrewremembered.com for supplying photographs.

Contents

Introduction xi
Map 1 xii
Ranks of the Armed Services xiii
Army Structure xv
Abbreviations xvi

1. The Earliest Armies 1
The Early Militias 1
The Birth of the English Army 3
The Napoleonic Wars 5

2. Victoria's Army 8
The Crimean War 8
A Modern Army 10
Life in the Army 14
Service Overseas 20
British North America 20
India 22
Afghanistan 31
Egypt and The Sudan 33
West Africa 37

3. The Anglo-Boer War 39
The War 41
The Flame Reignites 42
The End of the War 45

4. The Royal Navy 47
The Alscot Villages 48

5. The First World War 57
On the Eve of War 57
Kitchener's Volunteers 61
The Fighting Begins 65
The Western Front in 1915 68
The Desperate Need for Men 81
Love and War 89
The Battle of the Somme 91
The Royal Engineers (RE) 99
The Royal Army Medical Corps (RAMC) 101
The Machine Gun Corps 104
The Royal Artillery 105
The Army Service Corps (ASC) 110
The Labour Corps 116
The Royal Navy 118
The Gallipoli Campaign 123
The Mesopotamian Campaign 126
The Sinai and Palestine Campaign 128
The War in West Africa 131
The Canadian Expeditionary Force 132
The Battle of Arras 136
The Battle of Hill 70 141
The Australian Imperial Force (AIF) 142
The Third Battle of Ypres (Passchendaele) 143
The Battle of Cambrai 148
The Royal Airforce 151
The Western Front in 1918 152
The Michael Offensive 153
The Turning Point 160
The Hundred Days Offensive 161
The Aftermath 170
The Future 172

6. The Second World War 181
The Fighting Begins 182

The War Comes to Britain 187
Life on the Home Front 198
Feeding the Nation 204
The Army after Dunkirk 209
The North African Campaign 211
The Sicily and Italy Campaigns 217
The South East Asia Campaign 219
The Royal Navy 224
The Royal Airforce 229
The Return to France 235
After the War 242

7. RAF Atherstone on Stour (RAF Stratford) 247
Operational Use 265
The Training Wing 266
Airfield Life 269
The Air Crews 272
The Thousand Bomber Raids 283
Operations from 1943 287
The End of the War 291

And Finally… 297
Conclusion 298
Gazetteer of Military Personnel 299
Known Fatalities of RAF Stratford Airmen 305
Sources and Bibliography 309
Index of Surnames 311

Introduction

War has been a part of life for millennia, but over the past century it has shaped our world more than ever. The British armed forces created Queen Victoria's empire, and helped redefine the modern era through two world wars. Even the smallest communities have cheered their men as they marched away, and laid wreaths for those who didn't return.

During this time, four villages formed the core of the Alscot Estate in Warwickshire, which has been owned by the West family of Alscot Park for over 250 years. These are Preston on Stour, Alderminster, Atherstone on Stour with the hamlet of Ailstone, and Whitchurch with the hamlets of Wimpstone and Crimscote. They have all been unusually untouched by modern development, and so retained their sense of heritage and community into modern times. Many families living in these small villages today have connections stretching back generations. This makes the tragic cost of war even greater.

Over two hundred men and women from these villages served in the armed forces between Victoria's reign and the Second World War. Some enlisted in search of a better life or adventure. Others through coercion as the people around them volunteered. More still were conscripted. Men from the Alscot villages lie in graves in France, India, Iraq, Burma, South Africa and many other places besides. Some of their graves are remembered in perpetuity. Others are not.

History often focusses on those who didn't come home, but those who survived often paid a heavy price. None of those who went to war returned home the same. Physically and emotionally, their lives were changed forever, for better or for worse.

As conflict brings out the worst in people, it also brings out the best. This book tells of incredible feats of bravery. Humour amidst intolerable hardships. Dedication, sacrifice, camaraderie lasting decades. Men, women and children striving to do their best for their country. People simply getting on with things, because they had to be done.

This is their tribute.

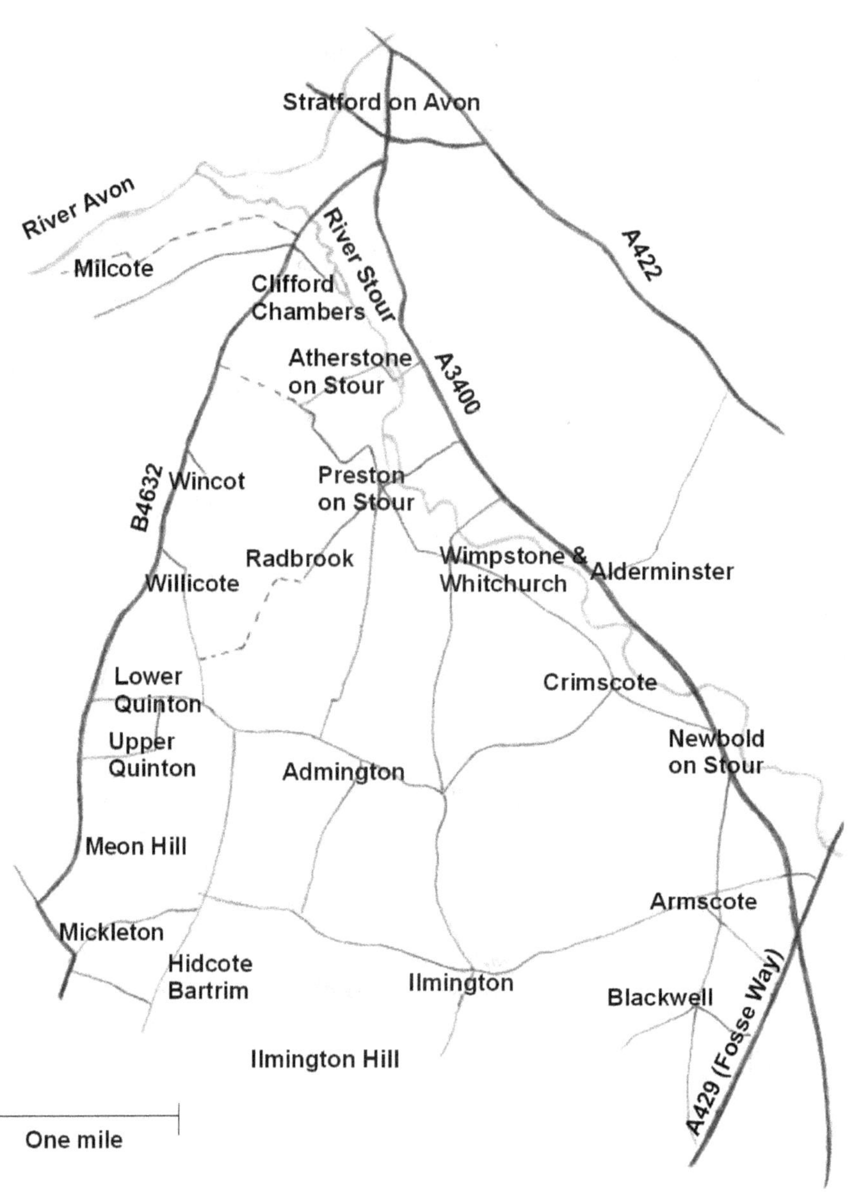
Stratford on Avon
River Avon
Milcote
River Stour
A422
Clifford
Chambers
Atherstone
on Stour
A3400
B4632
Wincot
Preston
on Stour
Radbrook
Willicote
Wimpstone &
Whitchurch
Alderminster
Lower
Quinton
Upper
Quinton
Crimscote
Newbold
on Stour
Admington
Meon Hill
Armscote
Mickleton
Hidcote
Bartrim
Ilmington
Blackwell
A429 (Fosse Way)
Ilmington Hill
One mile

Map 1.

Ranks of the Armed Services

British Army	**Royal Navy**	**Royal Airforce**
Commissioned Officers		
Field Marshal	Admiral of the Fleet	Marshal of the RAF
General	Admiral	Air Chief Marshal
Lieutenant General	Vice Admiral	Air Marshal
Major General	Rear Admiral	Air Vice Marshal
Brigadier	Commodore	Air Commodore
Colonel	Captain	Group Captain
Lieutenant Colonel	Commander	Wing Commander
Major	Lieutenant Commander	Squadron Leader
Captain	Lieutenant	Flight Lieutenant (FLt)
Lieutenant (Lt)	Sub Lieutenant *(Mate)*	Flying Officer (FO)
2nd Lieutenant (2Lt) *(Ensign)*	Midshipman	Pilot Officer (PO)
Non-Commissioned Officers		
Warrant Officer 1st Class (WO1) (Sergeant Major)	Warrant Officer 1st Class (WO1)	
Warrant Officer 2nd Class (WO2) (Sergeant Major)	Warrant Officer 2nd Class (WO2)	Warrant Officer
Staff / Colour Sergeant (SSgt/ CSgt)	Chief Petty Officer (CPO)	Flight Sergeant (FSgt)
Sergeant [1]	Petty Officer (PO)	Sergeant
Lance Sergeant		
Corporal (Cpl) [2]	Leading Seaman [1]	Corporal
Lance Corporal (LCpl)	Able Seaman [2]	Leading Aircraftsman (LAC)
Private (Pte) 3	Ordinary Seaman [3]	Aircraftsman (AC1 / AC2)
	Boy 1st Class	

	Boy 2nd Class	
[1] Corporal of the Horse in Guards units	[1] Sub-ratings include Leading Stoker; Leading Telegraphist	
[2] Bombardier in Artillery	[2] Sub-ratings include Stoker 1st Class; Telegraphist	
[3] Sapper in Engineers; Gunner/Driver in Artillery; Guardsman in Guards.	[3] Sub-ratings include Stoker 2nd Class; Ordinary Telegraphist	
Ranks in italics are now obsolete		

Army Structure

An army comprised 3-5 corps
A corps: 2-5 divisions
A division: 3 infantry brigades as well as supporting units
An infantry brigade (bde): 4 battalions
A battalion (bn): 4 companies, approx. 1000 men.
A company (coy): 4 platoons, approx. 250 men.
A platoon: 4 sections, approx. 50 men.

Abbreviations

AFC: Airforce Cross. Awarded for acts of valour, courage or devotion to duty while flying, not in the presence of the enemy.

ASC: Army Service Corps

ATS: Auxiliary Territorial Service

CWGC: Commonwealth War Graves Commission

DCM: Distinguished Conduct Medal. Awarded to lower ranks for gallantry in the field in the face of the enemy.

DFC: Distinguished Flying Cross. Awarded for acts of valour, courage or devotion to duty while flying, in the presence of the enemy.

DSO: Distinguished Service Order. Awarded to officers for distinguished service in wartime.

GC: Good Conduct. Refers to badges or pay.

HT: Horsed Transport section of the ASC

MGC: Machine Gun Corps

MM: Military Medal. Awarded for devotion to duty under fire in battle.

MT: Mechanical Transport section of the ASC

NCO: Non-Commissioned Officer

OTU: Operational Training Unit

POW: Prisoner of War

RAAF: Royal Australian Airforce

RAF: Royal Airforce

RAFVR: Royal Airforce Volunteer Reserve

RAMC: Royal Army Medical Corps

RASC: Royal Army Service Corps

RCAF: Royal Canadian Airforce

RFA: Royal Field Artillery

RGA: Royal Garrison Artillery

RHA: Royal Horse Artillery

RMLI: Royal Marine Light Infantry
RNAS: Royal Naval Air Station
RNZAF: Royal New Zealand Airforce
RSM: Regimental Sergeant Major. Position held by rank WO1.
RWF: Royal Welsh Fusiliers
SQMC: Squadron Quartermaster Corporal
USAAF: United States of America Airforce
WAAF: Women's Auxiliary Airforce
WAG: Wireless Operator/Air Gunner
WRNS: Women's Royal Naval Service

One: The Earliest Armies

The Early Militias

No formal standing army, controlled by central leadership, existed in Britain until the mid 17th century, excepting the Roman Army. But from the earliest days it was a necessity for almost all able-bodied men to be proficient with whatever weapons their means dictated. A statute decreed that all men must practice with the longbow, England's national weapon, on holidays and feast days. The law was enforced until the end of the 16th century when the development of firearms made it obsolete.

Following the Norman Conquest, land was typically held on tenure of military service. This meant that the landowner had to provide a specified number of armed men and equipment for his overlord as and when required. The first recorded freeholders in Preston – John Wylcotes and Thomas Franklin in 1419 – both held their land on tenure of military service. The largest landowners could field thousands of armed men and so wielded great political influence.

The private armies of the noblemen were curtailed from the 16th century. England was now ruled by the stable Tudor monarchy and removing the threat of these nobles – whose armies had driven the Wars of the Roses a century earlier – was expedient. And the wealthy were now less concerned with war and were diverting money away from castles and armed retainers into more peaceful pursuits.

The threat of foreign invasion, however, was still very real and a nationwide militia was vital. In 1547, the first year of Edward VI's reign, an order was issued throughout the country '*to have ready a good number of able horse[men] and foot [soldiers], either for the annoyance of our enemies or the defence of the realm*'. This was expanded during the reign of Elizabeth I with the increasing threat of invasion from Catholic Spain.

The militia was organised on a shire basis, and men would fight only within their shire borders. A general muster or formal inspection, which also provided basic training, was held every three years. All men aged between sixteen and sixty were obliged to attend. Each man had to bring arms ranging from a longbow and helmet for the peasantry to horses and full armour for the nobles. Preston Manor was also charged with providing one corslet [upper body armour] and one calyver [an early firearm].

The muster roll for Gloucestershire in 1608 records that Preston upon Stour, of which Sir Hugh Brawne was lord of the manor, had 27 eligible men. John Tymbrell and Giles Smith were the ancestors of long-standing farming families. Anthony Smith may have been Giles' brother. The Garfield family lived in the village until the late 18th century; the Robbins family until the mid 19th century.

Name	**Occupation**	**Age** **1: 20-40** **2: 40-60**	**Stature** **(see below)**
Thomas Bate	Servant of Hugh Brawne	2	c
Richard Smith	Servant of Hugh Brawne	1	m
Roger Edwards	Husbandman	2	c
John Tymbrell	Husbandman	2	m
Giles Smith	Husbandman	1	m
Anthony Smith	Husbandman	1	m
Adam Gybbs	Husbandman	2	c
John Harrod	Husbandman	1	p
Thomas Browne	Shepherd	1	c
George Harrod	Butcher	1	m
Robert Moore	Carpenter	2	m
Henry Peare	Labourer	1	p
Richard Winston	Wheeler	1	p
William More	Labourer	1	p
Richard Powel	Labourer	1	m
William King	Labourer	2	py
John Worrall	Labourer	2	py
Thomas Garfield	Labourer	2	py
Simon Jeff	Son of Thomas Jeff, husbandman	1	c
John Jeff	Son of Thomas Jeff, husbandman	1	c
William King	-	1	py
John Franklin	-	1	c

Humphrey Hunt	-	1	c
Michael Bravell	-	1	c
John Tompson	-	1	c
Nicholas Sheppard	Tailor	1	c
Thomas Robbins	Already a trained soldier	1	m

The tallest men were pikemen [p]. A pike was a 4m spear, eventually replaced by the bayonet. It was used in close combat against men and horses and great strength was needed to wield it.

Those of 'middle stature' were musketeers [m]. Muskets were long, heavy firearms with a drastic recoil. Upper body strength was essential to support its weight and master the recoil, so the strongest men who were not suitable as pikemen were armed with muskets.

Those of 'lower stature' were calyvers [c]. A calyver was one of the earliest firearms. A lighter predecessor of the musket, it was suited to the smaller and weaker men. 'Calyver' also refers to a soldier armed with this weapon.

Those of 'the merest stature' were fit to be 'a pyoneer [py] or of little other use'. The pyoneers were foot soldiers who cleared routes, dug trenches and performed other menial tasks.

Military tactics centred on a 'pike-and-shot' formation. Shots were fired into the enemy ranks in volleys, much as longbows were used in earlier centuries. The pikemen provided protection from attacking cavalry while the musketeers were laboriously reloading. Swords and javelins provided defence against enemy pikemen.

The pikeman was eventually replaced by the all-purpose infantryman, armed with both bayonet and firearm, who became the backbone of the army.

The Birth of the English Army

The roots of the English Army lie in the Civil War (1642-1649). Oliver Cromwell, leader of the parliamentary forces, saw the need for a centralised fighting force with common standards. He formed the New Model Army, and when King Charles I was defeated and executed, Cromwell became Lord Protector of England and his army remained.

When Charles II was restored to the throne in May 1660, he disbanded the force then raised a new army, under direct royal control. The first units were the 1st and 2nd Foot Guards, which became the Grenadier Guards and Coldstream Guards respectively. The army was brought under the control of parliament in 1689 and became the servant of the country rather than the throne. Its purpose was now to defend the realm and its overseas interests. It also maintained law and order, controlled riots, tackled highwaymen and escorted merchant convoys.

At first the army comprised infantry and cavalry. The infantry was divided into the footguards and regiments of the line, the latter denoted by numbers. The cavalry units were the most prestigious: only the wealthy could afford a horse. Each regiment had its own traditions and character, and its reputation and honour were a matter of fierce pride.

The ordnance or heavy guns, which later became the Royal Artillery, were next incorporated into the army structure, followed by the Royal Engineers. The Act of Union of 1707, which united the English and Scottish parliaments, saw the creation of the first British Army.

Army Officers

The army was a business enterprise, and all officers purchased their commissions and subsequent promotions, each rank considerably more expensive than the last. The officers were all from the upper classes of society who could afford the outlay. And only a gentleman was considered capable of leading British troops into battle.

Promotion was dependent on wealth rather than ability. A new officer could become a lieutenant colonel, in command of an entire regiment, within a few weeks if he had sufficient means. Promotion could take place without purchase on an officer's death: his place was filled by the most senior member of the rank below.

Other Ranks

Military service was officially voluntary, but press gangs were common. Army life was harsh, discipline brutal and the pay poor. Barracks were unsanitary and hugely overcrowded which led to myriad health problems. Enlistment was for life or until unfit to continue, and a posting to the disease-ridden tropics was considered a death sentence. The army attracted only the dregs of society who had little other option. Some were offered enlistment as an alternative to a prison sentence. The army was the subject of scorn and stigma – the Duke of Wellington called his troops the scum of the earth – and it didn't shake off this reputation until the 20th century.

Reform

Reforms in the 1790s improved barracks, rations and health care. Discipline was reduced, amidst much controversy. Many argued that severe punishments were vital to maintain order – the lower ranks were, after all, largely vagabonds and criminals – but it was decreed that courts martial could hand out a maximum punishment of only five hundred lashes. Good Conduct pay was introduced as an alternative to flogging. And contrary to concerns, the skill, discipline and quality of the soldiers increased immeasurably.

At the same time came a move to remove bad officers. The Royal Military Academy of Sandhurst was founded to train prospective officers. Free promotions were given to promising officers, with fixed periods of service before promotion. These reforms were instrumental in creating the cohesive fighting force that would achieve fame at Waterloo.

The Napoleonic Wars

The Napoleonic Wars began in 1792 when France began seizing territories in Europe and North America. Napoleon I, an acclaimed military leader, declared himself emperor of France in 1804. Britain was almost constantly at war for two decades, fuelled by the threat of French invasion, and the army and navy inflicted crushing victories on the French, including the battles of Trafalgar in 1805 and Waterloo in 1815.

The first known servicemen from the Alscot villages were serving at this time. Thomas Young was born in Preston in 1778, the eldest of six children of William and Martha Young. At least two of these died in infancy. William, a labourer, lived in a rented cottage and was classed in the Poor Register as 'very poor'. Thomas was probably an ideal illustration of a prospective soldier. He enlisted in the Royal Birmingham Fencibles – formed for defence in case of French invasion – in November 1799. The unit was disbanded the following month and in July 1800, now aged 22, Thomas enlisted in the 1st (Grenadier) Regiment of the Foot Guards, now the Grenadier Guards. This regiment was one of the first to land in Europe in 1793 and served in Holland and northern Spain. It is unclear where Thomas may have served.

His younger brother Richard (b1783) enlisted into the 39th Regiment of Foot in September 1803 and was transferred to the 95th Foot in August 1806. He may also have fought in Europe. He then enlisted in the Grenadier Guards on 3rd May 1815, a month before the Battle of Waterloo. He gave his age as 29, although he was actually 32. He may have been too old to transfer, or he may not have known his true age.

He was discharged with rheumatism in February 1823 after nearly nineteen years service. His discharge documents described him as 38 years old, of very good conduct, and with black hair, dark eyes and a swarthy complexion. He was also illiterate.

In the 1851 census, recorded as 65 and unmarried, he was living in the Royal Hospital for Invalid Soldiers in Chelsea. A pension system, managed by Chelsea Hospital, had been introduced in the 17th century for ex-soldiers. Out-pensioners received a pension but lived elsewhere, whereas in-pensioners gave up their pension for free board, clothing and medical care. Richard remained in the hospital until his death in February 1852. He was buried in the hospital's burial ground.

Thomas Young served for 24 years before being discharged in May 1824. His discharge certificate states he was about 45 years old, 5ft 7in in height, and like his brother he had black hair, dark eyes and a swarthy complexion. His general conduct was good and he also qualified for a pension. By 1851, now aged 70, he was married and living as an out-pensioner in Chelsea with his wife Frances. He died in 1861.

James Wheeler was born in Stratford in 1785, the son of William and Elizabeth Wheeler from Preston. The family lived in a public house called The Lyon, owned by James West of Alscot Park, and were also on the Poor Register.

James enlisted in the 7th Regiment of Foot and married Ann Handy, a nineteen-year-old Stratford girl, in 1803. Ann saw little of James who was presumably away with his regiment, but had a son Thomas in March 1807. James left her a few weeks later, leaving Ann penniless and with no idea when, or if, he would return. Ann was now the burden of her home parish, and was summoned before the officials of Stratford Union to discover who had responsibility for providing for her and her son. She believed that James, and by association his wife and child, belonged to Preston. This was confirmed and Ann and Thomas were delivered to John Mansell, overseer for the poor of Preston, within a fortnight.

Three years later in 1810, Ann returned to Stratford with Thomas. There was still no sign of James. She was living in Stratford with no legal settlement, a crime for the impoverished classes, and was summoned to JP John Lord Esq to answer her case. Ann pleaded guilty to the charge. Lord deemed her to be an idle and disorderly person and ordered her to be committed to a House of Correction for 14 days' hard labour.

The whereabouts of James all these years is unclear. His regiment was fighting in the Iberian Peninsula for several years and he may never have returned home. Or he may have simply grown tired of his idle and disorderly wife and gone to pastures new.

Two: Victoria's Army

The British Empire in the 19th century included a quarter of the world's population, ranging from North America to Australia. Britain dominated world trade and controlled the economies of several non-colonial countries. The Empire was vital for maintaining supplies of sugar, tropical fruits, precious metals, exotic cloths, tea, coffee and spices, all now staples in British society. A large and well-trained standing army was essential to defend these global assets against native uprisings and other European powers.

Queen Victoria came to the throne in 1837. The early years of her reign were marked by conflicts in Afghanistan and Punjab, then in 1854 came a crisis point for Britain and her army.

The Crimean War

The Crimean War grew from the long-deteriorating relationship between Turkey and Russia. Turkey was part of the crumbling Ottoman Empire, and Russia had set its sights on its assets. Russia's fleet crossed the Black Sea in November 1853 and destroyed the Turkish fleet. This caused alarm in Britain and France, who suspected that Russia would soon turn her attention to the Mediterranean and its coveted trade routes. Both countries sent fleets to the Black Sea, and war was declared in March 1854. The British and French troops landed in the Crimea, a peninsula of modern Ukraine, in September.

The Allies began fighting their way towards the fortress city of Sevastopol, the base of the Russian fleet. This was a formidable target: heavily fortified with gun batteries called the Redan and the Malakoff, surrounded by inlets and near unscaleable heights, and defended by Russian warships. The Allies laid siege to the city in October.

The siege lasted nearly a year and involved several battles, skirmishes and bombardments. The fleets of both sides were also engaged. The hardship the Allies endured is still proverbial today. The brutal Russian winter took a severe toll. The supply road from the coast became near impassable. Supplies of warm clothing never arrived. Shelter was lacking. Cholera and other diseases devastated the troops and medical treatment was deplorable.

Francis Henry Hastings (b1837) was a labourer's son from London who would eventually become the vicar of Preston on Stour. He enlisted as a naval cadet in January 1849, aged twelve, on HMS *Fisguard*, the harbour flagship at Woolwich. In 1854 he was serving on HMS *Sans Pareil*, a newly commissioned 70-gun ship of the Channel Fleet. She was dispatched to the Black Sea where she remained for the duration of the war. It is unclear what part Francis Hastings played in the war, but the *Sans Pareil* transported mortars and supplies to the Crimea, took part in the siege of Sevastopol, and also carried troops home after the war.

William Dalrymple Tompson (b1833) was the eldest son of William Currier Tompson, long-time vicar of Alderminster. He purchased a commission into the 17th Regiment of Foot in October 1852, then purchased the rank of lieutenant in March 1854. In January 1855, two months into the siege of Sevastopol, the 17th Foot were posted to the Crimea.

On 18th June 1855, eight months into the siege, the British began a massive assault against the Redan. The attack involved a charge across four hundred yards of open ground, amidst a storm of bullets. The 17th Foot was one of many regiments involved.

The attack was a failure. The British were driven back with losses of 2000 men. William Tompson came through unscathed and was Mentioned in Dispatches – a recognition of gallantry – by Lord Raglan, the British commander.

Three months later on 5th September, the Allies began a three-day artillery bombardment of Sevastopol. On the 8th, they attacked again. The British were to take the Redan; the French were to take the Malakoff. A day of fierce fighting ensued with over 2000 British casualties.

William Tompson again took part in the assault on the Redan. He was dangerously wounded by a musket ball which struck his chest. The French took their target but the Redan remained uncaptured.

But when the fighting lapsed that night, the Russians abandoned the Redan and Sevastopol fell. The Crimean War was effectively over. No more fighting took place over the winter and the Russians sued for peace.

A month after receiving his wound, William recovered sufficiently to leave the Crimea and returned to his father's home in Alderminster to recover.

Francis Hastings was awarded the Crimea Medal. William Tompson received the Crimea Medal with a clasp (issued for action under enemy fire) for Sevastopol. He also received the Turkish War Medal and was appointed a Knight of the Legion of Honour (KLH), a French gallantry award.

The Crimean War epitomised tactical, logistical and medical failures. Its cost was 20,000 British lives, three quarters of them through sickness. It was the first time that graphic reports and photographs of the horrors of warfare reached the wider public at home, and this caused a public outcry and demands for army reform.

Officers of the 17th Foot in the Crimea in 1855, taken by Roger Fenton, credited as the first war photographer. William Tompson is standing fourth from right.

A Modern Army

Drastic reforms followed the Crimean War. Battlefield medicine was transformed, in part due to the efforts of nurses such as Florence Nightingale. Sanitary and health problems were tackled. Overcrowded barracks were redesigned. The soldiers' diet improved. Military prisons began to replace flogging and much more emphasis was placed on training.

Further reforms were instigated by Edward Cardwell, Secretary of State for War from 1868-1874. His aim was to increase the appeal of the army and attract better quality recruits. He abolished flogging, increased pay and introduced free bread and meat, previously deducted from the soldiers' pay.

Cardwell also introduced shorter service terms. Enlistment had previously been for twenty years or for life. Men could now enlist for twelve years, spending half with the colours (the regular units) and the remainder in the newly created reserve, with an option of extending to 21 years service. Short service would attract fit, enthusiastic young men seeking a few years of adventure. Opponents countered that the men would have limited experience and be of little use in war.

Cardwell also affiliated the infantry (foot) regiments with specific districts. The 6th Regiment of Foot, for example, became the Royal Warwickshire Regiment. This was intended to create a local identity and attract recruits to 'their' regiment. The drive for recruits gained pace.

Recruits from the Alscot Villages

Many more men from the Alscot villages enlisted in the army from the mid 19th century. Most were farm labourers in their late teens. They were typically from large families who lived in run-down dwellings and followed their parents into the fields from early childhood. An agricultural labourer's wage barely stretched to basic necessities such as rent and a decent meal, and increasing mechanisation on farms caused further hardship. Unemployed labourers faced two options: the industrial towns or the army. Guaranteed pay and meals enticed many to the army.

Typical recruits were Joseph Hudson, (b1837) the son of farm labourer Benjamin Hudson of Goldicote Cottages in Alderminster. Benjamin died and left his widow Dinah a pauper with five young children. Joseph enlisted in the 97th (Earl of Ulster's) Regiment of Foot in April 1856, aged nineteen.

Joseph Horseman (b1861) was the son of Wimpstone farm labourer Richard Horseman. He was working as a labourer by age ten, then in January 1878 he enlisted in the Royal Horse Artillery. He stated he was eighteen although he was actually only sixteen.

William Seal (b1842) was one of eleven children of Alderminster farm labourer Henry Seal and his wife Jane. He enlisted in the 95th Foot in July 1858. He stated he was eighteen, the minimum for enlistment, although he was actually only sixteen. If anyone suspected his true age, they said nothing. There was no reason to turn a fit, willing young man away.

William's eighteen-year-old brother Henry joined the same unit a few months later. Although Henry was flat-footed and in-kneed, he was pronounced medically fit. The perennial need for recruits meant many seemingly unsuitable men were passed. Their younger brother David enlisted in the 95th Foot in October 1870. Two other brothers, Martin and Thomas, also served in the Royal Marines.

Herbert Horseman (b1868) was the eldest of fourteen children of Joseph and Emma Horseman of Crimscote. Herbert worked as a farm labourer then joined the Royal Warwickshire Regiment in February 1885, aged eighteen. His brother Harold joined the same regiment in 1901, giving his age as eighteen, although he was actually only fifteen. Their brother Albert, who was working in Derby as a footman, joined the prestigious Household Cavalry in 1900.

DECLARATION TO BE MADE BY RECRUIT ON ATTESTATION

I ***John Thorn*** of the Parish of ***Crimscote*** in or near the Town of ***Stratford on Avon*** in the County of ***Warwick*** do solemnly and sincerely declare, That I am to the best of my Knowledge and Belief ***20 7/12*** Years of Age; that I am not an Apprentice; that I am not married, that I do not belong to the Militia or to the Naval Coast Volunteers, or to any Portion of Her Majesty's Land or Sea Forces; that I have never been marked with the letter D; that I have never been rejected as unfit for Her Majesty's Service on any previous Enlistment; that I was enlisted at ***Warwick*** on the ***20th*** Day of ***December 1860***, at ***2*** o'Clock ***PM***, by ***Sergt James Pringle*** of ***1st Warwick Militia***, and that I have read or had read to me the Notice then given to me and understood its meaning; that I enlisted for a Bounty of ***Two pounds*** and a free kit, and have no Objection to make to the manner of my Enlistment; that I am willing to be attested to serve in the ***15th*** Regiment of ***Foot*** for the Term of ***Ten Years*** provided Her Majesty should so long require my Services, and also for such further term, not exceeding Two Years, as shall be directed by the Commanding Officer on any Foreign Station.

his
John **X** *Thorn* *Signature of Recruit.*
mark

OATH TO BE TAKEN BY RECRUIT ON ATTESTATION

I ***John Thorn*** do make Oath, that I will be faithful and bear true Allegiance to Her Majesty, Her Heirs and Successors, and that I will, as in duty bound, honestly and faithfully defend Her Majesty, Her Heirs and Successors, in Person, Crown and Dignity, against all enemies, and will observe and obey all orders of Her Majesty, Her Heirs and Successors, and of the Generals and Officers set over me. So help me God.

Witness my hand
his
John **X** *Thorn*
mark

Extract from an attestation (enlistment) certificate. The £2 bounty – more than a month's wages for a farm labourer – was a great enticement. The date and time of recruitment were recorded as a safeguard against unscrupulous recruiting sergeants, who would ply suitable candidates with round after round of drinks until the hapless man awoke with a sore head and no memory of having taken the Queen's shilling.

The Militia

The militia, an amateur army for home defence similar to the musters of earlier centuries, made up 20% of army personnel by the 1800s. Men undertook basic training in addition to their civilian work, and could be mustered in times of civil unrest. The militia was especially popular among farm labourers.

Following the Cardwell reforms of the 1870s, the militia battalions were attached to their local regiment to encourage men to transfer to the regular army.

Several men from the Alscot villages joined the militia. James Roberts-West of Alscot Park was commissioned as a major in the 3rd Warwickshire Militia in September 1808.

Giles Horseman (b1862) was the son of farm labourer Giles Horseman and his wife Mary of Preston. He joined a militia battalion of the Royal Warwickshire Regiment in March 1881 then a month later enlisted in the regular Derbyshire Regiment.

Moses Jacques George (b1876) was the illegitimate son of Hannah George, a Wimpstone dairymaid. He was born in the Stratford workhouse where he spent part of his childhood along with his mother and elder brother, also illegitimate. His name may hint at his father's identity: two farmers called Moses Jacques lived in the area. Moses worked as a farm servant and served in the 3rd (militia) battalion of the Royal Warwickshire Regiment before transferring to a regular battalion in 1893, aged 17½, stating he was 18½.

John Handy (b1871) was the son of farm labourer John Handy and his wife Ann of Whitchurch. John, a carter, joined the 3rd (militia) battalion of the Gloucestershire Regiment then transferred to the Army Service Corps in 1891.

Ernest Giles Horseman (b1890) was the son of William Horseman of Preston, who later moved to Bristol. He served in a militia battalion of the Gloucestershire Regiment then enlisted in the 3rd Dragoon Guards in 1906. He had just passed his sixteenth birthday.

Ralph Bailey (b1882) was the son of farm labourer John Bailey and his wife Catherine, nee Hone, of Preston. He was born in Wimpstone and by 1899 was living in Birmingham and working as a polisher for Messrs Brown and Marshall, a stagecoach and railway car manufacturer. He enlisted in the 4th (militia) battalion of the Worcestershire Regiment.

Frederick Beesley was the illegitimate son of Mary Ann Beesley of Atherstone on Stour, and was born in Stratford workhouse in November 1884. In 1901 was living with his grandmother in Atherstone and was working as a teamster. He then moved to Cannock in Staffordshire and found work as a collier. He joined the 3rd (militia) battalion of the South Staffordshire Regiment in 1905.

Life in the Army

From the mid 19th century soldiers often spent their entire service on home soil, which included Ireland and the Channel Islands. The home battalions trained recruits, supplied replacements for overseas battalions and helped maintain law and order, quelling riots and apprehending criminals. Those in Ireland tackled regular uprisings relating to political and religious grievances.

Henry Hicks (b1868) was born in Alderminster and in 1871 was living with his grandparents at Beecham Farm Cottage in Preston. He worked as a farm labourer then joined the King's Own Light Infantry in May 1886, aged 18. He spent time in Yorkshire, Gosport and Guernsey, was transferred to the reserve in 1893 and discharged in 1898 having never experienced any military action. This was now a fairly typical soldier's career.

William Horseman (b1823) was the son of farm labourer Giles Horseman and his wife Elizabeth of Crimscote. He enlisted in the 60th (Rifles) Regiment in May 1839, stating incorrectly that he was eighteen. It seems he regretted his decision. He deserted on 6th August but was apprehended two days later and court martialled. He was given two months confinement. On 7th June 1840 he again deserted. He rejoined his unit, seemingly voluntarily, at the end of August and was given six months imprisonment at his subsequent court martial. Four months after his release, he again deserted. He was apprehended four days later and this time given twelve months imprisonment, three months in solitary confinement and the remainder in hard labour, and he was also branded with the letter D. He was court martialled on another occasion for using insubordinate language and received a hundred lashes.

His unit moved to the East Indies in 1845, where William remained for thirteen years. It seems he now settled down and was of good character for the remainder of his service.

Good Conduct (GC) pay was introduced in the early 19th century as an alternative to flogging. After two years of unblemished service, a soldier was awarded 1d GC pay in supplement to his daily pay of a shilling, and wore a GC badge (an inverted chevron) on his uniform. After six years this was increased to 2d and two badges, and would eventually reach 6d after 28 years service. Any misdemeanour would revoke it at once. David Seal of Alderminster, serving in the 95th Foot, earned 1d GC pay in 1871, forfeited it in 1875 after a civilian offence, then maintained exemplary character for the next eighteen years until he was earning 4d GC pay.

Many soldiers were from impoverished families and never had the opportunity to attend school. In 1861 a three-tier education certificate was introduced, its attainment linked to promotion. In 1871 a fourth, lower certificate was added which involved basic reading and writing such as an eight-year-old would do today.

Albert Horseman of Crimscote, serving in the 1st Life Guards, attained his 3rd class education certificate in April 1901. This involved reading aloud a simple text, writing down dictation and simple arithmetic, and was necessary for promotion to corporal.

The 2nd class certificate, necessary for promotion to sergeant, involved reading and writing from complex texts, basic accounting and complex mathematics including fractions. Albert Horseman passed this in October 1903. The 1st class was much more complex and only those with serious ambitions attempted it.

Although many soldiers were of exemplary character in their military life, their life outside the barracks was often somewhat lacking. Until the introduction of sporting initiatives, schooling and reading rooms, soldiers' pastimes were limited to alcohol, prostitutes and gambling. A large proportion of hospital admissions was for endless bouts of venereal disease.

Henry Hicks of the King's Own Light Infantry spent two spells in hospital with severe gonorrhoea, although was otherwise of very good character. Sixteen-year-old Joseph Horseman, who enlisted in the Royal Horse Artillery in January 1878, was hospitalised eight times in three years; once wounded in an accident, three times with gonorrhoea, and four times with syphilis.

Nineteen-year-old Herbert Horseman of the Royal Warwickshire Regiment had eleven hospital admissions in five years, while serving at various bases in Britain and Ireland. Unusually, none was for venereal disease. He married Annie Pinfold from Quinton immediately on his transfer to the reserve in 1892: he was perhaps remaining faithful to her.

David Seal, the seventeen-year-old brother of William and Henry Seal, enlisted in the 95th Regiment of Foot in October 1870. He assumed the name Samuel Williams for unclear reasons. He received 1d GC pay after two years service, then in April 1875 was taken into custody by a civil power in Blackpool. David – now using his real name – and another soldier were charged with stealing a purse containing £5. Both pleaded guilty and were sentenced to three months imprisonment with hard labour. David then returned to his unit, having forfeited his GC pay and his pension.

He then became a reformed character. He was promoted to lance corporal two years later; sergeant in November 1879. In 1881 he re-engaged for 21 years service. A year later he was posted to the permanent staff of the regiment, now renamed the Nottinghamshire and Derbyshire Regiment, as a colour sergeant.

His personal life, however, was still somewhat lacking. He married Sabina Days from Quinton in Portsmouth in June 1884. Sabina was pregnant. David oddly stated on the marriage certificate that he was 26 – he was actually 31 – and was a private in the Royal Marines, living in the Marine Barracks near Portsmouth.

When the baby, Henry Elias Seal, was born, it became apparent – perhaps when David counted back the months – that the child was not his. The father was in fact his younger brother Martin, an enlisted Marine, who is the registered father on the birth certificate. It seems the marriage was quietly forgotten and Sabina married Martin the following year, stating she was a spinster.

Cuckolded David was probably secretly relieved. At the time of his marriage, he already had a wife and two children in Birmingham. The youngest was just five days old when he married Sabina. This presumably explains the lies on his marriage certificate.

David was discharged from the army in April 1890. He received a life-long pension and moved to Yardley near Birmingham, where he worked as a bricklayer's labourer. It seems his first wife had died and he remarried in 1892, had two further children and died in 1927.

Health Problems

All recruits underwent two medical examinations, but the need for recruits meant many unfit men were passed. A lifetime of poverty caused health problems which were exacerbated by military service, tuberculosis especially.

Richard Handy, 18, a labourer from Alderminster, enlisted in the 96th Foot in September 1859. He was of good conduct but suffered from tuberculosis, which was aggravated by exposure on duty. He was discharged as unfit for further service in April 1861. He died of tuberculosis at Alderminster in January 1862.

Thomas Neal (b1861) a farm labourer's son of Preston, was working as a farm boy by age nine and joined the 52nd Regiment of Foot (Light Infantry) in July 1880. After four months he was hospitalised with a clubfoot. Thomas believed it was the result of rheumatic fever six years earlier. Walking was painful and the problem was aggravated by military service, marching especially. He spent a month in hospital then returned to his unit, but was readmitted a week later for the same condition. He went before a medical board which recommended his discharge. After leaving the army Thomas moved to Warwick where he began work as a traction engine driver.

Thomas Gibbins (b1839) was the eldest son of Preston on Stour farm labourer William Gibbins. He worked as a groom then enlisted in the 24th Foot at Stratford in January 1863. He was of good character but didn't receive his GC badge because his name had been entered on one occasion into the regimental defaulter's book.

In January 1865, while in Cork, he was diagnosed as suffering from apertrophy (enlargement) of the heart, from which he had suffered for the past year. He also had chest pains and shortness of breath which made him unfit for labour. A medical officer believed this was caused by exposure and fatigue and he was discharged. Around 15% of recruits were discharged with heart disease, a problem linked to tightly buttoned uniforms and heavy awkward equipment.

He returned to Preston where he married, and despite being pronounced unfit for labour, he began work as a farm labourer. He had little other choice. He lived in Priest's Cottage for the remainder of his life and had nine children. He died in 1889 aged 50, from a carcinoma with which he had suffered for four months. His descendants lived in Preston until the 1970s.

Albert Fletcher (b1874) was the son of shepherd Joseph Fletcher of Atherstone on Stour. He worked as a labourer then joined the Royal Warwickshire Regiment in March 1890. He gave his age as eighteen years and two months, but he was actually only sixteen. He spent time in Fermoy, a large garrison in County Cork, then went to London. It seems he then developed a mental illness.

In January 1891 he was put in confinement awaiting trial for misconduct, but then was released and sent to hospital for observation. After three weeks no appreciable disease could be detected, and a court martial was held where he was sentenced to six weeks' hard labour. He was released after three weeks, perhaps because of continuing questions on his health, but a week later he was again in confinement. A second court martial sentenced him to four weeks' hard labour. He was soon returned to hospital, this time diagnosed with dementia. The 1891 census recorded him as a patient in the Grenadier Guards hospital in Westminster. His habits were described as 'peculiar' and his conduct 'indifferent'. A medical board declared him unfit for further service and he was discharged. He then disappeared from the historical record.

Alan George Rainbow (b1861) was the son of farmer Robert Rainbow. He was born in Alderminster and the family later took a farm in Ettington. In December 1881 he enlisted in the Royal Horse Guards and was posted to Windsor. He was of very good character and gained his 3rd class education certificate.

He was hospitalised in June 1884 suffering from a severe sprain after falling down some stairs, and again in December 1885 after an accident in the stables. In June 1886, now serving at Hyde Park barracks near Buckingham Palace, he was found to be suffering from a rupture, maybe caused by his earlier accidents, and was declared unfit for further service. He was then discharged. Eighteen months later he married and emigrated to New Jersey, where he took a farm and raised a family.

Crime and Punishment

By the late 19th century, the brutal punishment regime was obsolete, but discipline remained strict.

John Handy (b1871) was the son of farm labourer John Handy and his wife Ann of Whitchurch. He worked as a carter then in 1891 joined the Army Service Corps as a driver in the Horsed Transport section. He served in various places in the UK with no problems other than the usual hospital admissions with gonorrhoea and syphilis, and received 1d GC pay after two years. A month later he was awaiting trial for theft. He was convicted and imprisoned, then discharged for misconduct on his release. He then returned to Whitchurch where he returned to farm work.

Henry Holtom, a farm labourer from Alderminster, joined the Royal Warwickshire Regiment in January 1896 aged 21. He proved of particularly bad character, perhaps because of alcohol problems. He deserted after ten months, then was returned to his unit two years later in August 1898. He was put in confinement, court martialled and sentenced to twelve weeks imprisonment with hard labour. On his release he was sent to Malta and it appears he learnt his lesson. He passed his 3rd class education certificate and was appointed lance corporal in May 1899.

He was demoted less than a month later. He was put in confinement, tried and sentenced to six weeks imprisonment. He left Malta for the East Indies in September 1899, where he remained for three years without further trouble, returned to England in April 1902 and was again promoted to lance corporal.

Then he returned to his old habits. Just three weeks after his promotion he was demoted for misconduct. In December he was absent for a week. In July 1903, now in Dublin, he was convicted by a civil court for using threatening behaviour. He was given the choice of a ten shilling fine or seven days imprisonment. He took the latter. Three weeks after returning to duty he again went absent. He was sent back to prison, then the day after his release he went absent again. After his subsequent imprisonment he lasted six weeks before going absent for another week. This was the final straw. He was discharged for being 'incorrigible and worthless' in December 1903. His subsequent fate is unclear.

Army Officers

The proposed training of army officers was attracting controversy in the 19th century. Was it necessary, or was good breeding the only necessary qualification? Most believed the latter. British officers were a product of the public schools, where they were taught character and propriety above all else. They were epitomised by their unshakeable bravery: it was considered a disgrace to run away or even to duck if a bullet came close. They were expected to – and did – lead their men from the front, and often suffered the highest casualties. Even senior staff officers could be found amidst the thickest fighting.

It was decided in 1849 that prospective officers should pass exams, and many attended the officer training colleges at Sandhurst or Woolwich. The remainder were commissioned directly from militia units.

The purchase of commissions was abolished in 1871; commission and promotion were now dependent on ability. Men of all social classes could now gain a commission, but in reality the social divide between officers and other ranks remained well into the 20th century. A considerable private income was needed to supplement an officer's pay and the cost of uniforms and mess bills, often a groom and a personal servant, horses, polo ponies and other essentials excluded those without means.

Henry Stuart Tompson, (b1837) the younger brother of Crimean veteran William Dalrymple Tompson, purchased a commission as an ensign in the 51st (King's Own) Light Infantry in September 1856. He didn't attend military college which was not yet compulsory. He purchased the rank of lieutenant after two years, then captain in 1865. He spent several years in India then in 1869 sold his commission and took the position of adjutant (senior administrator) in the Durham Militia and later the Staffordshire Militia. He retired in 1884 as an honorary major, although he generally claimed to be a colonel, and moved to Bournemouth where he lived on a comfortable seven-shilling daily pension, in a large house he named Alderminster Lodge after his childhood home.

Bernard St John Warren Hastings (b1872) was the eldest son of Crimean veteran Francis Hastings, now vicar of Preston. He attended Sandhurst and was commissioned as a 2nd lieutenant into the King's (Liverpool) Regiment in February 1893. He reached the rank of captain then attended the schools of instruction for musketry, military engineering and riding. He served as adjutant of the 2nd battalion between 1899-1902, then attended the Staff College at Camberley. He was involved in training officer cadets from 1903-1907. He was promoted to major then retired. He rejoined his unit during the First World War but any further details are unclear.

Service Overseas

England became a stable nation during the Tudor period and turned her attention to acquiring overseas territories which would eventually become the British Empire. Maps were redefined as the age of exploration began. Columbus reached America in 1492. Dutch sailors reached Australia in 1606; New Zealand in 1642. Countless other territories were added to the map. Then came the race to claim and retain these valuable new lands.

The importance of a military base in the Mediterranean, the hub of global trade, was realised and Britain captured Gibraltar in 1704. Following the Peace of Utrecht, signed by several European states in 1713 after a decade of infighting, Britain was allocated the Spanish territories of Minorca and Gibraltar and the French territories of Newfoundland and Nova Scotia. Permanent garrisons were needed to safeguard these. Military presence in India was also vital for trade with the Far East; the Caribbean for the new trade in sugar.

India was the most common posting for the Alscot servicemen. A few served in Gibraltar, Canada or the Caribbean. Some fought on campaigns in Egypt and the Sudan. For most, their service abroad was relatively uneventful.

British North America

British North America comprised the lands remaining to Britain after the American War of Independence in 1775. These comprised Nova Scotia, Newfoundland, Quebec, Canada and the Pacific north-west. In 1867 Nova Scotia, New Brunswick and Canada were united to form the dominion of Canada, a self-ruling country with the British monarch as its sovereign.

Several men from the Alscot villages served in British North America. They were mainly involved in garrison duty with little action.

John Wheeler (b1836) was the grandson of James Wheeler of the 7th Foot and his idle and disorderly wife Ann. Their son Thomas had been removed to Preston following his mother's prison sentence in 1810 and remained for his life. He married Preston girl Esther Neale and their son John was born in 1836. Thomas was recorded as a pauper on the 1851 census. He suffered from chronic asthma and psoriasis of his whole body, probably due to his miserable living conditions, and this along with exhaustion caused his death in February 1852.

John worked as a groom then enlisted into the Horse Guards in September 1860. He served for nearly three years in British North America. He was of very good character, was awarded two good conduct badges, and was discharged in March 1870. He then disappeared from the historical record.

John Thorn (b1840) of Crimscote lived with his widowed mother Sarah, a charwoman. He was working as a farm labourer by age ten and enlisted in the 16th Foot in December 1860. He was posted to Halifax in Nova Scotia in December 1861. Crimean veteran William Tompson, a lieutenant in the same unit, arrived at the same time. John Thorn was of very good character and was, unusually, temperate. He also had no hospital admissions for venereal disease. He remained in Halifax until May 1866 when he was transferred to the West Indies. During John's three-year tour he had one hospital admission, suffering from an abscess. He returned to Ireland in February 1869.

William Tompson was promoted to captain in 1865 and transferred to Canada the following year. His promotion was without purchase, which indicates he was the most senior lieutenant to fill the position after another captain died. He returned to Ireland in May 1868.

William Best (b1851) was the son of farm labourer John Best of Alderminster. He was working as a farm labourer by age nine. His mother had died in his early childhood; his father in 1867. In May 1875 he enlisted in the army. He used the name William Jones for unclear reasons. He spent some time in Canada and was transferred to the reserve in 1881. He was discharged six years later. In 1911, now aged 59 and unmarried, he was working in a worsted mill in West Riding.

William Smith (b1852) was born in Alderminster. In 1861 was living with his widowed mother and his paternal grandparents, Robert and Ann Smith, on a farm in Upper Swell. In 1871 William was managing the farm alone. His grandfather, now in his late seventies and probably in poor health, was living elsewhere and died shortly afterwards. It seems William failed as a farmer, probably due to the agricultural depression of the time, and he joined the army in April 1874. He spent some time in Canada, then in 1901 he was living in St Pancras and working as a police constable.

India

Victorian India comprised the independent presidencies of Bengal, Madras, Punjab and Bombay, all annexed to Britain in the 18th and 19th centuries, as well as modern Pakistan, Bangladesh, Nepal and Thailand. India provided a crucial stepping stone to the Far East, and in the 17th century, the English East India Company, a powerful trade organisation, formed its own armies to garrison its trading stations, supplemented by the regular British Army.

In the 18th century Britain began to train the native population as soldiers. The native or 'sepoy' regiments were a success and by the 1880s over 150,000 native troops were serving. The sepoys had many benefits. They were plentiful; cheap to employ; immune to the local diseases; resilient to the climate; and were entitled to no pension. The British troops suffered heavily from myriad tropical diseases.

India was the most common overseas posting for British troops. Most completed their service in comparative peace, although campaigns and rebellions were frequent.

The Punjab Campaign

Punjab was an independent Sikh kingdom to the north of India. The Punjab army attacked British India in December 1845, and after several months of fighting amidst atrocities on both sides, the Sikhs were defeated and the British took possession of their capital city, Lahore. Two years later in May 1848, the province of Mooltan in southern Punjab rose in rebellion. The British won several victories over the next two months then besieged the capital city, also called Mooltan. The city was strongly fortified and after heavy losses the British were forced to lift the siege. They prepared siege engines and dammed the water supply, then on 27th December 1848 a greatly reinforced army resumed the siege.

William Horseman of Crimscote, serving with the 60th Rifles, had arrived in India in October 1845. His regiment was among those who took part. The opening assault captured the suburbs of the city; a week later the city itself was captured with the exception of a citadel where the rebel leader had retreated. After a fortnight of incessant shelling the British began their final assault. The rebels surrendered and Mooltan was taken.

19th Century India. Modern place names are in brackets.

The Sikhs were then joined by an Afghan force and began advancing on Lahore. They clashed with the British army near Gujarat on 21st February. The British artillery laid down terrific fire on the Sikh guns which were forced to retire. The infantry advanced and forced the enemy from several villages; the rapid advance broke the enemy ranks. The cavalry then charged and rode down the fleeing Sikhs for twelve miles. The Afghans were chased back across the Khyber Pass and the remaining Sikh army surrendered on 11th March. Punjab was then annexed to British India.

Willian Horseman was awarded the Punjab Medal with a clasp for the Battle of Gujarat. His regiment remained part of the occupying force in Punjab for several years to come.

The Indian Mutiny (First War of Independence)

In May 1857, the Bengal native soldiers mutinied against their British rulers, due to simmering resentment over their treatment and sparked by the use of pork fat, abhorrent to native troops for religious reasons, in gun cartridges. The rebellion spread to Delhi where European settlers were massacred. British troops, including the 60th Rifles, marched from Punjab and laid siege to Delhi. William Horseman's records state that he was involved in dispersing insurgent villagers in the Meerut district and destroying their villages.

Rebels attacked a small British force at Lucknow in June 1857. Despite being vastly outnumbered and starving, the British held out. Troops sent to relieve them in September were decimated. Another force arrived in November and the surviving troops escaped and Lucknow was abandoned to the rebels. The British were now in a precarious position.

Joseph Hudson of Alderminster, serving with the 97th Foot, was sent to India to reinforce the British troops and arrived in Bombay in November 1857. In February 1858, they formed part of a force which marched on Lucknow. They reached Chanda, a town in east India where 8000 rebels were stationed, on 19th February. The rebels fled but were soon reinforced. They were routed again with few British losses. The British won another battle on 23rd February and the siege of Lucknow began a week later. Fierce fighting lasted for three weeks before the rebels were routed and Lucknow was restored to British control.

The British then turned on the district of Rohilkhand to the north of Lucknow. The city of Shahjahanpur had claimed independence and was now a stronghold for the rebels. William Horseman fought in the Rohilkhand campaign. His regiment was part of the force which restored the city of Moradabad to British control on 25th April, then attacked and captured the city of Bareilly on 5th and 6th May. They then moved on Shahjahanpur. Their position was precarious after heavy fighting against a large rebel force, but the city was bombarded and the rebels defeated. Control was restored to the British on 11th May. The rebels then moved to the city of Mohammedi. The British attacked and destroyed their fort here on 26th May.

Amidst atrocities on both sides and savage fighting, the mutiny was eventually suppressed. Joseph Hudson was awarded the Indian Mutiny Medal with a clasp for Lucknow. The 97th Foot remained in India for several years, and Joseph died in Chanda on 2nd March 1859. There is no record of conflict at this time; he perhaps succumbed to sickness.

William Horseman was also awarded the Indian Mutiny Medal. He returned to Britain in January 1859 after thirteen years abroad and was discharged in October 1861. His records state he was: '*worn out by length of service in a tropical climate where he suffered much from hepatitis, dysentery and fever. Latterly his constitution has been much shaken by several sharp attacks of acute rheumatism. His disability is not attributed to vice or intemperance.*'

He was forty years old and had earned four Good Conduct badges, and he was awarded a lifelong pension. He married and returned to the Stratford area where he worked as a farm labourer and raised a family. By 1881 he was living in Aston near Birmingham, where he died in 1895, aged 72.

Reorganisation

The mutiny spurred a drastic reorganisation of Indian governance. The East India Company was dissolved and the British Raj, the Crown rule in India, was formed in 1858, giving a tighter control to the British government. Queen Victoria was appointed Empress of India in 1877.

Many more men from the Alscot villages now served in India. Henry Tompson, now a lieutenant in the 51st Light Infantry, sailed for the East Indies in April 1861, his second tour of the country. He remained for six years and was made adjutant while serving in the city of Campbellpore (modern Attock) in the Punjab.

The region between the Punjab and Afghanistan, known as the North West Frontier, was populated by many tribes who were violently opposed to colonial rule. In October 1863 the Eusufzai tribe rose in revolt, and a punitive campaign known as the Umbeyla Expedition was launched. The Eusufzai Field Force, including the 51st Light Infantry, struggled across mountainous terrain to the city of Peshawar, at the foot of the Khyber Pass, and were involved in constant fighting for several weeks. Henry Tompson, now acting major, became aide-de-camp (effectively a P.A.) to the commanding brigadier general. The campaign ended with the rebels' surrender in mid December and peace was uneasily restored. Henry Tompson remained fairly uneventfully in India until April 1867.

For most troops, their service was relatively uneventful. William and Henry Seal of Alderminster, both in the 95th Foot, embarked for Bombay in August 1860 and spent eight years in the East Indies, including time in the garrison city of Poona (modern Pune). Henry was appointed a drummer – who dictated the marching pace and firing drills – in October 1864 and was promoted to corporal in 1867. The 95th Foot returned to England in October 1868 and both brothers re-engaged to complete 21 years service. Neither served abroad again.

William was promoted to corporal in 1874 but was court martialled for unknown reasons the following year and was reduced to a private. He was never promoted again. Henry was made sergeant in 1870; colour sergeant in 1871; sergeant major in 1879. He was awarded the Long Service and Good Conduct Medal in 1879, awarded after eighteen years service with absolutely no fault.

William was discharged in August 1879. He was now married and he settled in Derby with his family where he worked as a labourer to supplement his meagre pension.

Henry married twice but it seems had no children. He re-engaged at the end of his 21 years and served as regimental sergeant major, the highest position for a non-commissioned officer, until his discharge in February 1881 when he was awarded a daily pension of 2s 3½d. His obituary in the *Stratford Herald* in 1918 stated he declined an offer of a commission, and over his career he had drilled no less than Lord Roberts, who commanded the British Army in the Boer War, and General Smith-Dorien, a prominent commander of the First World War.

John Thorn, serving in the 16th Foot, re-engaged to complete 21 years service in 1870. He was posted to the East Indies in February 1876 and remained for eight years. By 1878 he was earning 4d GC pay on top of his daily shilling but was never promoted, perhaps due to his lack of any education certificate. He left the East Indies in February 1884 and was discharged. His future from this point is unclear.

William Tompson of the 17th Foot purchased the rank of major in 1869 while serving in Ireland, and went to India in 1872. In 1874 he was serving in

Peshawar. In 1877 he was promoted to brevet lieutenant colonel. 'Brevet' was an honorary rank awarded for gallant conduct, used only when the officer was serving away from his own regiment. In 1878 William was serving in Bengal, then in October his battalion crossed the border into Afghanistan where another conflict was brewing.

Joseph Horseman, serving with the Royal Horse Artillery, embarked on the month-long journey to India in December 1880. He spent nearly two years in Umballa, a city in Punjab, then returned to England in November 1882. He was discharged in 1890, married Martha Holmes, his childhood neighbour, then moved to Enderby in Leicestershire where he worked as a stone quarryman. He retained strong links to Whitchurch: his son Richard was baptised there in 1894. Joseph died in 1895 after a quarry accident and was buried in his native Whitchurch.

Charles Bloxham (b1863) was the son of carter Joseph Bloxham. Joseph had married Hannah Parker, daughter of Preston's parish clerk, and the couple settled in Atherstone on Stour. In September 1881, Charles, now working as a farm labourer, enlisted in the Rifle Brigade. He was of good character and was also temperate. In January 1883 he sailed for India where he spent nearly five years. He served in Delhi and Meerut, a large garrison town. This included two month-long camps of exercise which provided training and experience of large-scale manoeuvres in the largely peaceful time.

He returned to England in November 1888 and was transferred to the reserve. In 1891 he was living with his mother in Atherstone on Stour and working as a farm labourer. He then married and moved to Birmingham where he worked as a labourer in a metal works.

John Dodd (b1864), the son of Alderminster farm labourer John Dodd, joined the Royal Warwickshire Regiment in February 1887. In January 1888 he sailed for the East Indies, where he remained for nearly four years. He served in Jubbulpore (modern Jabalpur); Rajmachi, a fort in Pune; and Mooltan in Punjab. He also spent six weeks at Dalhousie, a Himalayan hill station 2000m above sea-level, which was used as a summer retreat. In December 1891 he was transferred to Ceylon (Sri Lanka) where spent three years. He gained his 3rd class education certificate and was promoted to lance corporal. He then returned to England and was transferred to the reserve. He returned to Alderminster, married and returned to farm work.

Edwin Dyer (b1868) was the son of Preston farm labourer Charles Dyer. Edwin was one of eight children and was working as a farm labourer by age twelve. In January 1887, aged eighteen, he enlisted into the Manchester Regiment. Although recruits now typically joined their local regiment, they could state a preference to go elsewhere. The Manchesters had been in India for the past five years; this may have swayed Edwin's choice. The following year, his brother Frederick, aged 21 and also a farm labourer, enlisted into the Royal Artillery.

Edwin arrived in the East Indies on 21st March 1889 and remained for five years. He served at ten different stations including Meerut, Dinapore, Amritsar and Sialkot, all cities in Punjab, then in April 1894 he was transferred to Deolali, a transit camp near Bombay to await his transfer to Britain. Deolali was notorious for boredom and psychological problems – Edwin had to wait five months until the end of the monsoon season for a ship – hence the term 'going doolaly'.

He returned to Preston and farm work. He married and in 1901 he was working on a farm near Stratford; by 1911 he had moved to the town of Redditch where he was working as a cowman. He now had six children; only four still living. He eventually moved to Birmingham where he died in 1935.

Frederick was posted to the 68th Field Battery and joined his unit in Bengal in October 1888. He remained for seven years and served at various locations including Umballa, Peshawar and Rawalpindi. He was transferred to the reserve in January 1896 but it seems he suffered health problems. He was no longer fit for service when he was discharged in March 1900. He worked as a shepherd and later a bricklayer's labourer. He never married and remained living in Preston with his other unmarried siblings for his life.

Arnold Herbert (b1868) was the youngest of seven children of Preston labourer George Herbert and his wife Mary Ann. George died when Arnold was a baby and his widow then worked as a charwoman. Arnold worked as a labourer then moved to Handsworth near Birmingham, where he worked as a wheelwright's labourer. In October 1894 he enlisted into the Royal Artillery.

He went to India the following year and remained for three years. He was now married and it seems his wife Sarah and their baby travelled with him, as their second son James was born in 1897. Arnold was invalided home in October 1898 and transferred to the reserve in April 1902. He moved to Newport in Wales where he began work for a haulage company.

Sickness and Health

Sickness was a perennial problem for British soldiers in India. The unfamiliar climate and the myriad diseases to which they had no immunity took a severe toll. Exposure, cramped living conditions, hard labour and forced marching with entirely unsuitable uniforms exacerbated matters considerably. A report made in the 1860s on the army base at Dinapore in Bengal described a barracks crammed with over 300 men. There were no windows or other ventilation; the buildings were permanently damp in the wet season; open drains ran across the walkways; malaria, cholera and fevers were all prevalent and severe. The report concluded that it was next to impossible for barracks of this construction to be even moderately healthy.

Almost all servicemen contracted some form of tropical disease. The causes and distinctions between various illnesses were not – and often are still not – fully understood. 'Ague', 'debility' and 'fever' were used for many bacterial, viral and parasitic infections.

Malaria is caused by a mosquito-borne parasite which infects the red blood cells. The parasite matures and triggers a synchronised rupture of the blood cells to release a new wave of progeny. This rupture causes fever, immune-system overload, severe anaemia and often brain damage. The nascent parasites then re-infect new red blood cells to begin the cycle again. Thanks to this life-cycle, sufferers can continually relapse for months or years.

Henry Seal of the 95th Foot spent several spells in hospital during his eight years in India. The reasons included malaria; opthalmitis [eye inflammation] caused by cold and dust; fever caused by the climate and altitude; and on one occasion syphilis, caused by 'vice'.

John Thorn spent two periods in hospital during his eight years in the East Indies: once with 'SC fever', an unidentified tropical disease, and once with copitis [skin inflammation] and psoriasis.

Charles Bloxham spent two spells in hospital in 1884 suffering from ague; a particularly lengthy spell with gonorrhoea while in Delhi; and a period in Meerut with SC fever.

Edwin Dyer spent nineteen days in hospital with rheumatism and was admitted several more times with ague.

John Dodd seems to have avoided most of the ravages of tropical diseases during his four years in India. He had only one hospital admission with ague in October 1890, although he had two cases of gonorrhoea and one of syphilis.

Joseph Horseman, serving in the Royal Horse Artillery in the 1880s, spent several spells in hospital with ague, debility and 'remitt fever' [a recurring fever]. Joseph left India in November 1882 and suffered another attack of ague while on board the troop ship. He suffered continual relapses for the next two years, suffered from vertigo and convulsions, and on one occasion had a fit on parade. This resembles malaria, and may well have continued long after his discharge.

Frederick Dyer of the Royal Artillery suffered particularly badly. Within seven weeks of his arrival in 1888 he was hospitalised with SC Fever. He suffered from severe pyrexia [fever] followed by anaemia and cardiac debility, and was in hospital for nearly three months. He returned to his unit but less than six months later was again hospitalised, this time with malaria. He spent a total of three months over the next six in hospital. He was then admitted in March 1890 with dysentery. A fortnight later he was sent to Dalhousie, a hill station by the Himalayas, probably to try and recover his health. He remained for six months and it seems to have done the trick. He remained in India for another six years and remained in reasonably good health.

Giles Horseman of Preston, who joined the Derbyshire Regiment in April 1881, sailed for Gibraltar that December. He remained for a year, uneventful except for one case of gonorrhoea, then in October 1882 he sailed for India where he remained for five years. He was of very good character, good conduct and steady habits. He passed his 4th class education certificate and received 2d GC pay after four years. He had two spells in hospital in November 1885 with blistered feet caused by hard forced marching – the second for over a fortnight – then things became more sinister.

In March 1886, while serving in Dum Dum, he was admitted to hospital suffering from insanity and mental delusions, which consisted of 'elated ideas of his expected wealth and reduced moral causes'. He remained for seven months, his treatment a non-irking diet, exercise, and bromide of potash: a sedative and treatment for epilepsy. His condition improved, although he suffered attacks of ague – a significant point – and in January 1887 a medical board decided he was of sound mind. He then returned to his unit. The ague may give a clue to his illness. There is now a known link between tropical diseases, some of which infect the brain, and mental disorders.

Giles was readmitted in March 1887, again suffering from insanity. A new report stated that his state of mind was permanently impaired and recommended his discharge. His illness was caused by the Indian climate and 'not linked to intemperance, vice or misconduct'. He returned to England in May and was discharged. He returned to Preston, married, and in 1898 he became the sub-postmaster.

In February 1916, he didn't return from his daily round. His daughter Lucy and son William went to look for him. He was found face-down in a ditch near Churchill Farm in Alderminster. He had been dead for several hours. A post-mortem found heart problems and it was concluded that a heart condition made him faint as he was crossing the ditch. He had fallen face-down and drowned in three inches of water. His death was attributed to health problems caused by his service in India, thirty years earlier.

Afghanistan

Russia and Britain had always viewed each other with distrust, and Britain thought it expedient to gain control of Afghanistan as a buffer between Russia and British-ruled India. In the 1830s, the pro-British Afghan leader was deposed and Britain sent an army to restore his rule. The British lost control and withdrew from Afghanistan in 1842, but the Afghans continued to receive subsidies and arms from Britain.

In the 1870s the Afghans admitted a Russian envoy. The British uneasily demanded the Afghans also admit a British envoy. One was dispatched along with an escort force in September 1878 but was turned back. Two months later, the British invasion began.

William Tompson, now a major in the 17th Foot and in command of the 1st battalion, crossed the border from India on 13th November. The first target for the British was Ali-Musjid, a fort six miles from the border at the western end of the Khyber Pass. Ali-Musjid was flanked by artillery batteries and surrounded by near-perpendicular hillsides which concealed innumerable enemy soldiers. It was a formidable position to capture.

On 21st November, one division of the army began advancing on the fort. They came under fierce artillery bombardment but gradually advanced. A second division, which included the 17th Foot, had been tasked with taking a hill opposite Ali-Musjid and also capturing some Afghan gun batteries. They faced formidable obstacles, including an eleven-mile march in the dark across treacherous rocky hillside, but finally reached their objective. The Afghans fled and the fort was captured.

The 17th Foot then took part in fighting in the Chinar district in December,

Afghanistan.

then two expeditions into the Bazar Valley, inhabited by the hostile Zakka Khel tribe. These proved the most savage fighting of the war. In May 1879, a treaty was signed transferring control of Afghan foreign affairs to Britain, and hostilities ceased. William Tompson, now a lieutenant colonel, returned to the East Indies.

In September, Afghan rebels attacked the British residency in Kabul and killed all occupants. A British force fought its way to the city and took possession in October. The entire country was now very hostile. A huge rebel army attacked Kabul in November and desperate fighting lasted several weeks. The 17th Foot were part of a relieving force which raced from India to relieve Kabul. The city was close to falling and the winter snows, which would stop all troop movement through the mountain passes, were imminent.

The force reached Kabul. A huge Afghan army was drawn up in a good defensive position among the hills and the British had to fight uphill from ridge to ridge, but after a six-hour battle gained the victory. The rebels fled. William Tompson was Mentioned in Dispatches for his part in the battle.

The situation was uneasily settled for several months, then the British victory at the Battle of Kandahar in September 1880 brought the war to an end.

William returned to the East Indies and was created a Companion of the Bath (CB) for his services in Afghanistan. He also received the Afghan Medal with a clasp for Ali-Musjid. Shortly afterwards he was promoted to colonel.

He returned to England in March 1882 and retired in July 1884 aged 51, now ranked an honorary major general. He married shortly afterwards and died in 1916.

Egypt and The Sudan

The Egyptian War

The Suez Canal, running through Egypt between the Mediterranean and the Red Sea, opened in 1869. It halved the journey time between Europe and the Far East with vast implications for trade. European control of this asset was vital.

A nationalist revolution in Egypt in 1882 threatened its security. Britain prepared for war and troops began landing in August. Within three weeks, the British had moved up the Suez to occupy the city of Ismailia. The Egyptians, who held a strong position at Tel-el-Kebir, repeatedly attacked the British forces. The position had to be captured.

John Stowe (b1860) was the son of George and Ann Stowe of Atherstone on Stour. He was working as a farm labourer by age thirteen then joined the 39th Brigade in October 1880. He spent eighteen months in Malta then was among the first troops to land in Egypt. A few weeks later he took part in the assault on Tel-el-Kebir.

The position was surrounded by flat desert with no cover, and the enemy were also entrenched. A night assault was the only option. 14,000 British troops, including John Stowe, marched on Tel-el-Kebir in absolute silence through the night of 12th September. The Highland Brigade was in the lead. At 5am the next morning, the bagpipes struck up and the Scots charged the entrenchments. The rest of the army followed. They came under heavy fire and there was fierce hand-to-hand fighting until they took the first line of trenches. They then came under fire from a second line. This was assaulted and the enemy was routed. The British covered the 110km to Cairo within 24 hours and the city surrendered without a fight, bringing the campaign to an end.

John Stowe remained in Egypt as part of the occupying army. He was of exemplary character and two years later was promoted to sergeant.

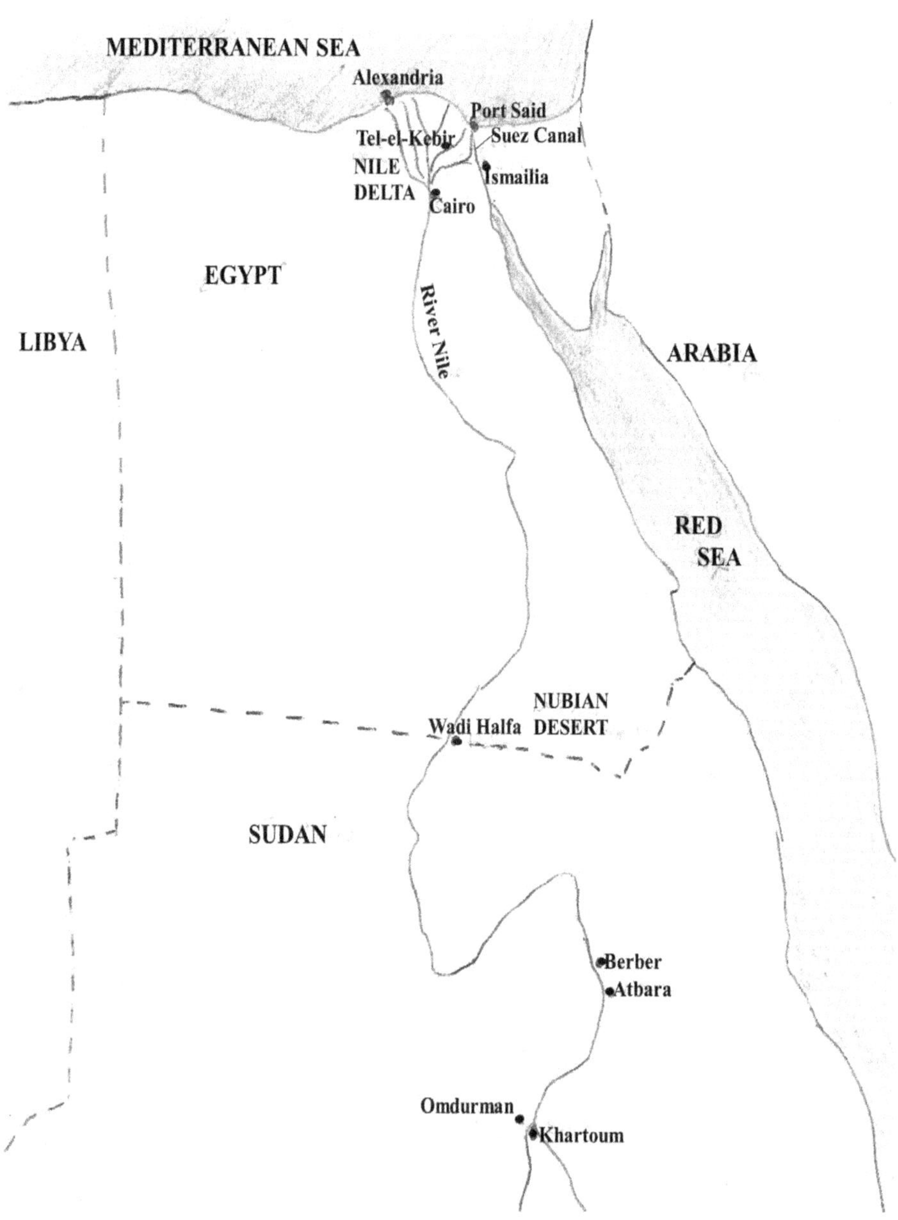

Egypt and The Sudan.

The Mahdi Campaign

A religious and political uprising led by a self-proclaimed Mahdi (Chosen One) began in 1883 in the Sudan, part of the Egyptian administration which was now under British control. Amidst increasing concern, General Charles Gordon led an Anglo-Egyptian force into the Sudan in the summer of 1884. His force was destroyed and Gordon was besieged in the Sudanese city of Khartoum. A 6000-strong force, including John Stowe, went to its relief.

The country near the Nile comprised swamps, forests and rich grassland. Further from the river it comprised mountains, deserts or rocky plains. The relief force began working their way up the treacherous cataracts and rapids of the Nile. Progress was slow – their boats often had to be unloaded, moved by hand and then reloaded – and they were twice attacked by rebels.

The force was eventually split. Half continued up the Nile; the rest took a hazardous shortcut across the desert. What water they found was polluted, and they had almost no food. The heat and dehydration caused heavy casualties among the force-marching soldiers. They finally reached Khartoum in January 1885.

They were two days too late. Khartoum had fallen and British defenders had been slaughtered. The Sudan was lost and the army withdrew to Egypt.

John Stowe returned to Malta. He was awarded the Egyptian Medal for the 1882 campaign with a clasp for Tel-el-Kebir; a medal for the Nile Expedition or Gordon Relief Expedition; and the Bronze Star or Khedive's Star issued by Egypt. By this point he had also received five Good Conduct badges.

He extended his service to twelve years with the colours and was posted to Ceylon where he was promoted to colour sergeant in April 1890. A year later he re-engaged in the Gordon Highlanders. He returned to England in March 1892 and extended his service to 21 years. He married and had six children. In 1893 he took a course to qualify as Company Sergeant Major (CSM). He was awarded the coveted Long Service and Good Conduct Medal in 1899 and when his 21 years was up, he extended his service even further. He was finally discharged in April 1903, aged 42. He re-enlisted in September 1914.

The Second Sudanese War

The conflict with the Sudanese continued throughout the 1880s, then in 1895 a new initiative was launched to reconquer the country. A well-trained and well-equipped Anglo-Egyptian army was formed and in March 1896, 11,000 men under the command of Major-General Horatio Kitchener entered the Sudan. Their first engagement came three months later when they wiped out a Mahdist force. Encouraged by this success, Kitchener planned a much more ambitious campaign. More British troops arrived over the coming year, including the 1st Royal Warwickshire Regiment in February 1897. This included Moses Jacques George of Wimpstone, who had enlisted four years earlier.

The Anglo-Egyptian army marched 140 miles over six days up the Nile from Abu Dis to Berber. At 4.30am on 7th April 1898, they advanced on an entrenched enemy force, 15,000-strong, by the Atbara river. After fierce hand-to-hand fighting, with enemy soldiers in every hut and trench, the British took the position and the enemy were scattered. The troops then went to summer quarters on the Nile – the relentless heat ended all campaigning – to prepare for their advance on Khartoum.

A campaign over vast distances of desert country was a major challenge, and Kitchener ordered the construction of the Sudan Military Railway, a hugely ambitious but vital asset for the movement of troops and supplies. More than 25,000 troops with horses and guns were moved 150 miles across enemy-held desert country towards the city of Omdurman in August 1898, a phenomenal achievement. They met the Mahdists in battle on 2nd September.

Kitchener's forces formed up against the Nile. The Mahdists attacked into colossal firepower and were mown down. The Anglo-British army chased the remnants seven miles towards Omdurman where the Mahdists were routed after a bitter fight. This effectively ended the war and Khartoum was captured two days later. Moses George wrote to his mother, subsequently published in the *Stratford Herald*, that the fight was a hard one. Their captain was directing the regiment to fire a volley and he had hardly spoken a word before he was struck by a dervish bullet and killed. He was buried at Omdurman the following day. British losses totalled 48; Sudanese 12,000.

Kitchener was awarded a peerage. Moses George was awarded the Khedive's Sudan Medal with the Queen's Egyptian Sudan Clasp and clasps for Atbara and Khartoum. He left Egypt for the East Indies, where he remained for four years. He underwent a court martial for unknown crimes and was sentenced to 28 days imprisonment with hard labour. This was his third prison sentence since enlisting. He returned to England in December 1902 and was discharged three years later. In 1911 he was working as a farm labourer. He died of tuberculosis in Stratford workhouse in 1914, aged 38.

West Africa

Charles Norrington Hastings, (b1874) who later adopted the name Wilfred, was the son of naval veteran and vicar Francis Hastings. He and his younger brother Cuthbert were well-known troublemakers. Rather than emulating their father's illustrious career, they indulged in a succession of petty crimes.

In April 1889, Wilfred, 15, and Cuthbert, 13, were summoned to court in Stratford. Along with two other boys, they had followed Fanny Harris, a respectable married woman, along the Shipston Road in Stratford and addressed obscene remarks to her, too disgusting to be repeated in court. When Fanny threatened to summon the police, the boys ran away. Fanny identified Wilfred in court but couldn't be sure about Cuthbert. Wilfred received a £1 fine and Cuthbert was acquitted.

Less than a month later, the two boys were again in court. This time they'd been caught trespassing in pursuit of game near Clifford Chambers. They were fined a shilling apiece, along with 12s 3d costs. On yet another occasion, the boys were fined for breaking public lamps.

Wilfred then went to live with Thomas Hook, a coffee-tavern keeper in Pershore. It seems to have done the trick. Cuthbert settled down, became a farmer and raised a family. By 1894 Wilfred had gained a commission into the 4th South Wales Borderers, a militia unit. The militia offered a 'back-door' route to a commission into the regular army. Commissions into the militia were less dependent on social requirements and promising officers could transfer to a regular regiment without the need to attend military college. Perhaps Wilfred, thanks to his troublesome background, couldn't gain a place at the college.

Four years later he was ranked a captain, and was dispatched on his first overseas operation.

The British colony of Sierra Leone in West Africa was established in 1792 for the resettlement of African slaves. Many other adjacent territories were annexed to Britain in the 19th century and the Sierra Leone Frontier Police, a military force comprising British army officers and native lower ranks, was formed to maintain law and order.

The financial burden of the territories was offset by the levying of Hut Tax. The Karene district, in the north of the colony, rose in rebellion in February 1898. The uprising spread and became what was known as the Hut Tax War.

The British reinforced their troops. Wilfred Hastings was seconded to the Sierra Leone Frontier Police that month and took part in a reprisal expedition into the Karene district. The British laid waste to the countryside and destroyed a hundred towns and villages. The uprising was supressed. Wilfred was slightly wounded on the expedition and was awarded the East and West Africa Medal with a clasp for Sierra Leone.

He spent eighteen months in Africa then, having proved himself a capable officer, was commissioned as a 2nd lieutenant into the Manchester Regiment, a regular infantry unit. Two years later he was again ranked a captain, and went on to an exemplary career serving in the Boer War and the First World War.

Three: The Anglo-Boer War

Southern Africa had been an important trade base between Europe and the Far East for centuries. The British and Dutch both laid claim to the Cape, and Dutch settlers, later known as Boers, began farming the inhospitable landscape which comprised a vast arid plateau known as the veld, dissected by a few unnavigable rivers and scattered with precipitous hills known as kopjes.

Britain eventually came to rule the Cape. The Boers moved north to form their own independent states of Transvaal and Orange Free State. The Cape Colony and Natal remained British colonies.

Transvaal was annexed to Britain in 1877 and rose in revolt three years later. The farmers armed themselves and the First Anglo-Boer War began. The British thought it would be an easy victory but lost battle after battle until their rout at the Battle of Majuba in February 1881. The war was lost and Transvaal was granted self-government.

A few years later, gold was discovered in Transvaal and prospectors flooded into the country. Britain used this pretext to prepare to reannex the state. The Second or Great Anglo-Boer War began on 11th October 1899 when Transvaal and Orange Free State rose in rebellion. Britain rushed her army to the Cape. Excited troops embarked to cheering crowds. It would be an easy victory. The farmers would be quickly defeated. Everyone would be home by Christmas.

The British had no experience of fighting a well-armed enemy with modern weapons. Their equipment and weapons were woefully inadequate. Innovations such as telephones were scorned by commanders. The Boers knew and understood the veld; the British did not. Most soldiers were city-born, and even those with rural backgrounds found nothing familiar about this arid landscape. British tactics centred on the bayonet charge, a disaster against modern rifles. Camouflage uniforms were considered cowardly. Unflinching bravery mandatory. The Boers had no ideals such as these.

A series of bloody battles shocked both sides. The Battle of Colenso in December

1899 was a disaster for the British with over 1100 casualties. The British-governed Cape was facing imminent rebellion. More troops were desperately needed.

The army reserve was mobilised. The militia and yeomanry volunteered to fight. Men surged to recruiting offices. The Commonwealth states of Canada, New Zealand and Australia also volunteered troops, and thousands of men poured into South Africa.

William Aquila Riley (b1871) was the son of woodsman William Riley and his wife Caroline of No.13 Preston. William worked as a labourer then in May 1890, aged eighteen, he enlisted in the 2nd Grenadier Guards. He served seven years in the UK and was transferred to the reserve. He married shortly afterwards. He was recalled on 20th December 1899, following the disaster at Colenso. His battalion left the UK on 18th March and arrived at the Cape three weeks later.

John Whiteman (b1876) was the son of Walter Whiteman, a farmer of British descent living in Wanganui in New Zealand. John, also a farmer, volunteered in January 1900 for the third New Zealand contingent to embark for the Cape. These were known as rough riders: good marksmen and skilled riders rather than trained soldiers. John left New Zealand on 4th March and arrived in South Africa on the 15th.

Wilfred Hastings, now commissioned into the 1st Manchester Regiment, also landed with his regiment at Durban in Natal on 16th March.

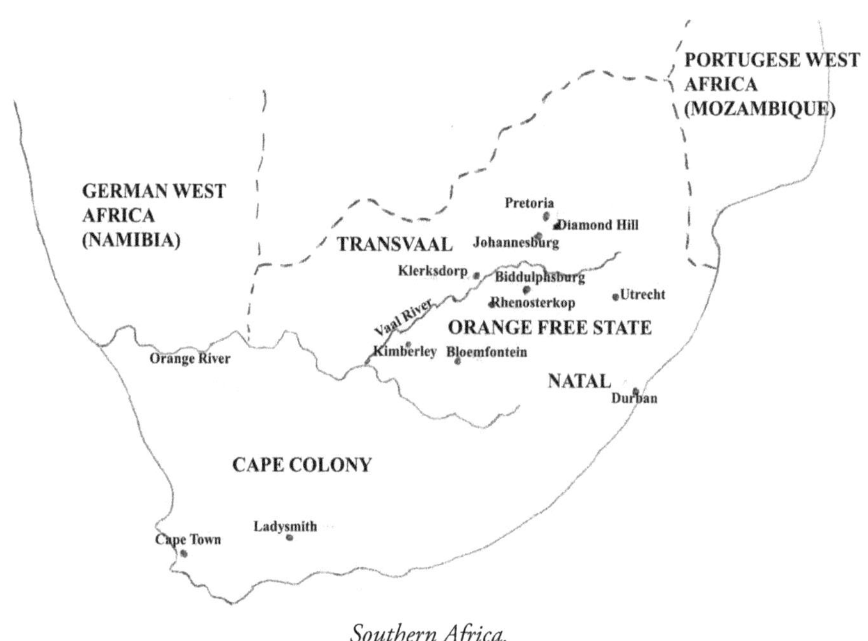

Southern Africa.

The War

Lord Frederick Roberts, a veteran of India and Afghanistan, took command of the army in December 1899 with Lord Horatio Kitchener as his chief-of-staff. In February 1900, Roberts invaded Orange Free State. A month later its capital, Bloemfontein, surrendered.

The third New Zealand contingent was sent straight to Orange Free State to aid in its occupation. Within two months, John Whiteman was recommended for a commission by Lord Roberts. It was rare for a soldier to be promoted from the ranks. John was accepted into the 2nd Middlesex Regiment on 15th May.

The Grenadier Guards, including William Riley, were also involved in the march through Orange Free State. They led a disastrous attack on an enemy-held hill in May. Shelling set fire to the long grass and many men, especially the wounded, were badly burned or killed. The Grenadiers fought their way to the foot of their target, and were then ordered to withdraw.

Wilfred Hastings spent time in Cape Colony and was soon promoted to lieutenant. He saw action at Biddulphsburg in Orange Free State in late May, where a detachment of British troops was attacked by a large enemy force. After reinforcements arrived, the British withdrew with no decisive result. Wilfred also saw action in the district of Wittebergen in July, where William Riley also saw action.

After Orange Free State was subdued, Roberts marched on Transvaal. John Whiteman was also part of this. He was present at the capture of Johannesburg in May 1900 and then the army continued to the capital, Pretoria, which also surrendered. The first British troops, including Whiteman, entered the city on 4th June.

On 11th June, Roberts left Pretoria with 14,000 men, again including John Whiteman, to engage a large Boer force near Diamond Hill. This battle lasted two days and reached stalemate. When the British renewed their attack the following day, they found the Boers had fled in the night.

Wilfred Hastings also took part in operations in Transvaal between August and November.

John Whiteman served in Transvaal for the remainder of 1900, including action at the hill of Rhenosterkop on 27th November. The Boers had been forced back to this position where they made a stand. The British, outnumbering the Boers ten-fold, made three attempts to take the hill with severe losses. The Boers, lacking food and ammunition, then abandoned the position during the night. The battle was considered a great victory for the British.

The Boers were defeated by the end of the year. Lord Roberts returned to Britain and most of the troops were sent home. Over 10,000 British men had died, with another 35,000 invalided home through sickness or injury. The war was considered a resounding success.

The Flame Reignites

Kitchener remained in South Africa with the remaining troops, and it was realised that the war was in fact far from over. The Boers began a guerrilla war with considerably more success than they had seen in open battle. They attacked isolated convoys, robbed trains and destroyed railway lines. The British retaliated by burning Boer farms.

Until now the war had been fought to chivalrous standards. Regular truces were held to tend the wounded; the British respected that the Boers didn't fight on Sundays for religious reasons. Now, it became more brutal. Rebels captured in Cape Colony were shot. Martial law was imposed. Women and children were put in concentration camps. Kitchener ordered the indiscriminate burning of all farms and the slaughter of their livestock.

The British were now hunting down parties of Boer commandos across Boer and British territories, and fought skirmishes rather than open battles. Relentless patrolling and sweeps across enemy territory had gradual success. Train wrecking was now a favoured tactic of the Boers. Railways were vital for transporting troops and supplies across the vast and barren landscape, and were an unmissable opportunity for the now starving Boers.

The Imperial Yeomanry was rapidly expanded. Troops were riding vast distances across the veld in search of the enemy, and anyone with horsemanship skills was a vital asset for the army.

Edward Simms (b1880) was the son of Henry Simms, who worked variously as a farmer, miller and gamekeeper. In the 1880s the family were living at Tithe Farm in Alderminster where Edward was born. In 1901 Edward was living in Wales and working as a groom. He volunteered for the 88th (Montgomeryshire) Company of the Imperial Yeomanry in February 1901.

Robert Ashby (b1878) was the son of farmer Nicholas Ashby, originally of Preston Pastures Farm. Robert later farmed at Tithe Farm in Alderminster. In March 1901, Robert, aged 23 and working on the family farm, enlisted as a shoeing smith in the 5th (Warwickshire) Company of the Imperial Yeomanry.

Three weeks later he left for South Africa. He and Edward Simms were both skilled horsemen and were ideal recruits.

Evan Horseman, 19, a railway porter and the son of Crimscote bricklayer Joseph Horseman, also went to South Africa in 1901 to work on the Imperial Military Railway. He was probably involved in assessing and repairing the constantly attacked lines.

John Whiteman, still serving in Transvaal, was promoted to lieutenant in October 1901. He commanded a unit of mounted infantry for several months, then commanded troops at the city of Utrecht, where he was complemented by senior officers for the defences he had erected. Wilfred Hastings also spent time on operations in Transvaal and was made a captain in December.

The 2nd Grenadier Guards, including William Riley, remained in Orange Free State throughout 1901 and 1902, taking part in endless columns trekking through enemy country, burning farms, capturing Boer commandoes and building blockhouses. They fought skirmishes with guerrillas almost daily.

The son of TW Wilkes of Preston on Stour, whose name and any other details are unfortunately lost, also served in South Africa. In October 1901 Wilkes was with twenty other men on a kopje (hill) a few miles from Doornfontein near Johannesburg. Another section of twenty men were on another nearby kopje.

At 4am, their sentry saw a group of mounted men making towards them. He woke the other soldiers. The intruders were dressed in khaki, so at first they were thought to be British troops. The men opened fire just to see who they were. And then the fight began.

Wilkes later wrote to his father, subsequently published in the *Stratford Herald*; *'Men came galloping out of the bush all around us like a pack of wolves, about 750 of them. They were Beyer's Commando, the train wreckers, and they attacked us on all sides.'* General Beyer was a Boer whose speciality was mining train-tracks and looting the subsequent wrecks.

Wilkes continued;

> *'Some of them got onto a high kopje behind us and were able to pour volleys right into our forts, and didn't forget to let us have it hot. I got out of the fort and among some boulders, and after ten minutes a bullet grazed my mouth, breaking off two of my front teeth but only skinning my lips. The enemy were creeping up on two sides of me, twenty yards distant. I couldn't single-handedly keep them back, and the fellows in the fort couldn't*

> *see them, so I made a dash for the fort. I only got a few yards when I fell, shot through the neck. I was quite dazed and couldn't move for a time, then managed to crawl between two large boulders, where I stopped for three quarters of an hour, bleeding heavily.*
>
> *'Our fellows had to surrender, for the Boers had fairly swamped us. They took everything from us but our breeches and shirts. Some saved their boots, but I couldn't as I lay there wounded. I put my purse with £30 in under a boulder, and my watch in my breeches, but hadn't time to hide £1 in silver which an old Boer took from me. Our fellows then came, dressed my wound and carried me into the fort.'*

The Boers told the British they'd sent a man under the white flag of truce to fetch a doctor, but they didn't actually do this until late afternoon. When the doctor arrived, one of the wounded had died. Another British man had been killed in the fight and five more wounded. The Boers wouldn't let the British witness the removal of their own dead and wounded but, Wilkes wrote, *'the niggers reported nineteen graves the next morning.'*

The Boers asked to bring two of their seriously wounded to the British hospital, which was allowed. One was wearing the tunic of an officer of the Gordon Highlanders, shot in cold blood in a train wreck at Naboomspruit in Transvaal on 5th June. It was believed the Boer was the man who actually killed him and he was executed.

When the Boers left, Wilkes' chum found his purse for him, but he'd lost his field glasses, two saddles and bridles, and everything else he had. He estimated the loss at £10 with no hope of compensation.

He was loaded onto a wagon for a terribly rough seven-mile ride to hospital. The shaking started his wound bleeding again but, he told his father, *'My wound is going on well. I am still in bed and am too weak to get up on account of losing so much blood, but am getting stronger every day.'*

His subsequent future is lost to history.

On 24th February 1902, Edward Simms was part of a convoy at Yzerspruit near Klerksdorp, a city in Transvaal. The convoy bivouacked on a farm for the night then left early the next morning. They marched for three kilometres then were attacked by a commando unit near a tributary of the Vaal river. The British put up strong resistance but were eventually forced to surrender with 187 men killed and wounded. Edward was shot and severely wounded, and died of his injuries a month later on 21st March.

Robert Ashby served in South Africa for a year and saw action in Cape Colony, Transvaal and Orange Free State. He was returned to the UK on 3rd April 1902 and discharged as medically unfit a month later.

The End of the War

The indiscriminate destruction of crops and livestock was taking its toll. The Boers' horses starved and the commandoes, near-skeletal and reduced to wearing grain sacks, were forced to admit that there was no point fighting any further. The peace agreement was signed on 31st May 1902.

Edward Simms was awarded the Queen's South Africa Medal with a clasp for serving under fire in Cape Colony, and the King's South Africa Medal with clasps for 1901 and 1902. He is commemorated on a memorial at Cathay Park in Cardiff and in St Mary's Church in Warwick.

Robert Ashby received the Queen's South Africa Medal with clasps for Cape Colony, Orange Free State and Transvaal; and the King's South Africa Medal with two clasps.

William Riley remained in South Africa until July 1902. He was awarded the Queen's South Africa Medal with clasps for Wittebergen and Cape Colony, and the King's South Africa Medal with two clasps. By 1911 he was living with his wife in Westminster and working as a housekeeper.

Wilfred Hastings left South Africa in October 1902. He was awarded the Queen's South Africa Medal with clasps for Transvaal, Cape Colony and Wittebergen; the King's South Africa Medal with two clasps; and the Distinguished Service Order (DSO). He had also been Mentioned in Dispatches in July 1902.

John Whiteman, who was Mentioned in Dispatches in July 1902, left South Africa in October 1902. He was awarded the Queen's South Africa Medal with five clasps including Cape Colony, Johannesburg, Orange Free State and Diamond Hill; and the King's South Africa Medal with two clasps.

The manpower and time needed to subdue the South African farmers had amazed the world. The climate was as much a problem as the fighting, and disease ravaged man and beast alike. The European cattle in the garrisons had no immunity to African diseases; Wilkes had reported that 4000 out of their 5300 cattle had died within four months. British leaders declared that a military catastrophe of this sort should never be allowed to happen again.

A decade later, it happened again. On an unimaginably greater scale.

John Whiteman wearing his South Africa medals with clasps. The badge on his collar is the insignia of the Middlesex Regiment.

Four: The Royal Navy

Ships were vital in Britain for defence, trade and conquest, war on the Continent, and maintaining control over the English Channel and North Sea. By the reign of Elizabeth I, England's navy was the most advanced in Europe. Piracy, especially of Spanish treasure ships, provided funds. Hostilities between England and Spain increased during Elizabeth's reign and the Spanish Armada arrived in 1588. The battle was a resounding success for the English Navy and England really did now rule the waves.

The Navy acquired its first steam ship in 1821. Ships could now navigate rivers and previously inaccessible coastal areas. In 1860 the Navy commissioned its first iron-hulled and armoured warship. Torpedoes and mines were added to the arsenal and naval warfare was fast redefined.

Until the 19th century, men typically joined a ship for a particular voyage rather than enlisting in the Navy as an institution. They were usually experienced sailors and when the ship reached port they would enlist on the next available ship. Pressed men often had no seafaring experience but quickly 'learnt the ropes' out of necessity. Every crew member needed to be highly competent if the ship was to survive an oceanic voyage. The wooden vessels were prone to leaks; could capsize in a squall if the sails weren't reefed fast enough; could run aground through poor navigation; or simply become lost or run out of food and water. Prospective naval officers had to pass exams two centuries before army officers. Gentlemen's sons were treated like the other ratings and learnt the same tasks.

The Royal Marines were soldiers under the control of the Admiralty, who served on and fought from ships and supported the army in land-based operations. They evolved into an elite fighting force capable of advanced amphibious warfare, a reputation which they retain today.

No men from the Alscot villages are known to have enlisted in the Navy or the Marines until the late 19th century. Most would never have seen the sea, let alone contemplated sailing on it.

Future vicar Francis Hastings, who had served on HMS *Sans Pareil* during the Crimean War, was transferred to HMS *Alarm* in June 1855 and rated a midshipman (trainee officer). A year later he passed the examinations to become a lieutenant. He remained on the *Alarm* for another year, now rated a mate: a midshipman who had passed for lieutenant and was waiting for a vacancy. In May 1858, now aged 21, he joined the officers' ranks as a lieutenant.

The following year he gained a first-class certificate in gunnery and joined HMS *Edgar* as a gunnery officer. The *Edgar* was a 91-gun, 600-horsepower steamship. The incessant operating of the heavy guns below decks, which were loaded, fired, hauled back into position after the recoil and reloaded, in complete darkness and with enemy missile exploding all around, needed great stamina and discipline. Francis was responsible for this, but a character report stated that although he was very zealous and active, he was not suited to be a gunnery officer as his manner was bad with the men.

In May 1861, the *Edgar* was near Aden when seaman William Skinner fell overboard. Francis jumped overboard into the shark-infested waters to try and save him. Skinner was heavy and couldn't swim, and drowned despite Francis' efforts. The following year Francis was awarded a silver medal by the Royal Humane Society for his gallantry.

Francis remained on the *Edgar* until July 1862. He spent time in the East Indies and the Pacific and was engaged in the suppression of the slave trade in East Africa. In September 1867 he was promoted to commander – in command of a small ship or second-in-command of a larger ship – and gained a second-class certificate in steam work the following year. In the 1871 census he was serving on HMS *Indus* in Devon. He married shortly afterwards.

He left the Navy in October 1873 to take Holy Orders, having been interested in church work for some time, but returned to the Navy in February 1874 and gained the rank of captain. He retired again in September 1882.

He spent some time in missionary work overseas then became vicar of Preston on Stour in 1887. Revd Harvey Bloom of Whitchurch noted with disdain that Francis often seemed to forget that he was in the pulpit rather than on board a ship, and unutterable words such as 'damn' would often find their way into his sermons. His obituary stated that his congregation admired him for his strength of character and the example he set to the village.

Preston's vicarage was now a private house and Francis lived in Stratford with his family. He remained the vicar of Preston for thirty years before retiring in 1917. He died in Stratford in 1921, aged 84, and was buried at Preston.

Henry Seal was the son of Thomas Seal, a farm labourer from Alderminster, and the cousin of David, Henry and William Seal of the 95th Foot. He enlisted as a boy sailor in November 1880 aged sixteen. In 1881 he was serving on HMS *Royal Adelaide*, a depot ship in Devon, and rated as a Boy 2nd Class. In January 1882 he became a Boy 1st Class, a promotion dependent on sufficient proficiency and a Good Conduct badge.

Henry reached his eighteenth birthday that June and enlisted for ten years as an adult sailor. He served on various ships as an ordinary seaman. He was generally of very good character although he spent six weeks in gaol for an unknown offence while on the cruiser HMS *Iris* in 1883. He was promoted to able seaman in August 1884. He then deserted or 'ran' at Portsmouth in May 1887. His subsequent fate is unclear, but he would have been brought to account if apprehended at any point in his life.

William Allcock (b1843) was the son of farm labourer Charles Allcock and his wife Ann of Alderminster. In 1861, aged eighteen, he was working as a cowman in Handsworth. He joined the Royal Marines for a twelve-year period in June 1866. His enlistment bounty was £1 and a free kit.

The 1871 census records him as a private in the Alverstoke Marine Barracks in Hampshire. He spent nearly eight years at sea, including two years on HMS *Valient* in Ireland and three years on HMS *Lord Warden* in the Mediterranean, was of very good character and gained two Good Conduct badges. He was discharged in July 1878, and in 1881 was working as a farm labourer. In 1891, now aged 48 and unmarried, he was living with his widowed mother in Claverdon and working as a farm labourer. His subsequent future is unclear.

Thomas and Martin Seal of Alderminster, the brothers of William, David and Henry Seal, all serving in the 95th Foot, both enlisted in the Royal Marines. Thomas, who was working as a farm labourer by age fifteen, enlisted in March 1864, aged eighteen. Like William Allcock, his bounty was £1 and a free kit. He served for nearly seven years, five of these at sea on HMS *Challenger* in Mexico and Australia, and was discharged at his own request in March 1871 on payment of £18, several months wages for a labourer. His subsequent future is unclear.

His younger brother Martin Seal was working as a farm labourer in 1871, aged thirteen. He enlisted in the Marines sometime afterwards and served until the 1890s. He seems to have had a long and successful career. His personal life, however, was not so illustrious.

In November 1884 Sabina, the new wife of his brother David, gave birth to a son, Henry Elias Seal. It then became apparent that Martin was actually the father. It seems Sabina had been involved with both men, and when she found herself pregnant and unmarried, she told the wrong brother he was the father. The earlier marriage was forgotten and Martin and Sabina were married the following September.

Sabina stated that Martin was a lance-sergeant in the Royal Marines on Henry's birth certificate; on their marriage certificate Martin stated he was a corporal and serving on HMS *Excellent*, a shore establishment in Portsmouth, while Sabina was living in Portsea, near Portsmouth.

Martin and Sabina had three further children. Martin John Days Seal was born in October 1887 in Alverstoke, near Portsmouth. Martin senior now stated he was a Marine sergeant. Herbert William was born in March 1889 at the same address, but Martin was now living at a separate address. Edna was born in 1891 and died in infancy.

Martin died of enteric fever in February 1899, aged 42. He had left the Marines and was now receiving a Navy pension and working as a hammerman – operating steam-powered hammers – in the Portsmouth dockyard.

Martin's sons all went on to naval careers. Henry (b1884) a boy sailor in the Navy, enlisted as an adult sailor in August 1902. He stated he was eighteen, but he was actually only seventeen. He served as a Domestic 3rd Class [a servant, steward or junior storekeeper] and was of very good character. He then deserted in October 1905 while the *Berwick* was in Halifax in North America. His subsequent future is unclear.

Herbert (b1889) enlisted in January 1903 aged fifteen. He spent time on HMS *St Vincent* as a Boy 2nd Class, was rated as a Boy 1st Class after nine months, and was rated as an ordinary seaman on his eighteenth birthday in May 1905. He was of very good character and ability and was rated an able seaman after a year. He was subrated as a seaman gunner (operating torpedoes) and then a gunlayer (sighting and aligning the guns to targets). He was rated a leading seaman in February 1912 while serving on HMS *Philomel.* She was loaned to the New Zealand Navy for much of the First World War and operated in the Mediterranean, escorted convoys and patrolled the Red Sea and the Persian Gulf. Herbert was promoted to petty officer in December 1916. He was discharged in 1922.

Martin (b1887) was a pupil at the Royal Hospital School in Greenwich in 1901 aged thirteen. This was a school for boys with seafaring backgrounds. A year later he followed his father into the Marines. His youth was obvious; he was only 4ft 9in on enlistment.

He spent eighteen months at Chatham dockyard then embarked on HMS *Fido*. He enlisted as an adult on his eighteenth birthday in 1905. He served as a bugler – conveying signals over deafening gunfire – until 1908. He was of very good character and ability and gained his 3rd class education certificate, swimming certificate, and qualifications in gymnastics, infantry work, sea service, musketry and field training. He also had a good knowledge of semaphore. He was serving in Egypt on armoured cruiser on HMS *Minotaur* when war was declared in 1914. He was promoted to corporal and served for the duration of the war. He was promoted to sergeant in 1922, was discharged in 1926, then remobilised in 1938, now aged fifty. He spent most of the Second World War in Chatham dockyards and was discharged in August 1945.

Edward Hibbard was the son of gardener Thomas Hibbard who lived in Alderminster and Whitchurch and was likely a relation of the gamekeeper's family of Preston. Edward, now working as a groom and a gardener, enlisted in the 18th Hussars in March 1911, aged nineteen – the 1911 census records him with this unit in Scalby in Yorkshire – but purchased his discharge two months later for £10. He enlisted in the Navy the following year.

He was rated a Stoker 2nd Class. Stokers kept the engines continually stoked with coal: hard and hot manual labour. He was of very good character and satisfactory ability, and was made a Stoker 1st Class after a year. He was serving on the *Prince of Wales* when war was declared.

In the mid 19th century the Navy became a fashionable career for gentleman's sons. Several members of the West family of Alscot Park served from this point.

James Alston-Roberts-West (b1842) served in the Royal Naval Reserve from November 1875 but never served on active service. In 1881 he was living in Ryde on the Isle of Wight with his wife and family, and rated as an honorary lieutenant. He inherited the Alscot Estate on his father's death in 1882 and returned to live at Alscot Park, but remained in the Naval Reserve. He lived at Alscot Park until his death in 1918.

James' sons, Harry and Reginald, both also followed naval careers. Harry began his career in January 1886 aged thirteen, as a naval cadet on the training ship HMS *Britannia* at Dartmouth, now the standard procedure for officer training. Harry passed as a midshipman in March 1889 and served for nearly six years on HMS *Tour Maline,* spending time in North America and the West Indies. He was attentive, of very good conduct, and had good physical qualities. He passed as a sub-lieutenant in October 1893 and began studying for the lieutenant's exams.

He failed in navigation in October 1893, for which he lost three months' seniority. Promotion was based on the date an officer reached each rank: Harry's was backdated three months. He failed in gunnery the following year, losing another month's time. In April 1894, he was charged with misconduct while at Portsmouth College – he had been sleeping outside the college, contrary to regulations – and was discharged to shore for three months. Only time at sea counted towards his promotion.

Harry finally passed all his exams, including seamanship, torpedoes and pilotage, and became a lieutenant in December 1895. He spent time on the *Dreadnought, Tauranga* and *Pembroke* and was noted as a smart and zealous officer, very good with all branches of signal work. He suffered continual bouts of malaria, remittant fever, enteric illness and appendicitis, probably through exposure in the tropics, and a report described his health as 'delicate'. Later still he was 'a bodily wreck from several ailments'.

In March 1898, while on the *Tauranga,* he awarded signalman John Brown a 'hasty and irregular punishment' and was court-martialled. He incurred seven days displeasure for his injudicious conduct.

In December 1901, his career took another blow. He was in command of the destroyer HMS *Salmon* when it collided with another ship en route for Amsterdam, causing the deaths of two men. Harry was court-martialled for negligence. He told the inquiry a month later that he considered the blame to be on the master of the other vessel. The adjudicating officers agreed and Harry was acquitted, but it seems his career never recovered.

He spent two years in command of HMS *Griffon,* which spent time in Australia, and was made lieutenant-commander in 1903, a rank issued after eight years as a lieutenant. In August 1904 was made flag lieutenant [personal assistant] to Rear-Admiral MacLeod on the *Aeolus.* He was considered a very good and zealous commander, with good aptitude for destroyer work, and had a great interest in wireless telegraphy. After two years he became flag lieutenant to Rear-Admiral King Hall, who recommended him for promotion, saying he couldn't speak too highly of his zeal and abilities and of the special interest he took in signalling work and telegraphy. Hall repeated his sentiments twice over the next eighteen months, adding that he considered Harry would do extremely well in the higher ranks, but no promotion was ever forthcoming.

In January 1908 Harry was placed in command of the minesweeper HMS *Skipjack* and served in Ireland in connection with the War Signal Station. A report stated his ship was admirably clean and the ship's company smart and well-drilled. Eighteen months later, in consequence of his knowledge of telegraphy work, he moved to the Padstow coastguard station in Cornwall as an Inspecting Officer, where he remained until the outbreak of the First World War.

Harry's brother Reginald also passed the examinations for a naval cadetship in March 1889, aged thirteen. He spent nearly two years on HMS *Britannia*, where his conduct and ability were very good, then spent three months on HMS *Aurora* in the Channel Squadron. The 1891 census records him on leave at Alscot, rated a navy midship junior; two weeks later on 17th April he joined the *Orlando*, where he passed as a midshipman and spent 3½ years in Australian waters. He was made a sub-lieutenant in May 1895 then returned to the naval college to prepare for his lieutenant's examinations.

He passed in seamanship but failed his college exams. He retook and passed these, then passed in gunnery and torpedoes but had to retake his pilotage exams. He spent time serving in Mauritius on the *Orlando* and was made lieutenant in December 1897. A year later a report described him as zealous and attentive, a good senior member of the gun room, but needed experience. Like his brother, he was physically delicate.

He spent several years on HMS *Centurion* in Chinese waters, then some time in UK waters – the 1901 census records him at sea near Plymouth – then served on HMS *Grafton* in the Pacific and commanded the *Thistle* in China. He had a very good knowledge of the pilotage of the Yangtse river and understood Chinese customs. He was interested in intelligence work and spent a month on reconnaissance with the military. He was recommended for early promotion.

In 1909 he was made commander but his conduct and ability, always described as very good, now dropped to satisfactory or average. In 1910 he moved to Shotley Barracks in Ipswich to command the naval training establishment. A report of 1911 described him as a little slow; a year later, as lacking initiative. He then returned to sea to command HMS *Vengeance* to the satisfaction of senior officers. He was serving on this ship at the start of the First World War.

Philip Douglas Roberts-West was the cousin of Harry and Reginald. He passed the examinations for naval cadetship in June 1890, aged fourteen, and went to sea on HMS *Victoria,* a new battleship of the Mediterranean Fleet, in February 1893.

Four months later, the *Victoria* was involved in an exercise near Tripoli when she collided with another vessel and sank. Half the crew drowned. Philip, now aged seventeen, saved a man from drowning and was awarded a bronze medal by the Royal Humane Society. A character report eight years later stated: *'this officer went down on the Victoria and was saved. I do not think he has ever recovered from the shock.'*

Philip was rated a midshipman a month after the disaster and served on the *Empress of India,* a twin-screw battleship and the flagship of the Channel Squadron. He failed his college examinations three times before gaining a third-class certificate, then scraped through his pilotage, gunnery and torpedo exams. He was made lieutenant in 1899. He served on several ships in China, Australia and the Mediterranean, and was made lieutenant-commander in 1907. Reports described him as hard working but slow; lacking in zeal; taciturn; and in times of emergency he appeared to become dazed. He needed to be more careful in making sure orders were carried out. An inspection of HMS *Hampshire* in 1908 stated he didn't exercise sufficient supervision over the clothing allocations, and he wasn't suitable for the command of a destroyer. In 1911 he overstayed his leave for twelve days but this wasn't considered a case for court martial. He was based on shore from July 1912, then joined HMS *Isis* when war broke out.

Charles William Keighly-Peach (b1865) was the son of Henry Peach Keighly-Peach and his wife Lucy. Henry was born in India, the son of Henry Keighly, a captain in the 3rd Cavalry Regiment in the East India Company, and later adopted his uncle's surname for inheritance purposes. He served as a captain in the 49th Madras Native Infantry and by 1891 he was living at Alderminster Lodge.

Charles passed for a naval cadetship in January 1879, aged thirteen. He was a promising officer and in October 1888 was posted to HMS *Pheasant,* a new six-gun gunboat, as a lieutenant. Six months later he merited special mention when his ship blockaded the river Opodo in Nigeria, and four months after this again distinguished himself when he assumed the role of Commanding Officer of the *Pheasant* after the death of the senior officer.

He served on various other ships and in September 1899 a senior officer said he had great zeal, very good judgement, was most trustworthy and deserving, and specially recommended him for advancement. He was promoted to commander the following year and married soon afterwards.

In 1906 he became commander of HMS *Hogue*, an armoured cruiser based in North America and the West Indies. An appraisal said that the *Hogue* was not in a satisfactory state, and there had been a lack of zeal and energy in getting her ready for sea. It seems Charles took note of this, for a report a year later said he was a capable officer, likely to make a good captain of a large ship, and was recommended for promotion. He was very slow in his manner, but this didn't prevent him commanding his ship efficiently. He was made a captain in June 1907 and remained on the *Hogue* for several years. In June 1914 he was transferred to the coastguard as war approached.

Francis George Burrows Hastings (b1874) was the son of naval veteran and vicar Francis Hastings. He was an actor with the Frank Benson company in the Royal Shakespeare Theatre, although not considered a great actor, and was a notable athlete and cricketer. He went to university and was ordained into the Church of England in 1904. A year later he enlisted in the Navy as a chaplain.

He served on HMS *Hecla*, a screw service torpedo vessel, and HMS *Hibernia*, a twin screw battleship, and spent time in Chinese waters. He was serving on HMS *Minotaur*, the same ship as Martin Seal, when war was declared.

Robert Arbuthnot was the eldest son of Sir William Wedderburn Arbuthnot, 3rd Baronet of Edinburgh and an officer in the 18th Hussars, and his wife Alice, the daughter of Matthew Tompson, long-time vicar of Alderminster. Crimean veteran William Tompson was his uncle.

Robert was born in Alderminster and joined HMS *Britannia* in 1877, aged thirteen. Two years later became a midshipman on HMS *Blanche* in North American waters. He was made a sub-lieutenant in December 1883 and lieutenant in August 1885. He was a first-rate officer and was awarded the Goodenough Medal, awarded annually to the best candidate taking the lieutenant's examinations.

He went on to serve in China, Japanese waters, Malta and Brazil – the 1901 census records him on the *Royal Sovereign* in the Grand Harbour in Malta – and he was made commander in 1897. He became the 4th Baronet of Edinburgh on his father's death and was appointed a Member of the Royal Victorian Order (MVO) in 1904. In 1907 he was made captain of HMS *Lord Nelson*, a brand new twin-screw battleship which became the flagship of the home fleet.

Robert now had a reputation as a detail-obsessed martinet, uncompromising, difficult to serve and merciless with discipline. A senior officer said of him: 'Arbuthnot is one of the finest fellows in the world, but his ideals are too high.' He was also courageous, dedicated, and won the grudging respect of all those under his command. Physical fitness, both in himself and his men, was a key aspect of his regime. He was accomplished at rugby and cricket, unbeatable over an obstacle course and also a champion boxer. When three of his men attacked him on shore, he hospitalised two of them.

His career took a blow in January 1910 when, during a speech at the Auto-Cycle Union, he made a serious attack on Germany and the British government and expressed the opinion that war was imminent. He was relieved of his command of the *Lord Nelson* following a formal complaint from Kaiser Wilhelm.

His career soon recovered. The 1911 census records him as commodore –commanding a small squadron of ships – on HMS *Boadicea* in Harwick harbour in Essex. The census return is covered in red stains and Robert added an explanatory note: *ink upset in rough weather.*

In 1912 he was appointed a Rear-Admiral, and in September 1913 he assumed command of the Second Battle Squadron of the First Fleet, as the Navy prepared for war.

Robert Arbuthot.

Five: The First World War

On the Eve of War

The 4th August 1914 marked Britain's entry into the war to end all wars.

Several men from the Alscot villages were serving in the army at this point, and their mobilisation began immediately. Troops were landing in France within a week as the German army swept through Belgium and into France, a massive surprise attack aiming to seize Paris and defeat France within six weeks.

Albert Horseman (b1879) was one of fourteen children of Joseph Horseman, a bricklayer's labourer, and his wife Emma of Crimscote. In 1891, aged twelve, Albert was working as a farm labourer. He then moved to Derby where he worked as a footman. In December 1900 he joined the 1st Life Guards, part of the prestigious Household Cavalry in Windsor. Local author Ursula Bloom wrote that when he came home on leave and attended church, resplendent in his scarlet cloak and white plumed helmet, the pews would be filled with young women hoping to catch his eye.

Albert passed his 3rd class and 2nd class education certificates and took an equitation course in 1903 to qualify as a rough rider. He was very reliable and willing to achieve, and his ability in all areas – riding, skill at arms, training a young horse and instructing – was good. He was promoted to corporal in October 1906. The only blemish on his record was in January 1908 when he was absent for 1 hour 55 minutes. For this he was 'severely reprimanded'.

He spent several spells in hospital including a month with orchitis [inflammation of the testicles] due to a horse accident and fractured ribs caused by an accident while training a horse. In 1909 he took another equitation course and was again of exemplary conduct. This covered elementary veterinary knowledge, pioneering, scouting and reconnaissance. He was promoted to corporal of the horse, the Household Cavalry's equivalent of sergeant, and in 1912 he re-engaged to complete 21 years' service. He married in 1910 and his son Albert was born in 1913. He landed in France with his squadron on 15th August 1914.

9/21

Cavalry Non-Commissioned Officers' Certificate.

No. 2315 Rank Corporal Name A. Horseman Regiment 1st Life Guards

Course 29th March to 30th October 1909.

Conduct during course Exemplary

PROFICIENCY.

Riding Maximum 100	Skill at arms Maximum 100	Training the young horse Maximum 100	As an Instructor Maximum 100	Horsemastership Elementary Veterinary knowledge Maximum 100	Cavalry Pioneering Maximum 100	Scouting and Reconnaissance Maximum 100
80	70	84	84	70·25	66 Qualified Instructor	60

Albert Horseman's certificate from the Cavalry School at Netheravon in Wiltshire.

Albert's younger brother Harold (b1886) enlisted in the Royal Warwickshire Regiment in December 1901. He was working as a labourer and stated he was eighteen, although he was actually only fifteen. He spent six years serving in Britain and Ireland and was promoted to lance corporal in February 1905. He qualified as the regimental watch bearer in 1904.

He was transferred to the reserve in December 1907 and in 1911 was living with his brother Evan in Great Bowden in Leicestershire, where both men worked as insurance agents. He had recently married and had a year-old daughter. In 1913, he re-enlisted to spend a further four years in the reserve. He would receive a worthwhile 3s 6d a week for minimal annual training. He was recalled on 5th August with the rest of the army reserve and posted to the 2nd Warwicks. He was promoted to corporal on 16th September and arrived in France two days later.

Frank Southam (b1892) was one of twelve children of gardener John Southam and his wife Ann of No.25 Alderminster. In 1911, aged eighteen, he was serving in the Royal Warwickshire Regiment at Budbrooke barracks in Warwick. He served in the 2nd battalion with Harold Horseman, and arrived in France on 6th October.

John (Jack) Garrett (b1885) was the son of farm labourer George Garrett and his wife Elizabeth. He was born in Whitchurch then the family moved to No.3

Crimscote. In 1901, aged fifteen, John was working as a groom in Tamworth. In 1904, just after his nineteenth birthday, he attested for the Royal Horse and Field Artillery. He was 5ft 7in, 144lbs and had a 39in chest. After six months' service and gymnastic training he had gained an inch in height, 16lbs in weight and an inch around his chest. In February 1908, he sailed for India where he spent nearly three years. He returned to England in November 1910 and was transferred to the reserve.

In 1911 he was living with his uncle in Kenilworth and working as a general labourer. He married the following year and his first son arrived six months later. In August 1914 he was living in Kenilworth with his wife Edith, who was heavily pregnant, and his infant son. He was mobilised on 5th August and landed in France two days later.

Ernest Giles Horseman (b1890) was the son of William and Sarah Horseman. William was born in Preston and worked as a waggoner before moving to Bristol where he worked as a railway horse keeper. In May 1906, Ernest, who worked as a striker and served in a militia battalion, enlisted in the 3rd Dragoon Guards. He stated he was eighteen, but he was actually barely sixteen and was discharged a fortnight later for this reason.

He enlisted again in August 1907, this time in the Royal Horse Artillery. He declared he had previously enlisted under-age, and stated he was now eighteen years and three months. He was still only seventeen, but this time he was accepted. He spent his entire service in Britain, and in August 1913 was transferred to the reserve. He was mobilised on 5th August and landed in France on the 15th.

Joseph Albert King (b1884) was the son of Robert King, a farm labourer from Tysoe. His mother Sally, nee Whiting, was from Alderminster where Joseph was born. The family moved to Bidford on Avon and in 1901 Joseph was living with his grandfather, William Whiting, in Wednesbury in Staffordshire where he worked on the railways. He enlisted in the South Staffordshire Regiment and in 1911 was serving in Lichfield. He landed at Havre on 13th August.

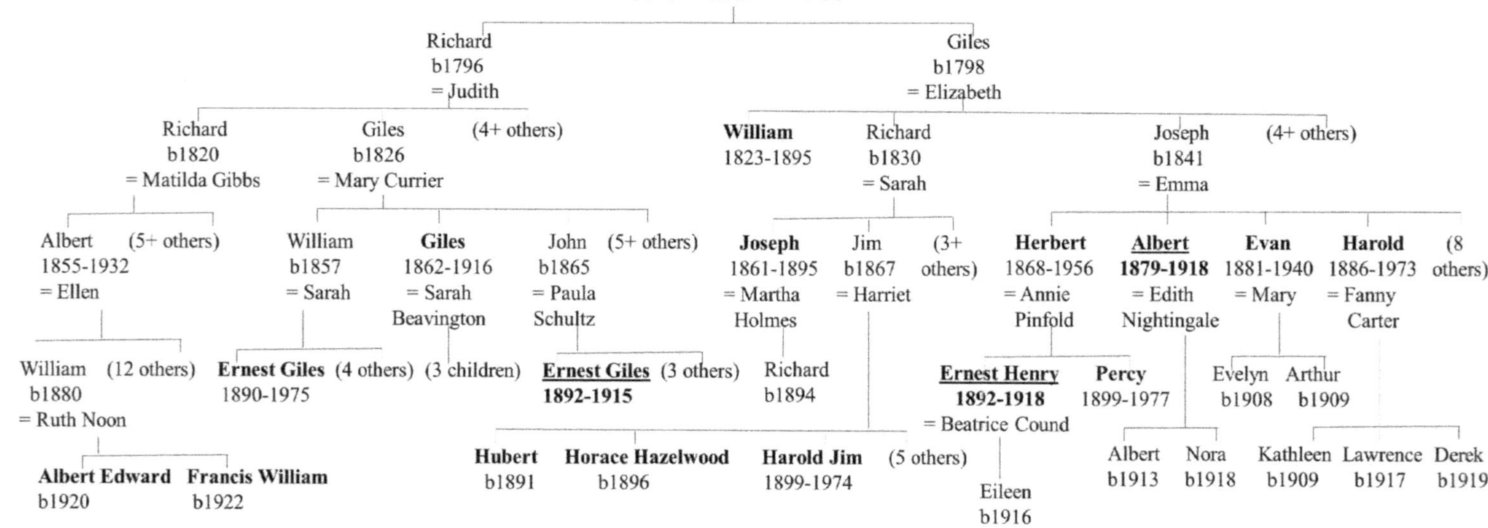

Horseman family tree. Names in bold served in the armed forces. Those underlined died on active service.

Kitchener's Volunteers

Field Marshall Lord Horatio Kitchener, veteran of the Sudan and South Africa and now Secretary of State for War, was one of the few men to predict a long and costly war and realised the British Army would be unable to cope with a major conflict. He had 750,000 men at his disposal, of which only one third were regular soldiers, one third of those being in India. France had mobilised 3.7m troops by the end of August, and Germany had 4.5m available troops.

Kitchener planned to create large voluntary armies. The first appeal for men began on 7th August. The nation was told it would be an easy conflict. That it was their duty to enlist. Recruiting parties toured towns and villages. Those who signed up were considered heroes. Those who didn't, cowards. By mid September nearly 500,000 men had volunteered.

> A meeting was held at at Alderminster on the green for all the Alscot Estate villages to attend. It gave information on the war and Mr Burra and Mr Archie Flower dwelled on the need for men and the obligation of young, able-bodied men to volunteer. Fourteen gave their names there and then and a half dozen more on Monday. All went to Birmingham for a medical, only one was rejected. All were to go to the depot on Wednesday, and on Tuesday a farewell service was held in Alderminster church by Rev. WH Morgan. The men were given a copy of the New Testament and each was presented with a packet of cigarettes. Mr Burra spoke a few concluding words of encouragement and three hearty cheers were given. The contingent left early Wednesday for the depot, Alderminster's bells ringing a farewell peal as they went.

From the Stratford Herald, 11th September 1914.

These men were all young and unmarried, probably itching for an adventure. They were exactly the healthy, fit, hard-labouring recruits the army wanted. They included James Paxford, 27, a farm labourer who lived with his widowed father at No.7 Preston. Arnold Herbert, who had served in the Royal Artillery in India two decades earlier, was his maternal uncle.

Robert William Dale, 22, was the eldest son of Edward and Esther Dale of Atherstone Hill Cottages. Edward was a shepherd at Atherstone Hill Farm, where Robert worked as a waggoner.

Arthur Thomas Burrows, 18, was the only son of baker's assistant George Burrows and his wife Sarah, who lived at No.13 Preston. In 1911, Arthur, aged fourteen, was working as a garden labourer.

Ernest Robinson, 18, who it seems was known as Jack, was the son of carter Richard Robinson and his wife Sarah. In 1911 the family were living in Atherstone where Ernest worked on a farm. By 1914 he was working in the Alscot gardens. The minimum age for enlistment was eighteen, but for overseas service nineteen, so younger volunteers were often encouraged to embellish their age. Whether Ernest and Arthur did this is unclear.

Harold Hyatt, 27, was the eldest son of carter William Hyatt and his wife Mary. The family moved to Whitchurch around 1900 then to Atherstone a few years later. In 1911 Harold was living at Alscot Park and working as a groom.

Thomas Bloxham, 21, was the son of farm labourer William Bloxham and his wife Sarah of Atherstone, and worked as a gardener. His uncle Charles Bloxham had served in the Rifle Brigade in the 1880s.

Frank Taylor, 19, was the son of John and Sarah Taylor of Alderminster Farm, and worked on the family farm.

Sydney Land was living in Preston. There is no record of this family name in the local area; he may have been an apprentice or farm pupil. Nothing else is known of his background.

These eight men were posted to the 11th Hampshire (Pioneers) Regiment, a newly formed battalion of Kitchener's Army. Men were usually posted to their local regiments, but some were overwhelmed with recruits while others were lacking, so men were often posted elsewhere to boost numbers. The Hampshires landed in France in December 1915.

Sidney Charles Hicks, 20, a farm labourer, was the son of cowman William Hicks and his wife Eliza. The family had recently moved from Tidmington to No.41 Alderminster.

William George Southam, 32, was one of twelve children of John and Sarah Ann Southam of Alderminster. His younger brother Frank was serving in the regular army. In 1901 William was lodging in Aston where he was working as a railway boiler washer. By 1911 he had returned to Alderminster and working as a farm labourer.

George William Hopkins, 20, a cowman, was the eldest son of farmworker

Josiah Hopkins and his wife Annie. The family lived in Atherstone Hill Cottages, next door to Robert Dale.

Stephen Bennett, one month past his 19th birthday, was one of eleven children of farm labourer George Bennett and his wife Flora. The family originated from Loxley but moved to Goldicote in Alderminster parish, where George worked as a shepherd for wealthy landowner Claud Portman. Stephen worked as a carter. His brothers George, Thomas and Frank also enlisted at an early stage in the war.

John Rimell, 24, was one of twelve children of David and Ann Rimell. David worked as a stockman and the family lived in various local villages including Preston and Wimpstone. In 1911 John was lodging at Milcote Hall and working as an under carter. In 1914 he was living in Wimpstone.

John's brother Edward, 19, also worked as a farm labourer and lived in Wimpstone.

These six men were posted to the 6th Dorset Regiment, a newly formed battalion with a large proportion of Warwickshire men. They arrived in France in July 1915.

Several other men enlisted by late September, and may have been among the first group of volunteers. They included William Henry Job, also spelt Jobe, 28, son of labourer Henry Job and his wife Mary of No.5 Preston. Henry died in the 1890s and Mary worked as a laundress. William worked as a farm labourer for Alscot Estate and was eventually put in charge of the agricultural machinery. His mechanical knowledge gained him the position of chauffeur in 1912. He was quickly discharged, probably for medical reasons, but was reenlisted in 1916 after manpower shortages led to lowering of physical standards.

Robert Henry Ashby, 19, was the eldest son of John and Rosa Ashby of Cottage Farm, Alderminster. In 1911, he was working on the family farm. He was also quickly discharged, but reenlisted in February 1916. His subsequent service history is unclear.

Wilfred Townsend, 17, was the son of carter Alfred Townsend and his wife Rosina of No.19 Wimpstone. In 1911, aged 14, he was working as a ploughboy. He presumably lied about his age to enlist. Nothing else is known of his service history.

James King, 27, was the son of farm labourer William King and his wife Elizabeth of Knavenhill Cottages, Alderminster. In 1911 he was working as a carter. Nothing else is known of his service history.

J. Thorp was living in Preston when he volunteered. It is unclear who he is and nothing else is known of his service history.

John Stowe, formerly of Atherstone and a veteran of the Egyptian campaign and the Nile Expedition in the 1880s, was now 54 and working as a dispatch clerk in Otley, Yorkshire. He re-enlisted on 4th September. Although well over the age for active service, he was accepted into the West Yorkshire Regiment as a colour sergeant in view of his military experience: slightly misstated as 22½ years in the prestigious Gordon Highlanders. He was appointed CQMS (Company Quartermaster Sergeant) and served in York for the duration of the war.

Algernon Claude Phillip Alston-Roberts-West, 36, was the youngest son of James Alston-Roberts-West of Alscot Park. He followed no particular career and was content to enjoy his privileged lifestyle. He was commissioned, as expected given his social status, as a temporary lieutenant in the 23rd (City of London) battalion of the London Regiment on 3rd October 1914. There was a dire need for officers to lead the thousands of recruits, and lengthy officer training courses were no longer feasible, so temporary commissions were given to suitable men from public schools and Officer Training Corps. Algernon arrived in France on 21st August 1917, nearly three years after his commission. He was wounded at an unknown point and subsequently discharged.

The rush for recruits meant many unsuitable men were enlisted. Men who were desperate to join in the fun did their best to cover up medical problems and recruiting staff, who received a bounty for each man enlisted, were not too careful about uncovering them.

Harold Hyatt was discharged after a month due to rheumatic fever which had made him unlikely to become an efficient soldier. Whether he contracted this before or after enlisting is unclear.

James Paxford was discharged in December for unknown reasons. John Rimell's initial medical had noted slight vasculitis [vein damage] on his leg and side. This was considered insufficient to reject him but led to his discharge at the end of October. His brother Edward was discharged on the same day: he suffered from cardiac debilitation.

Reginald Francis Hawkins, 20, was the son of gardener Thomas Hawkins and his wife Louisa, nee Francis, of a long-standing Alderminster family. Reginald, a motor mechanic, enlisted into the Warwicks on 26th August. He was 5ft 3in, the minimum height for enlistment, and weighed well under nine stone. He was discharged after four weeks' service, considered unlikely to become an efficient soldier.

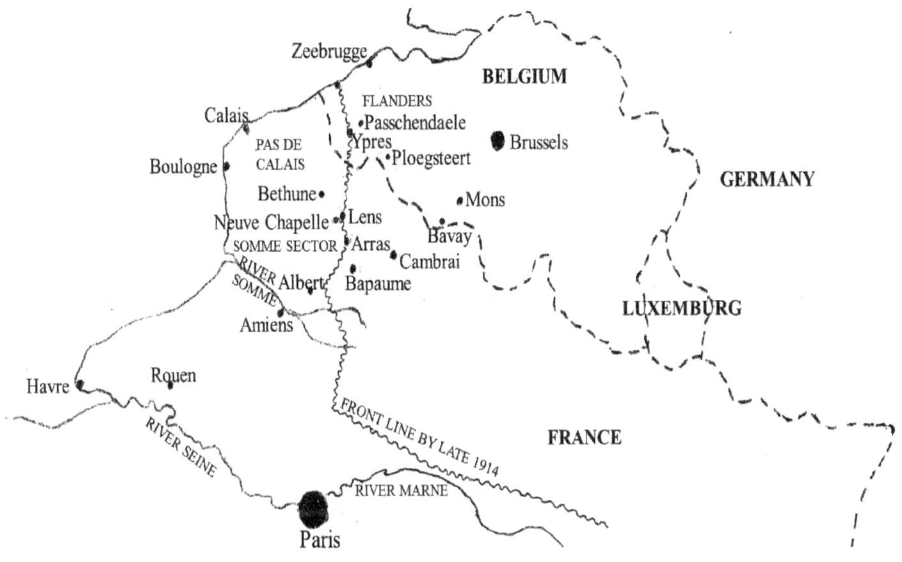

The Western Front in 1914.

The Fighting Begins

The 2nd South Staffs, including Joseph King, now a corporal, was one of the first units to land in France. Their war diary stated:

> *4 Aug 1914, Aldershot. OC [officer commanding] receives orders to mobilise.*
> *6 Aug 1914. Completed mobilisation.*
> *12 Aug 1914, 3.15am. Entrained for Southampton, embarked on SS Irrawaddy.*
> *13 Aug 1914, 7.30am. Disembarked at Havre, marched to No.1 camp, arrived 10.30am.*

The Staffs remained in billets for ten days then moved to the village of Harmignies, south of Mons in Belgium, on 22nd August, in preparation for the first British encounter with German troops.

The Battle of Mons took place on 23rd August. The British divisions had taken up a line south of the town of Mons, a landscape of slag heaps and pit villages. The Germans mounted a heavy attack on the British, and the much smaller but much better trained force checked the German advance. The Staffs came under slight enemy fire that afternoon, then witnessed a big artillery combat that evening. The battalion dug themselves into trenches and put Harmignies into a state of defence.

The British line was precarious due to the overwhelming German numbers. The French plan for a decisive victory proved disastrous, and they began to retreat after the enemy broke through their lines. The British had no choice but to fall back as well, the start of the infamous retreat from Mons.

The Staffs retreated with the rest of their brigade on the 24th. The men had a very long and hot day, and when they arrived that evening at Bavay, just over the French border, they had to dig themselves into trenches all through the night.

The retreat continued for several days, the Germans close behind. Little fighting took place apart from rearguard defensive action. The Staffs marched 236 miles between 21st August and 5th September. The Allies were forced back to the Marne, and after a week-long battle managed to check the German advance.

On the 10th September the Staffs' brigade surprised and attacked a German column, which surrendered after a 2½ hour fight. Apart from this, there was little fighting for the battalion.

After several more days of marching, the battalion received orders at 2am on 18th September to reinforce the 4th Guards Brigade at Soupir, which was under attack. The position was held and the Staffs remained there in trenches for two weeks.

The frontline stabilised and the Germans began to retreat. The Allies began push forward and the Staffs were then moved to Ypres.

William Lawrence of the King's Royal Rifle Corps is named on Alderminster's War Memorial. His identity is unclear. Two men of this name died while serving with the KRRC, both in 1914.

The first was born in Southwark in London, the son of box-maker Henry Lawrence, and joined the 1st KRRC in January 1910 aged eighteen. In July 1913, while serving in Aldershot, he married Eva Green, a homeless prostitute. His battalion arrived in France on 13th August 1914 and was involved in heavy fighting for the next two months. William was among many battalion casualties on 27th October, while fighting in the Ypres area. He has no known grave and is commemorated on the Menin Gate Memorial.

His family had lived in Southwark for at least two generations, and his widow remarried after the war and lived in Hampshire for her life. He has no identifiable connection to Alderminster.

The second William Lawrence was the son of Walter Henry and Ellen Lawrence of London and also has no obvious connection with Alderminster. In

1901 the family were living in Wandsworth where Walter was working as a road sweeper. In 1911 William, now fifteen, was boarding in Wandsworth with his elder brother Walter, and both worked as shop assistants.

William, aged eighteen, was serving in the 2nd KRRC when war broke out. Presuming he hadn't lied about his age, he hadn't been serving for long. His battalion landed in France on 12th August. He was recorded as missing in action on 14th September and is commemorated on La Ferte-sous-Jouarre Memorial in France.

There were two families named Lawrence in Alderminster at this time; a tailoring family which originated in Birmingham and a gamekeeping family which originated in Hampshire. Neither William seems to relate to these; he was perhaps working in Alderminster as an apprentice or in service before enlisting.

The First Battle of Ypres

Both sides were now trying to outflank each other in the race to secure the strategically vital coastal ports, known as The Race to the Sea, which culminated in the First Battle of Ypres in Flanders.

On 7th October, the South Staffs went into trenches at Ypres. Harold Horseman and Frank Southam, in the 2nd Warwicks, also moved to Ypres where they came under fire for the first time. The diary of the Warwicks stated on 10th October: *The firing started at 8pm. The French immediately retired to a position where they could conveniently enfilade [machine gun] our line, which they continued to do during the night.*

The battle began on 19th October. The Warwicks entrenched the next day at the town of Zonnebeke, where the British had formed a strong line. They were attacked at daybreak the following day and suffered many casualties. They retired to a new position at 1am on the 22nd where they entrenched and remained for two days.

On the 23rd October, the Staffs attacked some trenches which had been lost the previous night. These were regained after heavy fighting and many casualties.

At 6.30am on the 24th, the Warwicks were ordered to clear a wood of enemy troops. They were heavily shelled and the Germans retired obstinately, causing many casualties. The Germans then occupied a farmhouse behind the wood which the Warwicks were told to capture. They succeeded, despite coming under fierce rifle and machine gun fire and suffering heavy casualties. They were later told this had saved the British line.

The fighting continued for several more weeks. Attacks were repeatedly made by both sides with minimal achievement. On 31st October, Harold Horseman was wounded in the back by shrapnel. He was evacuated to England a week later and didn't return to the front line again. He was discharged as medically unfit, and as he had not completed the service period for which he had engaged, he was told he was not entitled to a bounty from the army.

The Staffs remained in the frontline at Ypres until mid November. Regular attacks were repelled with heavy casualties and they were subject to regular heavy shelling.

Joseph King, now acting sergeant, was killed in action on 18th November. The reason is unclear: there is no record of fighting in the battalion diary for this date. He has no known grave and is commemorated on the Ypres (Menin Gate) Memorial.

The First Battle of Ypres faded into stalemate at the end of November. Both sides were exhausted, low in morale and short of ammunition. The war now centred on attrition and trenched warfare, and the frontline remained largely static for the next four years.

The Western Front in 1915

The War of Attrition

For many of the troops arriving in France, the war now centred on trench life with little fighting. Trenches were permanently occupied and carefully constructed. They were deep enough to shield men from snipers, and zigzagged so raiding parties had minimal visible targets. Communication trenches led back to support trenches. Dugouts or underground shelters provided living quarters. As more and more trenches were dug, their layout became labyrinthine.

A strategy was developed where two of the four battalions of each brigade would be in the forward trenches, one would be in support just behind the lines, and one would be in reserve. They rotated every four days.

Trench routine involved strengthening, extending and repairing the trenches; working on the barbed wire; patrolling No Man's Land and gaining intelligence on German positions; and observing the Germans performing similar tasks. All work outside the trenches, including working parties which brought up rations and supplies, had to done at night. A sniper's bullet could strike whenever a man got careless. Most trenches were routinely shelled and raids were commonplace.

At first, life in the trenches was relatively pleasant, if monotonous. The weather was good, wildlife could be seen in the farmland and hedges, and the farmers' crops were still growing beneath the barbed wire. The surrounding villages and farms were adapted for tactical purposes.

In the winter of 1914, the weather deteriorated. Heavy rain meant the men were standing in waist-deep water. Attempts to pump out the trenches were futile. The Royal Engineers had the unending task of shoring up collapsing trenches and building platforms to keep the occupants dry. Trenches were now given names such as Muddy Lane, Rotten Row and Suicide Road. Rheumatism was rife, and constantly cold and wet feet caused circulation damage which could lead to necrosis and gangrene. This condition became known as 'trench feet'.

There were often no hard roads, and all routes were soon churned to deep mud. Endless shelling devastated the ground even further. Wooden walkways were laid but any man who fell into the deep mud could suffocate.

The landscape of France and Belgium turned to splintered trees, barbed wire, shellholes and mud. The occupied buildings were gradually wrecked by shelling. The war was now a matter of holding the line and waiting, as each side tried to wear down the other into capitulation. This would take another four years to achieve.

George Randolph Sheasby, 19, was the son of tailor Thomas Sheasby and his wife Lucy. He was born in Alderminster where the family lived for many years before moving to Stratford. In 1911 George was working as an apprentice barber. He had been in Stratford's Boy Scouts – later cited by many servicemen as providing vital skills for the frontline – and was a well-known local footballer. Sportsmen were especially targeted by recruiting drives.

George enlisted on 12th August 1914 and arrived in France on 23rd November, one of the first volunteers to do so. The unusually short time may suggest he had been in the territorial force or had some other military experience. He was posted to the 1st Royal Welch Fusiliers, which had suffered catastrophically at Ypres. By the end of October, just 86 men were left of the thousand who had landed three weeks earlier. George spent time in the trenches near Ypres with no substantial action then in March 1915 the battalion moved to northern France to fight in the Battle of Neuve Chapelle.

James Frank Holtom, 18, was the son of carrier Eli Holtom and his wife Catherine. Eli was born in Alderminster, moved to Birmingham where James was born, then returned to Alderminster around 1898. In 1911 James was working as a boot boy in Wootton Wawen. He enlisted in the 1st Warwicks on

13th August 1914 under the name Frank James Holtom and arrived in France on 3rd December. He spent several fairly quiet months in and out of trenches near Ypres, then fought in the Second Battle of Ypres in April 1915.

Walter Raymond Tilling, 20, was the son of George and Sarah Tilling. George worked as a carter at Wincot Farm then moved to Radbrook Cottages. In 1911 Walter was a private in the Royal Warwicks but it seems didn't serve for long. In 1914 the family were living in Atherstone and Walter was working as a porter. He enlisted in the 1st Hampshire Regiment on 9th November and arrived in France on 27th December. His previous military experience would account for his early arrival and his posting to a regular battalion. The 1st Hants went into waterlogged trenches at Ploegsteert in Belgium. There was little enemy activity except for almost daily shelling, but a hundred men each month were admitted to hospital, probably with problems such as trench feet and frostbite. They remained in and out of the same set of trenches until rushed to Ypres in April 1915.

Boer War veteran John Whiteman of the Middlesex Regiment had been posted to the East Indies after leaving South Africa in 1902, then arrived in Britain in February 1903 – probably the first time he had seen the country he was serving. He spent 3½ years in Britain and married Alice Gregg, of a wealthy Temple Grafton family, in 1905. A year later, he was promoted to captain. He spent more time in the East Indies, then in 1911 was living in Aldershot. His battalion arrived in France in August 1914 but John didn't join them until 20th December. They had suffered catastrophically at Mons and Ypres and reinforcements, especially officers, were desperately needed.

John spent several months in trenches near Ypres which, apart from regular artillery duels, was relatively quiet. The commanding officer (CO) of the battalion went sick in January 1915 and John Whiteman took his place. John was only a captain and the CO was normally a lieutenant colonel, but due to heavy casualty rates John was probably the most senior officer available. He remained in command for five weeks until a more senior officer arrived. His first major action was at Neuve Chapelle in March 1915.

Frank Southam of the 2nd Warwicks went into trenches in northern France in mid November. They remained in and out of the same trenches for the next month. On 18th December, they ordered to attack a line of German trenches. A heavy artillery bombardment was put down to cut the barbed wire and destroy enemy positions. The Warwicks advanced and were met with heavy rifle and machine gun fire. Despite very heavy casualties, some men got into the enemy trenches, but the attack proved a failure. The men in the trenches were captured and the remainder of the battalion withdrew. An informal armistice allowed the British to bury some of the officers and carry the wounded to the German lines to be made prisoner. Over 360 men were killed, wounded or missing. Their next action was at Neuve Chapelle.

Albert Horseman of the 1st Life Guards arrived in France on 15th August and joined the 4th Cavalry Brigade. The cavalry spent the first few weeks in mobile reconnaissance and scouting. The war was fast-moving and mobile, and the cavalry were a vital asset. They came into regular contact with German cavalry patrols but were involved in no serious fighting.

Albert rejoined the main body of the Life Guards, now in Flanders, on 11th November. The cavalry was held behind the line, ready to charge forward and consolidate the infantry's victories, but as the war turned to stalemate they were dismounted and sent to frontline trenches. Cavalry units were near-obsolete. Most of the work for this prestigious unit involved carrying supplies to the frontline, digging trenches and helping the local farmers with the harvest.

Neuve Chapelle and Festubert

In the spring of 1915, the Germans diverted large numbers of troops to the Eastern Front, aiming to quickly defeat the Russian army. The Allies seized the opportunity and planned a major offensive. The Battle of Neuve Chapelle, 10-13th March 1915, was the first British large-scale organised attack. The objective was Aubers Ridge, of tactical importance in the otherwise flat landscape.

John Whiteman of the 4th Middlesex was in trenches two miles south of St Eloi near Ypres. On 10th March, the battalion was ordered to make every endeavour to appear to be preparing for an attack, to divert attention from the real target. They dug a new communication trench; laid bridges over trenches for the benefit of aerial observers; started an artillery bombardment; then the men showed their bayonets over the parapet as if ready to go. The Germans shelled their lines immediately. The battalion then took no further part in the action.

Frank Southam, with the 2nd Warwicks, advanced on the German line on 12th March. They were held up by machine gun fire and darkness and were forced to dig in for the night. The exhausted men then began digging a communication trench to connect back to their former lines. Further advance was attempted by other units the next day. This was also held up. The Warwicks were ordered to attack a house occupied by the enemy, but were unable to leave their trenches due to machine gun and artillery fire. They remained in their position until relieved on the 15th. They had suffered 120 casualties during the past three days.

The village of Neuve Chapelle, now ruined by shellfire, was captured but Aubers Ridge and the second line of German trenches were not. Another attempt was made on 8th May. The Royal Welch Fusiliers, including George Sheasby, were in reserve but didn't leave the assembly trenches. The attack was a failure with 11,000 casualties and it was repeated the following week. This became known as the Battle of Festubert.

The Fusiliers were leading the attack with the 2nd Warwicks in support. The Fusiliers assembled in the assault trenches and at 2.15am on 16th May, the attack began. An officer wrote that: *'After half an hour's bombardment, the whole of our line with one leap were over our parapet. It was a sad spectacle owing to heavy rifle and machine gun fire mowing many of our poor chaps over, not to speak of high explosive and shrapnel shells.'*

Despite heavy casualties, the battalion took the first and second lines of German trenches. They were now in need of support, and at 4.30am the Warwicks were sent forward. They consolidated the captured ground but were unable to advance further.

The enemy held strong positions in nearby houses and orchards and their snipers caused many casualties. The British attacked these posts but not all were captured. The Germans shelled the captured trenches and the British were forced back. The following day the won and lost ground was taken again.

George Sheasby was working as a stretcher bearer throughout this operation and was noted for his gallant conduct in rescuing the wounded under heavy shell fire.

The Fusiliers remained in the frontline for another two days, by which time they had suffered nearly 600 casualties. They collected and buried the bodies of 110 men on the 18th alone. The Warwicks suffered 200 casualties. The battle was deemed a success.

Sometime after this, John Whiteman was invalided to England suffering from shellshock. He didn't return to France until December 1916.

The Second Battle of Ypres

A bulging weak point in the Allied line known as the Ypres Salient had been formed in November 1914. The Germans attacked on 22nd April 1915, a date significant for their first use of lethal chlorine gas, and a month-long battle to defend Ypres followed.

The French troops gave way under a German assault, leaving the Canadians on their flank exposed. They were forced back after heavy fighting. Walter Tilling, with the 1st Hants, and Frank Holtom, with the 1st Warwicks, were among many troops rushed to defend the line.

The Warwicks were ordered to attack a German-held wood early on the 25th, but the enemy trenches had been insufficiently shelled and with no support they were forced to withdraw after suffering over 500 casualties.

Later that day, the Hants were ordered to relieve the Canadians. But unknown to them, the Canadians had broken and fallen back. They passed Ypres, now blazing ruins with shells still crashing down, then learned of the Canadian withdrawal. There was a three-mile gap in the line which their brigade had to fill, but nobody knew the exact extent of the breach or the whereabouts of the enemy. The Hants were ordered forward to make contact with the Royal Fusiliers, who were holding the trenches at one end of the breach.

At 2.30am, they believed they were near the Fusiliers' lines. It was now less than two hours until dawn. The salient was exposed to artillery on three sides, and if the men were visible in daylight they would be annihilated by shelling.

They found some partly dug trenches and started digging while patrols made contact with the Fusiliers. The men were exhausted but dug fast: their lives literally depended it. Luckily, thick fog meant digging could continue past dawn.

When the fog lifted, the shelling began. Up to fifty shells a minute fell, with great accuracy, all day. The Hants lost a hundred men killed and many more wounded. They hung onto their position. When darkness fell they continued digging; fetched ammunition, water and rations; and carried the wounded three miles back towards Ypres. Reinforcements arrived and the breach in the line was finally sealed.

The shelling continued for eight days. The Hants spent sixteen daylight hours crouched in their trenches listening to the shells bursting, then eight hours of darkness desperately repairing and extending their trenches. Some men slept peacefully through the shelling; others barely slept and grew ever more exhausted.

After several failed attacks on the German lines, the Allies were told to prepare for withdrawal. On 3rd May, the shelling became heavier than ever. The battalion to the right of the Hants, entrenched in a small wood, was attacked. The Hants helped them drive the enemy back. Subsequent shelling left barely a tree in the wood standing, and a second attack drove the battalion back. The Germans then turned on the Hants, who held their line with heavy casualties. The Warwicks were also attacked, but despite being gassed were able to hold their line.

All units withdrew that night. The roads were heavily congested but the march of several miles was calm and all men and equipment got back safely. The Hants had suffered over 300 casualties during the past eight days; the Warwicks many more.

Five days later, the Hants were back in the trenches. They suffered regular heavy shelling; on 13th May the Germans bombarded them from 4am to 2pm, causing around a hundred casualties. They were relieved on the 16th and moved back to the support line. Two men were killed and nine wounded during the move. Walter Tilling was one of these. He was shot in the buttock, admitted to hospital in Versailles three days later, and evacuated to England on 28th May.

On 24th May, the Warwicks were ordered to support an advance on a German position. They were heavily shelled and gassed and the British attack was checked by heavy machine gun fire. The battalion returned to the support trenches having suffered nearly a hundred casualties. They were relieved two days later.

The Second Battle of Ypres ended on 25th May. The city was destroyed; the salient had been compressed but remained intact. The price was 87,000 Allied casualties.

Walter Tilling eventually returned to the frontline. He was transferred to the Corps of Dragoons and then the East Kent Yeomanry where he remained until the end of the war. Frank Holtom eventually transferred to the Machine Gun Corps and served until the end of the war.

The 6th Dorset Regiment

Stephen Bennett, William Southam, George Hopkins and Sidney Hicks, all posted to the 6th Dorsets in September 1914, landed at Boulogne on 13th July 1915. They went into the trenches for the first time at St Eloi, near Ypres, on 3rd August.

The trenches were in a shocking condition with practically no drainage and little work put into them, and the weather was also very bad. Their time behind the lines was spent under leaky canvas so they were constantly wet through.

On 10th August, Sidney Hicks was found asleep while on sentry duty. The men were constantly exhausted but this was a serious offence which could cost the lives of many men. He was given seven days' Field Punishment: he was put in handcuffs and fetters but otherwise continued as normal. This was to be his only offence.

On 10th November, William Southam received a gunshot wound to his right knee. The battalion was then behind the lines and providing working parties to the trenches. Four days later he was on the Hospital Ship *Anglia* en route for England. The next day Stephen Bennett was also invalided to England, suffering from trench feet and frostbite. He wrote to his parents, later printed in the *Herald*:

> *'We were up to our waists in mud and water and for three days I had no sleep. The corporal came along and said, 'Bennett, you'd better get some sleep if you can. You look bad.' I sat down in the mud and was so dead beat I fell asleep. When they came to wake me up they had to dig me out of the mud, and I was placed on a stretcher. I remember nothing more until I arrived at the dressing station where all my clothes were cut off me, my shirt and everything. I was washed and fed for I had no use of my hands and feet to do anything for myself. My right hand went black all over and I thought I should lose it, but now I am regaining use of it, thank God.'*

Stephen continued that although no one could realise what he'd experienced, he wasn't downhearted. He was proud to do his bit and wasn't slacking like some of the single chaps. There was a common and understandable resentment from those who had volunteered towards those who had not.

On the 17th November, the *Anglia* hit a mine off Dover and sank. William Southam was one of 135 people known or presumed drowned. His body was not recovered and he is commemorated on the Hollybrook Memorial in Southampton and the Alderminster War Memorial.

Stephen Bennett reached England safely. It was nearly a year before he was declared fit and returned to the frontline, where he was posted to the 1st Dorsets.

In December or early January, George Hopkins was wounded. The battalion was still in trenches near Ypres. He was probably evacuated to England, and eventually returned to the frontline.

Sidney Hicks remained with the battalion, which was posted to the Somme sector by July 1916 to take part in that battle.

The Battle of Loos

The Battle of Loos, which began in northern France on 25th September 1915, was the biggest British battle of the war so far. It was the first time the British used gas on the enemy and was also the first major action for several Alscot servicemen.

Frederick Churchill (b1881) was the son of farm labourer James Churchill and his wife Ellen. The family lived at Crimscote, and in 1901 Frederick was lodging in Edgbaston where he worked as a bread deliverer. He married, had two daughters, and in 1911 was living in Handsworth. He now ran his own bakery. He volunteered in 1914 or early 1915, by which time he was living near Cardiff, and joined the 1st Royal Welch Regiment. This was a regular battalion which may indicate he had prior military experience.

He arrived in France on 26th May 1915 and joined his battalion near Dickebrugh in eastern Flanders. The battalion diary reported that this draft of men was badly trained and showed great slackness in discipline. The battalion spent several weeks in trenches which needed a lot of work to make them dry and bulletproof, and men were regularly shot when carelessly looking over the parapet. By late September they were in trenches at Vermelles, preparing for the attack at Loos.

George Edgington (b1872) was a waggoner living at No.3 Wimpstone. He was married with no children, and enlisted into the 10th Gloucestershire Regiment on 17th November 1914. It was unusual for a married man of his age to volunteer. His earlier life is unclear but he may have been serving in the Royal Warwickshire Regiment in 1891, perhaps explaining his early enlistment. The Gloucesters landed at Havre on 9th August 1915. They had their first experience of the trenches ten days later, then a month later formed up near Hulluch near Loos.

John William (Jack) Ward, 31, was the son of George and Susanna Ward. George was the police constable in Alderminster for many years, and on his death in 1908 his family moved to Crimscote. John worked as a farm labourer and enlisted in the 3rd Grenadier Guards in January 1915. He had married Emily Taylor, the sister of Joseph Taylor of the Royal Artillery, three years earlier, and had two children with another on the way. His battalion arrived in France on 8th September and a fortnight later were preparing for battle.

Charles Edmund (Ted) Hyatt, 19, was the son of farm labourer William Hyatt and his wife Mary of Atherstone. In 1911 he was working as a waggoner. He then worked as an under gardener at Alscot Park. His elder brother Harold had been one of the first volunteers but was soon discharged. Charles, who was over six feet tall and very popular, volunteered around December 1914 and was posted to the 2nd Coldstream Guards. He arrived in France on 10th August 1915 and six weeks later was in trenches near Loos.

George Sheasby and Frank Southam, who had both seen action at Neuve Chapelle a few months earlier, were also involved in the fighting.

On 24th September, the Gloucesters, including George Edgington, drew up in battle position near the village of Hulluch. At 6.30am on 25th September, the attack began. The British released their gas but the wind was unfavourable and several of the Gloucesters were affected. They moved forward regardless. They lost direction in the smoke screen; the enemy wire was a considerable obstacle; they met heavy resistance; and their bombs had got wet and failed to explode. The assault pressed on. Most of the officers fell. The second and third lines of German trenches were taken, but that night, when the battalion reorganised, only sixty survivors assembled. Nearly a thousand men had disembarked the month before. More stragglers gradually rejoined and they were relieved on the 27th. The battalion later received commendation from the highest levels for their actions.

The 1st Welch Fusiliers, including George Sheasby, attacked at Vermelles at 5am on 25th September. The attacking units went right through the German lines but were left unsupported, and they met strong resistance from the Germans. After losing 450 casualties, the Fusiliers were forced to retreat back to their original lines.

George Sheasby was one of only two stretcher-bearers who didn't become casualties and was awarded the first Distinguished Conduct Medal (DCM) of the Stratford district. It was his third commendation. On one occasion he'd saved the life of a Bedfords captain; on another he'd rescued several men under heavy shellfire. He'd had several narrow escapes himself, in one case a bullet passing through his knapsack. He was soon promoted to lance corporal.

The 2nd Coldstream Guards, including Charles Hyatt, went into action on 26th September and consolidated the captured trenches near Vermelles. They remained in these trenches until the end of October.

11851 Private G. R. Sheasby, 1st Battalion, Royal Welsh Fusiliers.

For conspicuous gallantry when acting as a stretcher-bearer. After the capture of the first line of hostile trenches, Private Sheasby displayed great coolness and bravery in attending to the wounded under the most heavy rifle and shell fire.

From the London Gazette, 11th March 1916.

The 2nd Warwicks, including Frank Southam, were fighting near Les Harisoirs on 25th September. They advanced at 6.30am and took many German trenches by 9.30am, but that night the battalion could muster only 140 men. Nearly 250 had become casualties; another 270 were missing. The battalion held their new line until they were relieved on the 29th.

The 3rd Grenadiers, including Jack Ward, were fighting near Verquigneul, a village near Bethune. On 27th September, they attacked the German line. They suffered severe losses: only two sergeants were left and all the officers had become casualties. The men had to dig all day under heavy fire, hadn't had food for 24 hours, and were exhausted. It was too wet and cold to sleep and they were in constant anticipation of an attack. The trenches were very shallow but they couldn't dig down any further as the ground was full of bodies. There were fifteen dead Germans in the trench itself. Despite all this, the men were reported to be in extraordinarily good spirits and ready for the next attack. They were eventually relieved and marched six miles, absolutely dead beat, behind the lines to rest.

The 1st Welch Regiment, including Frederick Churchill, attacked a German trench called Little Willie near Vermelles, their orders to 'take it at the point of the bayonet, regardless of all costs'. At 8pm on 1st October, they climbed over the parapet like one man and moved forward in perfect silence. They were within a hundred yards of the enemy before they were seen. Then the machineguns opened fire.

The commanding officer's voice rang out, 'Get at 'em, Welch!' Within twenty seconds, 250 men were down. The remainder charged the trenches, bayonetting the enemy and firing on those retreating. The 'gallant little affair' gained most of its objectives but the Welch had to prepare at once for a counterattack. They had failed to capture a key communication trench so had no support. They had to dig all night to link back to their supporting units.

They didn't succeed. All night and the next morning they were in constant bombing battles with the enemy. Then their bombs ran out. The situation was now serious. The Germans were moving up and sending *minenwerfer* – massive and devastating trench mortars – into the trenches. They attacked that afternoon. The Welch charged them but were destroyed by a hail of bombs. The Welch then received orders to move back to their original line. They had suffered nearly four hundred casualties.

Frederick Churchill was killed on the 1st October. He has no known grave and is commemorated on the Loos Memorial and Whitchurch War Memorial.

On 4th October, the 3rd Grenadier Guards returned to the trenches near Vermelles. On 8th October, they were heavily attacked. The enemy bombed down their line, surprising their bombers and killing most of them. They also overran the battalion's machine gun position. The Guards were forced to retire, then more bombers were rushed up from the support lines and cleared the enemy from their trenches. They were heavily shelled the next day but no further attack followed. They remained in and out of this trench system for the rest of the month, with regular heavy shelling but no further attacks.

On the 5th October, the remnants of the 10th Gloucesters went back into the trenches. On 13th October, after an artillery and gas bombardment, they attacked the German line. They faced heavy rifle and machine gun fire and were forced back after suffering over 150 casualties – nearly a third of their number. They were relieved the following day.

George Edgington was wounded around this time. He was evacuated to England where he subsequently recovered. He was transferred to the Machine Gun Corps and eventually returned to France.

The Battle of Loos ended in mid October with nearly 60,000 British casualties. Little ground was gained; much of that subsequently lost. The situation on the Western Front remained relatively quiet as winter set in. No major attack could be mounted over the rain-sodden and snow-covered ground and both sides huddled miserably in their trenches, waiting for spring.

In early November, the 3rd Grenadier Guards, including Jack Ward, spent a week in very bad billets after a 26km march, then went into waterlogged trenches at Neuve Chapelle. They continued in and out of the trenches for several weeks, carrying out routine work and drainage. They were frequently raided but otherwise their time was fairly quiet.

Their tour ended on Christmas Eve. That day, the enemy shelled their trenches for two hours and enfiladed them. There were two casualties; Jack Ward was one of them. He was badly wounded and died in a casualty clearing station the following day. Six weeks later his widow received a letter from Captain Gordon, his company captain, stating;

> *'Your husband was hit by a German sniper on the night of December 24th. He was immediately taken to hospital but I am sorry to say he died on December 25th. I tender you the sincere sympathy of his comrades and myself and assure you he will be greatly missed by us all, as he was always cheerful and willing and very popular with us. He was buried by his comrades in the British cemetery at Neuville [La Neuville Communal Cemetery] in France and a cross erected in his memory. I am sorry to lose the service of a good soldier.'*

Charles Hyatt spent several more months in and out of trenches. He went home on leave in May 1916, and was killed in action near Ypres on 20th June. He was 20 years old. He had just finished his four-day tour of the trenches and was leaving the trench when a machinegun swept across it. He and three other men were killed instantly. He was buried in Essex Farm Cemetery near Ypres.

Frank Southam of the 2nd Warwicks, who was now a sergeant, returned home on leave in April 1916 and got married at Alderminster. His bride was Emily Cresser, 21, who was living at Beecham Farm in Preston, possibly as a servant. It was a quiet wedding as Frank's brother William had been drowned six months earlier. Shortly after the wedding, Frank returned to the frontline, and like many war brides, Emily began the anxious wait to see if her husband would return.

Mines

Both sides were now using mines to destroy enemy positions. These were tunnels dug beneath enemy lines by specialist miners and packed with explosives.

The 4th Middlesex, including John Whiteman, went into trenches near Hooge on the Belgian border on 18th July 1915 for a minor attack on the German line. A mine had been laid and the battalion was to seize the resulting crater and the adjoining trench.

At 7pm on the 19th, the mine exploded. The ground heaved and rocked for several seconds, then earth, bricks, wood and German bodies began to fall. Ten Middlesex men were killed by falling debris. Forty seconds after the detonation, the attacking columns went over the parapet and through a dense cloud of dust to their objective. Despite wild firing from the enemy they reached the crater, 200ft wide and 50ft deep, and fought their way into the trenches.

The Germans made a vigorous counterattack at 3am and the Middlesex were slowly driven back, but eventually the Germans were repelled and the new position was consolidated. The Middlesex were relieved that night, having suffered 300 casualties.

On 29th September 1915, while the Middlesex were in trenches near Ypres, the enemy sprung a mine of their own. German bombers then rushed one of their trenches and cleared it before the Middlesex could get into action. The enemy was prevented from advancing any further but the trench was lost. 127 men were missing. A counterattack the following day retook some of the lost ground at a cost of 150 further casualties.

Each side now kept a careful ear for any sounds of mining. The 1st Warwicks were in trenches in Flanders on 24th March 1915 when a boring machine was heard near the German lines, presumed to be mining under their trench. It was later discovered to be a bull frog heralding the approach of spring.

The Desperate Need for Men

Deferred Service

Volunteers were dwindling, and in May 1915 the upper age limit was raised from 38 to 40. Physical standards were also lowered. Recruits had previously been passed for frontline service or rejected; now, men fit only for garrison duty or home service could enlist, freeing up fitter men for frontline service. Those classed as Category A were fit for active service. Category B were fit to serve abroad in garrisons or on lines of communication. Category C were fit for home service only. Category D were unfit but may become fit in time.

In July 1915, the National Registration Act required all non-serving men aged 15-65 to give details of their employment and marital status. It found five million more eligible men. Edmund Stanley, Lord Derby, the Director General for recruiting, instigated the Derby Scheme: men could attest for deferred service and remain in the reserve until needed, with an armband to declare to public scrutiny that they were doing their duty. Over two million men attested for this scheme.

Frank Goodall, 27, was the son of gardener George Goodall and his wife Louisa of No.15 Preston. By 1911, Frank was working as an auxiliary postman. He attested for deferred service in December 1915 and was serving in France by September 1916. His unit is unclear but he served as a carpenter/wheelwright and was involved in making harness and equipment for horses and wagons. Dick Beavington wrote home in October 1916: '*I had a nice letter from F. Goodall. He was quite well, he said he often heard about me and was saying he always looked for the home news. I should just like to meet him. I could just picture him, how excited he got when he was talking.*' Nothing else is known of Frank's service history but he returned to Preston after his demobilisation.

Evan Horseman, 34, was son of Joseph and Emma Horseman of Crimscote. Four of his brothers had served in the army. He spent time in South Africa during the Boer War, and in 1911 he was living in Great Bowden in Leicestershire and working as an insurance superintendent. He was married with two children. He attested for deferred service in the 1st Life Guards, his brother Albert's regiment, on 11th December 1915 and was called up in October 1916. He served for 2½ years but never went abroad.

Walter Fowler, 35, was the son of painter Jonathon Fowler and his wife Sarah of No.37 Alderminster. Walter worked as a carter, attested for deferred service on 11th December 1915 and was mobilised into the Worcestershire Regiment in August 1916. He was quickly promoted to lance corporal and arrived in France on 31st December 1916. He joined his unit in the field a month later. He spent two years in France and in June 1918 was taken on as a batman: a personal servant to an officer. He remained in France until February 1919.

Cecil Vandelaur Keighly-Peach, 40, was the son of Henry and Lucy Keighly-Peach of Alderminster Lodge. His father was a retired army officer and his brother Charles was a naval officer. He was commissioned into the Mechanised Transport section of the Army Service Corps in September 1917. He served until the end of the war but never served abroad.

John Alfred Hicks, 19, was the son of cowman William Hicks of Alderminster. His brother Sidney had volunteered in 1914. John, a carter, attested for Lord Derby's scheme on 8th February 1916, joined the Worcestershire Regiment on 11th October and arrived in France on 30th December. He suffered a gunshot wound which severely fractured his leg on 23rd April 1917. He had an operation and eventually returned to the frontline. He was promoted to corporal and awarded the Military Medal in June 1919. He remained in the army after the war and in August 1919 was promoted to sergeant.

His leg injury was now causing problems. He suffered pain in walking and weakness in the knee joint. He was discharged as permanently unfit in May 1920. As he had fractured the same injured leg prior to joining the army, he was not entitled to an army pension.

Frederick Clark (b1890) was the son of George and Mabel Clark, teachers at Preston School. In 1911, Frederick was working as a telephone engineer in Salford. He enlisted at an unknown point and seems to have been invalided home around September 1918. Nothing else is known of his service history.

William Hopkins (b1891) known as 'Curly', was the son of waggoner Daniel Hopkins and his wife Jane of No.2 Preston. In 1911 William was working as a farm labourer, and he enlisted in an unknown unit by late September 1914. His cousin George Hopkins of Atherstone Hill enlisted at a similar time. Elizabeth Beavington wrote to her son Dick at an unknown date: '*Mrs Hopkins says tell Dick if he should see our Will to let me know. He is a bad lad if he is living not to write.*'

William lost his left arm at some point, which may be what Dick Beavington was referring to when he wrote home on 24th May 1916: '*I was sorry to hear about Billy's arm.*' He eventually returned to Preston.

Wilfred Victor Sivyour, 18, was the son of shepherd Charles Sivyour and his wife Emily, who lived in Timsbury in Hampshire. Wilfred moved to Wimpstone in his later life. He worked as a shepherd and was called up in April 1917. His employer sought exemption for him and Wilfred was granted exemption until 31st July. He was then enlisted into the East Surrey Regiment. He spent time abroad and suffered severe deafness from the incessant explosions, but nothing else is known of his service history.

John Milton James, 29, was the elder son of John and Leonora James of Whitchurch Farm. He trained as an architect, was appointed superintendent of structural alterations of Post Office and Municipal buildings, then became assistant agent for the Earl of Harrow's estate in Staffordshire. He was offered an appointment in Ceylon just as war broke out, but he felt it his duty to enlist. He was one of the first men to enlist in the three 'Birmingham Pals' battalions of the Royal Warwickshire Regiment. These battalions were recruited entirely from the Birmingham area and encouraged enlistment through peer pressure and local pride.

John joined the 16th (3rd Birmingham) battalion in October 1914. He landed at Boulogne on 21st November 1915. After three weeks training, the battalion went into trenches at Etinhem near the Somme. They spent several periods in these trenches over the next month.

Everyone thought highly of John, who was very willing and intelligent, and he was recommended for a commission. He was soon to return to England for officer training.

On 22nd January 1916 the battalion went into trenches at Bray-sur-Somme. John was killed the following day. His friend, LCpl Horseman, probably Edward Victor Horseman whose grandfather had hailed from Crimscote, wrote to his parents that John's platoon had just come off duty that afternoon and were asleep in their dugout. A shell killed John and two other men, and injured seven others. He was buried in Citadel New Military Cemetery in Fricourt. His mother chose for his headstone, *Until the day break and the shadows flee away.* He is commemorated on Whitchurch War Memorial.

Private Wilfred Sivyour.
Courtesy of Derek Bull.

Private John Milton James.
Courtesy of Robert Howe.

Conscription

The army could no longer be maintained by volunteers alone, and the Military Service Act of January 1916 allowed the conscription of single men aged 18-41. In May 1916, conscription was extended to married men. In 1918, the age limit was raised to 50.

Some of those called up were soon rejected. Edward Oliver Walter Goodall, 34, was the son of gardener George Goodall of No.15 Preston. He worked as a gardener, was married and lived in Kenilworth. He was called up in May 1916 and enlisted into the Royal Warwickshire Regiment. A subsequent medical examination didn't go well. He suffered from insomnia and neurasthenia, and his whole body was in a state of fine tremor, especially when ordered to do something. He also required dental treatment. He was pronounced permanently unfit for service and discharged after 37 days.

Albert Frank Noyce, known as Frank, 34, was a gamekeeper at Alscot Park and lived at Top Lodge in Preston with his wife and three children. He was called up on 6th June 1916, passed as fit and posted to the Durham Light Infantry. A second medical examination took place the following week, but, like Walter Goodall, the report was not good. He suffered from rheumatic pain in his legs and back, as well as arthritic damage to many of his joints. He was pale, anaemic and in poor general condition; the Medical Officer believed he would never make an effective soldier. He was discharged three weeks later.

Tribunals

Many who attested for deferred service appealed to defer their service longer, and tribunals were set up to hear their cases, most reported in the press. After conscription was introduced, the number of tribunals soared.

The Stratford tribunal board was made up of military officers and other officials. It included Thomas Salmon Smith of Park Farm in Preston, who represented the agricultural interest, and Robert Burra, Alscot's estate agent. Robert Burra may have been the 'Mr B' referred to in Dick Beavington's letters home in March 1916, who was very loath to grant exemption. '*I am glad he didn't have anything to do with me*,' Dick wrote. It was a matter of pride for many large estates to field as many servicemen as possible.

Nearly all cases from the Alscot villages related to agriculture. Many farmworkers had enlisted and farms were short-staffed, and the army's view of who was essential on the land was in severe conflict with that of the farmers. Thomas Smith complained that many men had been through the tribunal two or three times. Their cases have been thoroughly gone into, and most granted exemption. Some thirty men were each losing a day to answer a lot of useless questions, while they were told almost daily of the urgent necessity for farmers to get more out of the land, and he thought it was a wicked waste of time to bring these men and their masters here.

Mr. John James, the guardian for Whitchurch, wrote that his son had been killed on active service, his shepherd was called up some months ago, and his carter (who was starred) was being called up, and to keep his land in cultivation he was obliged to do the latter's work, so he had no alternative but to resign his seat as representative for Whitchurch. In doing so he desired to thank the chairman and members for the courtesy that they had extended to him.

Mr. J. H. Taylor said it was quite true, and he had seen Mr. James at plough without a boy.

A report of the Stratford Board of Guardians, May 1916. John James, 63, had said at a previous tribunal that he now had no option but to turn in and do the work himself, something he'd never expected to have to do at his age.

Arthur Coldicott, 19, a farm labourer's son from Ettington, attested for Lord Derby's scheme around February 1916. He was working at Whitchurch Farm for Alan Maxwell James. He was called up in March and Alan James applied for his exemption. Arthur worked as a ploughman and looked after the horses. The farm was 320 acres, 140 acres being arable, and a shepherd and a dayman had already enlisted.

The chairman asked Coldicott why he had attested. 'Because I should have been fetched if I had not,' he replied. He was granted three months' exemption and the chairman observed that if the war was still on at the end of this time, Mr James would have to do without him.

Alan returned to the tribunal in June to apply for a further period of exemption so they could get in 72 acres of hay and 120 acres of corn. Arthur was granted exemption to 30th September. His subsequent fate is unclear.

His brother George James Coldicott, 26, also worked for Alan James as head carter and looked after ten young horses. He had another brother already in France. He appealed in September 1916 and was granted exemption. Alan James was called up himself in August 1916 and was granted permanent exemption providing he remained on his farm.

In October 1916, Alan James applied for exemption for Harry Dyer, 35, who lived at No.21 Preston with his unmarried siblings and was passed fit for overseas garrison duty. He was granted exemption to 1st January provided he join the volunteers. He then appealed again, telling the tribunal he was now the only man working on the farm of 163 acres, and the work couldn't be done without someone. The tribunal agreed and Harry was given permanent exemption.

William Reason, 38, of the Old Thatch in Preston, was called up in June 1916. Bill worked for Thomas Smith at Park Farm and had been registered as a groom, but since the government had taken all Thomas' horses for the war effort, he had been working as a cowman. A cowman was a certified occupation; a groom was not.

Thomas requested absolute exemption. Bill had a club foot, so Thomas hadn't thought the military would trouble about him, else he would have registered him as a cowman instead. He also pointed out that he would be short at harvest as it was, and if he lost another man it would be very inconvenient. Bill was granted exemption until September, and Thomas was advised to get a medical certificate for him. Bill was subsequently passed as C3 – fit for sedentary work on home service – and granted permanent exemption.

William Coldicott, 40, was also called up in June 1916. William had been butler at Alscot Park for at least five years. James Alston-Roberts-West applied for exemption. West pointed out that it would be 'very inconvenient' if he were taken away. He also pointed out that there was no other person of military age now employed at Alscot. This swayed the panel – those with social standing received a better hearing than the farmers – and William was granted exemption until September, on condition he remained in his current employment. By that time he was over the age for active service and it is presumed he never served.

In July 1916, Ernest Morris, 30, a labourer of No.1 Wimpstone, applied for exemption. He was married with two children and was employed by Stratford rural district council on the roads. He also helped the farmers. The military comment was terse: 'Not assented to; he should go.' The applicant said he helped his father, who had 25 acres of land, including twelve of corn. He worked on the roads in winter and went to the farms when they wanted help. The prevailing view in the district was the man could be spared and the application was refused. Ernest joined the Royal Warwickshire Regiment on 26th July but was discharged after six weeks, declared unlikely to become an efficient soldier.

Charles Mayo, 38, of No.16 Whitchurch was called up in August 1916. He worked as a rick builder and thatcher for the Jaques brothers of Sweet Knowle Farm, who appealed on his behalf. Mayo had worked on farms since leaving school. The farm was 440 acres and Mayo was an all-round man who could do anything on the farm. There were twenty acres of hay to do, five working horses, seven milking cows, twenty young stock, sixty cattle and two hundred sheep to tend. Two of their men had gone to war and the farm was now worked by four men and a boy. One of these, Morris (probably Ernest's brother Albert) would shortly be called up.

Mayo was the only man in Whitchurch capable of digging graves, and Rev. Harvey Bloom described him as a most useful man. He was parish clerk and sexton and if he went there would be no one to dig graves but Harvey himself.

It was suggested if the two brothers did a little more work a man might be spared, but Mayo was granted three months exemption. In November, the brothers appealed again. Mr Jaques said so far he had kept his land planted. The military representative remarked that Mayo was passed for general service. Harvey Bloom stated that Mayo was practically the only able-bodied man on the farm. He was granted exemption to 31 March 1917. At a third tribunal he was granted permanent exemption.

Albert Morris, 25, the brother of Ernest Morris, worked as a labourer for the Jaques brothers. He was unmarried and lived at No.8 Wimpstone with his father Thomas, a roadman. He applied for absolute exemption in September 1916 on grounds that serious hardship would ensue if he was called up. His father had thirty acres and the applicant had to do the milking for him morning and night. Captain O'Flynn said the military wanted the man. Albert's father said he was the only one at home who could do anything for him. He had two sons in the army and twelve acres of corn to get in. He used to carry out haulage but was obliged to give that up. Albert said it would mean breaking up the home. Captain O Flynn said: 'Why, you only milk three cows!' He was granted one month's exemption. What happened to him then is unclear.

William Clarke Smith applied for exemption in November 1916. He lived in one of Silvester's Cottages in Preston with his father-in-law George Bennett, his wife Emma and four children, and worked as a bricklayer on Alscot Estate. The case was adjourned for Smith to be medically examined and he was subsequently passed fit for garrison duty abroad. He appealed again but his case was dismissed. What happened to him then is unclear.

In December 1916, Frederick George, 39, of Wimpstone, a wheelwright and agricultural repairer, applied for exemption. He was originally from Preston, where his family had worked as wheelwrights for three generations, and was employed by his father, aged 75. He did all the work on six farms and part of the work on two others. He said he had been requested by the farmers to appeal and a petition was presented by the local farmers, saying it would be in the interests of agriculture that he be retained.

The military representative observed there was another wheelwright at Alderminster. Thomas Smith said this man had more work than he could do already. Another of the board said he passed for general service. George said this was so, but it was a shoddy examination. If he joined it would mean closing his shop. He was given exemption to 1st February 1917, but would not be called up until two months after this date. What happened to him then is unclear.

Alfred Bishop, 34, who had recently taken over Beecham Farm in Preston, appealed in December 1916 and was granted permanent exemption providing he remain on his farm.

In January 1917, Frederick Ashby, 35, the youngest son of farmer Henry Ashby, married with two young children, appealed against his call up. His father rented Preston Pastures and Mansell Farm: a total of 387 acres. Frederick told the tribunal he was the farm manager for his father, now in his seventies, did all the shepherding and bought and sold livestock. The farm would suffer greatly if he went. The tribunal granted permanent exemption.

John Arthurs, 34, a cowman who worked for Arthur Ashby at Home Farm, Wimpstone, was called up in December 1917 and applied for exemption. He wrote that he did not propose to come to Stratford but would accept conditional exemption. Mr Hutton remarked: 'Very obliging of him.' Thomas Smith said the man could not well be spared; he was a full time agricultural worker. He was granted conditional exemption.

Love and War

The strict social conventions of earlier decades were crumbling, and men and women took whatever opportunity they could for fun. Whirlwind romances and fast marriages were common. Weddings took place while servicemen were home on leave, then the men returned to the frontline and the brides, sometimes with a baby imminent, faced the threat of quick widowhood or a disabled husband unable to support his family.

Emily and Gertrude Horseman were two of thirteen children of farm labourer Albert Horseman of Preston. In 1911 Emily, aged 20, was working as a housemaid in London. Gertrude, aged 17, was working as a servant for Preston schoolmaster George Clarke. She then joined her sister in London and began working as a servant in Notting Hill.

In October 1915, Gertrude got married. Her husband was Russell Herd, 24, a sergeant in the Army Service Corps. Russell, a plumber's son from Brighton, had served in the army before the war. His division was based in India and arrived in France on 22nd September 1914, where they remained for the duration of the war. Their honeymoon was presumably quite short and Russell returned to his duties.

Two months after Gertrude's wedding in December 1915, Emily also got married. Her husband was Ernest Maton, a sailor in the Royal Navy. Emily was now living in St Mary's Mansions in Paddington, an exclusive apartment block with high rents. How she came to be living there is a mystery; she wasn't working there as a maid, indeed wasn't working at all. She claimed on her marriage certificate that her father was a farmer rather than a farm labourer, which suggests she was living a bit above her station.

Ernest, a boot-maker's son, had been born in 1885 in Middlesex, and enlisted in the Navy aged fifteen in May 1900. He spent time on the boys' training ships HMS *Impregnable* and HMS *Ariadne* then joined the men's ranks for a twelve-year term on his eighteenth birthday. He was generally of very good character although he spent three periods in the cells in 1909. In 1911, now rated able seaman, he was serving in China, and he spent a great deal of the war in shore establishments including HMS *Pembroke* near London.

The time Ernest spent with his bride was presumably quite brief. Emily returned to Preston, but met her husband at least once over the ensuing four years. They had a daughter, Irene, born in August 1917.

Ernest was demobilised in March 1919 and joined his wife and daughter in Preston. He received a Navy pension and began work as a farm labourer. The couple went on to have eight further children and remained in Preston for their lives.

Russell Herd, now a staff sergeant, also returned home safely. The couple's first child, Stella, was born in London in 1919. They then moved to Preston where Russell began work as a painter. Their second child, Frederick, was born there in 1920.

Ursula Bloom, daughter of Whitchurch rector Harvey Bloom, married Arthur Denham-Cookes, a captain in the 24th London Regiment, in November 1916. He had enlisted in 1914 and spent the entirety of the war in England.

Arthur was the only son of wealthy widow The Honourable Mrs Denham-Cookes of Prince's Gate in London: an excellent match in the opinion of the Bloom family. Arthur telegraphed his mother the news. *Am engaged,* he wrote. *Am stunned,* was the unpromising reply. The wedding went ahead despite the sniffy disapproval of the Denham-Cookes family and their son Phillip was born the following year.

Arthur was troubled with ill-health for much of his service and was unfit to serve abroad. He contracted influenza and died on 5th November 1918. He was buried in his home village of Frinton-on-Sea in Essex.

The Battle of the Somme

The Somme offensive, which began on 1st July 1916, was intended to be a decisive attack by the British and French armies to end the eighteen-month deadlock on the Western Front. It involved 200,000 men along a twenty-mile line.

A week-long artillery bombardment was meant to destroy the enemy trenches, dugouts, barbed wire and gun emplacements. Over a million shells were fired; this was not nearly enough. As the British went over the top and walked across No Man's Land, the German machine-gunners crawled out of their barely damaged dugouts and opened murderous fire. It proved the worst day in the history of the British army with over 57,000 casualties, a third of them killed. The offensive continued until November, by which time its cost was over a million British, French and German casualties.

The 11th Hampshires, including Arthur Burrows, Ernest Robinson, Robert Dale, Sydney Land, Frank Taylor and Thomas Bloxham, arrived in France on 18th December 1915. As a pioneer unit, their main role was manual work such as building camps, huts and wells, shell-proofing buildings, digging and repairing trenches, laying barbed wire, and building parapets and firesteps. All this done at night and often under shell and machine gun fire. When out in No Man's Land they often encountered enemy patrols and came under fire. The battalion spent time in the Somme sector, then in September 1916, thanks to the manpower shortage, they took over frontline duties.

The 6th Dorsets, including George Hopkins and Sidney Hicks, were also in action in the Somme sector, as was Albert Horseman of the Life Guards.

George Sheasby of the Royal Welsh Fusiliers, and newly married Frank

Southam of the 2nd Warwicks, who had both fought at the Battle of Loos, were also saw action.

Frank's brother Ernest Edward Southam, 26, was also now serving in his brother's battalion. He was married and lived in Stratford where he worked as a clerk for Flower's Brewery. He had enlisted on 10th April 1916 and arrived in France in June.

Arnold John Reason, (b1888) one of eleven children of farm labourer Henry Reason and his wife Mary. Henry moved from Birmingham to Alderminster in the 1870s. In 1911, Arnold was boarding in Pontypridd in Wales with labourer George Pickering and his family, and worked as a fireman, stoking furnaces, in a colliery. Arnold married George's daughter Alice, who had a son, Leslie, a few months later. A second son followed.

Arnold joined the 10th Royal Welch Regiment, known as the Rhondda Pals and formed from the local mining community, at an unknown date. He probably arrived in France with his battalion on 3rd December 1915. Ten days later they went into the trenches in northern France, and trench routine and training was their life for the next six months. They were then moved to the Somme sector.

Thomas Frank Paxford (b1882) was the son of Maria Paxford, long-time widow of farm labourer Job Paxford. The family lived in several local villages including Preston, Wimpstone, Alderminster and Newbold. In 1911 Thomas was working as a farm labourer. He enlisted in the 10th Royal Warwickshire Regiment in October 1915. His unit was in the Somme sector by 1st July 1916.

James Baldwin, 21, was the son of Anthony and Johanna Baldwin of Wimpstone Fields. His father was a carter and in 1911 James, aged 16, was working as a ploughboy at Sweet Knowle Farm. He attested for Lord Derby's scheme in February 1916 and joined the 1/5th Warwicks on 18th May.

Percy Handy (b1895) was the youngest son of farm labourer Henry Handy and his wife Mary of Alderminster. His parents died young and in 1911 he was living with his brother-in-law Thomas George and was working as a horse lad for John Ashby of Cottage Farm, Alderminster. He then worked for Austin Motor Company Ltd in Northfield, Birmingham. Three of his brothers were already in the army. He also joined the 1/5th Warwicks and arrived in France on 1st September 1916, perhaps in the same draft as James Baldwin, and went into trenches in the Somme sector.

The battle began at 7.30am on 1st July. The 1st Life Guards, including Albert Horseman, were stood to, ready to charge forward and exploit the infantry's victory, their first real action since the start of the war. They were never called on.

The 6th Dorsets left their camp at 5.15am and arrived at the village of Meaulte at 6.30am, just as the artillery began their final hour's bombardment. It was a promising morning with a thickish mist over the low-lying ground. At 10am they saw the first batch of German prisoners passing by – an evil-looking, unkempt crowd, the battalion diary stated. The Dorsets remained behind the lines for several days until they were brought into action.

Frank Southam, Ernest Southam and George Sheasby were in position to attack the village of Fricourt. Both their battalions were in support for the initial attack. They waited as the leading battalions were mown down, then a company of the Fusiliers was ordered forward. They made little progress. More men went forward and their target trench was eventually captured. Two companies of the Warwicks were ordered forward to help take the now ruined village of Mametz. This was achieved and the Warwicks held the line until they were relieved on the 5th.

The Fusiliers attacked and took another enemy position on 2nd July, then were ordered to consolidate other captured trenches near Mametz Wood the following day. These were found to be still in German hands and they were forced to withdraw. They were ordered to capture them on the 4th, which they achieved, then faced more fighting at 1am on the 5th as the Germans attempted to retake them. The Fusiliers held the position, repulsed a bombing attack, and worked throughout the day to improve the position until their relief that night. These victories at Mametz were almost the only achievement of the opening stages of the offensive.

The 10th Warwicks, including Thomas Paxford, were in reserve until the afternoon of 1st July, when their brigade was told to take the village of La Boiselle. The attack was to start at 10.30pm, but the brigade didn't get into position in time and the attack was postponed. Their line was heavily shelled and at least six men were buried alive in the trenches. They moved forward over the next two days as ground was slowly gained and held. They suffered low levels of casualties and were relieved on the 5th.

On the 7th July, the 6th Dorsets attacked a German position near Fricourt, from which the Germans were attempting to counterattack. The Dorsets were forced back due to heavy machine gun fire. That night, British howitzers fired on the German trench and a Dorset bombing squad then rushed the German trench.

Sidney Hicks was the leading bayonet man in the attack and carried out his very nervous work with admirable courage and skill. He was the first man over the parapet and into the German trench, and led the way throughout the attack with fearless dash. The rest of the battalion then moved up and consolidated the position. They repulsed two counterattacks and held the position until their relief on the 11th. Sidney Hicks was awarded the Military Medal.

On 10th July, the 10th Welsh Regiment, including Arnold Reason, moved forward to attack Mametz Wood. The attack commenced at 4.15am. The Welsh were in support, but one of the leading battalions lost direction, leaving part of the wood unattacked. The Welsh were then brought up. They were enfiladed by machine gun fire and lost heavily. One platoon advanced into the machine gun fire and managed to capture the gun and part of the wood. The battalion then advanced to their first objective and dug in.

At 2pm, they advanced on their second objective. The Welsh suffered from machine gun fire and sniping and were forced back. They reorganised and went forward again, and this time achieved their objective. They dug in but suffered casualties from their own shelling. The following morning they were relieved, but were ordered back the same afternoon following a German counterattack. They suffered severe casualties and were relieved the next morning.

The battalion had now suffered over 300 casualties. Arnold Reason was reported missing, later reported killed in action. There is some confusion over whether it was the 10th or the 12th July. He was 28 and left a widow and two small children. He has no known grave and is commemorated on the Thiepval Memorial and Alderminster War Memorial. The capture of Mametz Wood was a crucial victory.

On 14th July, Frank and Ernest Southam with the 2nd Warwicks and George Sheasby with the Welsh Fusiliers moved into trenches near Fricourt for the Battle of Bazentin Ridge. The objective was to capture several villages and join up with flanking British positions.

The 2nd Warwicks took several German trenches then helped drive the Germans from Bazentin-le-Grand Wood. They moved on to the village of Bazentin-le-Grand but couldn't dislodge the enemy. They dug in and held their position under constant shelling until their relief on the 16th. They had suffered around 250 casualties.

The Fusiliers were in reserve for a simultaneous attack on Bazentin-le-Petit village. At 10am they were told the German line was broken and they were to consolidate the position, but the Germans then began a counterattack. The Fusiliers were rushed forward under heavy shellfire, but the ground was lost and another counterattack was coming. The Fusiliers were involved in fierce fighting until nightfall but managed to hold their line. They suffered continuous bombardment the following day and the Germans attacked other positions all along the line. When they were relieved on the 16th they had suffered nearly 300 casualties. The attack was considered a success.

The 10th Warwicks, including Thomas Paxford, attacked the German line at High Wood near Bazentin on 22nd July. The attack was to start at 12.30am under the cover of a barrage, but the guides didn't know the way so they weren't in position until 1.50am, by which time the barrage had lifted. The battalion attacked anyway, but heavy machine gun fire forced them back. Their line was heavily shelled but they were told to hold the line at all costs. The battalion was relieved the following day having suffered around 130 casualties.

On 30th July, they attacked the village of Bazentin-le-Petit, now entirely destroyed. They took their objective with 150 casualties. They were moved from the Somme sector to Flanders in early August.

Thomas Paxford died of wounds on 25th August. The line was quiet at this time with very few casualties; Thomas was probably an unlucky hit. He was buried in Baileul Communal Cemetery and is commemorated on Newbold War Memorial.

On 27th August, the Welsh Fusiliers attacked the German-held village of Ginchy. They gained little ground due to heavy shelling and lack of support. They began another attack which gained more ground. They held this line for two days, despite suffering heavy casualties, then on the 29th made three more attempts to rush the German line. They were forced back each time.

George Sheasby was killed on the 29th, aged 21. He has no known grave and is commemorated on the Thiepval Memorial and Stratford War Memorial. The *Stratford Herald* reported that: '*Many will regret his untimely though glorious end. The sympathy of all will go out to his parents with this sad blow.*' His parents attended the posthumous presentation of his Distinguished Conduct Medal in Birmingham in May 1917.

The commemorative plaque or 'Dead Man's Penny' was issued to the families of fallen servicemen. George Sheasby's was found in Stratford canal, near his family home, in 1960. How it got there is a mystery. Courtesy of Shakespeare's Birthplace Trust.

The struggle for Ginchy and the nearby village of Guillemont continued. The 2nd Warwicks assembled ready for another attack on Guillemont on 3rd September. Part of the battalion was held up by machine gun fire near Waterlot Farm, the scene of particularly bitter fighting, but the rest reached their objectives and dug in. They hung on for two days as the Germans mounted a counterattack. Captured positions were lost then regained. Most of the platoons were relieved, but some couldn't be reached. When the battalion was finally withdrawn, they had suffered 320 casualties. The battle was a success.

The British now turned back to Ginchy. The 11th Hampshires took over frontline trenches on 7th September. The army could now ill afford to have battle-fit men exclusively for pioneer duties. The battalion fought in the Battle of Ginchy on 9th September.

The Hampshires went over the top into immediate and devastating machine gun fire. Those left unhit took cover in shell holes, and the second line of attackers were brought up with difficulty. Despite heavy shelling, the remaining men managed to take the German trench, then a counterattack forced them back to their starting point.

Ginchy was eventually captured. Arthur Burrows was one of several Hampshires awarded a parchment certificate for gallantry. This news reached Dick Beavington in an inaccurate form. He wrote home, '*Fancy A Burrows winning the DCM. He would be proud of that, and his people I bet.*'

As winter approached, the trenches became a sea of impenetrable mud, choked with debris and bodies. All movement was through knee-deep mud covered with shell craters and barbed wire. The Somme offensive became a mere struggle for survival.

Many of the troops remained on the frontline through the winter. The 6th Dorests remained in trenches for several months. On 29th December, Sidney Hicks was wounded in the knee. Two days later he was evacuated to England where he spent several months in hospital. He rejoined his battalion in France on 15th August 1917.

The 1/5th Warwicks, including Percy Handy and James Baldwin, spent several months in the Somme sector. In February 1917, six weeks of frost gave way to rain and thaw. The trenches were now in a deplorable condition, many starting to collapse. When the Warwicks were relieved it took several hours to dig men out of the mud, in some places nearly four feet deep.

Percy was invalided home with septic poisoning in early 1917 and didn't return to France until June.

James suffered a severe gunshot wound to his leg at some point in February. He was evacuated to England where his left leg was amputated. His condition deteriorated and he developed septicaemia. He died in hospital on 7th April, aged 24 and was buried with military honours at Whitchurch. He is commemorated on Whitchurch War Memorial.

John Whiteman of the Middlesex Regiment had been evacuated from France with shellshock in 1915. He was promoted to lieutenant colonel and returned to France in December 1916 to command the Hawke Battalion of the Royal Naval Division (RND). This comprised Royal Navy and Royal Marine personnel not needed at sea. The battalion had fought disastrously in the Battle of the Ancre in November, one of the final battles of the Somme offensive, and was preparing for another major attack near the river Ancre.

John Whiteman's report stated that the attack began at 11pm on the 3rd February, and the enemy lines were quickly taken. At 3am the Germans

James Baldwin's grave.

began heavily shelling the captured lines. This was followed the next day by a counterattack which was broken by the British artillery and machine guns with heavy enemy losses. A series of small counterattacks all along the line took place at dusk which were beaten off.

An enemy strongpoint was directing heavy machine gun fire into the British lines, and had been attacked without success. Whiteman was told this must be captured at all costs. Then came a report that the left flank of the British line was in danger. The men preparing to attack the machine gun position were rushed to this point, arriving in the midst of the enemy attack. The Germans were forced back.

The planned attack on the machine gun emplacement successfully took place on the 5th. That afternoon, the Germans brought another machine gun up at close range but this was neutralised by snipers. The battalion was finally relieved late that night under very heavy shell fire. Whiteman concluded his report by saying that all objectives had been obtained and held; the officers and men carried out their instructions accurately; and the spirit of the men was admirable. Around 150 men were lost.

The 11th Hampshires moved to Ypres in November 1916. In May 1917, Ernest Robinson was commended for his gallant conduct. Three months later he was awarded the Military Medal for unknown reasons.

PIONEER ROBINSON'S GOOD RECORD.

Pioneer E. Robinson, of the 11th Hants Pioneers, has received a letter from Major-General Hickie, stating that he had read with much pleasure the reports of his gallant conduct and devotion to duty in the field, and had ordered his name to be entered in the records of the Irish Division. Robinson, who is a son of Mr. John Robinson, of Preston-on-Stour, joined the army in September, 1914, going to France in the following year. He was only 18 years of age when he joined, and was formerly employed in the gardens at Alscot Park.

From the Stratford Herald, 18th May 1917.

The Royal Engineers (RE)

The Royal Engineers were skilled craftsmen who did all construction and maintenance work. Carpenters, smiths, bricklayers and the like were typically posted here. The Field Companies worked on the frontline and dug and secured trenches, built camps, laid road, rail and water-based transport networks, laid wooden walkways through the deepening mud, designed front-line fortifications, developed responses to chemical weapons and laid communication systems. This was often in darkness and under artillery and sniper fire. They were often in action during attacks to repair and secure captured trenches before or during an enemy counterattack.

Albert Percy Dale, known as Percy (b1894) was the younger brother of Robert Dale who volunteered in September 1914. In 1911 he was working as a farm labourer, and he also enlisted early in the war. He was posted to the Royal Engineers and arrived in France on 28th August 1915. The prefix 'WR' of his service number indicates he spent time in the Waterways and Railways section which built, repaired and maintained these vital transport links. He was still serving abroad in September 1918 when baker Percy Beavington wrote home:

'*Fancy Percy Dale being at work round here. I hope I shall have the luck to see him.*' Nothing else is known of his service history.

William Paxton, 34, was the son of William and Ellen Paxton from No.18 Preston, the only boy amongst ten children. William worked as a carpenter like his father and grandfather, both lifelong Preston residents. He married Lily Ashby of Preston Pastures Farm in 1913 and moved to Stratford where he began work for the builder's firm G. Whatley and Sons. He had probably worked previously for Alscot Estate.

He volunteered in March 1915. His son William was ten months old and his wife was three months pregnant. He was old for a soldier, and was perhaps one of the many men pressured – by landlords, employers, and society in general – into leaving his family as recruiting became more ruthless. The volunteers now included older married men whose familial responsibilities had previously kept them at home.

William was posted to the Royal Engineers. His employer wrote in his reference that '*Mr Paxton worked for some months as a joiner and carpenter and we always found him a good, efficient and industrious workman.*' A week later the superintendent of the military workshops assessed him as 'skilled'. He was posted to 154th Field Company, based at Tidworth in Wiltshire. This consisted of 220 men, 60 mules, and workshops for carpentry, blacksmithing and other trades. They landed at Havre on 1st August 1915. William's daughter Ethel was born a month later.

He had a somewhat blemished record. While in Wiltshire in July 1915 he was charged with making a disturbance after lights out and confined to camp for five days. While in France in March 1916, he was absent from work for 3½ hours one afternoon; for this he forfeited ten days pay and placed under open arrest.

William's unit spent time in Belgian Flanders where they worked on the trenches. Two thousand infantrymen were attached to them to help. They were mainly deepening and draining existing trenches and riveting the sides to prevent their collapse. This was often under heavy shellfire. They spent a great deal of time constructing dugouts, set 16ft underground, using iron domes which would withstand shellfire. They also built machine gun placements and observation posts, fitted out buildings as hospitals, installed water supplies, strengthened roads for the passage of artillery guns, built latrines and made items such as waterproof grenade cupboards and drying hutches for clothing. They also spent a week threshing corn.

In May 1916 the unit moved to Bienvillers in the Somme sector.

Preparations were now underway for the Somme offensive, and for three weeks their company was constantly working on the frontline trenches and the wire. This involved incessant night work, almost always under machine gun fire and frequently under artillery fire. They also built and installed 74 gas emplacements with 1200 gas cylinders.

On 24th June, the week-long preparatory bombardment of the enemy lines began. The Engineers did little work except preparing bridges where the roads crossed the trenches.

The Somme offensive began on 1st July. At 6.30am, William's company was changing position near Bienvillers when two shells fell among them. Fifteen men were killed and seventeen others wounded. William was one of those killed. His commanding officer later wrote to his widow, who had two small children, that '*William was a willing and hardworking man, always ready to do his bit.*' He was buried in Bienvillers Military Cemetery, and commemorated on Preston War Memorial and Stratford War Memorial.

William Paxton's grave. Courtesy of Mick Jennings.

The Royal Army Medical Corps (RAMC)

The RAMC provided medical treatment and a large part of their work involved collecting and treating the injured from the battlefields, most often under heavy fire. The Geneva Convention stated that wounded men and medical personnel were not military targets, but even so it was dangerous work. Medical Officers (MOs) were usually medical professionals in civilian life; the other ranks generally had no previous medical experience and worked as stretcher-bearers, orderlies or combat medical technicians [paramedics].

Wounded men were collected by stretcher-bearers and taken to a Regimental Aid Post (RAP), set up in the safest place the MO could find on the frontline, for preliminary and often life-saving treatment. When this post was full or the frontline advanced, the wounded were left and a new RAP set up elsewhere. A Field Ambulance, a medical unit allocated to each brigade, collected and evacuated the wounded to dressing stations. These were set up in suitable buildings if possible; in dugouts or whatever cover was available if not. Motor ambulances were used if possible; more often horse-drawn wagons or hand stretchers were used. Casualties were often carried for over a mile, over waterlogged and shell-damaged terrain or through trenches, often under shellfire.

The casualties were then moved to an Advanced Dressing Station (ADS) further behind the lines then evacuated to a Casualty Clearing Station (CCS) which had advanced medical facilities and easy access to railways. From here men were transferred to civilian hospitals or evacuated to England. At each point their condition was assessed and the men were returned to duty where possible.

Those suffering from problems such as trench feet, rheumatism and infectious diseases such as trench fever and diarrhoea went through the same evacuation process. By October 1915, rest centres were set up for those suffering from mental strain or shellshock. This affected large numbers of soldiers and could persist for life. It was suggested – and recently proven – to be a non-visible concussion caused by exploding shells, although at the time was often attributed to weakness of character.

Physical and emotional stress, lack of washing facilities and cramped living conditions meant infectious diseases were prevalent and spread fast. Those serving in the tropics suffered especially badly with dysentery and malaria. Venereal disease was also a problem.

Reginald Thomas Neal (b1889) was the son of Moses and Annie Neal. Moses was a quarryman from Newbold on Stour and Annie, nee Newman, was from Whitchurch. The family moved to Leicestershire around 1890. He volunteered in 1914 or early 1915 and was posted to the RAMC. He arrived in France on 3rd June 1915. By 1917 he was serving with the 55th Field Ambulance. This unit had been based in the Somme sector from July 1915. Over the coming months they treated low numbers of casualties each day, the majority suffering from sickness.

On 25th June 1916, four battle stations were set up near the village of Carnoy ready for the coming Somme offensive. The assault began at 7am on the 1st July. By 9am the wounded began to arrive. By 3pm the unit had received over 700 casualties, including walking wounded and stretcher cases. The Field Ambulances were equipped to effectively deal with only 150 casualties.

The majority of wounded were evacuated to the casualty clearing stations, but this was very slow due to the condition of the roads. It was another day before their section of the frontline was cleared of wounded men. The next few days were quieter, then their division took part in another attack on the 8th July. The Field Ambulance was again inundated with casualties.

The unit remained in the area, operating where needed as the fighting continued, for another month until they were moved Tincquette in northern France. They were now involved in routine medical work, admitting up to fifty casualties a day.

On 26th September, the division took part in a major attack at Thiepval. The casualties soon began to arrive. Five hundred arrived on the first day. The offensive continued until the 4th October, by which time the unit had dealt with 2800 casualties.

The unit went out of action until 17th November, when they manned battle stations at La Boiselle ready for an attack the following day. They evacuated 250 casualties then were withdrawn two days later. They continued routine medical work for two months, then took over the Corps scabies station.

On 3rd May 1917, the division went into action at the Battle of Arras. It took four hours for the first casualties to reach the Field Ambulance; they then received a hundred casualties within 2½ hours. The following day they received nearly six hundred. They would treat 1850 casualties over the month. A hundred infantrymen were attached to the unit to help deal with the cases, as was a special surgical team.

In August, the division moved to Passchendaele. The Field Ambulance went to the frontline on 5th August and admitted nearly 8000 casualties over a fortnight, peaking with 2257 on the 17th. They were then moved to a quieter part of the line.

On 4th November they moved to Bleuet Farm near Ypres. On the 7th, Reginald Neal, now acting sergeant, was one of ten men to suffer gas poisoning. He died the following day in a casualty clearing station. He was 29 and left a widow and young daughter. He was buried in Dozinghem Military Cemetery in Belgium.

The Machine Gun Corps

Machine guns were automatic weapons capable of firing several hundred rounds a minute, and were crucial for defending frontline positions. Machine gun emplacements were usually a priority in an attack and machine gunners suffered particularly high casualty rates. Machine guns were initially operated by infantrymen, but in October 1915 the Machine Gun Corps (MGC) was formed.

Thomas Kingston, 35, was the son of Henry Kingston, a coachman and lodge-keeper who lived in the Lodge at Alscot Park. Thomas worked in the gardens of Alscot Park until 1905 when he married and moved to Northallerton in Yorkshire. He continued working as a gardener and later moved to Huddersfield. He enlisted in the army in 1915 and was posted to the Machine Gun Corps. He served in the 78th MGC in the Serbian Campaign. Austria-Hungary had invaded Serbia in 1914, and the Serbian army retreated south into Greece. An Allied force landed in Salonika (Macedonia) and mounted a long offensive against Austria-Hungary, recapturing Serbia in 1918.

Thomas was either injured or taken sick at some point and was declared no longer fit for frontline duties, and was subsequently transferred to the 968th Employment Company of the Labour Corps. He remained in Salonika until the end of the war.

He was admitted to hospital in Kalamaria in northern Greece shortly after the armistice, suffering from influenza. He died on 28th November 1918. He was buried in the Mikra British Cemetery in Kalamaria. He was 38 and left a widow and two young daughters. The inscription on his grave, chosen by his widow Amy reads; *Until the day break and the shadows flee away.* He is commemorated on Preston War Memorial.

Many men were transferred to the MGC as the war went on. George Edgington, who had served with the 10th Gloucesters, was transferred to the Machine Gun Corps at some point by mid 1916 and promoted to lance corporal. He contracted trench fever in August 1916 and was evacuated to England. It is unclear whether he returned abroad, but he was discharged as medically unfit on 26th February 1917.

Ernest Robinson, who joined the 11th Hampshires in September 1914, was transferred to the MGC sometime after May 1917. He remained in this unit until his discharge in March 1919.

Frank Holtom, serving with the 2nd Warwicks since 1914, was transferred to the MGC on 3rd October 1918. He remained in the unit after the war then transferred to the Royal Tank Corps in April 1921. He was discharged in August 1930.

The Royal Artillery

The Royal Artillery operated the heavy guns which had replaced cannons and siege engines. The Royal Horse Artillery (RHA) and Royal Field Artillery (RFA) operated light, horse-drawn field guns close to the front line. These could be galloped into position very quickly. The RHA typically supported the cavalry; the RFA supported the infantry. The Royal Garrison Artillery (RGA) operated relatively immobile heavy guns with a range of several miles and immense destructive power. Both sides put a great deal of effort into locating artillery batteries and mounting destruction shoots. Operating the guns under heavy shellfire was routine.

Each artillery battery comprised around two hundred men, six field guns and two hundred horses. The private soldiers were either drivers, who managed the horses, or gunners. The horses drew the guns and ammunition wagons. Many were requisitioned from farms and other businesses – all farms in the Alscot villages lost horses, as did Preston carrier Thomas Walton – and like the men, they suffered heavy casualties.

Shells were high explosive (HE); shrapnel; smoke, which masked advancing troops; and later in the war, gas. Artillery harassed moving troops and destroyed buildings, ammunition dumps and railways. The batteries were in constant readiness to respond to SOS flares from the infantry. Most infantry operations were preceded by artillery bombardment which destroyed enemy trenches, cut barbed wire, prevented supplies and relieving troops reaching the frontline, and also warned the enemy of the impending attack. The effectiveness of this barrage, as illustrated by the first day of the Somme, was often negligible.

The shelling wasn't always accurate. The diary of the 9th King's Royal Rifles (KRRC), in which Dick Beavington was now serving, bitterly described on 22nd October 1917:

> *'We suffered many casualties from our shelling today. The Forward Observation Officer apparently couldn't drag himself forward far enough*

to get observation worth having, so the infantry suffered accordingly. An altogether most trying day. Casualties 2 officers and 69 ORs wounded.'

Men on the frontline suffered routine bombardments. The diarist for the 9th KRRC described the shelling of their billets on 22nd November 1917:

'A house was blown over the signallers' billets, burying several of them in the debris. Long before the brickdust had dispersed a pink-tinted, gesticulating figure emerged, and broke all the laws of convention by traversing the public highway in its nether garments. Subsequent investigation proved this person to be the signal sergeant, whose trousers had been buried under the debris. Later, a shell penetrated the earth 2 feet from the Quartermaster's stores, but failed to explode. The force of its arrival, however dislodged two bricks immediately above the head of the RQMS, and the law of gravity was illustrated in a most amusing fashion. A hasty exit, followed by an incoherent explanation in the shelter of the RSM's billet, was the result.'

John Garrett, a gunner in the RFA, was mobilised from the reserve on 5th August and left for France two days later. His wife Edith gave birth to a daughter, Lorraine, three months later. In November 1914, a Soldier's and Sailors Tobacco Fund was set up in Kenilworth to send tobacco to local men. John was one of the recipients.

He was admitted to hospital at some point suffering from damage to his eardrum and partial deafness, possibly caused by an exploding shell, then returned to duty. He was transferred to the 119th Brigade in late July 1916. This unit was on the frontline in the Somme sector and involved in routine shelling of the enemy trenches and wire – they had a daily allocation of 137 rounds for this – as well as firing on any German activity reported.

The brigade moved to northern France in August where they remained for several months. John was admitted to hospital on Christmas Day 1916 with myalgia and rheumatism, probably caused by exposure. He was evacuated to England the next month with synovitis in his right knee. He spent three months in hospital and returned to France in June 1917. He was then posted to the 282nd Brigade.

He was injured on 3rd September 1917 and died of his wounds two days later in a casualty clearing station at Lozinghem in northern France, which was mainly receiving casualties from Passchendaele. John was 31 and left a widow and two children. He was buried in Dozinghem Military Cemetery in Belgium. Two months after his death his property – an identity disc, letters, photos, a pipe, cigarette lighter, religious book, knife, pen holder and a notebook – were sent to his widow. She chose the inscription *God's will be done. Never forgotten by all* for his gravestone. He is commemorated on the Kenilworth and Whitchurch War Memorials, and also on his uncle Thomas Richardson's grave in Whitchurch graveyard.

Walter Henry Keyte, 22, was the eldest son of shepherd John Keyte and his wife Mary. The family had recently moved from Brailes to Wimpstone. Walter worked as a farm labourer at Sweet Knowle Farm. He attested for deferred service on 8th February 1916 then appealed against his call-up in March. He said he was a shepherd and needed on the farm, but the military information was that he only did the shepherding when his father was ill. There were eight men employed on the farm, and Walter was refused and advised to join the army. He joined the RGA a fortnight later.

He served abroad with the 183rd Heavy Battery, which operated 60lbs guns towed by mechanical transport. These were predominantly used on large scale targets such as railways and ammunition dumps. No other details are known of his service history.

Ernest Horseman, who had served as a driver in the RHA since 1907, was mobilised from the reserve on 5th August 1914 and posted to the 3rd Brigade. He arrived in France on the 15th August and remained for the duration of the war. He was mainly based in the Somme sector and near Loos.

Ernest was made bombardier [corporal] in November 1915 but reverted to driver a week later. He was again promoted in January 1916 but demoted in September for neglect on duty while he was the NCO in charge of the observation limber. This was a portable ladder on wheels which was fixed to the ground and used to report on targets and accuracy. He was also deprived seven days pay in December 1917 for using obscene language. He remained in France without further incident until January 1919.

Henry Taylor, 21, was the eldest son of Josiah and Sarah Ann Taylor of Crimscote. Henry worked as a farm labourer and joined the RFA on 31st August 1914. He was posted to 109th Brigade which operated howitzer guns.

Henry was appointed a shoeing smith, tending the brigade's horses, and arrived in France on 29th August 1915. He spent a month in hospital suffering

Jack Garrett.
Courtesy of Richard Parnham.

Walter Keyte.
Courtesy of Pete Summerton.

from syphilis in May 1916. He was then readmitted suffering from renal calcitis – a kidney disease and probably a secondary stage of syphilis – and was evacuated to England. He returned to France in May 1917 and remained until the end of the war.

Joscelyn Bloom was the son of Whitchurch rector James Harvey Bloom. In 1911 he was living with his mother Mary, now separated from her husband. He joined the 1st Hertfordshire Battery of the RFA, a territorial unit based in St Albans, in October 1914.

He arrived in France on 19th October 1915 and the following year his unit was sent to Gallipoli and then Egypt. He became a saddler, making and repairing harness and other equipment, and reached the rank of corporal. He had an enjoyable time in the Middle East – he regularly raided tangerine orchards and stole chickens from the locals – but was also involved in fighting. On one occasion while in Cairo, an ambulance was set upon by hostile crowds and Joscelyn spurred his horse into the crowd and freed the ambulance, saving the female nurse's life. This was the first occasion he had to kill a man. A native was about to shoot him and he smashed his skull with the butt of his rifle. He remained in the Middle East until June 1919.

Joseph Taylor was one of thirteen children of farm labourer Martin Taylor and his wife Sarah of No.1 Crimscote. In 1911 he was working as a plough boy; by 1915 he had moved to Kenilworth and worked as a skin worker. He joined a territorial battery of the Warwickshire RHA on 6th May 1915, stating he was a day past his nineteenth birthday, when in fact he was two weeks short of it.

While in Canterbury in October 1916, he was charged with allowing himself to become verminous and not reporting the same. While lice were unavoidable on the frontline, barracks were kept clean and louse-free. He was confined to barracks for seven days and forfeited three days pay. He arrived in France in June 1917 and remained until May 1919.

John Boardman, 35, was born in Birmingham and worked as a tailor. He was widowed with an eight-year-old son and lived in No.8 Alderminster with his widowed mother Fanny. His brother William was serving with the Canadian Infantry. He joined the RGA on 30th August 1915. He served abroad but nothing else is known of his service history. He returned to Alderminster where he remained for his life.

James Richard Ashfield, 30, was the son of painter John Ashfield and his wife Sarah, nee Handy, of Alderminster. James moved to Birmingham where he worked as a grocer's assistant. He was married with one son. He attested for deferred service in December 1915 and was called up in April 1917. He was now working as a munitions worker. He was posted to the RGA and served in Palestine and Egypt where he remained until January 1920.

John Handy (b1890) was the son of farm labourer Henry Handy and his wife Mary Ann of Alderminster. He worked as a farm labourer then in February 1912 enlisted in the Royal Garrison Artillery. John served in the 3rd Mountain Battery and was probably in India when war broke out. It is likely he remained there for much of the war. He saw action in the Third Afghan War, which began in May 1919 on the perpetually troubled Northwest Frontier of British India. The Afghans crossed the border into British territory, probably spurred by the weakened state of the British Army, but were eventually driven back after three months of fighting. John received the Indian General Service Medal and a clasp for the Afghan Campaign. He was transferred to the reserve in February 1920 and discharged in 1924.

The Army Service Corps (ASC)

The army needed food, water, ammunition, transport, equipment, medical supplies and countless other things to reach the troops on a daily basis, wherever they were operating on or behind the frontline. This logistical feat was the task of the Army Service Corps (ASC) which at its peak comprised over 300,000 men. Different sections maintained mechanical and horsed transport; sourced, prepared and transported rations; provided fodder for horses and mules, including haymaking and harvest in summer; maintained railways; and many other things besides.

Mechanical Transport (MT) Section

The rapidly expanding Mechanical Transport (MT) section of the ASC operated and maintained all manner of motor vehicles from motorcycles to heavy tractors. Almost all men with experience of motor vehicles were posted to the MT section. The ability to drive at this time was a rare skill. Lorries and buses moved troops, ammunition and supplies to wherever they were needed. Near the frontline, the roads were often overcrowded and damaged from shelling. The work was often done at night, with little visibility and no hope of avoiding incoming shellfire. Dead mules and wrecked wagons littered the roadsides. When the motor transport could proceed no further on the shelled and mud-swamped terrain, the loads were transferred to horse-drawn wagons.

William Henry Sharpe was the eldest son of Henry Sharpe, a chauffeur and former coachman, and his wife Maria, of No.5 Alderminster. In 1911, William, aged fourteen, was working as a garden boy. He was also a bellringer and altar server at Alderminster church. He attested on 4th November 1915, stating he was aged 19 and 250 days. He was in fact only 18. He was working as a chauffeur and motor mechanic and was posted to the MT section. The recruiting officer wrote: *this is a capable young man, physically quite fit, and able for the work he now applies for. I should recommend his acceptance.*

He was posted to Grove Park, an MT depot in London, then left for Rouen on 25th February 1916. He spent a year with the Siege Park of the 56th Division, which supplied shells, mortars and ammunition to the frontline and also mechanical tractors for hauling massive artillery pieces. On 27th February 1917, he was compulsorily transferred to the 2nd Duke of Wellington's West Riding Regiment. The army was now desperate for men and anyone fit for the frontline was transferred to the infantry.

Edward Day, 39, was a chauffeur and former coachman, and married Emily Hathaway, a brickmaker's daughter of Broomfield in Alderminster. In 1911 the couple were living in Longborough in Gloucestershire and had two children. Edward attested for deferred service on 11th December 1915 and was posted to the MT section. He was called up in August 1916 and embarked for Salonika on 23th October. He served in Serbia and Salonika until the end of the war, then returned to the UK in March 1919.

William Jobe, a chauffeur at Alscot Park who had briefly served in 1914, was called up again in July 1916 and posted to the MT section. He was now married with a seven-month daughter. He was sent to Grove Park and was in France by October 1916, when Dick Beavington wrote home: '*Fancy W Jobe going to where I had just left. I wish I could have seen him there. I should soon have spotted him being so tall.*' William remained in France for the remainder of the war and reached the rank of corporal. He then returned to Alscot Park.

William Jobe.

John Edwin Howes, 18, was the son of Edwin Howes of Pershore, who had moved to No.16 Preston in the 1890s. Edwin worked as a groom and coachman for Alscot land agent Robert Burra. The family later returned to Pershore although John's two sisters remained in service at Park Farm in Preston. In 1911, John, now 13, was working as a draper's errand boy. By 1916, he was working as a chauffeur. He attested for deferred service on 12th December 1915 and was called up to the MT section in May 1916. He was sent in India in October where he spent six months before being transferred to Mesopotamia (Iraq).

In August 1917, he was working in a car shed in Baghdad when a blast of wind blew metal dust into his right eye. Some pieces of steel dust were taken out, but they left a permanent injury to the cornea. He suffered repeated infections to his damaged eye and six months later could barely see. His left eye had also started to deteriorate. A medical examination pronounced him unfit to drive but fit for home service, and stated that he now had total incapacity to earn a full livelihood. He was discharged in July 1918, with a voucher for a suit of plain clothes to the value of 55 shillings. As he was only twenty years old with no dependents, despite his permanent disability, he was deemed unworthy of an army pension.

Percy Horseman was the son of Herbert Horseman, a Crimscote army veteran now living in Aston. He enlisted on 24th February 1917, the day before his 18th birthday. He was apprenticed to a motor trimmer and was posted to the MT section. Three months later, he passed his learner's test for driving and motor vehicle management. He arrived in France on 5th September 1918 then went to Italy, which had entered the war on the Allies' side in 1915, and spent time in Arquata, a depot in northern Italy. In November 1919, he was charged with disobeying a lawful command by an officer. When the men were discharged to their duties, Percy did not do so. He was sentenced to eight weeks in a detention centre with Field Punishment No.2, namely put in fetters and handcuffs. He was transferred to the reserve in February 1920.

His brother Ernest Henry Horseman (b1892) was born in Preston and in 1911 was working as a clerk for an engineering works. He was married with a baby daughter and joined the MT section in March 1917. He joined the 695th Company depot as a stock-keeper and by December 1917 was serving in Baghdad.

He was admitted to hospital in August 1918. On 10th September he was moved to an isolation unit, suffering from smallpox. He died two days later. He was buried in the Baghdad War Cemetery, where his grave reads, *God Bless Daddy.*

Horsed Transport (HT) Section

Several men from the Alscot villages served in the HT section. They were generally farm labourers and experienced horsemen. Horse-drawn wagons transported supplies from motor vehicle dumps to the frontline where mechanical transport could not reach.

Harry Handy, 29, was the son of farm labourer Henry Handy and his wife Mary of Alderminster. Harry was working on a farm by age fifteen, and in 1911 was living at No.17 Alderminster with his sister Ellen Smith and working as a threshing machinist. He went to Worcester to volunteer on 24th February 1915. With him were his brother-in-law Thomas Ernest George, 33, and his cousin Wilfred William Handy, 19. Both also lived in Alderminster. Thomas, a carter, was married to Harry's elder sister Joyce and had two young children. Wilfred was the son of James and Ellen Handy and worked as a farm labourer. The three men were experienced horsemen and were posted to the HT section. They arrived in Aldershot two days later.

Harry's brother Thomas, 29, a carter who was married with a young son and lived in Nuneaton, attested for deferred service in February 1916. He was called up on 30th January 1917 and became a driver in the HT. He had a lymphatic chest due to typhoid but this was not sufficient to reject him. He never served abroad and was discharged in February 1919.

It seems Harry Handy also never served abroad. Wilfred Handy and Thomas George went to France on 1st June 1916 with the 292nd Coy of the 40th Divisional Train, a unit of 400 men, 400 horses and 150 wagons which supplied the 40th Division. The division was located near Bapaume for several months. The Train's railhead was occasionally shelled, as were many roads near the frontline. Wagons were ordered to keep at least a hundred yards apart to reduce the risk of drawing shellfire.

The division was fighting near Bapaume from October 1917, and getting supplies to the frontline became more difficult and dangerous. The men were warned that shellfire was not an excuse for non-delivery of supplies.

On 21st March 1918, the German Spring Offensive commenced. The supplies for the entire division had to be shifted from their railhead within 45 minutes, under heavy shellfire, as the Allied retreat began. Their task grew increasingly difficult over the coming days. The motor lorries were needed for ammunition; the wagons couldn't find the units they were supposed to be supplying; the enemy broke into their lines and attempted to stampede their horses; and the supply camps were shelled. The railheads supplying them were changed every few days.

In mid April, the situation stabilised and the division moved to Roubaix in Northern France where they remained until June 1919.

Thomas George received news that his wife Joyce had died of erysipelas and heart failure on 25th September 1918. He was given two weeks leave and returned to England on the 29th. It seems Joyce's sister Ellen took over the care of their two sons and Thomas returned to France. He remained until his discharge in March 1919.

Wilfred Handy returned to the UK on 14th July 1919 and was discharged the following month.

Harry Handy was admitted to Prees Heath military hospital in Whitchurch, Shropshire, on 13th February 1919. He was suffering from influenza and fever, which rapidly developed into virulent broncho-pneumonia. He died five days later, aged 32. He was buried in Stratford on Avon Cemetery and is commemorated on the Stratford and Alderminster War Memorials.

Farriers

Percy Richard Ladbury, 34, had married Emily King of Alderminster, the sister of Albert King who was serving with the Coldstream Guards. The couple lived in Yardley in Birmingham and Percy worked as a shoeing smith. He enlisted in the Army Veterinary Corps (AVC) on 25th October 1915. Over 800,000 horses and mules were taken to the Western Front alone to pull supply wagons and artillery pieces. Percy spent nine months at the School of Farriery in Woolwich where he was promoted to farrier sergeant. He served abroad, probably in the Middle East, and was demobilised in February 1919. While serving in Woolwich in August 1916, he was charged with disobedience of orders. He had been shoeing horses in the absence of pupils. His punishment was a 'severe reprimand'.

William Joseph Gilks (b1888) was the son of shoeing smith Joseph William Gilks of Idlicote. William also worked as a shoeing smith and enlisted in the Army Service Corps as a farrier in the early stages of the war. He arrived in France on 19th May 1915 and reached the rank of farrier staff sergeant. He later served in Salonika and was awarded the Meritorious Service Medal (MSM) in 1919.

He returned to the local area after the war and took over Preston forge in the 1930s, shoeing horses for all the surrounding villages, until the forge closed in 1948.

Bakers

The ASC were also responsible for feeding the army. Preparing food without modern electrical ovens, refrigerators or other conveniences was a challenge at the best of times; on the frontline even more so. Each division had a field bakery in which 92 men baked bread for 20,000 troops. Men who worked as bakers in civilian life were usually posted to these bakeries.

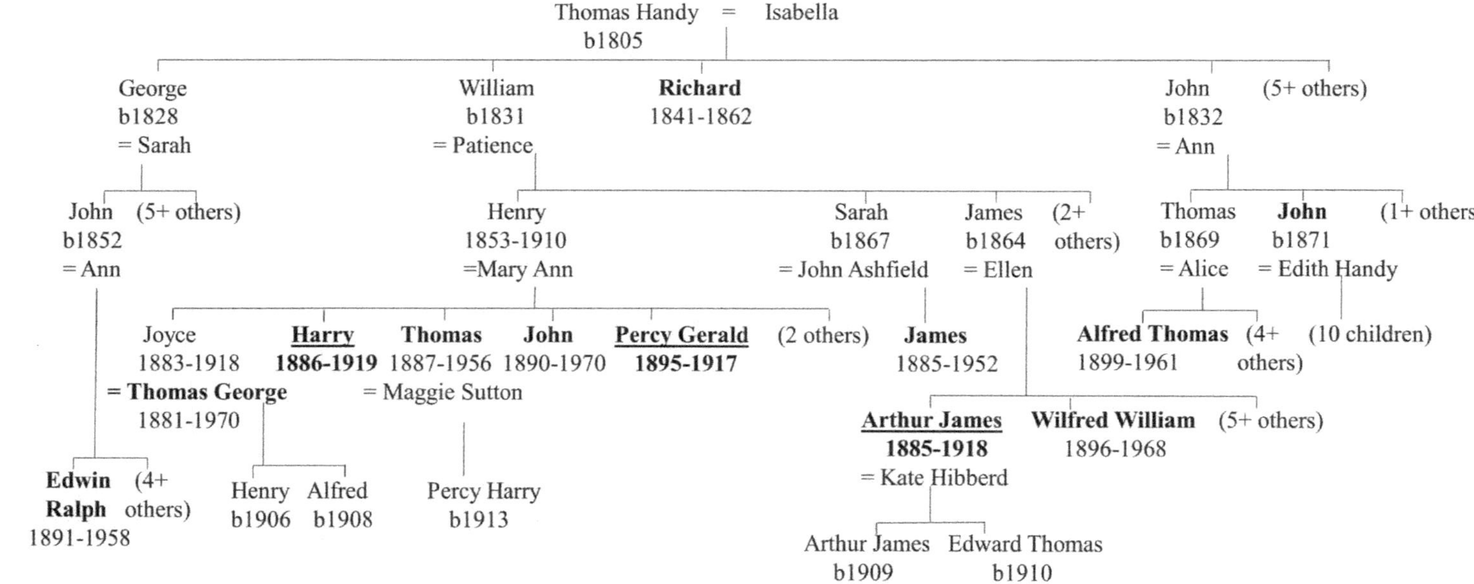

Handy family tree. Names in bold served in the armed forces. Those underlined died on active service.

Ernest Richard (Dick) Beavington, 22, was the elder son of Richard and Elizabeth Beavington of No.50 Preston. Richard had taken over the Preston bakery in 1887 and Dick and his brother younger Percy both worked in the business. Dick volunteered on 26th October 1915 and was posted to the ASC as a baker. His father Richard wrote in his character reference that '*I certify Ernest Richard Beavington, my son, has been helping me with my business as a baker and have always found him honest, industrious and a steady, good worker.*'

Dick went to France two months after enlisting on 17th December 1915. As he would not be fighting on the frontline he needed less training than the infantrymen. His field bakery was part of the 16th Division which included the 11th Hampshires, including several Alscot men. Dick served for two years as a baker then was transferred to 9th Kings Royal Rifle Corps, an infantry unit, in August 1917. Like William Sharpe, he was now needed on the frontline.

Dick's brother Percy, aged 18, was called up in April 1917 and Richard applied for exemption for him. Percy, passed fit for overseas garrison duty, worked in the bakery and filled in the time on the land. Richard told the tribunal that he was baking rather more than formerly. The new kind of bread – supplemented with rice, potato or barley flour thanks to shortages – didn't satisfy people as much. Percy was granted exemption to 1st September on condition he join the volunteers at Clifford Chambers. He then joined the ASC as a baker. He served abroad and was discharged in April 1920.

Harry Samman, also spelt Salmon, 36, was the son of sawyer Giles Samman and his wife Selina, lifelong Preston residents. Harry moved to Birmingham in his early twenties where he worked as a bread delivery man. In 1909 he married Elsie Wright, an unmarried mother with a two-year-old son, Walter. They had one further son, Frederick. Harry was called up for deferred service on 24th June 1916 and was mobilised in September 1917. He served in the ASC as a baker but never served abroad, and reached the rank of corporal. He was transferred to the reserve in October 1919.

The Labour Corps

The Labour Corps was formed in January 1917 for men unfit for frontline duties but fit for manual work. Many had served on the frontline but were no longer fit after illness or injury, such as Thomas Kingston of the Machine Gun

Left: Dick Beavington. Right: Percy Beavington.
Courtesy of Elizabeth Lyne.

Corps. They loaded and unloaded wagons and trains; built roads and railways; did repair work and many other things besides. This had been formerly the work of infantry pioneer battalions, but these battle-fit men were now needed on the frontline.

Harry Samman.
Courtesy of Janet Naylor.

Leonard Walton, 37, was the son of farm labourer William Walton and his wife Sarah of No.13 Alderminster. Leonard was working as a farm labourer by age fourteen then moved to Birmingham in the 1890s where he worked as a window cleaner. He married in 1904 and two children followed. By 1911 Leonard was widowed and living in a hostel in Birmingham. His elder child Elsie was in a children's home; the whereabouts of the younger is unclear. He attested for deferred service on 10th December 1915, was classed as BIII – fit for sedentary garrison duty – and posted to the 898th Labour Corps. He was called up in August 1916 and went to France on 3rd October 1916. He remained in France until May 1919.

Alfred Gibbs, 36, was the youngest of six children of Betsy Gibbs. His father Thomas, who farmed at Lower Farm in Preston in the 1870s, had died when he was a baby. The family then lived in Alderminster then moved to Blackwell where he and his brothers worked as drapers and outfitters. Alfred attested for deferred service in December 1915 and was called up on 20th April 1918. He served in the Labour Corps until March 1919 but never served abroad.

The Royal Navy

The Royal Navy was vital to the success of the land-based war. British military operations were dependent on transporting troops, ammunition and other supplies by sea to theatres of war around the globe. The Navy patrolled for enemy ships and submarines intent on sinking troop and supply ships, searched for mines and attacked enemy vessels. Apart from the occasional large-scale battle, the tactic for both sides was to wear down the other to gain supremacy of the seas.

Edward Hibbard, who had served in the Navy since 1912, was serving on HMS *Prince of Wales* when war broke out. He was promoted to leading stoker (maintaining the engines and stoking them with coal) in October 1916, then passed the petty officer's examinations in January 1918. He was transferred to the Royal Fleet Reserve in March 1919 and discharged in June 1921.

Charles William Keighly-Peach, who had served in the Navy since 1879, was transferred to the coastguard in June 1914 and commanded the Eastern District, based in Dover. A report said he did his duty conscientiously but lacked initiative and energy. In August 1917 he returned to sea as captain of HMS *Hindustan*, a battleship of the Northern Patrol which also took part in raids on the German-held ports of Zeebrugge and Ostend. He was now appraised as a steady reliable officer with sound judgement, with good health and physique, but was not recommended as a flag officer in command afloat. He was transferred to HMS *Alsation* where he remained until the end of September. He was then granted the rank of rear admiral and placed on the retired list. He was awarded the DSO for valuable and arduous services on convoy duties during the war and was later advanced to admiral.

Francis George Burrows Hastings, twin brother of army officer Wilfred Hastings, was serving as chaplain on HMS *Minotaur*, an armoured cruiser based in Egypt, when the war broke out. This ship spent most of the war patrolling the North Sea and was present at the Battle of Jutland in May 1916, although did not fire her guns. In January 1915, the crew were sent items of clothing from Stratford as one of many charitable initiatives, and Francis wrote to the mayor, subsequently published in the *Herald*: '*Will you convey to the ladies of Stratford on Avon the sincere thanks of the officers and men of HMS Minotaur for the very useful clothing which arrived today. As far as possible the items have been given to the men whose duties are on deck at night such as searchlight crews, gun crews and signal men.*'

In 1917 Francis began a two-year spell in the Royal Naval Hospital in Hong Kong then returned to England where he remained until his retirement in 1923.

Harry Alston-Roberts-West of Alscot Park, now married with three children, had served as a naval officer since 1886. He was at Padstow coastguard station in Cornwall when war broke out and remained there for much of the war. The coastguard was vital for maintaining defence against raiding ships, mines and submarines. In May 1917, Harry went to command Cattewater naval seaplane station in Plymouth. He was due to take up a telegraphist's position in Palestine but was too ill to take up the position – he had been plagued with ill health for much of his career – and he retired as medically unfit in March 1919. He was granted the rank of captain in recognition of his services rendered during the war.

Harry's brother Reginald was serving on HMS *Vengeance* when war broke out. He was serving in Malta in June 1915 when he had a nervous breakdown, possibly shellshock, and spent five months in hospital before being pronounced fit for service. He was transferred to the coastguard where he served until his retirement in August 1927.

Their cousin Phillip Alston-Roberts-West, who had served since 1891, was on HMS *Isis* when war broke out. He served on various ships throughout the war, including time on convoy duties near Gibraltar, and retired with the rank of commander in March 1921.

Walter Owen Handy, 18, was the son of shepherd Walter Handy and his wife Ruth, who moved to Alderminster in the 1890s. Their connection to the other Handys in the village is unclear. Walter, a farm labourer, enlisted in the Navy on 22nd September 1914. He spent three years on shore-based establishments then went to sea on HMS *Victory* in September 1917, where he served as a stoker. He was promoted to Stoker 1st Class in January 1918 and was discharged in November 1919.

Henry George Padbury, 18, was the son of wheelwright John Padbury and his wife Alice, nee Holtom, of a long-standing Alderminster family. The family lived in Kingham in Oxfordshire where Henry worked as a baker. He enlisted in the Navy in August 1915. He served on various ships as a stoker's mate before being transferred to the dreadnought HMS *Vanguard* as a cook's mate in June 1916. The *Vanguard* was mainly involved in patrolling the North Sea.

At midnight on 9th July 1917, while at anchor in Scapa Flow in Orkney after ironically practicing the abandon ship procedure, the ship suffered a massive internal explosion, probably caused by an unnoticed fire in the magazine. She quickly sank with only two survivors out of her 850 crew. Henry was among the fatalities. He is commemorated on the Chatham Naval Memorial for those lost at sea with no known grave.

Fred Pitt, 34, was one of ten children of farm labourer Thomas Pitt and his wife Charlotte of No.14 Preston. Fred, along with several of his siblings, set his sights on the city life and in 1901, aged 18, was working as a footman in Burntwood, Staffordshire. He over six feet tall and good-looking, with a fresh complexion, brown hair and blue eyes, ideal qualifications for a liveried servant. Ten years later, he was under-butler for an elderly widow in London. Soon afterwards, he reached the vaunted position of butler.

He enlisted into the Navy in early 1916. He was posted to the Royal Naval Air Squadron (RNAS), which operated the Navy's aircraft, airships and balloons and first saw action in May 1916. He remained in the RNAS until April 1918 when the RNAS was merged with the Royal Flying Corps to create a new service: the Royal Air Force.

Fred then spent time in Dover and Dorset and served as a batman: a personal servant to an officer. His background in service no doubt gained him this position. His main duties were conveying orders and messages, looking after the officer's uniform and equipment, driving his vehicle and any other tasks required. He was discharged in April 1920.

Albert Edward (Bert) Porter, 16, was the third son of Aubrey and Margaret Porter of No.8 Preston. His elder brothers Will and Jack were serving with the Canadian forces. In May 1917 Bert, who was working as a motor-car cleaner, enlisted in the Navy. He spent two years on HMS *Ganges* and HMS *Impregnable*, boys' training ships on the south coast of Britain. The boys and staff of these ships were involved in laying 600 miles of anti-submarine nets in coastal waters. He was of superb conduct and on his eighteenth birthday, two months after the armistice, he enlisted in the adult's ranks and remained for his working life.

Robert Arbuthnot, who had joined the Navy aged thirteen in 1877, was appointed a Rear-Admiral in 1912 and in September 1913 assumed command of the Second Battle Squadron of the First Fleet, as the Navy prepared for war.

Robert first encountered the enemy near Scarborough in December 1914,

Albert Porter (on right).
Courtesy of Maurice Porter.

Captain (later Rear Admiral) Robert Arbuthnot.

during a German raid on the north-east coast. He refused to fire on them as he had received no official orders to do so. By the time the orders arrived, the enemy ships had escaped. He assumed command of the First Cruiser Squadron in January 1915, and on 31st May 1916 he joined the biggest naval battle of the First World War.

The Battle of Jutland began on 31st May 1916 in the North Sea. It was the long-anticipated showdown between the British and German navies. The Germans planned to use decoy squadrons to divide the British Grand Fleet, then defeat it piecemeal. A section of the British fleet located and attacked German scouting ships, exactly as the Germans had planned. The two sides engaged, the shells began falling and two British ships were blown up and sunk. The remainder of the British fleet, including Robert Arbuthnot's squadron, joined in the fray, along with the waiting German High Seas Fleet. The battle continued well into the night with devastating losses on both sides.

Robert Arbuthnot brought his squadron forward into the area between the two fleets, possibly with the intention of attacking the German *Wiesbaden*. He had said before the battle, perhaps influenced by his failure at Scarborough, that he intended to take his ships within paint-scraping range of the enemy, but his 'mad rush for the enemy' was never satisfactorily explained. A British officer later reported, 'When I first saw them, I knew they were doomed.'

Robert's flagship, the armoured cruiser HMS *Defence,* was deluged with close-range heavy-calibre gunfire from SMS *Lützow.* It is possible a shell had disabled *Defence's* steering gear, leaving her unable to alter course. Captain Gunther Paschen, commanding *Lützow,* later reported, 'I recognised an old English armoured cruiser in the periscope, improbably close.' He gave the order to fire, and then came 'the now familiar sight of a ship blowing up.'

The *Defence* sank almost immediately with all hands following a massive magazine explosion, a loss of over nine hundred lives.

Robert, who left a widow and a ten-year-old daughter, was posthumously appointed a KCB for his services in command of the First Cruiser Squadron. His body was never recovered, and he is commemorated on the Plymouth Naval Memorial.

The British had lost fourteen ships and over 6000 men; the Germans eleven ships and 2500 men. Germany thus celebrated the battle as their victory, but in reality it was a strategic loss for both sides. The Germans retreated back to their home ports and no major naval battle was fought again. The war at sea now became one of stealth and subversion.

The Gallipoli Campaign

The British and French armies were also fighting against the Turkish (Ottoman) Empire, which had entered the war on Germany's side. This centred on a campaign at Gallipoli on the Mediterranean coast, also known as the Dardanelles Campaign, with a view to capturing the Turkish capital of Constantinople. The first landings took place on 25th April 1915.

The Turkish forces were greatly underestimated. The landscape, a mass of ravines and gullies, caused confusion. The troops were lacking in manpower, ammunition, water and leadership. The attack was a disaster. Both sides became entrenched with little progress possible. The heat was intense; drinking water scarce; dysentery and other diseases rife. In July the Allies planned a major new assault and began to land thousands more troops.

Ernest Giles Horseman (b1892) was the son of John and Paula Horseman of Preston. John worked as a shepherd then moved to Bilston to work on the railways. In 1911, Ernest, aged 16, was working as a junior clerk in the Bankfield

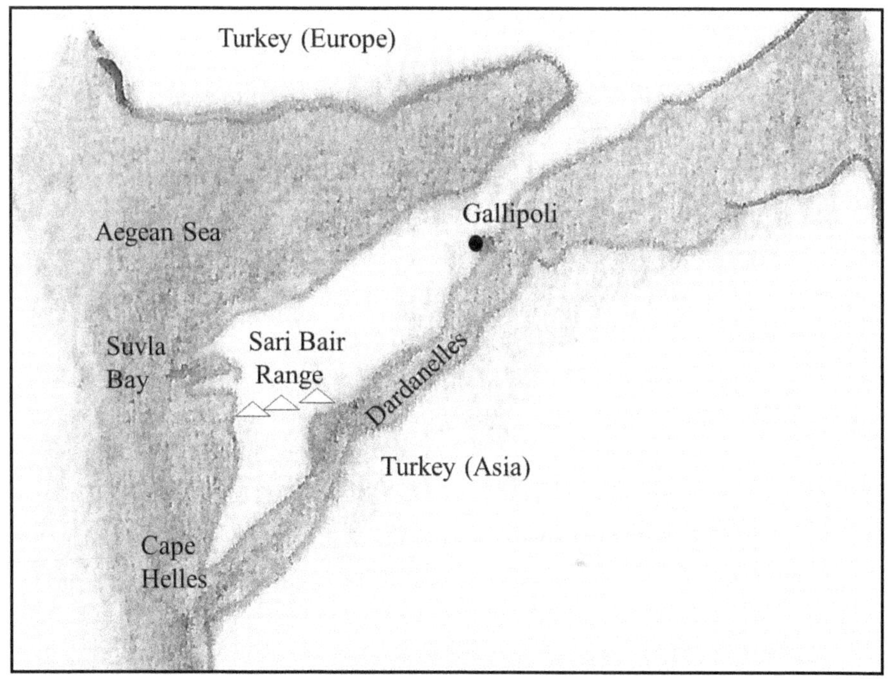

Gallipoli and the surrounding area.

Iron Works in Bilston. He enlisted in the 7th South Staffs in 1914 or early 1915 and landed in Gallipoli in July 1915. His battalion had only a few months training; not nearly enough for what they were to endure, a senior officer later wrote.

John Alec Clift (b1891) who enlisted under the name Alic, was the son of John and Julia Clift. The family had a farm near Chipping Campden in 1911 then moved to Atherstone shortly afterwards. Alic was serving in the Warwickshire Yeomanry, a territorial cavalry unit, by October 1914. He went to Egypt in April 1915, then Gallipoli shortly afterwards.

Waggoner George Bennett (b1890) a shepherd's son from Goldicote, enlisted in 1914 or early 1915. His younger brother Stephen had joined the 6th Dorsets in September 1914; his brother Frank (b1892) was serving in the Warwickshire Yeomanry and his brother Thomas, (b1888) was in the Army Service Corps in Serbia by 1915. George was posted to the 9th Warwicks, a new battalion formed in August 1914, and landed in Gallipoli in July 1915.

Sidney Hornsey (b1898) was the son of farm labourer and former police constable John Hornsey and his wife Margaret, nee Knight, a lifelong resident of Alderminster. The family were living at No.39 Alderminster in 1911. Sidney enlisted in the 9th Warwicks, aged 16 or 17, and landed in Gallipoli in September 1915.

George Bennett landed at Cape Helles on the night of 13th July. His battalion was in the frontline trenches the following day, and remained in trenches or digging trenches for the rest of the month. Ernest Horseman, now a lance corporal, landed on 21st July.

The Battle of Sari Bair began on 6th August. The Sari Bair range was a strip of Turkish-held high ground dominating the peninsula. Several battalions, including the Warwicks and the Staffs, landed at Suvla Bay in readiness to capture it. The Staffs was the first battalion to land and immediately began entrenching. They encountered a small group of Turks who ran away. The attack began.

The troops got confused in the dark and made minimal progress with heavy casualties, while the troops approaching overland got hopelessly lost in the tangled ravines. Little was achieved. The Warwicks went forward on 8th August and took part in a fresh assault the following day. The Staffs were also fighting on the ridge. They reached their objective but suddenly came under very heavy fire. The battalion on their flank gave way and exposed them to attack. Heavy firing set the undergrowth on fire which caused yet more casualties. The whole line was forced back. The Staffs had suffered 350 casualties.

The Warwicks also had immense difficulties. Their guides lost their way. They were attacking in full view of the enemy and were subject to enfilade fire. Even so, they reached the crest of the ridge and it seemed as if victory was theirs.

But support was unavailable. Nearly all the officers had fallen. They held on like grim death, but the Turks slowly forced them back. One officer forced retreating men back to the ridge at pistol point. They were now the only battalion left on the hill. One company was surrounded and it was supposed they all perished. The battalion now had less than half its number left, and a Turkish attack the following morning recaptured all the ground so painfully won.

A further attack on Sari Bair, known as the Battle of Hill 60, took place on 21st August. The Staffs were among the assaulting battalions; the Warwicks were in reserve. At 3.30pm the naval guns began bombarding the Turkish trenches and the troops moved out. They suffered very heavy shell fire and the Staffs lost 300 casualties, including all officers except two. The Warwickshire Yeomanry were also fighting and suffered heavy losses. Some ground was captured although the summits remained in Turkish hands, and the exhausted Staffs, suffering from heavy fighting, heat, dehydration and dysentery, were withdrawn on the 24th.

Ernest Horseman suffered a gunshot wound to the head and was evacuated to England. He suffered severe brain damage and paralysis of one side of his body, and spent three months in hospital in Bristol before he died on 10th December. He was 23 years old. He is commemorated on the war memorial of the Bankfield Iron Works, now in St Leonard's Church in Bilston.

The stalemate resumed. The Warwicks spent three months in frontline trenches with little action. Sidney Hornsey joined the battalion on 31st September along with other reinforcements but saw little fighting. On 26th November, a six-hour thunderstorm flooded the British trenches, swept away parapets and filled all the dugouts. Drowned Turks and horses were washed down into the trenches. The flood was followed by several days of hard frost, and the drenched men suffered hugely from exposure and frostbite. The Allies had 20,000 casualties in a few days.

The Gallipoli campaign was written off as hopeless. The evacuation of the peninsula began on 18th December, and was the most effective operation of the campaign. The troops were moved to the beaches and embarked in secrecy.

The ships left without incident. The last day of the evacuation cost only three casualties; the expected figure had been 20,000.

George Bennett, either wounded or suffering frostbite, was evacuated on 19th December. He eventually returned to active service in Mesopotamia. Sidney Hornsey was transferred to the 11th Warwicks and sent to France. Alic Clift was sent to Palestine.

The Mesopotamian Campaign

The campaign in Mesopotamia (modern Iraq) began in November 1914 between the British and the Ottoman (Turkish) Empire, who had designs on territory and oil fields. The fighting was limited to the areas watered by the rivers Tigris and Euphrates.

The British landed in the Persian Gulf and occupied Basra by late November 1914. During 1915, the Turks, whose priority was Gallipoli, retreated. The British captured the city of Kut-al-Amara on 26th September 1915. They pushed on towards Baghdad but after heavy fighting were forced to withdraw to Kut which was then besieged by the Turks. Both sides began to reinforce.

Frederick George (b1888) was the son of labourer Richard George and his wife Alice of Wimpstone. In 1901, aged thirteen, he was working as a teamster on

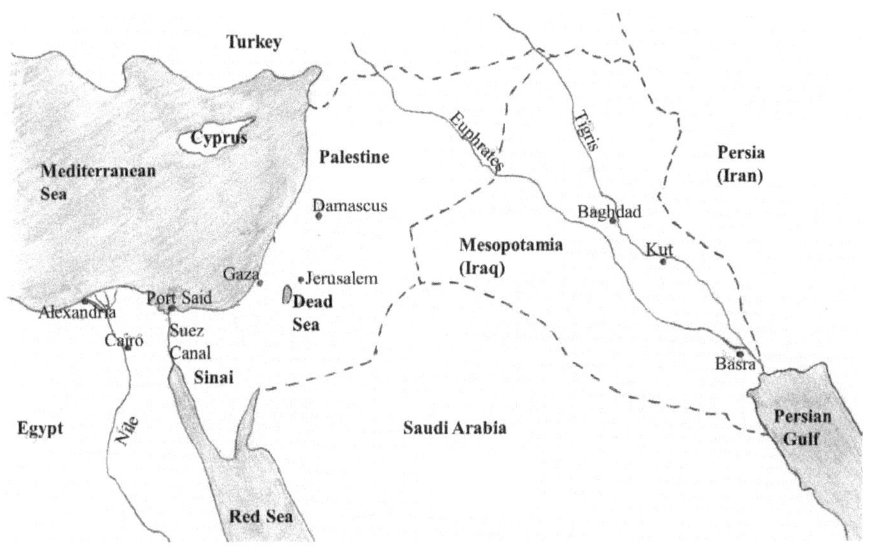

The Middle East.

a farm. In December 1909, he went to Birmingham to join the Royal Field Artillery. He went to India the following year, gained his 3rd class education certificate and was granted 6d proficiency pay in December 1911. In September 1914, his unit was recalled from India and began the month-long journey to France. He arrived on 14th October then left for Mesopotamia on 24th December 1915 after spending leave in Wimpstone. His battery reached Basra on 30th January 1916.

They spent several months on the banks of the Tigris, and had continual problems with Arabs stealing their horses and kit. Water had to be carried four miles and they had heavy losses from cholera, dysentery and jaundice. They moved to the Biblical city of Gomorrah in June, and exchanged some shelling with the enemy over the coming months. Frederick George was admitted to hospital on 26th July 1916, possibly with malaria, and rejoined his battery a month later.

The 9th Warwicks, including George Bennett, had left Gallipoli for Egypt in December 1915 and two months later sailed for Basra, landing on 7th March 1916. They advanced up the Tigris and were involved in heavy fighting over the next month against the Turks, who were trying to prevent troops reaching Kut. They lost heavy casualties and made little progress. They were also hindered by the flooding river.

Kut surrendered in April 1916 and all the British were taken prisoner. The Warwicks remained in trenches for several months. There were few casualties from fighting but they suffered heavily from sickness and heat-related problems.

An attempt to retake Kut began on 13th December 1916. The Warwicks attacked an enemy position the following day and ground was slowly gained. They took part in a major attack on 25th January. Frederick George's battery had spent four days firing 1500 rounds a day on the Turkish wire and trenches. The wire was well cut and the battalions took their objectives.

The British were slowly forced back by Turkish counterattacks, but Kut was finally recaptured on 23rd February 1917. The RFA diary reported that the infantry crossed the river at 5.30am while the Turks were still sleeping. They then fired on the moving Turks and prevented their reinforcement.

The British pressed on up the Tigris towards Baghdad. The Turks mounted a strong defence but Baghdad was captured on 11th March. The Warwicks were one of the first units to reach the city and the following day conducted a house to house search for firearms and ammunition.

The British advance stopped. The supply lines from the Persian Gulf were overstretched and the summer heat made campaigning near impossible. It was 122° in the shade and water was almost non-existent. Mesopotamia was a minor priority for both sides, and there was little further fighting.

The Warwicks remained near Baghdad until the end of the war, seeing little more fighting but with large numbers falling sick every day.

Frederick George spent a month in India in May 1917, probably because of continuing health problems, then returned to Basra on 18th July. He died of malaria the following day. He was buried in Basra War Cemetery in Iraq. Four months later, his mother received his education certificate, a photo and three watches, one broken, which accounted for his possessions. He is commemorated on Whitchurch War Memorial.

The Sinai and Palestine Campaign

A German-led Turkish force invaded Sinai, part of the British protectorate of Egypt, in an attempt to capture the Suez Canal in January 1915, and the area became the scene of protracted fighting. The British recaptured Sinai in January 1917, then suffered defeats in Palestine and Gaza over the coming months. In October 1917 they landed more troops, and captured Gaza and Jerusalem. Damascus fell in September 1918 and the Turks sued for peace.

Edwin Handy (b1891) was the son of carpenter John Handy and his wife Ann of Alderminster. By 1901 the family had moved to Fazeley in Staffordshire, where John was working as a quarryman. Edwin enlisted in the Staffordshire volunteer battalion in March 1909, aged 17½. He was now working as a collier. Eighteen months later, he joined the 1st Lancashire Fusiliers, a regular infantry battalion. His battalion landed in Egypt on 16th March 1915.

Edwin was among many of his battalion wounded at the end of May 1915. He was probably invalided home and was subsequently transferred to the Royal Engineers, perhaps in view of his civilian trade as a collier. He was transferred to the reserve in January 1919.

Robert Mansell Smith, 38, was the son of John Charles Smith, a farmer's son from Preston who founded the Stratford draper's firm JC Smith. Robert attended the King Edward VI grammar school and by 1901 was managing the shop in Stratford with his brother John. He was a prominent figure in the

Payton Street Baptist chapel and founded the local branch of the Boy Scouts. He was unmarried and lived with his parents in Stratford.

He was a corporal in the General Duty Reserve and enlisted in the Royal Army Medical Corps in January 1915. He served in the South Midlands Mounted Brigade Field Ambulance, then in January 1916 was commissioned into the Norfolk Regiment. He arrived in Egypt on 29th November.

On 24th July 1917 he received dangerous shrapnel wounds. A shell burst within three yards of where he was standing and he was struck in the breast and in the neck. He received first aid on the spot and it was found a piece of shell had embedded itself in his breast. His condition was too serious for an operation and he was sent on the four-day journey to hospital in Alexandria. The *Stratford Herald* reported on 10th August that: '*The legion of Stratford friends of this popular gentleman will learn with satisfaction that the last news respecting his progress is of a most favourable kind. The latest news from the patient himself is that he is progressing famously.*'

Subsequent letters received by his friends and published by the *Herald* gave encouraging accounts of his progress. '*He is so much better that at the time he last wrote he believed the attempt to extract the splinter would take place at once. These operations, he says, are so very common that success invariably attends them. The officer is rather optimistic regarding the close of the war.*'

Robert didn't return to the frontline and was eventually discharged as medically unfit.

Bernard David Walton, 40, was the son of Preston labourer George Walton and his wife Mary Ann. The couple moved to Stratford where George worked as a stationery engine driver. Bernard was called up in November 1916. He was single, lived with his parents, and had been employed in cellar work at the Flowers brewery since leaving school. He applied for exemption, pleading health reasons and saying he was the sole support of his recently widowed mother. He would be more usefully employed at the brewery. The appeal was dismissed and Bernard enlisted the following month. He passed his medical examination, although he needed an upper denture, and was posted to the 1/4th Norfolk Regiment. He arrived in Egypt in February 1917.

On 8th April, he was admitted to the field hospital suffering from dysentery. Ten days later, he was transferred to hospital in Alexandria, and on 26th April he was reported dangerously ill. At 4pm on 14th May, he died. He was buried in the Alexandria War Cemetery in Hadra, Egypt. His mother Mary was sent his personal effects, including his identity disk, purse, toothbrush, letters, postcards, and his set of false teeth. She chose the inscription *Thy will be done* for his grave. He is commemorated on Stratford War Memorial.

His bronze plaque or Dead Man's Penny was issued to Mary and when she died in 1931 the plaque was incorporated into her gravestone in Preston.

Bernard Walton's plaque. The gravestone reads:
In loving memory of Mary Ann Walton who passed away 6th March 1931 aged 82. Also of Pte Bernard David Walton 1/4th Norfolk Regiment, who died on active service in the Great War 1914-1918 and was interred in the military cemetery, Hadra, Egypt. May they rest in peace.

Richard John Green was born in Peckham, London, in 1898, the son of John Green, a tailor's cutter, and his wife Mary. Mary died shortly after the birth and Richard lived with his father for a few years in a poor area of Camberwell, then it seems his mother's unmarried sister Elizabeth Arnold took responsibility for him.

Elizabeth was comparatively well-off, recorded on the census returns as of no occupation and living on private income. She arranged for Richard to board at the fee-paying Thame Grammar School in Oxfordshire, where he started, aged nine, in September 1907. He left in July 1915 and moved to Preston where he became the farm pupil of Thomas Salmon Smith at Park

Farm. He may have had family living near Stratford. He was very keen to join the army and enlisted in the Royal Fusiliers soon after his eighteenth birthday in April 1916. As he couldn't serve abroad until he was nineteen, and was otherwise usefully employed doing farmwork, he was sent home until his next birthday.

In April 1917 he enlisted in the 1/4th Royal Sussex Regiment, which was serving in Palestine and took part in the Battles of Gaza and the capture of Jerusalem. Richard saw action in this theatre then his battalion moved to France in May 1918.

Thomas Canning (b1899) was the son of Thomas Canning of Crimscote Fields Farm. He was commissioned into the Warwickshire Yeomanry on 1st May 1917, a week before his 18th birthday, and arrived at Beersheba in the Middle East that November. A month later the unit was sent to Gaza. Alic Clift, who had fought with the Yeomanry in Gallipoli, also saw action in the Battles of Gaza and Jerusalem.

In March 1918 the Yeomanry were reorganised as a machine gun unit. They embarked on HMT *Leasowe Castle* on 26th May at Alexandria but the ship was torpedoed. Nearly all troops were rescued, and Tom in later years was scathing about the Japanese escort supposedly protecting them. The following month they reembarked and reached France on 29th June. They went into the front line at the end of August and remained in close fighting until the armistice, including regular gas attacks. Tom Canning was made lieutenant on 4th November. He and Alic were discharged in early 1919.

The War in West Africa

Vicar's son and Boer War veteran Wilfred Hastings went to West Africa in March 1903 to join the West African Frontier Force (WAFF), formed in 1900 to garrison the British colonies of Nigeria, Gold Coast, Sierra Leone and Gambia. The regiments comprised British officers and NCOs and native lower ranks. Africa was a brutal environment for the Europeans who rapidly succumbed to the climate, disease, terrain and wildlife. The benefit of native troops was understood by all colonialists.

Wilfred was attached to the North Nigeria Regiment and took part in the Munshi Expedition in 1906, an aborted expedition against the Munshi tribe of North Nigeria which had risen in revolt and burned a supply station. Wilfred was awarded the Africa General Service Medal with a West Africa clasp. He was posted to the Gambia Company in August 1906, then went to India in March 1909. His battalion remained in India until the start of the war.

Wilfred arrived in France on 27th August 1914. He was involved in staff work and was made assistant provost marshal of the Expeditionary Force, and was in charge of finding camping grounds for troops arriving from India. He was then invalided home, possibly with malaria.

In March 1915, in view of his experience in West Africa, he was promoted to major and sent to Africa to command the Sierra Leone battalion of the WAFF, fighting against the neighbouring German colony of Kamerun (modern Cameroon). There were limited troops available and no large-scale battles took place in the African theatre. Douala, the largest city in Kamerun, quickly surrendered to the British and the remainder of the war comprised minor skirmishes.

Wilfred arrived at Douala on 26th May 1915 and was promoted to lieutenant colonel. His battalion diary had nothing to report for most days. The troops were operating in Kamerun, which was largely unmapped bushland almost unpopulated by Europeans. They patrolled the area with some minor engagements. Natives reported settlements with enemy troops which were attacked. Often a counterattack pushed the British back again. Supply convoys, comprising native carriers and an army escort, were a regular target for both sides.

The last German settlement surrendered in February 1916, and the Kamerun Campaign was over. Wilfred Hastings remained in command of the Sierra Leone battalion for the remainder of the war.

The Canadian Expeditionary Force

The 19th century saw a surge in emigration to the British colonies. The Canadian prairies were ripe for exploitation and farm labourers especially were encouraged to emigrate. Many people, typically single young men, left the Alscot Estate villages for a better life abroad.

All territories in the British Empire were automatically brought into the war, although each government had the freedom to decide their nation's level of involvement. Many enthusiastically raised armies and urged their men to volunteer.

Henry George Walton (b1887) was the son of farm labourer William Walton and his wife Sarah of No.13 Alderminster. He emigrated to Canada and settled in St Thomas, Ontario, where he worked as a locomotive engineer. He enlisted on 1st May 1916, aged 28. His subsequent service record is unclear.

Edwin Plumb (b1867) was the son of labourer John Plumb and his wife Selena who lived in Crimscote and Wimpstone. In 1881 Edwin was working as a farm labourer. He served three years with the 9th Lancers and in April 1892, now aged 25, he left Liverpool for Montreal. He was in low water and had visions of improvement. He settled in Blackfields, Alberta, became a farmer, married and raised a family. By 1916 he owned 320 acres of land and was the biggest exhibitor of pedigree cattle and horses at the district stock show.

His eldest son John, 16, enlisted on 3rd June 1916 and two days later Edwin himself, now aged 49, also enlisted. He was now widowed and declared he was born in July 1872 – five years younger than his true age. He joined the 187th (Central Alberta) battalion and arrived in England in December 1916. The battalion supplied reinforcements to the Western Front as needed.

In April 1917, Edwin was serving in Hampshire. He revisited Wimpstone and told his story to the *Stratford Herald*. In his view, the report said, there were far too many Germans in Canada, and although long over qualifying age he was anxious to get at the enemy. His subsequent service record is unclear.

Horace Hazelwood Horseman (b1895) and his brother Hubert (b1891) were the elder sons of butcher and farm labourer Jim Horseman and his wife Harriet of No.5 Wimpstone. Both had red hair, blue eyes and numerous tattoos. Both were Baptists and worked as farm labourers.

In May 1911 Hubert, aged 20, left Bristol for Quebec. In April 1913 Horace, now 17, also sailed for Quebec. George Ward, a farm labourer from Crimscote, and his wife Ada travelled with him.

Hubert enlisted in the 1st Canadian Mounted Rifles on 30th December 1914. His unit arrived in England in June 1915 and landed at Havre on 22nd September. They were soon permanently dismounted: mounted troops were near obsolete. They formed working parties for a month then spent several months in and out of the trenches, involved in patrols, working parties and training with little action.

Horace enlisted on 1st March 1916. He was now nineteen and working as a farmer. He joined the 5th Canadian Infantry and arrived in England in October 1916. He saw little action until the Battle of Arras in April 1917.

Their brother Harold Jim Horseman, who lived in Wimpstone, joined the

1st Dorsets in early 1917, aged eighteen, and was later transferred to the 2nd Worcesters. He served abroad and promoted to corporal. Nothing else is known of his service history.

Hubert Horseman was on the frontline in Flanders on 2nd June 1916 when the Germans launched the Battle of Mount Sorrel, aiming to capture the strategically important heights near Ypres. The Canadian positions were overrun and the Rifles suffered 80% casualties. Rapid counterattacks regained most of the lost positions.

In August, the Rifles were in trenches in Dranoutre, a village south of Ypres, near a much fought-for hill known as Hill 60. On 12th August, the Germans began an intense 2½ hour bombardment with a view to capturing the hill. It was especially heavy on the Canadian communication and support trenches – a slight but costly German error. When the Germans attacked, the still-operational Canadian rifles and machine guns immediately checked their advance. The Germans suffered severe casualties and the attack was thwarted with only forty Canadian casualties.

Hubert received a shrapnel wound to his right knee. He was evacuated to England where he remained in hospital for several months then sailed for Canada in February 1917.

The day after the ship sailed, as was later reported in the *Stratford Herald,* Hubert was awakened by a great noise. He thought his ship had been torpedoed, but then he realised the Germans had torpedoed another boat which was burning furiously. The crew were rescued but a great number of horses drowned. Another ship was torpedoed soon afterwards and Hubert and the other passengers watched shells bursting all around them. They escaped undamaged but later heard the Germans had sunk twelve ships that night.

The rest of the voyage was uneventful except for heavy snowstorms and fog, and they landed safely in Canada on 11th February. Hubert went to a military convalescent hospital and then to a training college, probably to train recruits. His future from this point is unclear.

Francis William Porter, known as Will (b1891) was the eldest son of house painter Aubrey Porter and his wife Margaret. The family moved to No.8 Preston from Chipping Norton around 1895. By 1911, Will, aged twenty, was also working as a house painter for Alscot Estate. He was much liked by everyone in Preston, both as a boy at school and afterwards as a young man.

He left Liverpool for Quebec on 11th July 1912. The following year his younger brother Aubrey John, known as Jack, joined him. With him was Edith Keyte, a domestic servant from Wimpstone, who would shortly become Will's wife.

Jack, who had worked as a carpenter and a wheelwright, enlisted on 14th December 1914. He was posted to the 2nd Divisional Supply Column of the Canadian Army Service Corps (CASC) and arrived in England in April 1915. The unit landed in France on 10th September. Jack was gassed at some point and subsequently evacuated from the frontline.

Will enlisted in the 21st Canadian Infantry on 14th March 1916. He was now working as a painter and living in Ottawa with Edith and their young son Maurice. He left for England on 25th October. Edith and Maurice had recently returned to Edith's family home in Wimpstone. She probably didn't want to remain alone in a strange country, and it would be easier to see her husband when he had leave.

Will arrived in France in May 1917 and joined his battalion on 11th June. He went into the trenches for the first time a few days later. His first major action was the Battle of Hill 70, a prelude to the Third Battle of Ypres (Passchendaele) in August 1917.

William Barton Boardman (b1882) was the son of William Boardman, a blacksmith, and his wife Fanny, a tailoress. The family lived in Birmingham until the 1900s then Fanny, now widowed, and her son John moved to No.45 Alderminster.

In 1901, William was working as a bicycle fitter. He served eight years in the Royal Artillery then in April 1913 left Liverpool for Canada. He was now thirty and working as a fitter. He had a dagger and a butterfly tattooed on his chest and a cross and his initials on his left arm.

He settled in Vernon, British Columbia, and worked as a bricklayer. He enlisted in the 54th Canadian Infantry on 28th September 1915 and landed at Havre on 13th August 1916. His battalion went into trenches near Ypres a week later. On leaving the trenches after their first tour they were severely bombarded; several men were buried when the parapets collapsed. During the several months they spent around Ypres, things did not much improve.

In November, they took part in an assault on the German line near the village St Eloi near Ypres. After spending six days waiting in the frontline, now bitterly cold with rain and snow, the barrage began at 6.10am on the 18th November and the battalion advanced. Their objective was captured and held until the battalion was relieved. The subsequent report stated that the men showed the greatest courage, intelligence and endurance during the operation.

In April 1917, the battalion took part in the Battle of Arras.

Aubrey John (Jack) and Francis William (Will) Porter.
Courtesy of June Thompson.

The Battle of Arras

The Battle of Arras was a six-week Allied offensive which began on 9th April 1917, and was intended to bring the war to a decisive end. The aim was to capture German-held ground, the formidable defences known as the Hindenburg Line, and divert forces from the French front further south. It was the most costly battle for the Alscot servicemen.

William Boardman of the 54th Canadians and Horace Horseman of the 5th Canadians took part in the opening stages. Sidney Hornsey, who had fought at Gallipoli, was now a lance corporal serving with the 11th Warwicks in the Arras area. Stephen Bennett, who had been invalided with frostbite in November 1915, had returned to France in October 1916 and posted to the 1st Dorsets. He had fought in the Battle of the Ancre, the last battle of the Somme offensive, and was now serving near Arras.

Frank and Ernest Southam, serving in the 2nd Warwicks, also saw action at Arras, as did John Whiteman, now commanding the Hawke Battalion of the Royal Naval Division. Ernest Horseman of the 3rd Royal Horse Artillery (RHA), in France since August 1914, was providing artillery cover for attacking troops.

Frederick Reuben Knight (b1897) was the son of William and Emily Knight. In 1911 the family were living in Moreton in March and Frederick, aged 13, was working as a farm labourer. The family moved to Wimpstone and in 1916 Frederick was working as an under gardener. He attested for Lord Derby's scheme in February 1916, and was called up just after his 19th birthday on 18th May 1916. He joined the 15th Warwicks and arrived in France on 21st January 1917. Arras was his first major action.

Percy Harold Dove (b1898) was the son of Percy and Miriam Dove of No.12 Preston. The family moved to Preston around 1902 when Percy took the position of electrical engineer at Alscot Park. By 1916, Percy junior was living in Stratford and an assistant clerk in the civil service. He was unusually keen to enlist – perhaps still cushioned by boyish dreams of heroism – and applied six times before being accepted in October 1916 for the 14th London (London Scottish) Regiment. He arrived in France on 19th March 1917, just after his 19th birthday.

Charles Benjamin Waters, 23, was the son of shoemaker Albert Waters and his wife Elizabeth of Hatton, near Warwick, although he had some connection to Alderminster. This was possibly employment related, although several peoples named Waters lived in Alderminster in the later 19th century. Charles joined the Warwickshire Yeomanry, a territorial cavalry unit, in November 1914. He was transferred to the 11th Warwicks, Sidney Hornsey's battalion, in December 1916 and arrived in France on 21st March 1917.

Jack Brown, known as Jacky, 18, was the son of John Brown, a kennel-man and groom for the Warwickshire Hunt at Kineton. John was widowed by 1901 and moved to Houndshill Cottages in Alderminster. Jack went to Ireland where he became second whip – managing the hounds during the hunt – to the East Galway Hunt, where he was highly respected. He returned to England to enlist and joined the Royal Warwickshire Regiment on 21st November 1916. His elder brother Harry was serving in Salonika. He arrived in France on 22nd March.

Vimy Ridge

The battle began on 9th April with a Canadian assault on Vimy Ridge, a four-mile escarpment which commanded the area. William Boardman of the 54th Canadians had been part of an attack on this ridge on 1st March after a gas and artillery bombardment. The gas had no effect on the Germans who retaliated with gas and machine gun fire. Nor had the wire entanglements been cut. The attackers were forced to retreat with heavy casualties.

The attack was now repeated after a week-long bombardment. The 54th Canadians were again at the front of the attack. Horace Horseman of the 5th Canadians also took part. The 15th Warwicks, including Frederick Knight, were lent to the Canadian Corps for the attack.

A tremendous barrage was put down at 5.30am and the attack commenced. The leading battalions took their objectives easily and the Warwicks moved up to consolidate the captured trenches. They spent the rest of the day and night digging a new trench and consolidating the ground. No counterattack followed. Vimy Ridge was captured and the day was considered a major success.

Horace Horseman was severely wounded in the back during the battle and was evacuated to England. He survived his injuries but his subsequent fate is unclear.

Percy Dove with the London Scottish took part in a follow-up attack on the same day. The pipe major played the battalion from the assembly area – a nod to its Scottish origins – and they then attacked three German trenches. The objectives were 1400 yards away and the battalion took too long to cross the difficult muddy ground, thus losing the benefit of their artillery barrage. They suffered heavily from shelling and machine gun fire but one company reached its objective and captured 300 prisoners. The objectives were finally taken the next morning. The expected counterattack came a week later. The Germans recaptured part of the line; the British quickly retook it. The London Scottish were then relieved.

Ernest Horseman, serving with the 3rd RHA, was in action for several days during the action at Vimy Ridge, providing artillery support for the attacking infantry. The unit diary reports they had 'a successful shoot' on the 11th April, catching several parties of the enemy in the open and silencing an artillery battery. One of their own batteries was then heavily shelled by the Germans with seven men and 33 horses becoming casualties. They were then withdrawn.

The Battle Continues

Sidney Hornsey and Charles Waters, serving in the 11th Warwicks, were part of a follow-up attack near Cambrai on 10th April. The Germans brought down heavy artillery fire and the battalion on their flank was held up. The Warwicks enfiladed the German positions but the attack stalled. Communications were lost with the rest of the brigade and some battalions had been forced back. No artillery support was available and the Warwicks dug in. The next day, they continued the attack. The Germans counterattacked but were repulsed with heavy losses. The Warwicks were withdrawn. They had suffered over 200 casualties. Jack Brown, recently arrived in France, was transferred to the battalion with other desperately needed reinforcements. He joined them in the field on 20th April.

Stephen Bennett, with the 1st Dorsets, attacked Cepy, a village overlooking the Hindenburg Line, on the 14th April. The village was captured but the following day the British suffered a constant bombardment with heavy casualties. Stephen Bennett, aged 22, was one of those killed. He has no known grave and is commemorated on the Thiepval Memorial and Alderminster War Memorial.

The Battle of the Scarpe

The 6th Dorsets, which many early volunteers had joined, attacked the Scarpe, high ground near Arras, on 12th April. They left the trenches and were at once subjected to heavy machine gun fire. Their artillery bombardment had missed the machine gun emplacements. The battalion reached its first objective with heavy casualties and with all but one officer down. Reinforcements were brought up and their position was consolidated. The other attacking battalions had failed to gain their objectives, so orders were issued to withdraw to their original line.

They made another attack on the position on 23rd April. The Dorsets again suffered heavy casualties but the high ground and nearby villages were captured and the attack considered a success.

The Hawke battalion, commanded by John Whiteman, were also fighting in the Battle of the Scarpe. They attacked the village of Gavrelle at 4.45am on 23rd April and took their objective easily. They then came under machine gun fire. The emplacement was rushed and the gun captured along with its crew. The battalion headquarters moved to a new position in the old German front line at midday, but several bursts of shrapnel fell over the party as they moved. John Whiteman and the battalion's adjutant were both wounded. They were evacuated and the battalion spent the remainder of the day defending against constant counterattacks until they were relieved. John Whiteman died of his wounds on 25th April. He was buried in Aubigny Communal Cemetery in France and is commemorated on a memorial in Temple Grafton church.

The 11th Warwicks were fighting in the Battle of the Scarpe. They moved forwards at 3.30am on 23rd April. They were subject to heavy enemy artillery all day, then in late afternoon were ordered to attack. They suffered from heavy machine gun fire and were unable to advance further. They dug in and held their position until 3am on the 25th when they were relieved.

Sidney Hornsey, aged 19, was killed on 23rd April. Jack Brown, also 19, was killed on the 25th. Both men have no known grave and are commemorated on the Arras Memorial and Alderminster War Memorial.

On 28th April, the Warwicks made another attempt on their objective. All officers and NCOs except two became casualties, but this time the line was captured. Charles Waters, aged 25, was reported missing on 29th April. His fate was never discovered but he was presumed killed on this date. He is commemorated on the Arras Memorial and the war memorials at Alderminster, Ettington, Hatton and St Paul's in Warwick. His younger brother Ernest, who had enlisted underage and arrived in France in May 1915, aged 17 or 18, had also been killed in August 1916.

The Battle of Bullecourt

On 3rd May, the Allies attacked the village of Bullecourt on the Hindenburg Line. The village was honeycombed with dugouts and was a maze of underground passages. It was also heavily fortified with machine guns and wire. The Battle of Bullecourt involved eight waves of infantry which suffered disastrous losses and gained nothing.

The 2nd Warwicks, including Frank and Ernest Southam, attacked at 12.30am on 4th May. Little ground was gained and commanding officers had no idea of its extent. A few men dug in. Other survivors were scattered in shellholes, unable to move for enemy fire. 630 men went into the attack; only half came out.

That night, the remainder of the battalion, now only 200 men, was ordered forward again. The enemy machine gunners allowed them to reach the second line of barbed wire before opening fire. The Warwicks suffered severe casualties.

Ernest Southam, aged 27, whose brother William had died two years previously, was reported missing on 4th May, later presumed killed. He has no known grave and is commemorated on the Arras Memorial and on Alderminster and Stratford War Memorials.

After several more attempts, Bullecourt, now utterly destroyed by the artillery bombardment, was eventually captured.

The Final Phase

At 2am on 9th May, the 15th Warwicks, including Frederick Knight, attacked the village of Fresney. Their supporting barrage moved too slowly and the attackers became pinned between their own shelling and the enemy's counter-barrage. They suffered heavy casualties in consequence but reached their objective. They were in a weak position and met heavy machine gun fire, and were forced to withdraw with 200 casualties. Frederick Knight was wounded but returned to duty the same day. The battalion remained in trenches in the area for several weeks before taking part in the Battle of Passchendaele.

The London Scottish, including Percy Dove, attacked a German position on 11th May. They left their trenches at 8.30pm; the German SOS went up 1½ minutes later. The enemy barrage came down but the battalion avoided it and reached their objective. The Germans had been caught by surprise; most ran away. Others were seen trying to withdraw from another trench and these were picked off with snipers and machine guns. A captured machine gunner was persuaded to explain how his gun operated and this was also turned on the fleeing Germans. The line was held until the 13th when the battalion was relieved.

The Battle of Arras ended on 16th May. A substantial amount of ground had been captured and it was considered a success, although its strategic importance proved minimal.

The Battle of Hill 70

The Battle of Hill 70 began on 15th August 1917 near Lens in northern France. The intention was to divert German troops away from Ypres, thirty miles to the north. It was the first major action for Francis William (Will) Porter. Ernest Horseman's battery of the RHA was providing support for the Canadians.

Farm labourer Harry Wilfred Knight, 21, was the son of William and Emma Knight of Wimpstone. His brother Frederick served with the 15th Warwicks and Sidney Hornsey of the 11th Warwicks was his cousin. Harry joined the 6th Oxford and Bucks on 4th January 1915 and arrived in France in July 1915. Shortly after his arrival he was charged with losing by neglect a tube of iodine. He was confined to barracks for five days and told to pay for the tube. In October he was evacuated to England suffering with trench feet, spent two months in hospital then returned to France on 26th November 1916, despite having suffered permanent damage to his feet. He moved to Flanders on 21st July 1917 and took part in this battle.

At 4.25am on the 15th August, a barrage of hundreds of machine guns, howitzers and artillery opened for several miles along the German line. The 21st Canadians were keen and in the highest spirits as they attacked. The barbed wire provided little obstacle. The enemy began a counter-barrage but their frontline trench was taken, followed by further trenches. Several counterattacks were mounted before daybreak. One of these regained a foothold but the enemy were forced out. The Canadians held the captured ground against repeated counterattacks for another four days until they were relieved.

The RHA observers saw the enemy massing for a counterattack and the battery fired on them for an hour. Many other targets were engaged and the battery fired 7000 rounds during the day. They'd had limited opportunity to view their target ground but their very accurate and effective barrage, thanks to their discipline and high standard of gunnery, received commendation from the highest levels.

The 6th Ox Bucks, including Harry Knight, moved into position for an attack near Langemarck, near Hill 70, which began at 4.45am on the 16th August. They advanced under a smoke barrage but met heavy opposition from strongly held German positions. They were also held up by deep mud. Despite this, they reached and took their objectives with little loss – less than 200 casualties, 38 being killed – and consolidated their position. They were relieved two days later. The fighting at Hill 70 continued for another week and was considered a success.

The Australian Imperial Force (AIF)

Reginald Frank Hicks (b1889) was the son of Frederick and Harriet Hicks of No.3 Alderminster, of no known relation to servicemen Sidney and John Hicks. Frederick was a woodman on Alscot Estate, and Reginald spent five years apprenticed to James Roberts-West as a woodman. He then left England for Queensland, Australia, on 23rd October 1911. With him were John Charles Reading and Arthur Goodway from Alderminster. All three were members of the Alderminster football team.

Arthur Goodway was a wheelwright's son. John Charles Reading, known as Charles (b1887) was the grandson of Alderminster blacksmith Edward Roberts. He lived with his grandfather and uncle, to whom he was apprenticed for five years.

Reginald settled in Ipswich in New South Wales and worked as a carpenter. His brothers Albert and Oliver soon followed him to Australia. Charles Reading also settled in Ipswich where he worked as a blacksmith.

On 2nd March 1916, Reginald, aged 26, enlisted in the 20th battalion AIF. He left Sydney in August and arrived in Plymouth two months later. He arrived in France on 4th February 1917 and joined his battalion in the Somme sector a week later.

Charles Reading enlisted in the 41st battalion AIF on 14th April 1917 and left for Britain two months later. He arrived in France on 5th February 1918 and saw action in the closing stages of the war.

The 20th Australian Infantry were involved in the first attack in the Battle of Bullecourt on 3rd May 1917. They went into a heavy German barrage at 3.20am on the 3rd and were forced back with severe losses. Another attack was organised with the same result, and the battalion was withdrawn. A few months later, the battalion was again in action at the Third Battle of Ypres, also known as Passchendaele.

The Third Battle of Ypres (Passchendaele)

The frontline around Ypres had changed little since 1915; the British held the city while the Germans held the surrounding high ground. The Allied plan was to break through the German line and capture the Belgian ports used as German U-boat bases. Fighting began in May 1917. The Third Battle of Ypres, also known as Passchendaele, began on 31st July and lasted nearly four months.

The area of Flanders was flat, silty and prone to flooding, and the summer of 1917 saw the worst rain for forty years. The drainage ditches and canals had been destroyed by shelling, and the area was now the impenetrable quagmire of mud for which Passchendaele is infamous.

William Boardman of the 54th Canadians, who had fought at Vimy Ridge, saw action at Passchendale, as did Harry Knight of the 6th Ox Bucks; his brother Frederick Knight of the 15th Warwicks; Reg Hicks of the Australian Infantry; Will Porter of the 21st Canadians; Dick Beavington, a baker now transferred to the Kings Royal Rifles; and Frank Southam of the 2nd Warwicks who had now lost two brothers in the conflict.

Albert and Frank Silvester, aged 19 and 21, of Coombe Farm, Alderminster, the sons of Thomas and Mary Silvester, attested for deferred service in February 1916. Both had worked on the farm for several years. Mary managed the farm: Thomas, in his seventies, was perhaps an invalid.

Both brothers were called up in March 1916 and Mary appealed on their behalf. She said that no one was employed on the farm of 216 acres except the two lads, and she would be very sorry if either of them went away. They were granted three months' exemption. At the end of July, Mary applied again. The military said one of them should go. The chairman asked Mary: 'Don't you think you could spare one of these boys?' 'No sir, it's difficult to get anyone,' she replied. Frank said there was 45 acres of hay to do and his mother had fifty head of young cattle. Albert said: 'I don't want to go into the army.'

Frank was given exemption to 1st January; Albert one month. In September, Mary made a third plea for Albert. She said she couldn't get anyone else to work on the farm. The chairman said: 'We can't extend the time. He is a single young man and must go and fight for his country.'

What happened to Albert then is unclear. Frank joined the Royal Warwicks on 17th January 1917 and arrived in France on 20th May. He was posted to the 11th Warwicks, the same battalion as Sidney Hornsey, Jack Brown and Charles Waters, and went into the trenches near Ypres in July. The battalion suffered high casualty rates over the subsequent months then fought in the Battle of Poelcappele in October.

Percy Handy of the 1/5th Warwicks had been invalided home with septic poisoning early in 1917, and returned to France on 12th June. His battalion was in northern France and involved in training and working parties. They were also hay-making. Ten men worked on the frontline for several nights – they would come under fire in daytime – to cut the hay which was then carted behind their lines to be dried. At the beginning of August the battalion moved to Flanders. They went into trenches near the village of St Julien, where the battalion suffered numerous casualties over the following weeks. On 21st

August, they moved into position for a joint infantry and tank attack on the German line.

At 10.30pm they moved forward. The leading waves of the battalion cleared all the ground within 150 yards of the enemy line without serious opposition and the enemy machine gun emplacements were captured after protracted fighting. The tanks were supposed to move forward and capture the enemy trenches, but didn't do this – perhaps bogged down in the mud – and the German line, the main objective of the attack, was left uncaptured.

The next morning the enemy counterattacked and drove the Warwicks back to their original position. That night one company recaptured and occupied a German gunpit, and held it until 3am on the 24th when the enemy counterattacked in force and with flamethrowers. The Warwicks were driven out. The position was retaken the following day and further attacks continued over the next two days. Communications were very difficult throughout, due to the state of the ground and the severity of the enemy's fire, and the runners – vital for carrying messages along the line and key targets for the enemy – suffered many casualties.

Percy Handy, aged 22, was killed on 25th August. His platoon officer wrote to his sister;

> *'I regret to say your brother, in my platoon for some time, was unfortunately killed in action in a very dangerous part of the line. He was one of the best men I had, and he was killed while acting most bravely as battalion runner. We all miss him very much and my sincere sympathies are with you in your loss. We can ill afford to lose our best men like that. We hope this knowledge and our sincere sympathies may help make your sorrow less difficult to bear.'*

Percy has no known grave and is commemorated on the Tyne Cot Memorial and the Stratford War Memorial.

On 5th September 1917, the 54th Canadian Infantry, including William Boardman, was involved in an attack on German outposts. The enemy were positioned in ruined houses and inflicted heavy casualties. The Canadians were beaten back. They cleared their wounded and attacked again. This time they cleared the houses of the enemy by hand-to-hand fighting with bombs and bayonets. The Canadians then attacked and cleared an enemy trench.

The Germans counterattacked and regained some of their lost ground. The

Canadians had now suffered 80% casualties. Despite this they reorganised and recaptured the ground. They held it until they were relieved two nights later.

William Boardman, aged 35 and now acting corporal, received gunshot wounds to his chest and armpit. He was taken to a casualty clearing station in Bracquemont in Normandy where he died on 11th September. He was buried in Noeux-les-Mines cemetery in Pas de Calais. His gravestone reads: *Deeply mourned by mother, brother and sister.* He is commemorated on Alderminster War Memorial.

At 2am on 20th September, the 6th Ox Bucks, including Harry Knight, formed up to attack the German line. The attack began at 5.40am. Oil drums were set alight by the enemy which illuminated the attackers, and as the leading lines crested the ridge in front of the German trench they met heavy machine gun fire. One company lost all its officers and most of its NCOs. The attackers pressed forward and one company got within fifty yards of the German trench before they were held up. The reserve troops went forward but were unable to reach them. The survivors got into shellholes and dug in, where they remained under constant sniper fire. A fresh attack was ordered that evening. The German trench was shelled and two of the remaining officers collected all the men they could and went forward. They reached the trench and the enemy surrendered. They then proceeded along the trench with bombs, meeting little opposition, and linked up with other advancing units. They dug a line of posts and held their position until they were relieved on the 22nd.

The 15th Warwicks, including Frederick Knight, fought at the Battle of Broodseinde on 4th October. Frederick suffered gunshot wounds to his hand and left shoulder during the action. He was taken to hospital in Boulogne and a day later he was on a hospital ship for England. He remained in hospital for six weeks then returned to active service.

The Battle of Poelcappele

On 1st October, Reg Hicks, with the 20th Australian Infantry, moved to Flanders. They spent the next week pumping out dugouts and laying duckboards across the deepening mud. The trenches were collapsing and the battalion diary described conditions as 'unbearably miserable'. The tracks were now threads between quicksand and shellholes, and troops were easy targets for enemy artillery. The stretcher-bearers had to carry casualties across 1000 yards of quagmire, and most became casualties themselves.

On 9th October, the battalion, despite being reduced to only 120 men, was ordered to attack the enemy lines. The barrage began at 4am, followed immediately by an enemy counter-barrage. The Australians took their first objective but the line was weak and their position critical. One company – only 35 men to start with – were almost all casualties. The attack pushed on but lacked weight, and the attackers withdrew. A German counterattack was neutralised with artillery fire and the Australians' line was held until their relief the following night.

The 2nd Warwicks, including Frank Southam, were also fighting at Poelcappele. They attacked at 5.30am but were machine gunned by enemy in a nearby copse. They suffered heavy casualties including many officers and it was the following day before the copse was cleared of enemy and the battalion could move up and link with their line. They had lost 320 casualties.

Frank Silvester, with the 11th Warwicks, was also fighting at Poelcappele. The battalion formed up at 5.20am on 9th October and soon took their objectives. Within half an hour the Germans began an intense retaliatory artillery bombardment which lasted 24 hours. The battalion held their line until relieved the following day.

Frank, aged 23, was one of 33 men from the battalion killed. He was buried nearby then reinterred in Zantvoorde British Cemetery in Belgium after the war, one of the few bodies which could be identified. He is commemorated on Alderminster War Memorial.

The battle was a German victory.

The End of the Fighting

The 21st Canadians, including Will Porter, moved to Passchendaele in early November. They had 1½ hours of hard marching through mud and shellholes to reach their destination. They then dug themselves in with such protection against the weather as was possible. They suffered high casualties from shelling, injury and gunfire. Will Porter was admitted to hospital on 11th November suffering from a septic finger, and was out of action for nearly two months before returning to the frontline.

The village of Passchendaele and the surrounding high ground were finally captured in mid November, and the Third Battle of Ypres was at an end. British losses were 245,000; German losses 400,000. The misery for the troops, however, was far from over.

The 20th Australians remained in the trenches for three more months. By January 1918 the trenches were 3½ feet deep in water. They were working in knee-deep mud with the endless task of draining, clearing and riveting the collapsing trenches. They were finally withdrawn in February.

Dick Beavington, who had served for two years as a baker, was transferred to the 9th Kings Royal Rifles Corps (KRRC) on 27th November 1917. Anyone fit for frontline duties was now being transferred to the infantry. The battalion spent some time in the Passchendaele area, then left for some very comfortable billets. The burning question, the battalion diarist asked, was: '*how long are we to remain in such luxury?*' The answer was 72 hours. They then moved back into trenches near Passchendaele with accommodation for battalion headquarters 'such that no self-respecting dog would dream of using', which involved a seven-mile walk along slippery duckboards, and 'all the deathtraps in the world seemed to fall upon us'. There were many casualties with sprains and broken limbs.

They were withdrawn on 25th December, and three days later had a lavish Christmas dinner with pork, beef, plum pudding, nuts and beer. This was followed by a snowball fight.

The Battle of Cambrai

The Battle of Cambrai began on 20th November 1917 as the Passchendaele offensive ground to a halt. Cambrai, a town in northern France, was a key supply point for the Hindenburg Line and its capture of strategic importance. New tactics were employed with great success. It was the first large-scale tank attack in history, and the tanks easily crushed the enemy wire. A lack of prior bombardment kept the battle a surprise and an impressive amount of ground was captured.

Ernest Horseman of the 3rd RHA was in action at Cambrai. The attack began at 6.20am and all available guns opened fire. The batteries fired on German defences for the next 3½ hours as the attacking infantry moved up. They remained in action over the next two weeks as the offensive pushed forward, covering subsequent attacks and laying down harassing fire.

The 6th Ox Bucks, including Harry Knight, were amongst the leading battalions. They had practiced the operation and took the German trenches easily. They then moved forward to the Hindenburg support line which they occupied and held for the next few days.

Percy Dove, with the London Scottish, was in reserve for the initial attack then went into action on the 22nd to continue the attack along the Hindenburg Line. The offensive was now losing momentum. The attack began at 6.30am but a German machine gun post enfiladed all the trenches and held up the attack until mid afternoon when the post was captured. The battalion took their objective but the enemy immediately counterattacked. One company beat off the attack; two others were forced back. They began preparations to recapture the lost ground but the enemy mounted another attack and forced all companies back with heavy casualties.

Percy Dove was severely wounded and was evacuated to England on 29th November. He was transferred to hospital in Edinburgh where he had an operation. It was later reported to the *Stratford Herald* that he was 'doing well'. He eventually returned to the frontline.

Albert Edward King (b1889) was the son of farm labourer William King and his wife Elizabeth of Knavenhill Cottages in Alderminster. In 1911 Albert was living in Yardley in Worcestershire with his brother Charles and working as a nurseryman. His brother James had enlisted in 1914. Albert enlisted at an unknown date and served in the 4th Coldstream Guards, a pioneer battalion which never fought on the frontline, although they were routinely shelled and gassed. Following the successes at Cambrai, the battalion spent several days clearing mud and obstructions, including two demolished bridges, from the Canal du Nord to enable its use by the British. As more ground was taken, work of this type continued.

On 30th November, the 6th Ox Bucks, including Harry Knight, were ordered to attack Quentin Ridge, a strongly held enemy position. The battalion advanced close to the ridge and dug in. It was now dusk and any further advance impossible. The commanding officer believed the attack hopeless and explained this to the high command. He was ordered to mount a new attempt on the ridge. This began at 10pm. The battalion went forward but were forced back by German fire. Another attempt at 6am the following day met the same result. Some ground was taken by other units over the day and this was held until the battalion was relieved on the 3rd December.

Oliver Summerton, the son of bricklayer James Summerton and his wife Lucy of No.6 Alderminster, enlisted in May 1916, a month short of his 17th birthday. He was apprenticed to builder Thomas Minett as a carpenter and wheelwright and was also a keen member of Alderminster football club. Many his friends were in the army and he – and probably the public in general – thought he should do the same. He joined the 2/7th Royal Warwickshire Regiment and arrived in France in late 1917. He was a good marksman and served as a sniper.

His battalion was sent into newly-captured trenches on the Hindenburg Line on 2nd December. They were subject to severe bombing attacks and repeated counterattacks as the enemy attempted to retake the trenches. Constant artillery bombardment almost entirely demolished some of their trenches. Troops came to relieve the now severely depleted battalion on the 5th, but an enemy attack at the same time meant more heavy fighting and many trenches were lost. The fresh troops mounted a counterattack and the positions were recaptured. The battalion had now lost around 230 casualties. This may be the action later recalled by Oliver, who remembered that machine guns in cellars caused severe losses among his unit. His officer ordered the men forward, and was cut in half by machine gun fire after just one step. Only seven men, including Oliver, remained from his section.

The battalion was relieved after this and went into support for several weeks.

Oliver Summerton.

Courtesy of Pete Summerton.

The Royal Airforce

The benefit of aircraft for observing and bombing enemy lines, monitoring attacks and transmitting progress to high command, and intercepting enemy aircraft engaged in similar activity, led to the rapid expansion of the Royal Flying Corps which became the Royal Airforce in April 1918.

Thomas Bloxham, a gardener from Atherstone now living in Whitehaven in Cheshire, joined the RAF in September 1918 aged 48. He served with 67 Wing in Taranto in Italy and remained in the Adriatic Sea area until January 1919. He was then transferred to the reserve and discharged the following year.

William Hutchings (b1899) was the son of farmer William Hutchings and his wife Sarah. William died a few months after his son's birth, and in 1901 Sarah and her baby were living at Churchill Farm in Alderminster with her father-in-law, also called William. They then moved to Shirley where William worked as an engineer for XL-All Ltd in Birmingham, which manufactured motorcycles and then war equipment.

He was enlisted into the 34th Training Reserve Battalion, which trained recruits, in September 1917, aged 18. He joined the Royal Flying Corps, later the RAF, in March 1918, spent three months training then was commissioned as a 2nd lieutenant and went to 199 Night Training Squadron for advanced bomber training. He was passed as medically fit as an observer but not as a pilot. He went to France in September 1918, was wounded six weeks later and admitted to a French hospital, then returned to Britain in December. He was discharged in June 1919. His future from this point is unclear.

Walter Henry Hathaway was the son of brickmaker John Hathaway and his wife Elizabeth of Alderminster. In 1901 Walter, aged 19, was boarding in Yorkshire and working as a railway porter. By 1911 he was married and living in Luton, working as a licenced victualler. He enlisted in the army at an unknown point and served in the Royal Fusiliers, then transferred to the Royal Flying Corps on 8th May 1918. He seems not to have served abroad. He was working as an aeroplane mechanic in Hendon, Middlesex, when the aeroplane he was flying crashed. He sustained fatal injuries and died on 8th June 1918. He was buried in Hendon Cemetery.

Those called up during 1918 were mainly those who had just come of age. Anyone who was fit for service was already in the army.

Franklin Baker was the son of tailor Franklin Baker and his wife Rose of No.41 Alderminster. Franklin was called up in February 1918, just after his 18th birthday, and posted to the West Somerset Yeomanry. He served for a year but never went abroad.

Alfred Thomas Handy was the son of carter Thomas Handy and his wife Alice of Wimpstone. Alfred was called up on 22nd May 1918, twelve days after his 19th birthday, and sent to the 5th Cavalry reserve regiment in Tidworth in Wiltshire, then four months later transferred to the Tank Corps. He never served abroad.

Herbert Victor Knight was the son of farm labourer William Knight and his wife Eliza of No.10 Alderminster, of no known relation to brothers Harry and Frederick Knight. He was called up on 1st June 1918, just after his nineteenth birthday, and was posted to the Irish Rifles where he served in the UK for nine months.

Thomas Hadland, 43, an unmarried gardener with deformed feet, was the son of widow Eliza Hadland of Alderminster. He was called up for the 13th Somerset Light Infantry in May 1918. He performed light duties only and was discharged on 6th November 1918 without going abroad.

Thomas Gibbins, 17, was the son of woodman William Gibbins and his wife Hannah of No.1 Preston. He was called up in September 1918 and Dick Beavington wrote home: '*I was sorry to hear Tom Gibbins has got to go but hope he won't pass.*' He probably didn't see active service.

Percy Dove, 46, of No.12 Preston, was electrical engineer at Alscot Park. His son Percy was serving in France. Percy senior was called up in June 1918 and Dick Beavington wrote home; '*I was sorry Mr Dove has to join up seeing as Percy is out here as well, but I suppose they have all got to do their bit, but I should have thought he would have got off as he is a very clever man.*' His subsequent service is unclear, but he probably didn't serve abroad.

John Thomas Truslove, the son of groom John Truslove and his wife Esther, was called up in December 1916, just after his nineteenth birthday. The family lived in The Lodge of Ettington Park and John worked as a shepherd and ploughman for Alan James at Whitchurch Farm. Alan applied for exemption, saying he was shepherding up to 250 sheep. John said he supported his mother and father. He earned £1/week and gave 12s to his parents. The military representative said he passed for general service and was just the sort of man the army wants.

Thomas Smith asked: 'If the military can find a substitute, would Mr James be willing to let Truslove go?' Mr James replied: 'Certainly.' John was granted exemption to 1st March 1917, and the military would use their best endeavours to find a substitute. He was called up on 27th February and arrived in France on 10th November 1917. He was posted to the 10th Worcesters and joined his battalion on 4th January 1918. They were in reserve in the Somme sector, then went into the muddy and waterlogged trenches.

On 30th January, John was admitted to a field hospital after being gassed. The battalion diary reported one casualty. Perhaps having just reached the frontline, John was too inexperienced to avoid exposure. Six weeks later he was evacuated to England with gas poisoning and trench fever. He spent 2½ months in hospital and didn't return to the front line again.

The Michael Offensive

The war between Germany and Russia ended with the Treaty of Brest-Litovsk, signed in March 1918, and the Germans began to transfer their troops to the Western Front. A major offensive was planned. This was their chance to win the war.

On 21st March 1918, the Germans launched their spring offensive, known as the Michael Offensive. This was a disaster for the British who were caught entirely by surprise. The Germans advanced fourteen miles in three days, a phenomenal distance, and the Allies retreated in confusion.

The 11th Hampshires were in the frontline near Villers-Faucon in the Somme sector when the offensive began. Robert Dale was still serving with the unit; it is unclear whether the other men who had enlisted with him, including Sydney Land, Thomas Bloxham, Arthur Burrows and Ernest Robinson, were still present.

At 4.30am on 21st March, a German barrage started on their line, with high explosive and gas shells. Battle stations were manned immediately. The battalion's horses and mules panicked and were about to stampede, but they were moved to the rear and a stampede narrowly avoided. Robert Dale, now acting lance sergeant and a horseman in civilian life, was noted for his courage and coolness in this achieving this.

The enemy attacked at 10.30am. The battalion was soon moved to defend another part of the line. They suffered very heavy shelling and considerable casualties and the Germans gained some ground. The following day the enemy sent down more barrages and made gradual gains. The fighting continued for two days and the Hampshires' division was steadily forced back. The men were now exhausted. They were relieved from the frontline at 11.30pm on the 23rd and began a six-hour march to billets to rest. The battalion was congratulated for their splendid discipline and the way they had fought. Robert Dale, who had been awarded a certificate for gallant conduct in April 1916, was awarded the Military Medal.

Robert Dale's service medals. The Military Medal, awarded for bravery in the field; the 1914-15 Star, for service in these years; the British War Medal for service overseas; the Victory Medal for service in a theatre of war.

Courtesy of Fred Dale.

Sidney Hicks of the 6th Dorsets, who had been wounded in the Somme sector in December 1916, rejoined his unit in France in August 1917 and was now a lance corporal. His unit was in frontline trenches in Havrincourt when the offensive began. They were subject to an intensive bombardment at 4.45am on the 21st, then the attack began. The Germans gained some ground but the

British troops immediately counterattacked and retook it. That night the British began to withdraw.

The enemy advanced further over the following days. They made several attacks, including one with flamethrowers but gained no footing. The Dorsets were subject to very accurate sniper fire, and machine gun and rifle duels caused further casualties. They fought a rearguard action from ridge to ridge as the brigade withdrew, then the remnants of the battalion made a stand near Henencourt near the Somme. They were placed in reserve for a day then sent into position ready for a suspected German attack. This didn't materialise and the battalion were moved to lines near Albert. They were relieved on 31st March. The battalion had suffered 200 casualties killed, wounded or missing.

Sidney Hicks, aged 24, was killed on 30th March. He has no known grave and is commemorated on the Arras Memorial and Alderminster War Memorial.

Dick Beavington was serving with the 9th King's Royal Rifles near Jussy in the Somme sector when the bombardment began. It lasted nearly five hours, then the Germans advanced. The battalion diary stated that details as to what happened next were almost entirely lacking.

Two companies were killed or captured to a man. A few men from the third escaped. Some parts of the line held out for some hours – the Germans had lost their way in the mist – and it seemed the fourth company, now surrounded by the enemy, held out into the afternoon. But by evening, the battalion had ceased to exist. The few stragglers were collected and attached to another battalion. 650 men were lost.

Dick Beavington received a gunshot wound to the head and was evacuated to England on 28th March. He didn't return to the frontline again.

Arthur James Handy (b1885) was the son of labourer James Handy and his wife Ellen of Alderminster. In 1901, aged fifteen, he was boarding in Birmingham and working as a draper's porter. He married Kate Hibberd, a gardener's daughter from Alderminster whose brother Edward was serving in the Navy, and had two children. In 1911, the family were living in Birmingham and Arthur was working as a stableman for Mitchell and Butler's Brewery. He was also a member of the brewery-based St John's Ambulance Brigade. He enlisted in the 2nd Royal Berkshire Regiment at an unknown point. The battalion had suffered heavily on the first day of the Somme and also fought at Ypres and Passchendaele in 1917.

They were behind the lines when the offensive began, and on 22nd March the battalion was rushed to the village of Guillaucourt in the Somme sector to aid in rearguard action.

Arthur Handy, aged 24, died of wounds on this date. Further details are unclear. He has no known grave and is commemorated on the Pozieres Memorial and Alderminster War Memorial.

Arthur Handy.
Courtesy of Andy Warren.

The 2/7th Warwicks, including Oliver Summerton, were in billets in Germaine in the Somme sector. At 5am on 21st March they were ordered to man battle stations ready for a counterattack on the German line, but eventually did nothing but cover the withdrawal of other battalions. Faced with massing enemy troops, and with no artillery support and near-useless trenches, the demoralised troops began to retire under heavy machine gun fire. Senior officers stopped their retirement with difficulty and reformed their line. The withdrawal continued amidst confusion for several days.

Oliver Summerton, a battalion sniper, was wounded in March, possibly during this operation. Snipers set up position in No Man's Land, overlooking enemy positions, and picked off any target that should cross their sights. They were key sniper targets themselves. When Oliver was in No Man's Land, a bullet hit his rifle which exploded and blew one of his fingers off. He tried to get back to his own lines but was becoming weak from blood loss. He came across two stretcher-bearers who turned out to be British, and he was taken to a dressing station for treatment. He was evacuated to England and admitted to hospital in Lancashire on 30th April. While there he helped the nurses tend the more seriously wounded, including on one occasion helping a double amputee to climb through the window on knotted bedsheets to attend a party in town. He didn't return to the frontline again.

William Sharpe had been transferred from the Mechanical Transport section to the 2nd West Riding Regiment in February 1917. They were in trenches near Arras when the offensive began in the south, and saw no action in their part of the line. The division to their right retreated the next day and the battalion formed a defensive flank to prevent further German advance. The enemy attacked and entered the West Riding's trench on the 23rd, but were bombed out and caused only seven casualties.

On the 28th, they were shelled with high explosive, shrapnel and gas, and the enemy attacked their line. The British were forced back, then dug and held a new line. The West Riding Regiment suffered sixty casualties during the day. William Sharpe may have been one of these. He was admitted to a casualty clearing station on 30th March with shrapnel wounds to his face and right knee. He died of his injuries the following day, aged 21. He was buried in Duisans British Cemetery in Pas de Calais and is commemorated on Alderminster War Memorial.

The artillery played a crucial part in holding up the German advance and covering the retreating troops. Ernest Horseman of the 3rd RHA was in action near Rouez in northern France. On 22nd March they were shooting hard all day with excellent targets, and they held up the German attacks completely until the light faded. The following day they supported a French counterattack, but a fresh German attack forced them back and the batteries were withdrawn. Over the next few days they were constantly moving the guns then bringing them back into action, keeping pace with the retiring line. This continued until 2nd April. Each battery had been firing 1500 rounds a day, an incredible feat of endurance and hard labour.

The 20th Australians, including Reg Hicks, were rushed to Hangard in the Somme sector on 4th April; a seven-hour night march on a very wet and muddy road. The enemy had captured 300 yards of the frontline. The Australians went into the line immediately and a counterattack recaptured all lost ground. On the 7th, they launched an attack on Hangard Wood. The objectives were taken but a heavy counterattack forced them to withdraw. They suffered 150 casualties, but killed an estimated 750 enemy troops. They were reinforced and the attack continued. They faced heavy machine gun fire and many casualties from snipers, and were relieved on the 9th.

Reg Hicks was working as a stretcher bearer throughout this action. He and three other men worked incessantly for 48 hours without rest, bringing in and tending the wounded under very heavy machine gun fire. All cases had to be carried over 2000 yards of heavy ploughed ground. Their devotion to duty and determined grit saved the lives of scores of their comrades and their action inspired all those who came into contact with them. All four were recommended for the Military Medal.

The Battle of the Lys (Fourth Battle of Ypres)

On 7th April, the German offensive turned north. They attacked the Allied line in Flanders on a 40km front from Ypres to Bethune. The Germans broke through and the towns of Messines and Bailleul and the hard-won ground at Passchendaele were lost. By now the Allies had lost 90,000 prisoners and on the 10th April, Field Marshall Haig issued his 'backs to the wall' message: *Every man must stand and fight and fall.* A message issued to the 20th Australians stated that: *The time has arrived in this war when every man who can possibly be put forward to kill Germans must be employed on that duty and no other. They only way to defeat the enemy is to KILL, KILL, KILL.*

Frederick Knight, who had been evacuated to England with a gunshot wound in October 1917, returned to France on 24th March 1918. He was posted to the 10th Warwicks in the frontline near Passchendaele, a mass of waterlogged shell holes and old trenches. At 2.30am on 10th April, the enemy heavily shelled their trenches. Then small parties of the enemy attacked their flanks and gradually worked forward. The Warwicks began to withdraw under heavy shell and machine gun fire. The withdrawal continued throughout the day. The next day the enemy attacked part of the line, and although the battalion's machine guns inflicted severe casualties, they were forced to withdraw again. The men were exhausted, having had no food, water or sleep. They were also under continuous shell fire. Two hundred men were missing. The battalion, now half its original strength, withdrew further and was relieved early on the 14th April. They were ordered back into the frontline trenches the next day for a counterattack on part of the newly lost line.

On the 17th, the battalion was subject to heavy shelling with 25 casualties. Frederick Knight was one of them. He suffered wounds to his right hand and shoulder and was admitted to hospital in Boulogne. It wasn't a 'Blighty wound' and he rejoined his battalion a month later.

George William Brookes, 18, was the eldest son of George and Martha Brookes of Atherstone Hill Farm. He was called up in August 1916 and applied for exemption. George was a cattleman and had been doing the milking since he left school at fourteen. He was too young to go overseas, and Thomas Smith on the tribunal asked what use it was to take young men of eighteen who were doing useful work on the farms. He cited his own farm pupil, Richard Green, who was eighteen and was anxious to get into the army. He had joined the Royal Fusiliers but had been sent back until he was nineteen.

The only labour on the farm was George, his two younger brothers and a waggoner. The farm was 200 acres and there were 35 cattle and seven horses to see to. He was granted exemption until his birthday on condition he joined the volunteer corps at Clifford Chambers.

He turned nineteen soon afterwards and was given two further months exemption to see if a substitute could be found. When the case was heard for the third time in December, the military had found a substitute but the man was not suitable. The chairman said: 'It's almost impossible to let the man off.' The military representative said George passed fit for military service, and there were other sons who could help. One of the board recommended exemption to the 1st April as he did the milking. Another brother, eighteen-year-old Frederick, was due to go next April – Frederick was ultimately granted exemption and remained on the farm – and a third was nearly seventeen. Mr Brookes had done the best he could to get another man. It was decided the other sons could do the milking and the appeal was dismissed.

George joined the Royal West Surrey Regiment in February 1917 and arrived in France on 22nd September. On 11th April 1918, the battalion was rushed to the village of Meteren in Flanders. An attack was imminent. The next day they were told to move at once to occupy a defensive position covering the village. This high ground was covered by enemy machine gun fire but they suffered few casualties.

The enemy began attacking in waves but were easily stopped. They dug in and began shelling the British line. They sent patrols to try and break through the lines without success, but by midnight the British situation was precarious.

The Germans made continual attacks the next morning and eventually drove one company from their position. The West Surreys mounted an unsuccessful counterattack and were forced to withdraw. The enemy immediately followed up. Fierce fighting took place throughout the day as the battalion gradually withdrew.

The following morning, after the battalion had been continually fighting for two days, the Germans overran some of their positions. Their situation was now critical. No artillery support was available and the battalion was forced into a continual withdrawal throughout the day, the enemy on their heels. They were relieved at 3am the next morning, then were brought back into action when the enemy captured part of the village. When they were withdrawn they had suffered over 350 casualties. They were congratulated by high command for their magnificent stand and their splendid heroism.

The Turning Point

The German offensive began to lose steam. Transporting heavy artillery pieces, ammunition and other essentials over the shell-blasted and near roadless ground in the wake of the advancing troops was a logistical nightmare, and the German infantry was hugely overstretched. The Allies slowly checked the advance, and began to prepare for their own great offensive.

Percy Dove of the London Scottish returned to France on 5th April 1918, four months after being wounded. The battalion was then in Mont-St-Eloi near Arras. At 4.20am on 19th April, they mounted an attack on the German line. This went exceptionally well thanks to a provident heavy hailstorm which obscured their advance. The enemy were caught by surprise and all objectives were taken with a large number of prisoners. A few half-hearted counterattacks were easily repulsed. A stronger counterattack forced the battalion from some of the captured positions, and then the battalion withdrew.

Percy Dove was likely one of those wounded during the attack. He was evacuated to England on 23rd April and didn't return to the frontline again.

Albert Horseman of the 1st Life Guards, who arrived in France in August 1914, had been admitted to hospital with pleurisy on 15th February 1917. It developed into pneumonia and he was invalided to England on 2nd March, the first time he had been home since the start of the war. His wife Edith conceived another child soon after his discharge from hospital.

The Life Guards was formally dismounted in March 1918 and became the Guards Machine Gun Regiment. By this time Albert had been awarded the

Military Medal and the French Medaille Militaire, and was promoted to SQMC (squadron quartermaster corporal). He joined his new unit in Etaples on 18th May.

The following day the camp suffered a three-hour air raid, during which two bombs fell on the Guards' camp, killing 42 and injuring 83 more. Albert, aged 35, was one of those killed. He was buried in Etaples Military Cemetery and his effects – photos, wallet, tobacco pouch, three medal ribbons, and a watch presented to him by the NCOs and men of the Life Guards wishing him luck in his new unit – were sent to his wife Edith. She chose for his grave the inscription *Well done, thou good and faithful servant, thou has given thine all.* He is commemorated on Whitchurch War Memorial.

Charles Reading, who had emigrated with Reginald Hicks and joined the 41st Australian Infantry, arrived in France on 5th February 1918 and joined his battalion on the Belgian border. Three weeks later, he was accidently shot in the thigh, although it wasn't sufficient for hospital treatment. His records state he was not to blame. On 3rd March, he received shrapnel wounds to his hip and chest. He was evacuated to England a week later. He remained in hospital for nearly a month then returned to France on 6th June. His battalion was now in the Somme sector, and on 1st July some of the first American troops to arrive in France were attached to them.

The Australians fought in the Battle of Hamel which began on 4th July, known as 'the Glorious Fourth'. The joint Australian and American operation achieved all objectives within 93 minutes. Charles Reading saw little action here: thanks to the overwhelming success his battalion wasn't needed. They relieved the attacking battalions and remained in the line for the next few days, consolidating captured ground and digging new trenches. They then prepared for the Battle of Amiens.

The Hundred Days Offensive

The Battle of Amiens

The Battle of Amiens, which began on 8th August, was the opening of the Allies' Hundred Days Offensive and marked the beginning of the end of the war. The attack depended on surprise rather than weight. There was more emphasis on guns, tanks and aeroplanes: the army could ill-afford high casualty rates. There were no more men to replace them.

Will Porter of the 21st Canadians, who had been admitted to hospital in November 1917, rejoined his unit in January 1918. They saw little action but skirmishing. On 4th March, while in frontline trenches near Lens, they were subjected to their heaviest yet artillery bombardment then 300 enemy troops raided their lines. The Canadians killed around forty Germans but the enemy captured one part of the line and also bombed their dugouts. The Germans were eventually forced out.

Two days later, the Canadians mounted their own raid on the German line. The Germans were occupying buildings and after the Canadians got through the wire they attacked the dugouts and cellars – not easy to find due to the smoke and brick dust – and caused as much damage as possible before retiring. A few months later they preparing to lead the attack at Amiens.

The 41st Australians, including Charles Reading, were moved to Corbie in the Somme sector at the beginning of August in preparation for the attack. The 20th Australians, including Reginald Hicks, also assembled near Villers. Low-flying aircraft masked the noise of assembling tanks. The entire Canadian Corps was also assembled, Will Porter's battalion near Bois l'Abbe. The men were radiant and confident, and almost all were thinking of home. Many were writing letters; for many it would be their last message. One sergeant said, 'I don't know what this show will be called, but I'm sure it will be a great day in Canadian history.'

Despite the secrecy, the enemy noticed the unusual activity near the Canadian lines and commenced very heavy bombardment just before the attack. This caused no casualties, and at 4.20am the attack began.

The barrage opened like one gun. The 21st Canadians' chaplain wrote that a blaze of crimson lit the horizon for miles. Three seconds later came the deafening roar from hundreds of guns. Shells screamed overhead like countless legions of destroying angels and the green turf was churned by an invisible harrow. All along the line, men leaped onto the parapet and went over the top. Wave after wave of the attackers passed.

The Canadians met heavy resistance. Thick mist lay on the ground and the supporting tanks lost their way, but they took their objectives. It proved their most successful operation and they suffered only light casualties. They consolidated their position and other battalions pressed forward the attack.

The 20th Australians also took their objectives. Their tanks gave every assistance to the infantry and they suffered few casualties. The 41st Australians captured their first line of trenches and other battalions leapfrogged past. This battalion alone captured a mile of frontline up to 1500 yards in depth. This near impossible feat was almost entirely due to the high morale and confidence of the troops. It was the Australian Corps' most successful operation.

Eight miles of ground were taken – the greatest gain in a single day of the entire war – and 30,000 Germans were killed, wounded or taken prisoner. Will Porter was awarded the Military Medal for his part in the attack.

The advance continued over the coming days. Ernest Horseman of the 3rd RHA was in action for much of the fighting, providing covering barrage for the advancing infantry. This was the last time his unit would fight.

The 20th Australians supported another attack on 9th August, which was hindered by machine guns and snipers and cost the battalion eighty casualties. They formed a defensive line which they held for three days until they were relieved.

The 41st Australians captured a German position on 11th August, with difficulty and with heavy losses. The Canadians also rapidly advanced into enemy territory. Gas shells caused many casualties but the advance continued for several more days.

Will Porter, 21st Canadian Infantry.

Courtesy of Pete Summerton.

The Second Battle of the Somme

Following the successes at Amiens, a fresh Allied offensive was mounted in the Somme sector on 21st August. This began with the Second Battle of Bapaume which would last for a fortnight and aimed to capture the town.

William Henry Hopkins, 20, was the son of Josiah and Annie Hopkins of Atherstone Hill Cottages and the brother of early volunteer George Hopkins. He worked as a gardener and enlisted in the Royal Marine Light Infantry in March 1917. The Marines were part of the Navy but operated on land as well as at sea. William arrived in France on 13th May 1918 and joined the 1st Marine battalion, in frontline trenches in the Somme sector.

They were fighting on the first day of the battle. The attack began at 4.55am. The lead division took their objectives and the Marines pushed through and attacked a German-held wood. They met obstinate resistance from enemy machine guns but these were eventually cleared and the objectives taken. They repulsed several counterattacks and then pushed forward to capture more ground over the coming week.

William Hopkins was reported wounded and missing on 21st August. It later transpired that he had been taken prisoner. The Germans recorded that he had suffered a *schrapnellverletz* [shrapnel wound] to his *recht unterschenkel* [right lower leg]. He was taken to Limburg an der Lahn POW camp in Germany. It seems that news of his capture didn't reach his family for some time; Percy Beavington wrote home in September 1918: *'I was sorry to hear about poor old Bill Hopkins.'* And a week later: *'Will you let me know how Will Hopkins is getting on as I should like to know and hope his wound isn't too bad.'* It was on 9th October that he wrote: *'I was sorry to hear that old Will Hopkins was a POW but hope he has the luck to come back safe and soon. He will have something to talk about when he does come home.'*

William remained a prisoner until his liberation two weeks after the armistice.

On 26th August, the 21st Canadians led an attack on the German line. They advanced under barrage at 3am and the German artillery didn't respond until 3.11am, by which time the Canadians were well across No Man's Land. The German trenches were captured and their machine gun posts bombed and rushed. All objectives were taken. Other battalions pressed forward the attack, and two days later the 21st again went forward. They were now fatigued and were up against a well-constructed and well-wired enemy line. They were enfiladed

COPIÉ FICHE V 31 17 Oct. 1918 P.A. 39121

1 Lfd. Nr.	2 a) Familienname b) Vorname (nur der Rufname) c) nur bei Russen Vorname des Vaters	3 Dienstgrad	4 a) b) Truppenteil c) Komp.	5 a) b) Gefangennahme (Ort und Tag) c) vorhergehender Aufenthaltsort	6 a) Geburtstag und -Ort b) c) Adresse des nächsten Verwandten
17	HOPKINS William PO 2569	Sold	Royal Marine L.Inf. C.	21 8 18 Bapaume Fr nt.	27/10/1897. Alterstone Hill. Joseph Hopkins. Alterstone Hill. Stratford-on-Av n.

Limburg

P.A. 39412 COPIÉ

1 Lfd. Nr.	2 a) Familienname b) Vorname (nur der Rufname) c) nur bei Russen Vorname des Vaters	3 Dienstgrad	4 a) b) Truppenteil c) Komp.	5 a) b) Gefangennahme (Ort und Tag) c) vorhergehender Aufenthaltsort	6 a) Geburtstag und -Ort b) c) Adresse des nächsten Verwandten
20	Hopkins William P.O.2569	Gem.	R;Marine L.I. C.	Bapaume. 21.8.18. Schrapnellverletz. r. Unterschenkel. Front.	27.10.97. Atherstone, Warwickshire. Vater: Josiah, unbekannt.

Limburg

The records compiled by the International Committee of the Red Cross. The language barrier no doubt accounts for the inaccurate spellings.

with machine gun fire and the German line resisted all attempts to take it. They suffered heavy casualties and the advance stalled. The Canadians were sent back behind their lines.

The 41st Australians took part in an attack on the 27th, and took their objectives after heavy fighting. They advanced 1000 yards and captured 100 prisoners and twenty machine guns. The fighting was now on open ground rather than from trench to trench, but the men adapted well and despite heavy losses inflicted six times more casualties on the enemy. Charles Reading was accidentally injured on 1st September and admitted to hospital. He didn't return to his unit until after the armistice. The Allies were suffering heavily, but the German army was all but broken. The outcome of the war was now a foregone conclusion.

On 29th August, the 20th Australians were advancing across ground near Feuilleres in the Somme sector when shelling caused five casualties. Reginald

Hicks was one of them. He suffered a shrapnel wound to the lumbar region and was admitted to a casualty clearing station the following day. He died of his injuries three days later on 2nd September. He was buried in Daours Communal Cemetery and is commemorated on Alderminster War Memorial.

Frederick Knight, with the 10th Warwicks, went into the frontline trenches in northern France on 10th August after two months in reserve. They mounted a raid on a farmhouse where the battalion captured two machine guns and killed seven of the crew, then on 3rd September they attacked a position near La Bassee. They took their objectives and were heavily shelled, but the following day they pushed on to capture and consolidate another line. Frederick Knight suffered shrapnel wounds to his face on 3rd September and was evacuated to England a week later. He didn't return to France again.

George Brookes, with the 1st West Surreys, was in the frontline on 29th September when some gas shells fell among them. The gas alarm was given and the shells were later declared safe, but the next morning the gas began to take effect. It mainly affected the eyes and around 150 men were admitted to hospital. George was one of them. He was evacuated to England and admitted to hospital near Chichester. His parents at Atherstone Hill Farm received a postcard from him a fortnight later saying he was now 'going on fairly well'. He didn't return to the frontline again.

The Closing Stages

The 21st Canadians attacked the Hindenburg Line at Avesnes-le-Sec in northern France on 11th October. They began to assemble at 2am. At 5.30am the Germans saw the activity and began shelling their lines. This caused few casualties and the Canadians attacked at 9am.

The machine gun retaliation was prompt. Within thirty minutes the battalion had suffered severe casualties, including half of the officers and NCOs, but the attack went on. The enemy withdrew, then counterattacked with tanks. The Canadians were forced to withdraw with over 300 casualties.

Will Porter, aged 27 and now a lance corporal, was one of those killed. He left a widow and a young son. He was buried in the Niagara Cemetery in Iwuy near Cambrai, alongside many other Canadian soldiers. He is remembered on his father's gravestone at Preston and is also commemorated on Preston War Memorial.

Tom Job Lowe (b1899) was the son of shepherd Albert Lowe and his wife Eleanor. The family were originally from Whichford then moved to No.53 Alderminster.

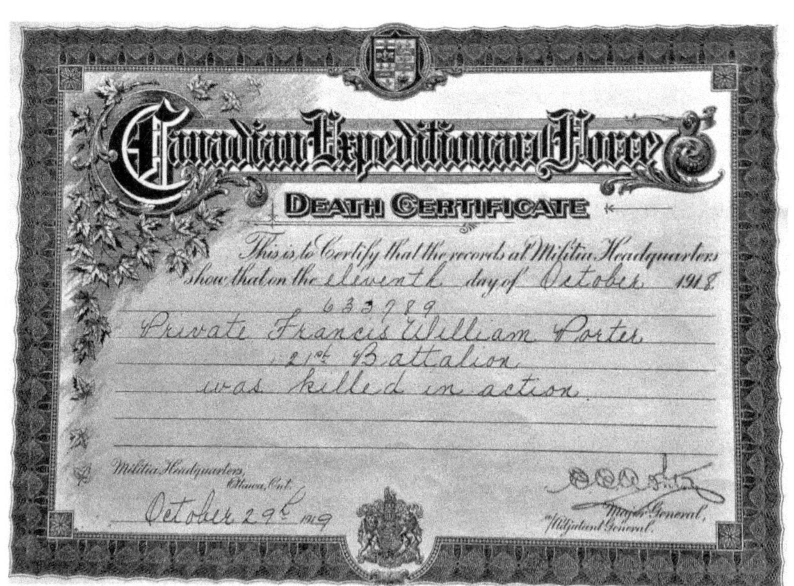

Canadian Expeditionary Force

DEATH CERTIFICATE

This is to Certify that the records at Militia Headquarters show that on the eleventh day of October 1918

633789
Private Francis William Porter
21st Battalion
was killed in action.

Militia Headquarters,
Ottawa, Ont.
October 29th 1919

Major General,
Adjutant General.

Will Porter's death certificate.

Courtesy of Pete Summerton.

Will Porter's grave.

Courtesy of Elizabeth Lyne.

In 1911, Tom, aged twelve, was working as a farm boy. He enlisted in the Dorset Regiment at an unknown date and was later transferred to the 1st Wiltshires, now following the German retreat across France.

On 1st September 1918 the battalion attacked the village of Beaulencourt. They went forward under barrage at 2am. The village was strongly held and covered by machine guns but the Wiltshires attacked with such determination that the opposition was overcome and the village captured by 5.30am. A counterattack was easily repulsed. Enemy resistance broke down and the attackers swept forward and captured several more villages. A fortnight later, the Wiltshires were in trenches when the enemy attacked, and some of their positions were lost. An immediate counterattack recaptured them.

During October the battalion were involved in several attacks on the Hindenburg Line. On the 23rd, they attacked the village of Ovillers. They were masked by mist until the last minute, but then this cleared and their forming-up line was revealed to the enemy. They were heavily shelled but the attack began as planned. They reached the village and took all their objectives, with 25 men killed and 120 wounded.

Tom Lowe, aged 19 and now a lance corporal, was killed during the attack. He was buried in Ovillers New Communal Cemetery.

Arthur Burrows of the 11th Hampshires, who had served sinceSeptember 1914, was transferred to the 2nd Devons in April 1918. Frank Taylor, now a lance corporal, and Thomas Bloxham were transferred at a similar time. On 31st October, Arthur Burrows was wounded by shrapnel in the wrist, leg and ear. He was transferred to hospital in London where he recovered from his injuries. He didn't return to the front line again. Frank Taylor and Thomas Bloxham probably remained with the Devons until the end of the war.

Richard Green, serving with the 1/4th Royal Sussex Regiment, left Egypt in May 1918 and spent time in France and Belgium. He was given leave in October 1918 and returned to Preston. In contrast to his early enthusiasm to join the army, Dick Beavington wrote home of him: '*I was pleased to hear Dick Green has been home. I don't expect he does want to go back if he has to do what you put in the letter.*'

On 2nd November, two weeks after returning to the frontline, Richard was attending the wounded in a dressing station when he was hit by an exploding shell during an air-raid and killed. He was twenty years old. His death cast a gloom over the whole of Preston where he was a universal favourite. He was buried in the Harlebecke New Military Cemetery near Ypres. His aunt, Elizabeth Arnold, chose for his headstone the inscription *We loved thee well, but Jesus loved thee best. Goodnight.* He is commemorated on Preston War Memorial and the Thame School Memorial, where his name is read out at a memorial service each November.

Richard Green's grave.

Courtesy of Elizabeth Lyne.

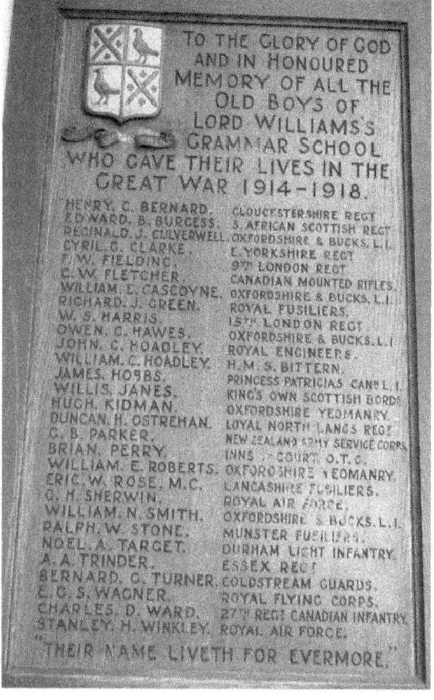

The War Memorial in Thame School.

Courtesy of Graham Thomas.

The Armistice

By November the war was all but over, and the Germans sued for peace. The diary for the 11th Hampshires, now in the village of Taintignies in Belgium, reads for 11th November:

10.40am. Information received that the armistice has been signed and hostilities to cease at 11.00 today. Band played in square at 11.00. Work continued as usual.

The Aftermath

After the fighting ended, the troops were gradually demobilised and returned home. They, and the families of those who had fallen, were left to pick up the pieces of their lives as best they could. Many were permanently scarred, physically and emotionally. Many had left home as boys, keen for an adventure. They were returning as hardened soldiers, killers. Many could never speak of what they had endured.

Adjusting to civilian life was a wrench. The loss of comradeship, the bond and identity which gelled a unit together, and the sheer normality and safety which they had waited for so many years, was hard to bear.

Demobilising the army took over a year. Most servicemen were transferred to the Class Z reserve, to immediately remobilise should the peace talks collapse. Those who had a job to return to were demobilised first. For the rest, their time was focussed on preparing them for civilian life. Classes for horse-shoeing, agriculture, gardening and carpentry were held over the coming months.

Spanish Influenza

Although the fighting was over, the deaths were not. A new disaster was spreading in the wake of the demobilising armies. In the spring of 1918, an unusually severe strain of influenza known as the Spanish Flu had begun to spread across the battlefields of Europe. The demobilising troops took the virus home with them and it affected 500 million people worldwide. It proved fatal in up to 20% of cases. Physical and emotional stress, overcrowding and malnutrition among the servicemen, exacerbated its severity. Several men from the Alscot villages contracted the illness. Three of them died.

On 16th November 1918, Henry Taylor of the RFA was admitted to a field hospital in France suffering from influenza. He returned to England on 10th January 1919, and four days later was admitted to a military hospital in Nottingham with the same illness. Ten days later he was sufficiently recovered to be discharged.

Franklin Baker of the West Somerset Yeomanry, serving in the UK was hospitalised with influenza in December 1918 and was discharged a week later.

Harry Handy of the Army Service Corps, who had served four years in England, was admitted to hospital in Shropshire with influenza on 13th February 1919. It rapidly developed into broncho-pneumonia and he died five days later. He was buried in Stratford on Avon Cemetery.

Thomas Kingston of the Machine Gun Corps was admitted to hospital in Greece with influenza shortly after the armistice. He died on 28th November 1918 and was buried in the Mikra British Cemetery in Kalamaria. He is commemorated on Preston War Memorial.

Albert King, in the 4th Coldstream Guards, was admitted to hospital in Charleroi in Belgium with influenza on 23rd November 1918. Ten other men from the unit were admitted the same day, and more fell sick each day. Albert, aged 29, died on 7th December. He was buried in Charleroi Communal Cemetery and is commemorated on Alderminster War Memorial.

Harry Handy's grave.

Remembrance

In the years following the war, communities began to think of memorials for those who had fallen. Preston's War Memorial was unveiled on the village green; those for Alderminster, Atherstone and Whitchurch were erected in their parish churches.

The Imperial War Graves Commission, now the Commonwealth War Graves Commission (CWGC) was founded to ensure that the graves of fallen soldiers would not be lost. The Commission began recording graves and securing permanent cemeteries and sites for memorials. Each soldier was treated equally and had a uniform headstone.

The British Legion was formed in 1921 to support former servicemen, and a branch for the Alscot Estate servicemen held its first parade in November 1935. Around forty ex-servicemen attended. This became an annual event and rotated between each parish church. An annual dinner was also arranged by Captain Reggie West, owner of the Alscot Estate.

Left: Preston War Memorial soon after its unveiling (courtesy of Pete Summerton). Centre: Whitchurch War Memorial. Right: Alderminster War Memorial.

The Future

Ernest Horseman, a regular soldier with the RHA, left France after 4½ years on 20th January 1919 and was transferred to the reserve. He was of exemplary character, a continually hardworking man who could ride and drive, and had

two Good Conduct badges. He returned to his parents' address in Bristol. He married the following year, raised a family and remained in Bristol for his life. He died in 1975.
Robert Dale, serving with the 11th Hampshires since 1914, was transferred to the reserve in March 1919 and returned to Atherstone Hill. He married his childhood neighbour Sarah Hopkins a few weeks later, resumed work at Atherstone Hill Farm as a carter and had two children. He suffered from chronic heart problems and in April 1940 he fainted, fell into a pond on the farm and drowned. He was 48 years old. A post-mortem linked his condition to his military service.

Frank Taylor of Alderminster Farm, who had enlisted with Robert in 1914, was discharged to the reserve in February 1919; Thomas Bloxham from Atherstone a month later. Ernest Robinson was transferred to the reserve in March 1919. Their future from this point is unclear.

Arthur Burrows had been evacuated from France in October 1918. He was transferred to the reserve in March 1919, returned to Preston and resumed his work as a gardener. He married in 1924, had one daughter, and died in 1947.

George Hopkins, serving in the 6th Dorsets since 1914, had been twice wounded on the frontline. He was transferred to the reserve in March 1919, married and raised a family.

His brother Will, taken prisoner in August 1918, was repatriated to England on 29th November. He remained with the Royal Marines in Portsmouth until his discharge in March 1919. He later married and raised a family.

Their cousin William 'Curly' Hopkins of No.2 Preston, who lost his left arm, returned to Preston. He perfected the art of lighting a cigarette one-handed. His mother Jane died in 1925 and he lived with his father Daniel and brother Phillip until the 1950s when all three went into an old people's home. William died in 1955.

Walter Handy, who had served as a stoker in the Royal Navy since 1914, was discharged in November 1919. He married, raised a family, and spent 42 years working as a stoker at a power station. He died in 1972.

Jack Porter, who joined the Canadian ASC in 1914, returned to Canada in September 1920, perhaps after spending time with his family in Preston. He suffered from ill-health for the rest of his life thanks to being gassed in France.

He continued to work as a carpenter, mainly involved in house-building, although his health problems prevented him working a great deal of the time. He married Englishwoman Ida Anderson in 1922 and had a daughter. He remained in Canada until his death in 1973.

Dick Beavington, who was evacuated to England with a gunshot wound in March 1918, was transferred back to the ASC and resumed work as a baker. He spent the remainder of his service in England and was discharged in April 1919. Because of some permanent disability, he was awarded a pension of 5s 6d a week which continued for his life.

Dick Beavington in 1956. A former comrade recognised his picture in a local newspaper, forty years on, and cycled to visit him. Such was the bond formed between men on the frontline.

His brother Percy was discharged in April 1920 and both brothers spent their working lives in the family bakery in Preston, until it closed in 1970. Dick married district nurse Margaret Hayward in 1942 and had one daughter. Percy died in 1984; Dick in 1991.

Thomas George of the ASC left France in March 1919 and was demobilised a month later. His wife had died six months earlier, and in 1920 he married her sister Ellen who was caring for his two sons. He remained in the Stratford area for his life and died in 1970.

Wilfred Handy, who had enlisted with Thomas George in February 1915 and served alongside him throughout the war, returned to the Stratford area, married and had at least five children. He died in 1968.

Harry Knight, serving with the 6th Oxford and Bucks since January 1915, suffered a hernia in April 1918. He was declared unfit for frontline duties and transferred to the Labour Corps in August, where he remained until his discharge in May 1919. He had some permanent disability thanks to trench feet in October 1915, and was awarded a pension of 5s 6d a week.

His brother Frederick, who had been invalided from France in September 1918 after being injured for the third time, was discharged as physically unfit in September 1919. He married and had eight children.

Harry Samman, a baker with the ASC, was demobilised in October 1919 and returned to his family home in Birmingham. He continued working as a delivery roundsman for much of his working life, and lived in Birmingham until his death in 1954.

ROYAL ARMY SERVICE CORPS.

CERTIFICATE of* ~~Discharge~~ / Transfer to Reserve / ~~Disembodiment~~ / ~~Demobilization~~ Z on Demobilization. Army Form Z. 21.

214060

Regtl. No. S/363551 Rank a/Cpl

Names in full SAMMAN HARRY (Surname first)

Unit and Regiment or Corps from which *~~Discharged~~ Transferred to Reserve Z: ROYAL ARMY SERVICE CORPS

Attested on the 24 - 6 - 1916

Called up for Service on the 15 - 9 - 1917

For ROYAL ARMY SERVICE CORPS (Here state Regiment or Corps to which first appointed)

Also served in

Only Regiments or Corps in which the Soldier served since August 4th, 1914 are to be stated. If inapplicable, this space is to be ruled through in ink and initialled.

†Medals and Decorations awarded during present engagement: authorised prior to 11-11-18 N.L.

*~~Has~~ Has not served Overseas on Active Service.

Place of Rejoining in case of emergency: Oswestry. Medical Category B2

Specialist Military qualifications: Baker. Year of birth 1883

He is* ~~Discharged~~ Transferred to Army Reserve ~~Disembodied~~ ~~Demobilized~~ Class Z on 16 - 10 - 1919 in consequence of Demobilization.

Signature and Rank.

for RASC Officer i/c Records. Woolwich (Place).

* Strike out whichever is inapplicable. † The word "Nil" to be inserted when necessary.

N.B.—Any person finding this Certificate is requested to forward it in an unstamped envelope to the Secretary, War Office, London, S.W.1.

WARNING.—If this Certificate is lost a duplicate cannot be issued. You should therefore on no account part with it or forward it by post when applying for a situation.

(23741). Wt. W 1139-P.P. 2444. 600m. 6/19. D & S. (E 1256.)

Harry Samman's demobilisation documents.

Courtesy of Janet Naylor.

George Brookes of the Royal West Surrey Regiment, evacuated from France after being gassed in September 1918, was eventually posted to the Labour Corps. It is unclear whether he returned to abroad. He returned to Atherstone Hill Farm after his demobilisation then ran his own farm in Stratford. He went blind in his later years, perhaps linked to the gas damage. He died in 1980.

Charles Reading of the Australian Infantry rejoined his unit in France in December 1918 after being injured three months earlier. They were now taking classes such as telephony, agriculture, accountancy and book-keeping. He returned to England in March 1919 and was granted three months leave to return to Alderminster to help in his family's blacksmith's business. He returned to Australia in July. His future from this point is unclear.

Joscelyn Bloom, son of Whitchurch rector Harvey Bloom, was discharged from the RFA in March 1920. Like many young ex-soldiers, he had no training for any trade and he lived with his sister Ursula, herself a war widow. He struggled through a succession of temporary jobs then trained as an artist, and eventually became a well-known landscape painter and engraver. He died in 1978.

Wilfred Hastings, commanding officer of the Sierra Leone Battalion, was appointed Colonel-in-Command of the West African Frontier Force. He retired in 1922 due to ill-health after contracting malaria. He died three years later.

His twin brother Francis, a chaplain in the Royal Navy, became chaplain to the Royal Marine barracks and Chatham Dockyard in Kent in 1919. He retired in 1923 and became vicar at St Mellion in Cornwall. He died in 1933 and was buried in his home town of Stratford.

William Jobe, serving with the Mechanical Transport section, returned to Alscot Park after his demobilisation in 1919. Harry West had kept his chauffeur's position open and sent for him after the conclusion of hostilities. He became a special constable and received a long service medal in 1932. He had four further children, one of whom died in childhood.

In January 1933, he collected two passengers from Leamington Station to take to Alscot. His car crashed into another vehicle near Oxtalls Farm on the Warwick Road near Stratford. William was killed instantly and the other parties involved were seriously hurt. The reason for the crash was never ascertained. William's widow Sarah and their four children had to leave their cottage in Alscot Park and moved to Preston where Sarah became the school caretaker.

The wreckage of Captain West's Standard car.

Walter Keyte of the Royal Artillery returned to the local area, married Florence Roberts in 1922 and had one son. Florence died in 1926 and Walter then lived with his widowed sister until his death in 1967.

Oliver Summerton, who had enlisted underage in 1916, returned to Alderminster on his discharge in April 1919. He worked as a carpenter for Alscot Estate, a trade which, despite the gunshot injury to his hand, he continued for his life. He married Walter Keyte's sister Emma in 1923 and the couple moved to Stratford where they raised a family. He died in 1978.

Thomas Canning returned to his family farm in Crimscote and later set up business in Birmingham. He suffered permanent ill health on account of being gassed and was declared unfit for service when he applied to rejoin in 1939, although he subsequently served in the Birmingham Home Guard, as well as serving on the War Agricultural Executive Committee. He died in 1952.

Frank Southam, whose brothers Ernest and William had died on active service, returned to his bride in Alderminster and went on to have three children. He died in 1955.

Walter Tilling was transferred to the Royal Tank Corps in December 1918.

Thomas Canning, Home Guard, 1941.

Courtesy of Gay Jennions.

He was transferred to the reserve in March 1919 and returned to Atherstone. His subsequent future is unclear.

Wilfred Sivyour was discharged from the army and moved to Clifford Chambers to work as a shepherd. He married local woman Ethel Harding in 1923 and two daughters followed. He never spoke of his experiences, and his family said he was now an entirely different person. He later had a nervous breakdown which may have been caused by his experiences on the frontline. He lived at The Stalls at Alscot Park and No.17 Wimpstone where he remained until his death in 1976.

Robert Mansell Smith, wounded by shrapnel in Egypt, was discharged and returned to Stratford. He continued his work for the local community and was elected mayor of Stratford in 1930. He later moved to The Gables in Preston. He was appointed OBE for public services to Stratford in 1952, and died later the same year.

War Widows

The young widows, many of whom had small children, faced a life of poverty. They received a pension from the War Office but it could take months to arrive and was barely adequate to live on. Many remarried as a necessity.

Edith Garrett, widow of John Garrett who was killed in 1917, had two young children. She married Harold Timms of Kenilworth two years later. Edith wrote to the War Office in 1920, '*I married last September but I have 2 little children of my late husband and I think the plaque and scroll should be forwarded to me. Also if there is any more money as I think 17/6 is poor pay to bring up to [sic] little children who's father gave all to his country.*'

William Paxton's widow Lily, who had two children, wrote to the War Office asking if any money was due, and also asking if any letters or articles were found in William's pockets at the time of his death. The reply stated that no effects were found, and six months after William's death she was awarded a pension of 21 shillings a week.

Lily remarried in September 1920. She was 39 and her new husband was her next-door neighbour Ernest South, aged 23. Ernest was himself an army veteran and had been wounded at Passchendaele in October 1917, two days after his brother Frederick was killed in the same battle. Ernest was living on his army pension and later worked as a labourer. He died in 1941 from tuberculosis, probably linked to his military service. Lily remained a widow until her death in her nineties.

Alice Reason, the widow of Arnold Reason who was killed in July 1916, had two sons. She remained in Pontypridd and it seems never remarried. Their eldest son Leslie, a sergeant in the Royal Artillery, died on active service in 1944. Father and son are commemorated on the Ynysangharad Memorial in Pontypridd.

Edith Porter, widow of Will Porter who was killed in October 1918, had a young son, Maurice. Maurice was killed in a motorbike crash in 1934 and Edith remarried the following year. Her new husband was Stratford resident Walter Collins. The couple lived in Tiddington until Edith's death in 1974.

Jane Waters, widow of Charles Waters who was presumed killed in April 1917, had one daughter. She received a pension of 18s 6d a week. Her future is unclear.

Annie Neal, widow of Reginald Neal who died in November 1917, had one daughter. She remarried in early 1919 and moved to Surrey.

Edith Churchill, the widow of Frederick Churchill who was killed in October 1915, had two children. She remarried Frederick Powell in 1922.

Emily Ward, widow of Jack Ward of Crimscote who was killed in December 1915, had three children. Their future after Jack's death is unclear.

Alice Whiteman, widow of John Whiteman who was killed in 1917, moved into Alderminster Lodge where she remained for many years and became closely involved in local events and initiatives.

Edith Horseman, widow of Albert Horseman who was killed in May 1918, had two children. Their future after Albert's death is unclear.

Beatrice Horseman, widow of Ernest Horseman who died of smallpox in 1918, had one daughter. She remained a widow for her life.

Amy Kingston, widow of Thomas Kingston who died of influenza in November 1918, had two daughters. She never remarried and remained in Huddersfield for her life.

Kate Handy, widow of Arthur Handy who was killed in March 1918, had two young sons. She received a £10 1s 9d gratuity from the War Office in August 1919. She did sewing work to help make ends meet, possibly with a sewing machine provided through government assistance, and remarried in 1927. Her new husband was Harry Wills, a war veteran who had contracted gangrene and now had a metal leg. Harry died in 1938, and Kate took over the care of her grandchildren for several years. She died in 1965, aged eighty.

One of many broken families. Will Porter with his wife Edith and son Maurice.

Courtesy of Pete Summerton.

Six: The Second World War

On 3rd September 1939, Britain declared war on Germany. The conflict then escalated into a worldwide war. It had been considered inevitable for years, but even so Britain was woefully ill-prepared. The army comprised a small force of regular soldiers who, thanks to years of economising, lacked rifles, ammunition and tanks and had little training in large-scale operations. For the territorial soldiers and conscripts, the situation was even worse.

The National Service (Armed Forces) Act was passed on 3rd September 1939, declaring that all men aged 20-41 would be eligible for conscription, although those who worked in occupations of national importance such as agriculture were eligible for exemption. The men were called up as needed, but could volunteer earlier if they wished.

160,000 British servicemen occupied the Franco-Belgian border in September 1939, in readiness for the German advance. Unlike their counterparts in 1914, they would have eight months to prepare for their first major battle.

The war had far greater impact on life at home than any other war in British history. Air raids were expected; invasion likely. Children were evacuated from the cities. German U-boats attacked merchant shipping and triggered years of rationing. Every available plot of land was forced into food production. This war could not be won by the military alone. The entire British nation had to come together to do their bit, and this spirit came to epitomise Britain during the Second World War.

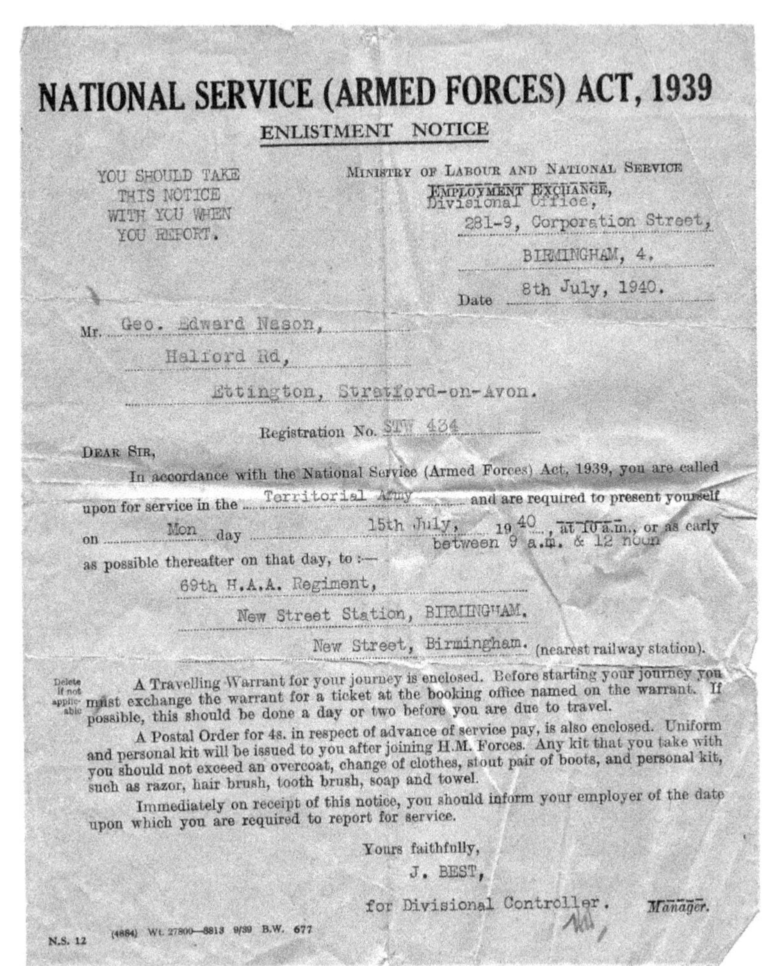

NATIONAL SERVICE (ARMED FORCES) ACT, 1939

ENLISTMENT NOTICE

YOU SHOULD TAKE THIS NOTICE WITH YOU WHEN YOU REPORT.

MINISTRY OF LABOUR AND NATIONAL SERVICE
~~EMPLOYMENT EXCHANGE~~,
Divisional Office,
281-9, Corporation Street,
BIRMINGHAM, 4.

Date 8th July, 1940.

Mr. Geo. Edward Nason,
Halford Rd,
Ettington, Stratford-on-Avon.

Registration No. STW 434

DEAR SIR,

In accordance with the National Service (Armed Forces) Act, 1939, you are called upon for service in the Territorial Army and are required to present yourself on Mon day 15th July, 1940, ~~at 10 a.m.~~, or as early as possible thereafter on that day, between 9 a.m. & 12 noon, to:—

69th H.A.A. Regiment,
New Street Station, BIRMINGHAM.
New Street, Birmingham. (nearest railway station).

Delete if not applicable

A Travelling Warrant for your journey is enclosed. Before starting your journey you must exchange the warrant for a ticket at the booking office named on the warrant. If possible, this should be done a day or two before you are due to travel.

A Postal Order for 4s. in respect of advance of service pay, is also enclosed. Uniform and personal kit will be issued to you after joining H.M. Forces. Any kit that you take with you should not exceed an overcoat, change of clothes, stout pair of boots, and personal kit, such as razor, hair brush, tooth brush, soap and towel.

Immediately on receipt of this notice, you should inform your employer of the date upon which you are required to report for service.

Yours faithfully,
J. BEST,
for Divisional Controller. ~~Manager~~.

N.S. 12 (4864) Wt. 27800—8813 9/39 B.W. 677

George Nason's call-up papers.

Courtesy of Jane Spencer.

The Fighting Begins

Several men from the Alscot villages were serving in the regular and territorial armies at the start of the war.

William Reginald James Alston-Roberts-West, known as Reggie (b1900) was the eldest son of Harry Alston-Roberts-West, the owner of the Alscot Estate. After attending the Royal Military College of Sandhurst he was commissioned into the 3rd Grenadier Guards. He was promoted to lieutenant in 1922 and captain in 1930. He left the army following his father's death in 1931 and returned to Alscot Park to take over the estate.

Reggie was a keen sportsman. He was a member of the Warwickshire Hunt and an amateur jockey, and would dismount and run up the steep Larkstoke hill in Ilmington – expecting his grooms to do the same. He was president of the Stratford Football Club, captain of the Alscot Park Cricket Club, president of the Royal Warwickshire Agricultural Society and president of the Alderminster and District Shire Horse Society. He was also a JP for Warwickshire. He married Isolde Grosvenor in 1930 and had two young sons. He rejoined his unit when war was declared and arrived in France with his unit three weeks later.

Lieutenant (later Major) Reggie West.

Courtesy of George West.

Albert Victor (Bert) Hathaway (b1913) was the son of Alderminster farm labourer John Hathaway and his wife Sarah. He enlisted in the Royal Artillery in January 1933 and was stationed at Woolwich Arsenal in London where he trained as a gun-fitter and locksmith. He was transferred to the reserve after three years and was remobilised the day after war was declared. He served in an anti-aircraft regiment and then moved to the 53rd anti-tank regiment, which went to France on 5th January 1940.

William (Bill) Simms, (b1918) was the son of Henry and May Simms. He was born in Newbold on Stour then moved to No.39 Alderminster where he grew up. He enlisted in the army at an early stage in the war and was serving in France by 1940.

William (Bill) Gibbins (b1902) was the son of woodsman William Gibbins and his wife Hannah of Preston. His grandfather Thomas had served in the army in the 1860s. Bill married Gladys Walton, the daughter of George and Elizabeth Walton of No.36 Preston, and moved into No.6. Two daughters followed. He also worked as a woodsman for Alscot Estate.

He served in the 1/7th (territorial) battalion of the Royal Warwickshire Regiment and reached the rank of corporal. He was mobilised shortly after war was declared and went to France with his battalion in early 1940.

Corporal William Gibbins, 1939.

Courtesy of Jenny Wilkins.

The first major battle between the British and German armies took place on 10th May 1940. The French army was collapsing and within days the British were forced into a desperate retreat.

Reggie West, recently promoted to major, was fighting in Flanders on 21st

May when the Germans attacked their line. They used rafts to cross a canal in front of their position and Reggie, increasingly worried for his unit's safety, went forward to see about organising a counterattack.

He came across Lt Nigel Forbes who had been shot in the leg. Reggie asked him if he wanted to be left and taken prisoner, or risk being pulled back to the Regimental Aid Post. Nigel chose the latter. He later recounted: '*Major West… pulled me along the ground by my shoulder straps, rather like a dead stag is pulled off the hill by its antlers. We hadn't gone far before I passed out.*' Nigel subsequently recovered from his injuries.

Reggie was later seen running along the canal bank, exposed to enemy fire. This was the last recorded sighting of him alive. After a bitter battle the Guards retreated, with over sixty of their number killed. The Germans buried the bodies including, they recorded, Major West, the leader of the counterattack. 'It was very seldom the English left their dead behind,' a German officer commented.

Reggie's body was never subsequently recovered and he is commemorated on the Dunkirk Memorial and Preston War Memorial. An anonymous friend later wrote to *The Times;*

> *'His only thought since the war started was to remain at the front leading his own men against the enemy. This brave and kindly man died as he had lived; a superb example of an English guardsman and a country gentleman.'*

The army reached Dunkirk and an emergency evacuation began. Troopships, ferries, fishing smacks and all other available vessels struggled through mines, shells and air raids to bring the army home as the Germans closed in.

The 1/7th Warwicks, including Bill Gibbins, were fighting in Belgium and on 16th May were one of three much-depleted units sent to defend the Ypres canal zone and hold up the German advance. Thousands of lives depended on them. They held off an assault by three German divisions on 27th and 28th May, by which time the defenders were reduced to a third of their original strength. 70,000 more men were taken from Dunkirk in this time. Only 215 men of the 1/7th Warwicks reached Dunkirk themselves. Bill Gibbins reached Britain safely.

Bert Hathaway of the 55th Anti-Tank Regiment was also fighting in France. They came under a German attack on 10th May and inflicted heavy enemy losses as their division retreated. They were then ordered to destroy their guns and the much-depleted unit retreated towards Dunkirk. Bert carried an injured man for three miles to the beachhead and helped him onto a ship which brought him safely to England. The man's wife later wrote to the Hathaway family and they remained in contact for several years. Bert was safely evacuated himself on HMS *Halcyon.*

Bill Simms of Alderminster was also fighting in the battle for France. He was one of the last troops to be evacuated, finding passage on a grain boat. It was attacked while crossing the channel, costing the lives of several men on board, but Bill reached England safely.

Bert Hathaway's future brothers-in-law, Albert, Stanley and Douglas Ward, were the sons of Alderminster builder Harry Ward and all worked as builders before serving in the army. Albert and Stanley were fighting in southern France and were cut off from Dunkirk. They managed to cross the border into Spain and then got a ship back to England.

Dunkirk, an unparalleled military disaster, was lauded a feat of brilliance, saving 339,000 British and French troops from annihilation. But almost all of continental Europe was now under Nazi control, and the invasion of Britain seemed certain.

Memorial to Reggie West in Preston church.

The Local Defence Volunteers (The Home Guard)

On 14th May 1940, in response to the disaster in Europe, the Local Defence Volunteers (LDV) was formed and recruited 400,000 volunteers within a fortnight. It was later renamed the Home Guard. The local unit was the 4th Warwickshire (Stratford) battalion, which had its headquarters in Stratford and had several platoons in local villages including Ilmington and Clifford Chambers.

The Home Guard has been much satirised as a motley group of old men and boys, but the units did sterling work throughout the war. They manned coastal defences and were prepared to defend nationwide stop-lines where an invading army could be thwarted. They would also remove road signs and lay roadblocks. One of these was prepared at Preston bridge. The Home Guard positioned a tree-trunk with a cartwheel fixed to it, ready to roll across the bridge. They would then remove the wheel.

Joe, Bob and Guy Spencer at Park Farm, Preston.

Courtesy of Mary Watts.

Left: Sergeant Oliver Summerton.
Courtesy of Pete Summerton.

Sergeant Robert Stredder with his son Robert.
Courtesy of James Stredder.

Several local men enlisted in the Home Guard. Many worked in agriculture and were exempt from the army; others were waiting their call-up. Joe, Bob and Guy Spencer were farmer's sons from Park Farm in Preston. Eric Dale from Preston also worked at Park Farm. Oliver Summerton was a carpenter and First World War veteran from Alderminster. Peter and James Jones were the sons of shepherd William Jones of Preston. Peter later joined the regular army. Ray Russell was a farmworker from Atherstone. Robert Stredder was an accountant from Preston. Henry Ashby was a farmer's son from Home Farm in Wimpstone.

There was little action for the Home Guard in the area. They did exercises with live ammunition if they could get it, and on one occasion mounted an attack on Snitterfield airfield after a mock German landing. They were often stationed at night on Meon Hill watching for enemy aircraft, and they also guarded the electricity substation on the Fosse Way near Tredington. Often one remained on duty while the others played snooker at The Gables in Preston. They then went off to a full day's work on their farms.

The Clifford Chambers platoon. Third left, back row: Ray Russell.
Courtesy of Richard Parnham.

The Battle of Britain and The Blitz

The Luftwaffe mounted a series of raids to destroy ships and clear the skies of British fighters prior to the planned invasion. The first bombs fell on 3rd July 1940 and the Battle of Britain began. Amidst aerial dogfights, German bombers targeted docks, airfields, aircraft factories and storage depots. On 24th August, the first bombs fell on central London and 24 hours later, Bomber Command launched a retaliatory attack on Berlin. On 7th September, the war reached a new level when a vast fleet of bombers headed for London and the Blitz began.

Wilfred George Newey (b1907) was the eldest son of James and Ouida Newey of Solihul. James ran a business manufacturing hooks and eyes and later moved to Stratford. The family lived at Whitehill farmhouse in Preston, the farmland rented out separately. By the 1940s Wilfred, now married with two sons, was living at Talton House in Newbold and was a director of the Birmingham manufacturing firm Messrs Newey and Taylor Ltd, probably his father's original business.

Wilfred joined the territorial army in 1923 and in 1936, now ranked a major, he joined the 69th (Royal Warwickshire Regiment) Heavy Anti-Aircraft

The Ilmington platoon of the Home Guard.
Back row: 1) Tommy Wilkins; 2) Henry Ashby; 5) Sam Freeman; 7) Herbert Sabin.
Middle row: 1) Charlie Sabin.
Front row: 1) Bert Empson; 3) Butcher Handy; 4) Sam Handy; 7) Captain Learmouth; 11) Bob Spencer.
Courtesy Richard Parnham.

Regiment of the Royal Artillery. This was a new territorial unit which was mobilised on the outbreak of war.

George Nason (b1916) was the son of gardener Leonard Nason and his wife Amy of Ettington. He worked as a painter and was courting Florence Molly Westbury, daughter of farmworker Harry Westbury of Preston. He was called up for the 192nd (Heavy Anti-Aircraft) Battery of the Royal Artillery in July 1940.

The anti-aircraft batteries played a crucial role defending the West Midlands against the Luftwaffe. Wilfred Newey's battery was based in King's Norton until early 1941. George Nason was based in Edgbaston.

The bombing had a great impact on civilian life, and everybody was issued with rubber gas masks. These smelt horrible and Vicky Young, nee Harwood of Alderminster (b1929) hated them. Babies were put in a special protective cradle. The children had to take their masks to school and practiced getting under their desks in event of a raid.

The government began top-secret preparations to evacuate to Stratford, and the Ministry of Works began to requisition all major hotels. The Welcombe Hotel would be used by the Treasury; peers would stay in the Falcon Hotel; MPs would find lodgings in local guest houses. The theatre would be the debating chambers for the Houses of Lords and Commons. These plans never came to fruition.

Over four million bombs were dropped on Britain before the end of 1940, but the Luftwaffe failed to ground the RAF and in October 1940, the German plans to invade Britain were abandoned. The Battle of Britain was over.

The anti-aircraft batteries were no longer as necessary for home defence, and Wilfred Newey and George Nason were both sent to the Middle East in early 1941.

George Nason.

Courtesy of Jane Spencer.

Air Raid Precautions (ARP)

The ARP wardens were responsible for ensuring blackout precautions were in place – unnecessary in the villages which had no electric lighting – and for marshalling people, ambulances and fire engines during raids. The bombing posed little threat to the Stratford area. The control centre in Stratford library was connected by telephone to ARP posts in the town and outlying villages.

This had some difficulties. Ernest Morris, a gardener in his fifties, was the ARP warden for Whitchurch. When the first air raid warning sounded in September 1939 he had to get on his bicycle, pedal three miles to The Bell in Alderminster which had a telephone, collect his orders and his whistle, then pedal back again to assume his duties. By this time the raid was over.

Charlie Horseman, a gardener at Alscot Park, Reg Ashby, a farmer who lived at the Old Vicarage in Preston, and Harry Smith of Lower Farm in Preston were also ARP wardens. They presumably had to go through a similar procedure. Vicky Young of Alderminster remembers the village policeman pedalling through the village blowing his whistle to warn of a coming raid.

Two incendiary bombs fell into Preston Bushes on one occasion; it was thought a farmer had gone out to check his hens with a hurricane lamp and a Luftwaffe pilot had seen the light, although they may have been jettisoned by a bomber returning from one of the city raids.

Alan Noyce of The Kennels in Preston (b1937) remembers a bomb falling in a nearby field one night. The explosion left a huge crater in the field but neither he nor his brothers were woken by the noise.

Few enemy aircraft were seen, with one exception. On 14th November 1940, the Luftwaffe raided Coventry. Waves of bombers were flying over Preston for eleven hours that night and everybody could see the glow in the sky, 25 miles to the north, as the city burned. The people of Crimscote all climbed up Talton Hill to watch the bombers pass, and Eric James of Whitchurch Farm (1926-2016) remembered their cellar door rattled throughout the night from the vibrations of falling bombs.

The National Fire Service (NFS)

The raids caused devastating fires and incendiary bombs caused even more problems. The NFS had branches in every district. The NFS in Stratford were at first equipped with only a tin hat and an axe per man, and a few old cars in lieu of a fire engine. Nevertheless, they did sterling work as far afield as Coventry, Birmingham and Wales and also attended accidents at Atherstone airfield.

Victor Browett, who lived at Sutcliffe Avenue in Alderminster, served in the NFS. Harvey Bloom, the former rector of Whitchurch who was now living in London, also applied. He truthfully stated his age to be 'over sixty'. He was in fact 79. He was soon dismissed on fitness grounds when he failed to squirm through a series of barrels on his stomach, much to his annoyance.

Edward (Ted) Coomber lived in London with his wife Queenie and their two children. He sold fruit and vegetables, first from a barrow and then from a horse and cart, and joined the NFS at the outbreak of war. His wife and children moved to Preston around 1940 while Ted remained in London. They stayed with the Beavington family for a while and their son Roger was born in Preston in 1943. After the war, Ted was transferred to the Stratford fire station and the family remained in Preston for good.

The Royal Observer Corps (ROC)

The ROC, the eyes and ears of the RAF, watched for enemy aircraft. Their reports on the numbers, type and direction were used to plot their progress across the country and their observations were instrumental for launching air raid warning systems and mounting interceptions by the RAF. They also logged aircraft crashes.

An observer station was built in a field next to Barton Farm in Alderminster which was manned round the clock. Two men at a time worked eight-hour shifts. Their reports were conveyed by telephone to a central control in Coventry which passed the information to the RAF Fighter Command.

Several local men served in the ROC. Jack Thorp, who ran Thorp's garage in Alderminster, was the Head Observer. Patrick Haycock, the head gardener at Ettington Park, was a Leading Observer. Other observers at Alderminster were George Mumford, a gardener at Ettington Park; farmer David Wells; farm worker Phillip Coleman; Wilfred Attewell, a motor engineer and coal merchant; Bert Lowe of Preston, a gamekeeper at Alscot Park whose brother Tom had been killed in France in 1918; gamekeeper Bill Noyce; and William Hicks of Preston who worked for Alscot Estate.

A searchlight station was located on the Stratford side of Alderminster beside the A3400, in a field now known as Searchlight Field. This was managed by Philip Green, a former artillery captain and Boer War veteran of No.11 Alderminster. Local people remember the strong beams of light probing the sky. The wooden huts were dismantled after the war and used to build Preston village hall.

Evacuations

Plans were put in motion to evacuate children and expectant mothers from the cities. Several hundred Birmingham children arrived in Stratford within a week of the outbreak of war and were distributed around the town and outlying villages. Anyone with a spare room was expected to accommodate somebody.

Twenty eight children and three teachers from St Catherine's Roman Catholic School arrived in Preston in September 1939, along with five mothers and eight babies. Thirty six children, seven mothers and twelve babies went to Alderminster. Thirteen children went to Whitchurch.

Schoolmaster Harry Lord was the billeting officer for Preston and allocated their new homes. Those at Preston attended the village school, were included in the annual prize-giving, and received the traditional Christmas orange from Mrs West. Those in Alderminster were taught in the school in the morning while the local children were taught in the afternoon.

The evacuees were a culture shock for the villagers. Many were dirty, full of lice, ate with their fingers and didn't know how to say grace. The children themselves often found their new life hard. They wanted fish and chips; asked where the cinema was; didn't realise that milk came from a cow; and were horrified when vegetables were brought from the garden covered with dirt. A Whitchurch woman saw with dismay her charges were putting onion sauce onto ginger pudding. One boy called Albert ran into a patch of stinging nettles without realising they stung.

They didn't stay long. With no bombing forthcoming, many evacuees returned home to see what happened.

When the bombing began in earnest, people began to seek places of safety. George and Elsie Harding moved from London to Preston in 1940 and lived in the lodge gates of Alscot Park. Bob and Doreen Stredder and the Coomber family also came to Preston and all settled in Preston for good. A family called Jones from Birmingham lived with Bill and Ada Noyce at The Kennels for much of the war.

Bill and Lily Walton lived in Fulham with their young son Derek. Bill was friends with George Harding, and Lily's sister Florence had married George's brother Tom, who also came to Preston. Lily and Derek moved to Preston in June 1944 and stayed with George and Elsie Harding before moving to No.37 Preston with Florence. Bill Walton and Tom Harding were both in the army by this point. Derek's baby book reads: *First journey: June 24th 1944. To Stratford on Avon to get away from the flying bombs.*

Bill Walton at Alscot Lodge with his wife Lily and son Derek, September 1944.
Courtesy of Derek Walton.

The lack of mains electric, water and gas was something of an ordeal, but the families remained in Preston until the end of the war. The Waltons returned to Fulham, then in 1954 returned to Preston. Tom and Flo Harding settled in Atherstone and Tom worked as a butler at Alscot Park.

Arthur and Marian Jaques lived on a farm in Essex with their two young daughters, Valerie and Barbara. Bombs started falling only a few miles from their farm, so Arthur decided to move to Warwickshire where he had roots. They moved into Atherstone Hill Farm where their third child, Norman, was born in 1941.

Reg and Nell Stoppard were living in Hall Green in Birmingham with their two small children. In 1940 a bomb fell just outside their house and the next morning, Reg said to Nell; 'When I get home from work tonight, you're to be in the countryside somewhere safe.' So Nell gathered everything she could carry into a pram, took the children and walked to the train station, where she caught a train to Stratford. A friend had given her the name of Ned Hutchings in Alderminster, and she found his farm. Ned and his wife let her stay for a while then she moved in with the Jaques family in Atherstone Hill Farm.

Despite having no electric, water or inside toilet, both families enjoyed their experience. The Stoppards became country children and came to love the farming life. Reg was called up for the RAF while Nell was pregnant with her third child, Mary, born just after Reg went abroad.

The Stoppards returned to Birmingham after the war, but they missed Atherstone so much they came back again. They eventually emigrated to New Zealand, while the Jaques family moved to Stratford, but both families have remained solid friends and still visit the place that provided the happiest days of their lives.

More evacuee children came to Preston in June 1940. Nine-year-old Joan Hulbert, nee Knight, was one. She had been evacuated from Dagenham in Essex in 1939, along with four of her siblings, 12-year-old Violet, 11-year-old Harry, 8-year-old Doris and 6-year-old Mary. They were permitted to take only a small bag of clothes, their gas mask, a day's supply of food and their label. Their two younger siblings were kept at home.

The children were taken to Halesworth in Suffolk, but with the increasing threat of invasion the area was no longer considered safe, and Joan and her siblings, along with many other Dagenham children, were loaded onto a train and sent to Stratford. They were then taken to Preston.

Joan and Doris were taken in by Charlie and Rose Horseman of No.8. Mary and Violet went to Gladys Gibbins of No.6, and Harry went to Elizabeth Walton of No.36. Mrs Walton could be very strict with children. When they climbed the tree outside her cottage she would come out with her stick and chase them away. Harry could be a bit naughty, which didn't suit Mrs Walton's temperament. He tried to run away and was eventually moved to another home.

Many other families took in evacuees. Ethel Hicks from No.13 Preston, the wife of William Hicks, took in 12-year-old Sylvia Luck and another girl called Winnie. Frank and Myra Noyce of Top Lodge took in a girl called Elsie.

The women who opened their homes for uprooted and frightened children are, in Joan's opinion, the forgotten heroes of the evacuation process. Joan remembers that Rose Horseman was strict but always fair and treated them no differently to her own son John. She didn't believe in idleness and taught the girls to cook, darn and sew – their work always thoroughly inspected – as well as providing the love and stability they needed. Her husband Charlie was also a wonderfully kind man; Joan remembers him putting a hot brick in her bed to warm it on cold nights.

The expedition to the outside toilet at the top of the garden, in the dark and with a pig grunting in the pigsty next door, was terrifying. Joan never got used to this, although they quickly adapted to using oil lamps and had fun with the water pump. The local children were generally friendly although they got teased a bit at first.

In their five years away, Joan and her siblings only saw their parents a couple of times. Returning to Dagenham after the war was almost as traumatic as leaving. Their parents had become near strangers, and she had to say goodbye the new family they'd found.

It was just as difficult for their parents. They had said goodbye to their children five years earlier, without knowing if they would see them again, and now they had to come to terms with the fact that they had grown up without them. Joan had left Dagenham a child; she was now a young woman. Even the youngest girl was almost a teenager.

Joan and her family remained in constant touch with the Horsemans, and seventy years after she returned to Dagenham, Joan still looks back on her years in Preston with fondness, and acknowledges the enormous influence, all entirely for the good, her experience has had on her life and the person she became.

Figure 60. Ethel Hicks with evacuees Sylvia Luck and Winnie and her son Billy.

Courtesy of Bill Hicks.

The war effort was the main focus of everybody. Molly Westbury of Preston worked in the NC Joseph armaments factory in Stratford, which made bomb cases. Emily Sivyour, later Ridgard, who lived at The Stalls in Preston and later at No.17 Wimpstone, also worked at Joseph's welding bomb cases. Vera Perry who purchased Preston Pastures around 1950 worked as an ambulance driver. Winifred Hartwell of Preston was also involved in war work in the area.

Fred Lockwood of Crimscote was a senior engineer for Messrs Balls Brothers, an engineering firm in Arden Street in Stratford. When the war started they began making bomb casings, ammunition cases and barrage balloons, and Fred was granted exemption from military service to continue his work.

Elsie Harding, who moved from London to Preston in 1940, had worked as a seamstress in Harrods with her sister before the war. Elsie was directed to stitch parachutes, while her sister made tents for soldiers. Both sisters also met trains bringing wounded soldiers up from Dover and would give them tea, cigarettes and a welcome smile.

As most of the police force were serving with the forces, Special Constables, also known as the Police War Reserve, were drafted to take their place. Many were in reserved occupations or were unfit for active service. Andrew Simpson, who took Alderminster Farm in 1941, served as a Special Constable.

As well as dealing with criminal activity, the Specials helped enforce wartime regulations. On 28th October 1939, Police War Reserve Hicks, his identity unclear but based at Alderminster, was on duty in Wimpstone when he saw a bright light in a field. He found a gypsy encampment with two fires. Hicks pointed out to the two women, Louisa Sherriff and Ivy Smith, that they were committing a serious offence: no lights could now be shown after dark. Hicks eventually persuaded the women to put the fires out and both were summonsed to Stratford Magistrates Court. They promised to obey the regulations in future and were fined five shillings each.

Metal was desperately needed for tanks and armaments, and all unnecessary metal was commandeered by the government. The iron railings outside Preston School and those surrounding many graves in the churchyard, which had survived a similar trawl during the First World War, were taken away. The stumps remain today.

The oak trees at Preston Pastures were cut down for gun carriages. The heavy horses used to haul the timber were stabled in Harvey Smith's farm buildings on the Admington Road, for which the carpenters made him an oak sideboard. Lumberjacks and lumberjills were lodged with the Harwoods at No.26 Alderminster. One of these, John Saunders from Derbyshire, was a conscientious objector and was granted exemption from military service.

Meat, sugar, eggs and butter were rationed, as was petrol, soap and clothing. Milk rationing was introduced in 1941. Everyone was issued a ration book with weekly coupons for each item. Joan Hulbert remembers they gave up sweets for Lent and hoarded their rations until Easter Sunday. Rationing was less of a problem in rural areas, as people could easily grow vegetables, keep hens, and acquire extra produce from farms on the sly. The black market thrived. Valerie Bliss, nee Jaques, living at Atherstone Hill Farm, remembers her parents' friends from Kidderminster bringing them an illicitly-killed pig one Christmas. The pig was hidden in the back of the car under some blankets, and they were terrified they would be caught en route.

Fundraising

The government instigated a nationwide fundraising and savings scheme to fund the war effort. This was the forerunner of the present National Savings scheme. Savings stamps were issued and the money could be withdrawn after the war.

Specific fundraising efforts were arranged. For Navy Week in September 1941, Stratford district aimed to raise £200,000 towards the hull of a destroyer which would be given a name commemorating the district. For Warship Week a month later, Stratford was to raise another £100,000. Preston and Atherstone had a combined target of £3500; they raised an incredible £11,246. Whitchurch raised £5154 and Alderminster £7692, both greatly exceeding their targets. Collectors in Alderminster visited every household and often had 100% success in collecting donations. Stratford raised nearly £230,000 during Warship Week in February 1942. The money helped build HMS *Farne*, launched the following year with the town's coat of arms on its quarterdeck.

In May 1943, Stratford had a target of £210,000 for the Wings for Victory campaign to purchase eight Spitfires and four Lancasters. They exceeded this by over £80,000. Preston and Atherstone alone contributed £3995. Alderminster raised £5183 and Whitchurch £2375. Alderminster's efforts included dances, a whist drive, a film show and sporting events.

Vicky Young, nee Harwood, was given a box of chocolate bars – a nearly non-existent treat – by the NAAFI of the Atherstone aerodrome which she raffled for the Spitfire Fund. Valerie Bliss, nee Jaques, of Atherstone Hill remembers her father giving her and her sister Barbara £100 each to take to Stratford for one campaign.

The fundraising efforts continued throughout the war, and by May 1944 Stratford had contributed over £61m to the war effort. These figures would have been considered impossible before the war, Britain's leaders enthused. Everybody was coming together to do a sturdy job for the nation and fundraising efforts also provided a valuable contribution to village life.

Smaller but no less valuable efforts included a dance at Alderminster in February 1942 which raised £10 10s for St Dunstans, a charity for blind ex-servicemen. Another dance three weeks later raised £10 for the British Sailors' Association. The Red Cross Rural Pennies Collection, where workers donated a few pence of their wages, raised £6 18s from Preston, £10 from Atherstone and £7 6s from Whitchurch and Crimscote in September 1944. In October 1944, Elsie Spencer and Sarah Jobe of Preston organised a dance which raised £8 15s for the British Sailors' Association. A comedy performance in February 1945 raised £25 for the Duke of Gloucester's POW fund. A rummage sale held at The Gables in Preston in April 1945 raised £15 for the Red Cross Agricultural Fund. The Whitchurch

Harry Lord, Preston's schoolmaster from 1922-1942, with his wife. Harry served on HMS Malaya during the First World War and lost parts of his fingers. The Malaya suffered heavily in the Battle of Jutland. Harry may have been wearing his old uniform in conjunction with Navy Week.

Courtesy of Richard Parnham.

Girl Guides held a monthly whist drive. Former vicar's daughter Ursula Bloom organised a campaign to raise money for machine gun bullets, which cost 1½d and stood a chance of bringing down a German plane.

Alan 'Mac' James of Whitchurch Farm, who worked as a grader for the Ministry of Food, donated a fat bullock to be auctioned for the war effort in March 1943. The auction, held at Stratford Market, raised an incredible £10,251 for the RAF Pilots and Crews Fund.

Prisoners of War

Low-risk prisoners of war were kept at a camp in the grounds of Ettington Park. At first it housed Italian prisoners, and then Germans captured after the D-Day landings. In December 1946, 66 German POWs, all of them anti-Nazi, joined a church service at Alderminster and their padre, captured after D-Day, preached in German and English.

POWs were put to work of non-military nature. Some worked on local farms, most of which were short of labour. They were often used for the sugar beet harvest. Others worked in Knavenhill Woods in Alderminster, cutting down trees. They walked from the camp through Alderminster and up New Road to each day with a military escort. Some of the prisoners made a wheelbarrow and a wooden battleship, which they named HMS *Alderminster*, for David Hathaway (b1940) who lived on New Road. They took a shine to him because he had blonde hair and blue eyes.

Many POWs remained in Britain after the war, having few prospects in

HMS Alderminster.

Courtesy of David Hathaway.

their homeland. Many were given work on local farms. A German POW named Rudolph worked for Harvey Smith at Lower Farm in Preston, living in one of the farm cottages and eating his meals with the family. He couldn't speak English and was very moody, and the Smith children were quite scared of him. He had a family back in Germany, who were probably suffering greatly without him. Two German POWs worked for Andrew Bishop at Beecham Farm. They enjoyed their time there and in later years returned to visit the family.

Weddings

As in the First World War, the conflict kindled romance, and several local girls married servicemen.

Kathleen Hartwell, the daughter of Preston's roadman Fred Hartwell, married Leonard Skidmore. Leonard was from Coventry and had enlisted in the 1st Gloucestershire Regiment in June 1940. He joined his battalion in India, where it had been serving for several years, and then in early 1942 they joined the Burma campaign. Leonard was one of thirteen men of his battalion reported missing in action on 17th April. He rejoined his unit safely shortly afterwards. He was one of several men wounded on 1st May. The battalion then returned to India where they remained for the remainder of the war. Leonard returned to Britain in February 1945 and promptly married his sweetheart in Preston church. He was discharged in April 1946, shortly after the birth of his son, also called Leonard. The couple settled in Coventry where Leonard worked as a gardener and chauffeur.

Four weeks after Kathleen's wedding, her sister Winifred also married. Her husband was Alfred William Maull, a corporal in the 13th Royal Corps of Signals. Alfred was born in Solihul and later moved to Wellesbourne. He was serving in Greece by early 1941. On 28th April 1941 he was one of thirty men reported missing in action; he and several others subsequently rejoined their unit. He came home on leave in March 1945 after five years overseas, and he and Winifred were married. The couple remained in the Stratford area after Alfred's discharge and had two children.

Ethel Paxton, the daughter of Preston carpenter William Paxton who had been killed in action in 1916, married Percival Wheeler in August 1945. Percival was her neighbour in Percy Street in Stratford and served for four years in the Royal Army Medical Corps in Burma. The couple were married on his return home.

Emily Sivyour and her sister Frances, daughters of First World War veteran

Wilfred Sivyour, were sitting on their garden fence at Salt and Pepper Pots in Clifford Chambers in 1941 when two soldiers on bicycles stopped to chat to them. One was Arthur Ridgard from Ashbourne in Derbyshire. Arthur was serving with the Pioneer Corps and was constructing the runways on RAF Long Marston. Two years later in 1943, he and Emily were married. 'You know how soldiers will stand and talk to you,' Emily later recalled. 'My sister and I used to watch the soldiers go by to Long Marston, but nothing came of the other soldier and my sister.'

Arthur then served in Cardiff and Liverpool while Emily remained in Stratford. He was unfit to go to France in 1944 and eventually returned to the Stratford area where he guarded prisoners of war at Ettington Park. Like David Hathaway, he was impressed by their woodworking and carving skills. The couple went on to have two children and lived in Alscot lodge gates then No.17 Wimpstone where they remained for their lives.

Arthur Ridgard.

Courtesy of James Ridgard.

Feeding the Nation

In 1936, the War Agricultural Executive Committee (War Ag) was set up to tackle the major deficiencies of British agriculture. The depression of the 1920s meant a great deal of land had been abandoned by struggling farmers, and had reverted to scrub. The remaining farmland was woefully under-productive and 70% of British food was imported. Any blockade in the imminent war would be a disaster.

All unproductive land had to be cleared and cultivated. If landowners were unable or unwilling to do the work, it was taken over by the War Ag. Many farmers were still using heavy horses, incapable of drastic clearance work or hauling a plough through heavy, stony ground, and the War Ag would arrange machines to do the work. A 'bush-pusher' was a huge crawler which bent the stems of small trees, cut through them, then scooped out the roots. They were pushed into heaps and burned, the fires dowsed at night. Ridge and furrow grassland was broken up using a 'ridge-breaker' which simply split the ridges in two and tipped the soil into the furrows either side.

Nardey Bush near Whitchurch, a shooting ground and fox covert owned by Alscot Estate, and Crimscote Downs were reclaimed in 1943 despite protestations about disturbing the foxes. The grounds of Ettington Park, mainly scrubland, were also ploughed up with crawlers.

Daylight Saving was extended by an extra hour in summer. Harvey Smith of Lower Farm believed this was too much for the livestock, so he kept two clocks: one set to the 'correct' time and one an hour earlier to manage the farm work.

A drive to bring tractors, combine harvesters and other machinery onto the farms pushed farmers forcibly into the mechanised era. The number of tractors tripled during the war years. They were originally painted orange but these were an easy target for the Luftwaffe, who would bomb stockpiled machines and strafe them in the fields, so they were later painted green for camouflage.

In August 1940, Warwickshire was told to plough another 100,000 acres of land, amidst protests from the National Farmers' Union. Much of the land was heavy clay, hopeless for growing any sort of crop. The NFU said many farmers, especially livestock farmers with no experience of growing cereals or root crops, would be forced into ruin, and the land was best left as pasture. It had little effect.

Potatoes and sugar beet were priority crops with each farm given quotas.

Potatoes were spun out of the ground by machine then picked up by hand, often a women's and children's job. Sugar beet was lifted by hand in winter. This was often done by prisoners of war. Eric Reason of Alderminster, who was held prisoner of war in Germany, also spent time working at his captors' sugar beet harvest.

All out for the 1943 Harvest

This is the most critical year of our history. Hitler still aims to sink our ships–to starve us out. You are fighting the "Battle of the Fields" to defeat him. Every possible ship that might bring us food must now carry tanks and planes and guns. Every extra acre of tillage crops you can grow in 1943 will help to release ships and bring the day of victory nearer.

THE NATION MUST HAVE BREAD
– grow all the wheat and barley you possibly can.

THE NATION MUST HAVE POTATOES
– we can never have too many. They are your country's "iron rations" – an insurance against hunger and defeat.

THE NATION MUST HAVE MILK
– it is vital for young children. Grow the crops needed to keep your herd in full production, especially next winter.

These crops are vital. To make sure that the Nation gets enough of them we must plough up more grass-land that is not essential to maintain your dairy herd–any seeds area that can go into the tillage pool—must grow these war-winning crops.

Plan your part
to the
food production battle

ISSUED BY THE MINISTRY OF AGRICULTURE AND FISHERIES

From the Stratford Herald, *January 1943.*

The Women's Land Army (WLA)

The WLA, or land girls, made up much of the labour shortfall while the men were at war. The women lived on farms or in hostels and travelled to local farms as needed for harvest, threshing, root harvest and sack-making. Hostels were built at Whitehill Farm and at Long Marston. Andrew Simpson of Alderminster Farm had a land girl named Pat who lived at the farm for much of the war, doing milking, tractor work and other tasks.

Many land girls had no agricultural experience. Some were as young as seventeen and away from home for the first time. An appeal was made to the local women to help at the hostels, cleaning, preparing meals and providing sympathy and care to the young girls. Rose Horseman of Preston often had land girls round for tea.

The local Girl Guides held an annual three-week summer camp at Alderminster, where they stalked and canned plums. They processed an average of eight tonnes of fruit each day, all loaded onto lorries to be sent to serving troops.

Land girls remained at Whitehill Farm for several years. In April 1947 these included Betty Chamberlain from Chiswick, aged 18, Emily Saunders from Middlesex, and Lilian Nicholls. Betty was hit by a lorry and killed as the three girls walked back from Newbold one evening.

In December 1947, Florence Mary Isobel Hamilton of the Whitehill hostel was asked by another girl to steal her a hen for Christmas. Florence went to Elizabeth Spencer's hen house on Whitehill Farm, took a hen and wrung its neck. She appeared in Stratford Magistrates Court a month later where she was dismissed but ordered to pay £1 costs.

Land girls at Crimscote. Note the neatly thatched ricks.

Courtesy of Joan Hughes.

Mary Watts, nee Spencer (b1923) of Park Farm in Preston was working as an apprentice hairdresser when war broke out. She faced the choice of the women's forces or farm work, and returned to work on the family farm. Mary's first job each morning was feeding the calves, kept in the old stables. This involved lighting a fire under a copper in the old wash house, heating water, making gruel and carrying it out in buckets. She grew adept at both tractor and horse-work. The bulk of the hard labour was done by the men; Mary would drive the tractor at harvest time while her brother Bob worked the binder. If there was no farm work to be done, she would work in the garden or in the house.

Mary married farmer Bertie Watts in 1946 and they moved to their own farm. Her new skills proved very useful; the work force comprised only Bertie and herself.

The threshing engine owned by Austin Izard of Quinton, at Home Farm Wimpstone, 1944. Pictured are Betty Staines; Austin Izard; Reg Ashby; Joan Allen; Bert Morse. Both women were land girls who worked for Austin Izard.

Courtesy of Richard Parnham.

The Pig Club

Pig Clubs surged in popularity during the war years. Preston and District Pig Club was formed around 1940, and by 1946 had swelled to 110 members from Preston, Alderminster, Clifford Chambers and Atherstone. Members would rear a pig and have a supply of meat when the animal was slaughtered, in return for giving a quantity of the meat to the government and forgoing their meat coupons. Members pooled their expertise in pig-keeping. Many houses had their own pigsties and others were kept in yards and gardens. They were fed on household scraps and vegetable peelings.

Each member paid an annual four-shilling membership fee which included an allocation of meal or corn, purchased in bulk by the committee, and insurance should their pig die. In 1946 it was decided that a member of the committee had to inspect and approve each pig before it was insured, as three members had claimed for pigs that year.

Schoolmaster Harry Lord was the secretary until his death in 1942, then replaced by accountant Bob Stredder. The secretary had to be notified if a pig were slaughtered or sold, and the necessary forms dealt with. Baker Percy Beavington was the treasurer, and the sacks of meal were kept in one of the outbuildings next to the bakery. William Fletcher was the village pig-killer or 'pig-sticking man', helped by gamekeeper Bill Noyce. The pig, weighing up to twenty stone, had to be tied up, its mouth secured so it couldn't bite, and manhandled onto a pig-killing bench for the job to be done. The blood was collected for black pudding – every part of the pig could be used except the squeak – and the carcass was singed over a fire to remove the bristles, scrubbed with boiling water then butchered. Offal was eaten quickly; the bladder was blown up to make a football; the larger joints were salted and hung by the fireplace or from bacon racks.

The Pig Club was still attracting a good attendance in 1948. Mrs Isolde West was now the president; former mayor Robert Mansell Smith and his brother-in-law Cecil Lees from Mansell Farm were vice presidents; farm worker Eric Dale was secretary and army veteran Peter Jones treasurer. It was disbanded as obsolete shortly afterwards.

Preston and District Pig Club cup.

The Army after Dunkirk

After the fall of France, Britain was standing alone in Europe against Germany, and new theatres of war opened in North Africa and the Far East. A new modern army was developed which eventually comprised three million men and 300,000 women.

The National Service (No.2) Act of December 1941 decreed that all men aged 18-60 should be in some sort of national service, and also that unmarried women aged 21-30 were eligible for call up. The women could choose between industries such as ammunition or aircraft factories; agriculture; civil defence; or the women's armed services. The latter comprised the ATS (Auxiliary Territorial Service), WRNS (Women's Royal Naval Service or Wrens) and WAAF (Women's Auxiliary Air Force). They worked as clerks, storekeepers, telephonists and drivers; operated searchlights, radar, communication systems and anti-aircraft guns; packed parachutes and crewed barrage balloons.

Joan Ashby, later Spencer (b1914) was the daughter of farmer Arthur Ashby of Wimpstone. She trained as a secretary and excelled at shorthand and typing. She worked in a garage in Stratford then joined the ATS. Her sister Olive (b1920) served in the WRNS, and their sister Kath (b1909) who had been captain of the Whitchurch Girl Guides, served with the Girl Guides International doing relief work in Europe.

Joan spent time at Donnington Park in Leicestershire, a former motorcycle circuit requisitioned as a military vehicle storage depot, and her secretarial skills were put to good use. She was often woken in the night to minute important meetings and prepare faultless documentation. She was outstandingly efficient with an extremely pleasant personality, was promoted to lance corporal and was awarded a certificate of merit in September 1943. She was demobilised in 1946.

Olive spent several years in Glendower in North Wales where she reached the rank of chief petty officer. Here she met her future husband, sailor Joe Parnham. She was demobilised in February 1946.

Audrey Bishop of Rough Farm (b1919) worked for the National Farmers' Union in Stratford and was then called up for the ATS.

Diana Walsh, later Langley, who spent her later life at No.6 Alderminster, served in the WAAF. She worked as a radar operator and spent a lot of her service at the naval base in Orkney.

Left: Joan Ashby, ATS. Right: Olive Ashby, WRNS.
Courtesy of Richard Parnham.

Joan Canning, later Hughes, was the daughter of Thomas and Kathleen Canning. Thomas, a First World War veteran, owned Crimscote Fields Farm and sett up business in Edgbaston. Joan joined the WRNS in November 1942 and served as a radar operator at RAF and naval bases around the UK. She was noted as a sensible and reliable rating and able to take responsibility. She was sent to Ceylon in July 1944 where she worked in the naval offices at a racecourse with Tamil clerks. She married Lieutenant Commander Ian Hughes on 13th August 1945 at Colombo and left Ceylon a month later. She was demobilised in November 1945.

Ian, originally from Fife in Scotland, spent time on HM Submarine *Trenchant* in the Far East. Its most significant action of the war was the sinking of the Japanese cruiser *Ashigara*, carrying 1600 Japanese troops, in the Bangka Straits in June 1945. Shortly after this, Ian was awarded the Distinguished Service Cross for gallantry and meritorious service in Burma and was Mentioned in Dispatches for 'courage and initiative while engaged in secret hazardous operations'. This may have been related to the *Ashigara* sinking.

Joan and Ian returned to Crimscote Fields and spent many years in the large-scale rearing of chickens. Joan was later awarded the MBE.

Left: Joan Canning in 1942. Right: Joan and Ian Hughes' wedding in Colombo, 1945.

Courtesy of Gay Jennions.

Heron	Wren	S	Radar	M	4 Jan 44	3 July 44	
HMS Pembroke III	Wren	S	Radar (G.C.I.)	M	4 July	17 July	
HMS BHERUNDA.	WREN	Spec:	RADAR OPERATOR	M	18th July 1944	4th October 1944	
HMS HIGHFLYER	WREN	Spec:	RADAR OPERATOR	M	5th October 1944	20 April 1945	Pay
HMS UKUSSA	WREN.	SPEC.	RADAR.	M.	21/4/45	15/9/45	RELEASED IN CLASS "A"
H.M.S. VICTORY IV P.D.D.	Wren	AFO 1050/45	Radar Operator	M.	16 Sept 1945	13 Jan 1946	Suitable for re-entry

Extract from Joan Canning's service record. HMS Bherunda, HMS Highflyer and HMS Ukussa were naval naval bases in Ceylon.

Courtesy of Gay Jennions.

The North African Campaign

Britain, France and Italy all had colonies in North Africa. Libya was an Italian colony; Egypt a British protectorate; Algeria, Tunisia and Morocco were French colonies now ruled by a Nazi-controlled puppet government. British troops were stationed in Egypt, maintaining security with occasional action against local factions.

Italy declared war on Britain and France on 10th June 1940, aiming to capture the British and French territories in North Africa. British troops crossed from Egypt to Libya a few days later and captured some Italian positions. In December 1940, after several months of fighting, the Italian army was crushed. The British advanced 500 miles into Libya and captured 130,000 POWs, the first decisive British victory of the war. In February 1941, Erwin Rommel and the German Afrika Korps were dispatched to North Africa to reinforce the Italians. Rommel began his offensive a month later and the Allied forces, known as the Eighth Army, were gradually forced back into Egypt. The fighting continued for the next year, with both sides repeatedly gaining and losing ground.

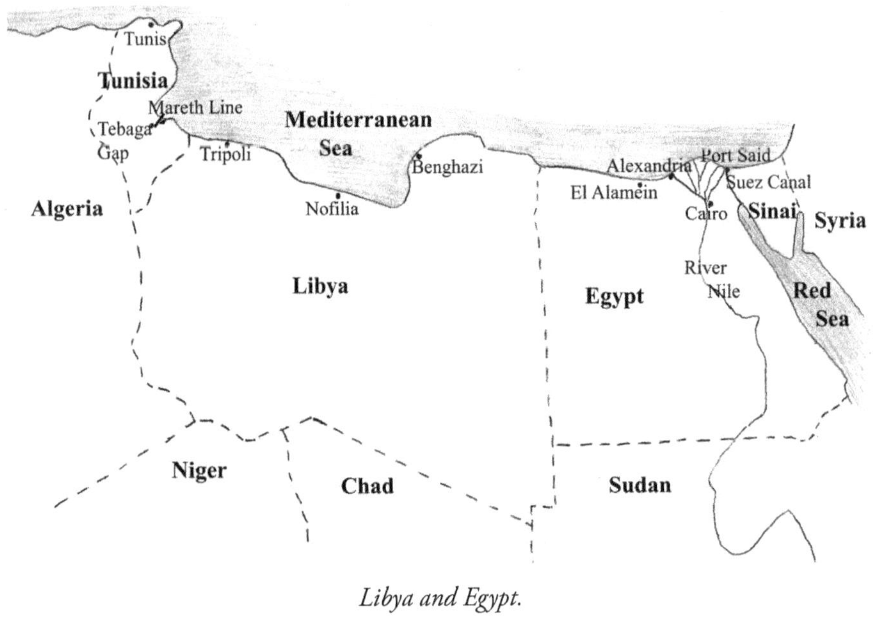

Libya and Egypt.

Leslie Francis (b1918) was the son of Frank Francis, who spent several years as farm manager to Alan James of Whitchurch Farm. Leslie was serving in the Warwickshire Yeomanry, a territorial cavalry unit, when war was declared. He arrived in the Middle East in January 1940. He was now a sergeant in D Squadron. The desert was one of the few theatres where horse cavalry still had any advantage: motorised vehicles frequently got bogged down in the sand.

Albert Horseman (b1920) and Francis (Frankie) Horseman (b1922) were the sons of William and Ruth Horseman of Preston. Both brothers also served in the Warwickshire Yeomanry during the war but their service history is unclear.

George Nason, serving with the 192nd anti-aircraft battery, left Liverpool

Leslie Francis in 1939.
Courtesy of Ray Francis.

for Egypt in March 1941. At first he delighted in the scenery and wrote enthusiastically of the Nile and the pyramids. But as the months passed, his diary entries grew more homesick and melancholic. He missed his sweetheart Molly and wrote long reminiscences of the Warwickshire countryside.

Wilfred Newey, with the 69th anti-aircraft battery, arrived in Egypt to join the Eighth Army in November 1941 and saw action throughout Libya. Now acting lieutenant colonel, he was awarded the Distinguished Service Order (DSO) in April 1942.

The Warwickshire Yeomanry were converted to a tank regiment in October 1941. Over the next year they spent time in Iraq, Syria, Persia and Palestine, mainly training in their new roles. Leslie Francis was promoted to SSM (Squadron Sergeant Major) and was then commissioned into the Royal Scots Greys, another tank regiment in the Eighth Army.

Bill Simms, who had been evacuated from Dunkirk, also joined the Eighth Army in Egypt. He drove a truck but his unit is unclear.

Walter Henry Hathaway (b1918), the brother of Dunkirk veteran Bert Hathaway, lived at No.16 Alderminster and worked as a baker at Valender's bakery. His uncle of the same name had been killed on active service a month before his birth. He spent time in North Africa and Malta but nothing else is known of his service history.

The Grand Old Clock of England Chimes On and On

When Mars again from slumber rose and loosed the dogs of war
When evil birds with wings outspread attacked our peaceful shore
When over the seas foul death appeared and chilled the hearts of men
A sound there rose that spurred them on, the chimes of old Big Ben

Above the roofs of London town, above the river's wall
Above Westminster's stately pile, the abbey and the hall
Above the fears of those below, when home and hearth were gone
The grand old clock of England chimed, chimed on and on and on

They sought to smash it from its tower, they sought its voice to still
By night, by day, they struck again, to force their Fuhrer's will
Upon that dauntless grand old face, so dear to England's men
But still the chimes went pealing out, the chimes of old Big Ben

The word went forth from Nazi chiefs to all their flying spawn
That come what may that tower must go, before another dawn
Their foul birds came and struck again, their countless bombs screamed down
But England's grand clock chimed out, chimed on and on and on

So desperation seized the Hun, in towering wrath he swore
To smash that clock at any cost, to hasten on his war
And so once more the brood flew out and crossed the seas again
To still the heart of London town, the chimes of old Big Ben

They hurled destruction from the air, they wrecked the streets nearby
In frenzied hate their bombs lit up then blackened out the sky
But through the smoke pall and the glow, the peals rang out 'ding dong'
As England's grand old clock chimed out, chimed on and on and on

And so throughout the world today, a voice calls loud and clear
That seems to speak to all free men and bids them have no fear
From Norway's icy northern coast to Grieves hill and fen
The voice calls out for faith and hope, the voice of old Big Ben

It matters not, it calls to us, if all our buildings fall
If now we're fighting dogged with our backs against the wall
It only matters that out faith stays dauntless till we've won
Thus in our hearts Big Ben chimes out, chimes on and on and on.

A poem written by George Nason in July 1941.

The British began to suffer catastrophic defeats. In May 1942, the Eighth Army lost 30,000 men captured along with vast stores of rations and petrol. The First Battle of El Alamein a month later checked Rommel's onslaught, less than a hundred miles from the vital assets of Alexandria and the Suez Canal. Lieutenant General Bernard Montgomery then took over command. Bill Simms was proud to meet him on one occasion.

The Second Battle of El Alamein began on 23rd October. It was the first British offensive for two years and proved a turning point. The battle, predominantly between artillery and tanks, lasted for twelve days. Wilfred Newey's battery was involved in the fighting, as was George Nason's battery and the Warwickshire Yeomanry who were now operating Sherman tanks.

A huge five-day barrage opened on the German minefields then the armoured troops began to advance. The Scots Greys were part of a diversionary attack to the south. The Warwickshire Yeomanry were held up by a minefield which hadn't been cleared by the barrage, and after limited success the army was ordered back.

Another attempt was planned. The advance began during the early hours of the 2nd November after a four-hour barrage, but again the minefields caused delays. The Yeomanry were caught exposed in daylight and were slowly picked off by enemy shells. By 10am, only seven of their tanks were still operating.

The attack pushed on over several days. Rommel's tanks were slowly picked off, but the British were in a poor state with endless breakdowns. Then the Afrika Korps broke and was driven west towards Tunisia.

The Scots Greys followed the retreat for the next 1½ months. Their only major action was on 15th December at the village of Nofilia in Libya. They overran the village's defences and captured many POWs, then thirty German tanks entered the fray. The subsequent engagement was inconclusive, with losses on both sides, but the Germans withdrew. The Scots Greys were withdrawn from the front in January 1943. The Eighth Army pushed on through Libya and reached the Tunisian border in March. Then the campaign to conquer Tunisia began.

Eric Reason (b1915) was the only son of farm worker Bill Reason and his wife Mary of The Old Thatch in Preston. Eric worked as a painter for Alscot Estate, married Connie Southam in 1939 and moved to Alderminster. He enlisted into the 7th Oxford and Bucks Light Infantry in May 1940. They sailed for an unknown destination in August 1942. Eric's wife was now pregnant with their first child.

A month later, Table Mountain in South Africa came into view, and the men had a few days to experience the delights of Cape Town. A few weeks later they arrived in Bombay, their final destination still under speculation. At the beginning of November they arrived at Basra. They travelled to Baghdad, then crossed the Syrian Desert, the Jordan River, the Sinai Desert and the Suez Canal. They reached the Eighth Army in Tunisia at the end of April 1943 after a 3000-mile overland journey.

The German and Italian forces were holding a line of fortifications across Tunisia known as the Mareth Line. The Eighth Army went south to a mountain pass called the Tebaga Gap to outflank these positions. On 9th May the 7th Ox Bucks took part in fighting here. The Gap was breached and the army closed in on Rommel's forces. They were forced to surrender and on 13th May the war in North Africa was declared over.

Eric Reason, Oxford and Bucks Light Infantry.
Courtesy of Chris Daniell.

Leslie Francis returned to England where he became a tank gunnery instructor for the rest of the war, and much of the Eighth Army was transferred to in Italy. Wilfred Newey's battery left for Italy in October 1943. The Warwickshire Yeomanry arrived in Italy in May 1944 after a year of refitting in Egypt. The 7th Ox and Bucks, including Eric Reason, were also sent to Italy.

George Nason went to Italy where he reached the rank of bombardier (corporal) and remained until the end of the war. On one occasion he guarded Italian POWs on a recently surrendered warship which gave George a view of Vesuvius. He also spent time in Rome and visited the opera. He got back late to camp and was challenged by the guard. 'Is that you, George Nason?' The guard was also from his home village of Ettington.

The Sicily and Italy Campaigns

In July 1943, following the successful campaign in Northern Africa, Britain mounted an invasion of Sicily which was captured in September, and then the

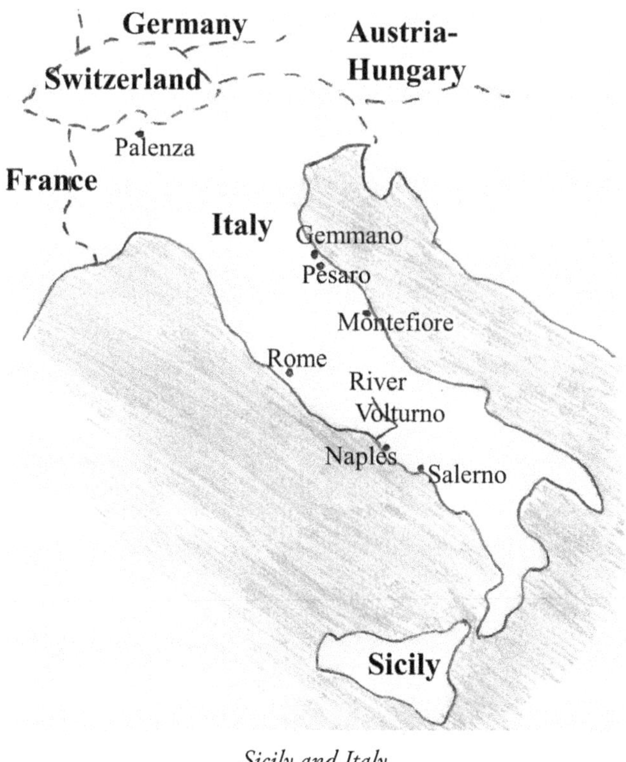

Sicily and Italy.

Allied forces landed in Italy. The Italians at once surrendered and the Allies faced the German army.

Reverend Montague Laban Hunt had been appointed vicar of Preston and Whitchurch in 1930. He was a Civil Service clerk's son from London and had been among the earliest volunteers in September 1914, enlisting in the Royal Field Artillery aged seventeen and serving in France. After his demobilisation he attended Leeds Clergy School. He reenlisted in the army after the outbreak of war and served as a chaplain to the forces in Italy, where he remained for much of the war.

Eric Reason with the 7th Ox Bucks spent some time training in the Libyan mountains then embarked for Italy on 5th September 1943. They reached Salerno three days later. An assault landing was intended to capture Naples. The invading force of infantry and tanks faced heavy German opposition but landed and made slow advances. Bitter fighting lasted for ten days as the Germans made ferocious attempts to force them back. Eventually the beachhead was secured. The campaign then made slow progress across Italy with heavy losses. The 7th Ox Bucks saw more action at the Volturno, and Rome fell in June 1944. The Allies then advanced rapidly but the Germans rushed reinforcements into Italy and formed a line of defence across the mountains near Pesaro. Breaking this line was essential. On 27th August, 7th Ox Bucks went into battle.

The British advanced against a surprised and confused enemy. The Allies pressed home the advantage. The 7th Ox Bucks advanced into German minefields, and on 3rd September were ordered to attack the small but strategically important hillside village of Montefiore at first light the next morning.

The enemy had reinforced their positions and the fighting lasted all day before the village was taken. Several counterattacks were unsuccessfully mounted and the Allies were shelled. Casualties for the 7th Ox Bucks were light, but Eric Reason was reported missing, believed taken prisoner. Two months later he was confirmed a prisoner in Germany. He was taken to Stalag 11A, an *arbeitskommando* or work camp near Berlin. He had served as a sniper, for which the Germans would have likely shot him, as happened to his comrade. He asked to go to the latrine, and as no guards came with him he dropped his incriminating papers into the hole.

The Geneva Convention agreed that POWs could be set to work of non-military nature, and Eric had to work eighteen-hour days harvesting sugar beet

ALDERMINSTER MAN BELIEVED PRISONER

News has been received that Pte. E. J. Reason, of Alderminster, is missing and is believed to be a prisoner of war. Formerly employed on the Alscot Estate, he had served in Italy for 11 months. Mrs. Reason has one child, born just after her husband went abroad.

From the Stratford Herald, 27th October 1944.

on German farms. Despite international rules regarding the treatment of POWs, they had little food and no beds, blankets or washing facilities. Eric didn't remove his clothes or boots during his imprisonment and had lice constantly crawling through his clothing. He once pulled a handful of grass to eat on his way to the field and got a rifle butt in his stomach.

On 3rd May 1945, the Americans reached the camp with truckloads of rations and medical teams. Five days later on VE Day, the camp was officially liberated. Eric was then flown home by the Americans.

The South East Asia Campaign

The Japanese Empire invaded the French colonies in the Far East in September 1940. On 7th December 1941, they bombed Pearl Harbour – which brought the USA into the war and ultimately decided its outcome – and attacked Hong Kong, the Philippines, Thailand, Singapore and Malaya. Hong Kong fell on 25th December. Singapore surrendered in February 1942 with 130,000 British personnel taken prisoner. Japan then invaded the British colony of Burma in January 1942. The capital city, Rangoon, fell in March and the British were evacuated. Preparations were made for a Japanese invasion of India.

Reginald Henry Maton (b1921) was the eldest son of Ernest and Emily Maton of Preston. Emily, nee Horseman, had married Ernest in 1915 while he was serving in the Royal Navy.

Reg worked for the Alscot Estate then for a builder in Stratford. He was of

The South East Asia Campaign.

a jolly disposition and respected by everyone in the village. He enlisted in the Royal Warwickshire Regiment and later transferred to the 1st Royal Berkshire Regiment. He went to India in January 1943.

Cyril William Wood (b1918) was the son of Ernest Wood of Alderminster. He married Mary Day, daughter of Preston woodsman Jack Day, in 1937 and the couple lived with Jack at No.51 where their two sons were born. Cyril worked as a carpenter and enlisted in the army at some point after 1943. He served in India and Burma and reached the rank of sergeant. He may have served in the East Lancashire Regiment and spent time with the 11th (East Africa) Infantry Division. This was formed mainly of colonial troops from East Africa; Cyril was probably seconded to this division.

Figure 78. Left: Cyril Wood. The rhino insignia is the 11th (East Africa) Infantry Division.

Courtesy of Dave Wood.

Right: Reg Maton.

John Bishop (b1917) of Rough Farm served in the military police and spent most of the war in India.

William Haylock (b1918) was originally from Burton on Trent but was living in Alderminster by 1939. He worked for Messrs Bosley and Harper in

Shipston and was also the church organist. He was called up in early 1940, around the time of his marriage to local girl Muriel Sutcliffe, and joined the 1st Cambridgeshire Regiment. His unit fought in the Malayan campaign and the Battle for Singapore, in which they defended their position for two days before being ordered to surrender to the Japanese when Singapore fell on 15th February 1942. William was reported missing in action on this day; over two years later in August 1944, he was finally reported a POW in Japanese hands in Thailand. He remained in captivity until October 1945, when he returned to Alderminster. While in captivity William had suffered diphtheria, jaundice, eighteen attacks of malaria, four of dysentery, and other illnesses besides. This, he later stated, was a clean sheet: he'd never had cholera or beriberi. The *Herald* reported: *'Although not fully restored to health, his physical condition is surprisingly good while his spirit is impaired.'* His subsequent future is unclear.

Michael Alston-Roberts-West (b1905) was the younger brother of Reggie West, killed in action in May 1940. Michael went to Sandhurst in 1923 and was commissioned into the Oxford and Bucks Light Infantry two years later. Like his brother, he was a keen sportsman and was an army champion for the ¼ mile and the high jump. He went to India in 1935, and by 1939 was ranked a major. In 1942 he was promoted to lieutenant colonel and placed in command of the 2nd South Lancashire Regiment, which was dispatched to Madagascar for his first major operation of the war.

In April 1942, the Japanese forced the British Eastern Fleet from Ceylon to Kenya. Both sides then looked towards Madagascar. This was a French colony now controlled by the Nazis, and if Japan gained control it would be a base for attacking the British fleet and the ships supplying the Eighth Army. Britain decided to occupy it as a precaution.

The Battle of Madagascar began on 5th May 1942 with an amphibious landing of British troops, including Michael West and the 2nd South Lancashire Regiment. The French had good defences and the British were soon at deadlock. After some hard fighting they managed to break through, and then the fighting was all but over. Low levels of fighting with minimal casualties lasted for several months, the French aided by Japanese ships and submarines, then the capital city was captured and an armistice was signed on 6th November. Michael West was Mentioned in Dispatches for gallant and distinguished service.

The Allies made repeated attempts to liberate Burma over the next two years.

The impenetrable jungle terrain was plagued with mosquitoes; there was no transport infrastructure; and the monsoon season limited campaigning to six months a year.

Reginald Maton arrived in Chittagong, near the Burma border, in January 1943. By May the battalion had moved to south-west India for jungle training. They remained for nearly a year then moved to Assam district on the India-Burma border. A Japanese invasion was imminent.

In March 1944, the Japanese invaded India, aiming for the major cities of Imphal and Kohima. A British counter-offensive began and bitter fighting lasted for three months.

The Battle of Kohima began on 4th April. The Japanese captured the Kohima Ridge which dominated the British supply road. The British were under siege, enduring constant shellfire and running short of water and supplies. The Japanese occupied well-dug and well-hidden bunkers which withstood any attempt to take them. The monsoon, starvation and disease took its toll on both sides. The steep, muddy hillsides made progress near impossible. The 1st Berks entered the battle near Kohima on 20th April and endured three weeks of fighting in horrendous conditions, suffering nearly 50% casualties.

Michael West, now a brigadier, arrived in Burma in May to command the 5th Infantry Brigade. Later cited as one of the finest tactical brains at Kohima, he was instrumental to orchestrating the eventual breakthrough. The British made gradual progress and the Japanese, now at the limit of their endurance, began to retreat. When Kohima Ridge was taken it had become a rat- and fly-infested wilderness with half-buried human remains everywhere.

The Battle of Kohima ended with British victory on 22nd June. It was a turning point for the campaign and is now considered Britain's greatest battle. Michael West was awarded a bar to the Distinguished Service Order for his services.

In November 1944, the Allies began their campaign to recapture Burma. The 11th (East Africa) Division, possibly including Cyril Wood, were involved in driving the Japanese from Imphal, and fought in decisive battles which led to the recapture of Rangoon and the liberation of Burma in May 1945.

On 1st January 1945 the 1st Berks moved to Taze in north Burma. On 3rd January Reg Maton wrote to Blanche Taylor, nee Reason, a childhood friend. He was more than pleased to have news from home and to know people were still thinking of him, despite being so long away. *'I shall be pleased to get back home. Preston is only a small place but it is home to me.'*

He wrote wistfully about how his family was growing up: *'I have two sisters married, Rene and Rose, and I shall have to look out else I shall be left behind. But all I want is to get this war over with so we can all get back to normal.'*

The next day the battalion went into action. Reg was one of five members of his unit to be killed. He was 24 years old. He was buried in the Taukkyan War Cemetery and is remembered on Preston War Memorial.

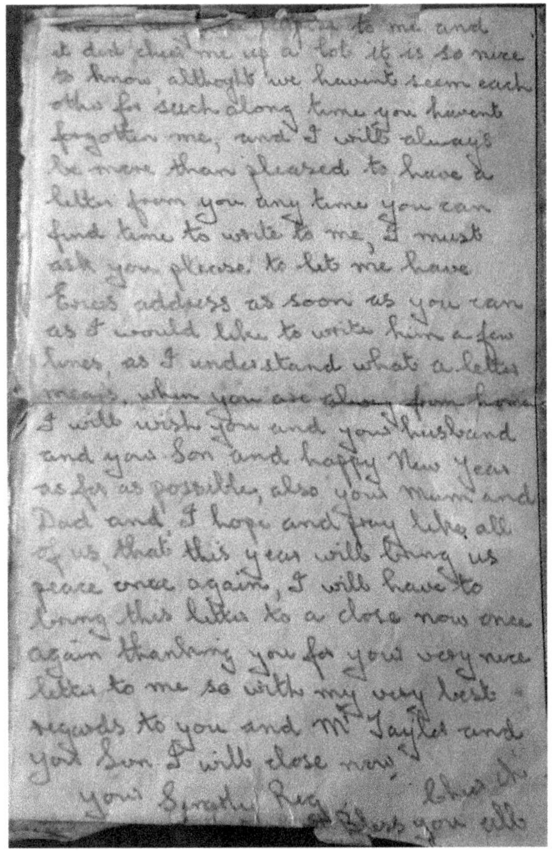

to me and
it did cheer me up a lot it is so nice
to know although we havent seen each
other for such a long time you havent
forgotten me, and I will always
be more than pleased to have a
letter from you any time you can
find time to write to me, I must
ask you please to let me have
Erics address as soon as you can
as I would like to write him a few
lines, as I understand what a letter
means, when you are away from home
I will wish you and your husband
and your Son and happy New Year
as far as possible, also your Mum and
Dad and I hope and pray like all
of us, that this year will bring us
peace once again, I will have to
bring this letter to a close now once
again thanking you for your very nice
letter to me so with my very best
regards to you and Mr Taylor and
your Son I will close now,
Yours Sincerely Reg
God Bless you all

Extract from a letter written by Reg Maton to Blanche Taylor.
Courtesy of Chris Daniell.

The Royal Navy

Thomas John Bloxham (b1910) was the son of John and Lucy Bloxham of Atherstone. John worked in the Alscot gardens and eventually became head gardener. Thomas' elder brother Francis, born shortly before his parents' marriage, had enlisted in the Worcestershire Regiment and died of tuberculosis in 1933, aged 24.

Thomas worked as a farm labourer then enlisted in the Royal Navy as a boy sailor in October 1926. He transferred to the men's Navy on his eighteenth birthday in January 1928. His first spell on board a ship was on the *Emperor of India*, a battleship of the Atlantic fleet. He was of very good character and served as an Ordinary Telegraphist, operating the ship's signalling systems. He married Gladys Blanchard in Guildford in August 1933. He was now serving on HMS *Nelson* and he was given an oak clock from the ship's wireless staff. In 1939 he transferred to the Fleet Air Arm which operated the naval aircraft, and was seconded to the RAF Fighter Command. He served as a telegraphist at HMS *Peregrine*, a Royal Naval Air Station in Sussex, then transferred to HMS *Daedalus* in Dorset where he was promoted to leading seaman. He spent a few months in 1943 at HMS *Goshawk,* a station in Trinidad, then returned to the UK where he was promoted to petty officer. He remained in various stations in the UK and Northern Ireland for the remainder of the war.

James Hathaway (b1910) was the son of Arthur and Ruth Hathaway of Alderminster. He worked as a gardener then enlisted in the Royal Navy on the same day as Thomas Bloxham. He transferred to the men's Navy for a twelve-year period in December 1928 and spent a year on board the *Emperor of India.* His service history from this point is unclear.

Joseph Parnham (b1916) was a coalminer's son from Derbyshire. He wanted to see the world rather than go down the pit, so he enlisted in the Navy in 1934. He served on the heavy cruiser HMS *Norfolk* in the East Indies Station from 1935-1937, operating in the Indian Ocean and the Persian Gulf as far as East Africa, India and China. He then joined the battleship HMS *Rodney* in 1938 where he remained for most of the war. The *Rodney* spent time on convoy duties in the Atlantic, then in May 1941 she joined the hunt for the *Bismarck,* one of the most powerful warships in the world. After withering bombardment from several ships including the *Rodney,* the *Bismarck* was scuttled by her own crew.

The *Rodney* then went to Boston in America to have her boilers repaired while the crew enjoyed a long shore leave in the land of plenty. As the city was home to a lot of German immigrants, the sailors received a mixed welcome. Some went into a German bar by mistake and were speedily ejected.

The *Rodney* provided coastal bombardments for the North African Campaign in 1942-43 and the D-Day landings in June 1944, and Joe was also involved in the Arctic convoys to Russia, Britain's ally and under blockade by the Nazi fleet. The convoys, which ran between 1941 and 1945, took food, fuel, armaments and weapons to the northern Russian ports, primarily Murmansk, facing severe trials from German ships, sea ice, treacherous currents and, in winter, constant darkness. While at Murmansk, Russian lorries arrived with crates of gold which was loaded onto the *Rodney* under heavy guard. This was payment for the goods supplied. Joe also visited Iceland, where Churchill once stopped to address the troops.

Joe was then stationed at Glendower in North Wales from 1945 until his demobilisation in February 1946, where he met Wren Olive Ashby of Wimpstone, who would later become his wife.

Petty Officer Joe Parnham, with two Good Conduct badges, 1944.
Courtesy of Richard Parnham.

Charles Lindsay Keighly-Peach (b1902) was the son of naval veteran Charles William Keighly-Peach, formerly of Alderminster Lodge. He became a naval cadet in January 1916 aged thirteen, and was awarded the Meritorious Service Medal in 1919. In April 1925, now a lieutenant, he received a temporary

Joe Parnham (2nd left) with other Royal and US Navy personnel and some local girls in Boston, July 1944.

Courtesy of Richard Parnham.

commission into the RAF as a flying officer and flew Woodcocks, a new night fighter aircraft. In 1927 he transferred to the Fleet Air Arm, which operated the Navy's aircraft, and spent time on HMS *M2,* a submarine aircraft carrier, flying Parnall Peto seaplanes. In 1932 he was promoted to lieutenant commander, then commander in 1938.

He commanded the Royal Naval Air Station at Lee on Solent between 1939 and 1940, then returned to sea to command HMS *Eagle*, an aircraft carrier based in the Mediterranean. The *Eagle* destroyed a number of Italian ships and aircraft – Charles himself shot down five enemy aircraft – and he was awarded the DSO in September 1940 for 'courage, enterprise and devotion to duty'. In September 1941 he was appointed OBE for 'skill and judgement in directing operations on HMS *Eagle* which led to the sinking or scuttling of the Italian Destroyer Force in the Red Sea'. He was made captain in 1943 and the following year was appointed commander of HMS *Heron*, the naval fighter school in Somerset, and then RNAS *Changi*, a naval base in Singapore, where he remained for the remainder of the war.

Albert Porter was the son of Aubrey Porter of Preston. His elder brother Will had been killed in action in 1918. He joined the Navy as a boy sailor during the First World War. He was awarded the Long Service and Good Conduct Medal in 1934 and a year later he was promoted to petty officer. He was now married with three children. He served on HMS *Nelson* between 1935 and 1938. He served throughout the Second World War and was involved in the convoys to Russia. He retired from the Navy in October 1945.

William (Bill) Paxton (b1914) was the son of William Paxton of Preston, who had been killed in action in France in July 1916. He married Ruth Ashby of Home Farm in Wimpstone in 1936 and had one son. He enlisted in the Royal Army Medical Corps and spent much of his service on board troop ships, travelling as far afield as South America, Canada, New Zealand and Australia as wounded personnel were taken home.

Left: Petty Officer Albert Porter with three good conduct badges; the Defence Medal (First World War); the second unknown; and the Naval Long Service and Good Conduct Medal. Courtesy of Maurice Porter.

Right: William Paxton on board a troop ship. Courtesy of Richard Parnham.

Alderminster School adopted the destroyer HMS *Verity*, which spent much of the war in convoy defence, took troops from Dunkirk where she took casualties from coastal guns, and escorted military convoys to North Africa in 1942 where she rescued troops from a stricken ship. The children wrote to the crew and knitted them socks and scarves. The captain later visited the school to thank them, and gave them an ensign which was displayed on important occasions, one being the Queen's coronation in 1953.

The Royal Airforce

William Leslie James, known as Sam (b1921) was the second son of Alan Maxwell and Alice James of Whitchurch Farm. He worked on the family farm then left to join the RAF at an early stage in the war. He served at first as ground crew, then became a member of the air crew. He trained as a flight engineer, monitoring the engines and aircraft systems. Without constant attention, the engines and propellers were prone to failure in flight. He spent six weeks training at RAF Sandtoft in Lincolnshire in summer 1944, practicing circuits, landings, cross-country flying, bombing and air-to-sea bombing. In September 1944 he moved to 166 Squadron at RAF Kirmington, then a month later moved to 153 Squadron at RAF Scampton in Lincolnshire and was on bombing operations within a week.

Sgt Sam James.

Courtesy of Joan James.

Sam's first operational flight was to the French port of Le Havre on 10th September 1944. Over the next month he flew on several more operations including bombing raids on marshalling yards at Frankfurt; emplacements at Calais; coastal guns in Holland; and an air-to-sea firing mission. On 15th October he was transferred to 153 Squadron, which was based in RAF Scampton in Lincolnshire and flew Lancaster bombers. He flew on missions to Cologne; the Urft Dam in Germany; Dresden; Denmark; railways yards at Bonn; and an oil plant at Meresburg. On a nine-hour mission to Munich on 7th January 1945, the last 5h 20m were flown on three engines, a very testing time for the flight engineer.

On 3rd March 1945 Sam flew his 34th operation, laying mines off the coast of Denmark. The crew took off that evening with four other Lancasters, and failed to return. The area was subject to heavy and accurate flak and also night-fighter activity, and other crews reported an aircraft was shot down into the sea. No trace of the aircraft or crew was found, and six months after his death, Sam's father received official notification that: *'In view of the time which has elapsed since your son, 941154 Sergeant W.L. James, was reported missing and the absence of evidence of his survival, it must be concluded that he has lost his life.'*

Sam, who was 23, and the other six crew are commemorated on the Runnymede Memorial in Surrey for Airforce personnel with no known grave.

The crew from 153 Squadron. Courtesy of Joan James. Those in bold lost their lives on 3rd March 1945. Back: Unknown crewman; **F/O Leo Gregoire***; unknown crewman;* **FSgt John Sabine; Sgt Sam James***; W/O Cosby; unknown crewman;* **W/O Kenneth McCoy**. *Front:* **W/O Douglas McGregor; P/O William Webber; W/O Marvin Sandomirsky.**

Tel. No.: GERRARD 9234, Ext.

Correspondence on the subject of this letter should be addressed to THE UNDER SECRETARY OF STATE AIR MINISTRY [P.4 (Cas.)], and should quote the reference

P.430070/L/P.4.A.3.

Your Ref.

AIR MINISTRY
73-77 OXFORD STREET
LONDON, W.1

11th January, 1946.

Sir,

I am directed to refer to your letter of 24th November, 1945, and to say that the Lancaster aircraft in which your son was flying, was one of five which left base on the night of 3rd March, 1945, to carry out a sea-mining operation in the sea area between Aebestoft Peninsular, Samsö Island and Sjaelland, Denmark.

The enemy defences consisted of slight light anti aircraft fire, with searchlights co-operating; no news has however been received which would indicate the reason for the aircraft's failure to return, nor has anything been heard of any of the occupants.

With reference to your enquiry as to the circumstances in which your son and the other members of the crew were briefed for this particular operation, I am to say that this Branch is not in a position to reply to such questions; enquiries are however, being made of your son's Squadron, and should it be possible to obtain information, a further letter on the subject will be addressed to you.

I am, Sir,
Your obedient Servant,

[signature]

for Director of Personal Services.

A.M. James, Esq.,
Whitchurch,
Stratford-on-Avon,
Warwickshire.

Memorial for Sam James in Whitchurch church.

John Edward James (b1918) of Whitchurch Farm was Sam's elder brother. He worked in the accounts department for the National Farmers' Union. He was called up for the RAF, did his basic training and was sent to Algiers in North Africa, where local belly dancers made a lasting impression on him. He served in the RAF Police and returned to Whitchurch to farm after the war.

Raoul Alfred Gerald Tucker (b1916) was born in Peckham, the son of hairdresser's assistant Alfred Tucker and his wife Edith. Raoul was living in Whitchurch by the 1940s and enlisted into the RAF Volunteer Reserve in 1940. By August 1942 had reached the rank of flight sergeant. He was then commissioned as a pilot officer and in June 1943, now a flying officer, he was awarded the Airforce Cross for gallantry.

He served in No.7 Squadron which flew Short Stirling heavy bombers. The squadron flew to Rotterdam in February 1941 and on 1000-bomber raids to Cologne, Essen and Brennen in May and June 1942. The squadron was then transferred to the Pathfinder Force where it remained for the rest of the war. The Pathfinders located and marked targets and also dropped flares along the routes to aid navigation and keep the huge formations compact.

In March 1945, Raoul, now a flight lieutenant, was awarded the Distinguished Flying Cross, a more prestigious gallantry award. The citation in the *London Gazette* read: '*Flight Lieutenant Tucker has, through numerous sorties, set his example of efficiency to his squadron. He is captain of a crew whose confidence in operating is in no small measure due to his cheerful courage, skill and devotion to duty.*'

He probably remained on active service until the end of the war.

John Smith (b1920) was the son of Harvey and Nellie Smith of Lower Farm in Preston. He had little interest in farming and worked as a motor mechanic, serving an apprenticeship with a local business. He volunteered for the RAF soon after war was declared and served as an aircraft mechanic. He spent time at an airbase near London and also in France. He married Rene Guy from Uxbridge, near his base, in 1943 and had a son Neville the following year. His family saw little of him during the ensuing six years apart from when he had leave. He served until the end of the war and reached the rank of corporal.

Reg Stoppard (b1907) lived in Hall Green in Birmingham with his wife Nell and their two young children. He worked as a pay clerk in the Gas Department. His wife and children moved to Atherstone Hill Farm in 1940 to escape the

John Smith and Rene Guy's wedding, 1943. Front: Bob Smith; Janet Smith; John Smith; Rene Guy; ?; Rene's sister; Rene's mother. Back: Harry Smith; the best man; Rene's father.
Courtesy of Ruth Vanderzalm.

bombing while Reg remained in Birmingham. He was now working as a special constable as well as his day job, and could visit them only on rare occasions. He was called up for the RAF in 1942 while Nell was pregnant with their third child. He tried unsuccessfully to delay his overseas posting, and his daughter Mary was born while he was in Egypt. He remained for four years then returned to Britain. His family, including three-year-old Mary whom he hadn't yet met, travelled to Liverpool to meet his troopship.

Reg Stoppard in Egypt.
Courtesy of John Stoppard.

Cyril George (b1913) was the son of wheelwright Frederick George, originally of Preston and later of Wimpstone. Cyril was living at No.15 Wimpstone in the 1940s. He ran a radio shop in Stratford, and served in the RAF as a radio fitter. He returned to the area after the war and remained until his death in 2006.

George Randle lived in the Schoolhouse in Alderminster. He worked as a foreman bricklayer for a Stratford builder and his wife Ceretha was headmistress of Alderminster School. He was employed as a builder on the Atherstone aerodrome during the early stages of the war, then had an argument with his wife which culminated with him saying he was going to volunteer for the RAF. Ceretha said they wouldn't have him. He was enlisted shortly afterwards.

He trained as an air gunner for Lancaster bombers. He flew on 36 missions as a rear gunner but never fired a shot in anger. After VE Day he was given 48h leave – his son Rob was born nine months later – and then went to India where he spent time in Poona and New Delhi. He was now commissioned as a flight lieutenant. He returned to Alderminster on his demobilisation.

Walter Morris (b1912) was the son of ARP warden Ernest Morris of Wimpstone. He lived at No.2 Wimpstone with his wife and three children and worked as a builder. He served in the RAF, possibly as an engine fitter, and may have spent time in Italy.

William Reginald Hicks (b1912) was the son of William Charles Hicks of No.11 Alderminster, and second cousin of Reginald Hicks who was killed in 1918. William senior worked for Alscot Estate as a woodman all his life apart from during the First World War, where he did war work in Birmingham, possibly building wooden sectional buildings, and cycling home for the weekends.

William junior lived at No.13 Preston with his wife Sylvia and family and worked for Alscot Estate as a chauffeur. He spent some time in the Royal Observer Corps and worked on the construction of Long Marston airfield. He then served in the RAF as an engine fitter, working on bomber aircraft. His family later moved to Clifford Chambers where they remained.

Robert Elliott Storey Wyatt (b1901) was an acclaimed test cricketer and captain of the English cricket team from 1930-1937. He moved to The Forge in Wimpstone in 1936. He volunteered for the RAF at the outbreak of war and was called up in 1941, by which time he had used his cricketing status to raise huge amounts of money for service charities.

After his call-up he undertook officer training and was commissioned. He played many matches for the RAF cricket team: he was rather old for military service and his fame was a huge morale booster. He was posted to RAF Honiley in Warwickshire, where his main duty was the physical fitness of the station personnel. He was then posted to RAF Little Staughton in Cambridgeshire and promoted to flight lieutenant.

In 1944, he was the captain of the RAF cricket team playing the army team at Lords. A flying bomb was heard approaching, and everyone abandoned the game to take cover. The bomb exploded a mile away at Regents Park. Bob continued to play cricket for the remainder of the war, including five victory matches which attracted vast crowds, and was demobilised in December 1945.

Bob Wyatt in 1944.

Courtesy of Richard Parnham.

The Return to France

The D-Day landings on 6th June 1944 was the biggest amphibious military operation in history. Alan Noyce of The Kennels (b1937) remembers watching convoy after convoy of American troops passing along the main road as they headed for the south coast. 'Got any gum, chum?' he and his brother would shout. They collected enough sweets and gum to fill an entire drawer in their chest-of-drawers. David Hathaway of Alderminster (b1940) remembers seeing his first black men in the convoys of American troops.

155,000 Allied troops landed on beaches in France as the long-awaited invasion of Normandy began. This was the first step towards the liberation of France and the beginning of the end of Hitler's Third Reich.

The Germans were waiting. In many places the landing troops faced murderous fire, but the invasion was a success. The Allies began to fight their way across Normandy.

William Thomas (Bill) Paxford (b1917) was the son of James Paxford of Preston, who had served briefly in the army in 1914. Bill worked as a gardener at Alscot Park and married in 1940 and his first son Kenny was born in 1943. He was enlisted into the Royal Warwickshire Regiment and took part in the D-Day landings.

William Jones and his wife Lilian moved to Preston from Atherstone on Stour, where William worked as a shepherd for farmer John Clift. Their son Thomas (b1903) was serving in the Royal Armoured Corps in the Far East by 1940; Stanley John, known as John (b1905) served in the Coldstream Guards; Hubert (b1912) served in the Royal Artillery in Iraq; and Arthur (b1914) served in the Royal Army Service Corps in the Middle East. Their son Sidney Walter, who later adopted the name Peter, (b1908) enlisted into the Royal Warwickshire Regiment and took part in the D-Day landings.

From the Evesham Journal, 4th April 1942.

Left: Bert Hathaway. Right: The School of Artillery, Larkhill, where Bert attended in 1941.

Courtesy of David Hathaway.

Bert Hathaway of the Royal Artillery, who had been evacuated from Dunkirk and was now married with two small children, landed in France on 21st June. He was now in the 53rd Heavy Regiment which fought in the battle for Caen and other action around Normandy. He supported Canadian troops along the coast as far as the Danish border. As a trained locksmith it was his job to gain entry to any locked buildings. He was now acting lance bombardier, and trained troops in new modifications to the guns. He saw action in Holland and Germany and remained overseas until November 1945.

The 1/7th Warwicks, including Bill Gibbins who had been promoted to sergeant in 1943, had spent two years in Northern Ireland then on 29th June 1944, they landed in France with the British Second Army, whose aim was to capture the city of Caen. On 8th July, they took part in their first major action when they were ordered to capture the village of St Contest. This was a hard-fought battle against the first rate 25th Panzer Grenadiers, but they eventually took their objective. On 16th July, the battalion was camped in an orchard near Caen when they were attacked. Bill, now acting sergeant major, suffered severe shrapnel injuries and several other men were killed. Bill was evacuated to England where his right leg was amputated, ending his military career.

William (Bill) Walton, whose wife and son had now moved from Fulham to Preston, was serving in the Devonshire Regiment. He visited his family in September 1944, 'borrowed' a bike to get to Oxford to catch the train back to camp, and landed in France the next month. He fought through France and

Bill Gibbins on his promotion to sergeant, 1943.

Courtesy of Jenny Wilkins.

Portrait of Bill Walton by a German artist in Berlin 1945.

Courtesy of Derek Walton.

Holland and finished in Berlin, where he was transferred to the Military Police. He remained in Germany until March 1946.

Wilfred Newey, now a lieutenant colonel, left his regiment for staff work and in early 1945 was part of the War Cabinet Map Room staff. On 1st February 1945, he was on board an aircraft carrying Foreign Office personnel and army officers involved in the Yalta conference, aimed to reconcile the differences between the West and Russia. They were trying to reach Malta, but the aircraft got lost and crashed into the sea. Wilfred one of twelve fatalities. He was 37 years old and left a wife and two children. He was buried in the Imtarfa Military Cemetery in Malta and is commemorated on Preston War Memorial.

After several months of bloody fighting, Normandy was liberated. The Allies swept into Belgium and towards Germany. The Germans mounted an unsuccessful counter-offensive in December 1944, and in March 1945, the Allies crossed the Rhine. The noose drew tighter and on 8th May 1945, Germany surrendered. Italy followed, and Victory in Europe was announced.

On 8th June 1945, a VE Day celebration was arranged for the Preston children by Isolde West, whose husband Reggie had been killed in 1940. A lavish tea was held on tables decorated with flags and ribbons, followed by jelly and ice cream and a sports programme. Prizes were awarded, a magician made an appearance, and all youngsters were given a gift supplied by the American Junior Red Cross. The Alderminster children were also treated to a lavish tea with jellies, trifles, cakes and ice cream.

The new panel added to Preston War Memorial.

Relief Work

The Guides International Service was a scheme of adult volunteers set up by the Girl Guides Association to do relief work in Europe. Two hundred former Guides were chosen after a gruelling training and selection procedure. The women had to be adept at lighting fires and cooking good meals in darkness and rain; deal with sanitation and crowd control; learn at least one European language; know how to treat fear and mental breakdown; display extreme levels of physical and emotional endurance and deal calmly with any emergency that should arise.

Kathleen Ashby, a farmer's daughter and former Guide captain of Wimpstone, was one of those selected. The women landed at Ostend in Belgium in April 1945 and began following the liberating army across Europe.

Kath worked in a seven-ton mobile kitchen, capable of feeding 600 children a day. A letter she wrote to a friend, published in the *Stratford Herald* in April 1945, spoke of: '*the breathless moment when the vehicle, the heaviest in the convoy, is driven aboard on the 3rd attempt with a lurch which rattled all the plates and cups and almost shook the harbour.*'

After spending time in Antwerp, the Guides entered Arnhem as soon as it was cleared by British troops. The fighting was just three miles away. Derelict tanks were by the roads; the town itself was dead. It was their first sight of war.

They were billeted in a schoolhouse with shell holes piercing the tower, the windows blown out, and with no fuel, water or lighting, and at once set up their kitchen at a transit camp, where displaced people of multiple nationalities, many of them forced labourers, were starting their long trek home. They were under strict orders to feed only refugees, a hard job when faced with hungry and begging local children. Epidemics of disease were expected among the starving and homeless population and the Guides were responsible for maintaining hygiene and treating typhus outbreaks as well as feeding the thousands of refugees.

Following VE Day, the Guides negotiated a series of mined roads to reach the concentration camp at Amersfoort in Holland, liberated a day earlier. There was nobody left but starving patients in filthy, louse-infested bunks. When faced with the emotional horrors of the Nazi regime, their only option was to carry on regardless.

Then they moved to Rotterdam, where 17,000 homeless people were living on potato peelings and sugar beet. Two thousand people turned up for food on their first day. They had equipment for two hundred, but Kath and her team fed them all for three days. They received more equipment and kept this up for six weeks.

By August 1945 they were in Germany, where over 15 million homeless people and former slaves were in need of food and shelter. The Guides remained in Germany for several years and were instrumental in helping people rebuild their lives in Germany or abroad.

Left: Kath Ashby, Rotterdam 1945. Right: washing up at the mobile kitchen.

Courtesy of Richard Parnham.

The Guides team in Holland, 1945. Kath Ashby is third from left, back row. The women in caps are Dutch hospital workers. Several women are Dutch Guides. The others are Dutch helpers and drivers.

Courtesy of Richard Parnham.

After the War

Bill Gibbins, who lost his leg in France, returned to Preston after six months in hospital. No longer fit for physical work, he started work as a clerical officer at Long Marston army camp. He was fitted with a prosthetic leg and rode to work on a specially adapted one-pedalled bicycle. Motor cars were still an unaffordable luxury. He remained in Preston until his death in 1973.

Eric Reason returned to Alderminster and his second daughter, Christine, was born in 1946. The family then moved to Preston. Eric was badly affected by his experiences as a POW; he became fanatical about hygiene and never refused food again. He worked on local farms then started work in the Alscot Park gardens, where he remained for the rest of his working life. He received the Long Service Medal from the Royal Horticultural Society, kept an immaculate allotment, and was a regular winner in the Preston Flower and Produce Show. He died in 2009.

Eric Reason's medals. The 1939-1945 Star, issued for 180 days operational service. The Italy Star, issued for service in the Italy Campaign. The Defence Medal, issued for operational or non-operational military service. The War Medal, issued for 28 days fulltime operational service.

Courtesy of Chris Daniell.

George Nason and Molly Westbury's wedding day.

George's medals and ID badges or 'dog tags'. Defence Medal; possibly an Italian souvenir; War Medal 1939-1945; Italy Star; Africa Star with 8th Army clasp; 1939-1945 Star.

George Nason of the Royal Artillery had remained in constant contact with his sweetheart Molly Westbury during his five years service. He returned home on leave in July 1945 and the couple were married in Preston church a week later. They moved into No.40 Preston and remained for their lives. George found the village he had left five years earlier much changed; the beautiful meadows full of wildflowers were now ploughed and growing wheat crops. He kept an immaculate garden, won regular prizes in the Preston Flower Show, and was a bellringer at Preston church for over fifty years.

Peter Jones and his brother Hubert both returned to Preston, married and lived in Silvester's Row. Peter was killed in a motorcycle accident in 1959. Hubert, himself now widowed with three children, then married Peter's widow Kathleen.

William Hicks returned to Clifford Chambers after his demobilisation. He found work at Stratford Tractors, working on the new Ferguson system and using his mechanical skills learnt in the RAF. He then became a service and sales manager for Tredington garage. He died in 1996.

John Smith of Lower Farm left the RAF but found it hard to adjust to civilian life, missing the excitement and camaraderie of active service. An Australian pilot whom he had served with sponsored his emigration to Australia, offering him a job in his family's car business. John, his wife and son left England in 1948. After a while John set up his own garage business and remained in Australia for his life.

Joan Ashby was demobilised in 1946 and returned to Wimpstone. She married Preston farmer Bob Spencer, had one son and remained in Preston for the rest of her life.

Olive Ashby returned to Wimpstone, married former sailor Joe Parnham, whom she had met at Glendower, in 1949 and had two sons. The couple remained in Wimpstone for their lives.

Kath Ashby returned to England and married in December 1946, with the Girl Guides forming a guard of honour. Her husband was Kenneth Saunders, a banker from Newmarket who had been serving in the Army Pay Corps. The couple had met in the town of Benthe in Germany. They moved to Cambridge and named their new home Benthe.

William Paxford returned to Preston and had two further children. His eldest son Kenny, aged twelve, was tragically killed in 1955 when he was hit by a car while waiting for the school bus. He had dropped a toy which rolled into the road, and ran after it. The car which hit him had no chance of avoiding him. The family left Preston soon afterwards.

Bert Hathaway returned to Britain on 1st November 1945 and was transferred to the reserve in January 1946. He returned to live at Alderminster with his family, apart from a spell living on the Atherstone aerodrome. He found work on the Stratford railway, working variously as a signalman, guard, porter and ticket collector. As a trained locksmith, he was always the first suspect when Alderminster's PC Turner was investigating any local burglary. This eventually got Turner moved to another area.

Reverend Montague Hunt returned to Whitchurch after his demobilisation. He left for a new parish in Lincolnshire in 1952.

George Randle left the RAF in 1946 and returned to Alderminster. He set up his own building business which he ran until his death in 1971.

Thomas Bloxham remained in the Navy after the war and in 1960 was awarded the Long Service and Good Conduct Medal. He retired in 1961.

Raoul Tucker had married Marjorie Darby in Pershore in 1941, and their son Colin was born in 1945 in Thanet, perhaps where Raoul was stationed. Their daughter Karen was born there in 1948. Nothing else is known of his future.

Bill Simms returned to Alderminster, married and raised a family. He rarely spoke of his experiences again.

John James, whose brother Sam was killed in March 1945, was demobilised from the RAF and married in December 1946. He took over Wimpstone Farm, had three children and eventually retired to Stratford. He died in 1999.

Cyril Wood returned to Preston and worked as an engineer. He rarely spoke about the war. He had a third child and remained at No.51 until his death in 1989.

Reg Stoppard joined his family at Atherstone Hill Farm after leaving the RAF. It was fifty years before he spoke of his military service. The family emigrated to New Zealand in 1951, and still retain connections with the area today.

Bob Wyatt was demobilised in December 1945 and returned to Wimpstone. He continued to play professional cricket until 1951. He lived in Wimpstone until 1966, and spent his later years in Cornwall where he died in 1995, aged 93.

Charles Keighly-Peach, now a captain in the Navy, left Singapore in 1947 and was appointed commander of the 3rd Destroyer Flotilla in the Mediterranean. In 1951 he was appointed Assistant Chief of Naval Staff and was attached to the Canadian Navy. He retired in 1953, aged 51. His son Peter, also a pilot with the Navy, was awarded the DSO for services in the Korean War in 1953.

Michael West served in the Korean War from 1952-53 as General Officer Commanding (GOC) of the 1st Commonwealth Division, and was the architect of British strategy in this war. In December 1953, he was awarded a second bar to his DSO for services in Korea.

He then became head of British Defence Staff in Washington DC and was the UK representative on NATO from 1962-65. He was considered for even higher levels of command, but was believed too provocative and unpredictable. He retired in 1965.

Seven: RAF Atherstone on Stour (RAF Stratford)

In 1938 the Aerodromes Board began to search for suitable sites for the rapidly expanding RAF, in readiness for the almost unavoidable war. Altitude, topology and local climate were important; local objections were not. Over 4000 sites across Britain were considered, and 400 airfields were built. Britain was likened to a massive, unsinkable aircraft carrier.

One site spanned Preston and Atherstone on Stour. It had been proposed for a municipal airport by prominent Stratford businessmen in 1933, but the plans were abandoned as war loomed. The Air Ministry then took over the investigative work. The site was approved in June 1940 and work began.

Work went on almost around the clock. Woodland, hedgerows and buildings were bulldozed, ponds and watercourses filled in, tumps were levelled. A 13-acre plum orchard near the railway line belonging to Heath Farm was grubbed out.

Locals with building skills were set to work on the site, including George Randle, a bricklayer from Alderminster, and gangs of itinerant Irish labourers were bussed out each day. The site foreman, an Irishman, was billeted with Bill Bowie at Wimpstone Farm and got Bill to spend a great deal of time in The Bell at Alderminster, to the great detriment of his farm.

The machines were supplied by the firm John Laing on the Birmingham Road in Stratford, owned by Pat Barrett of Clifford Chambers. Harry Jaques, who had moved to Atherstone Hill Farm with his family to escape the bombing, managed the company, and lorries, tractors, trailers, dumper trucks and other vehicles were parked in the fields at Atherstone Hill. Jesse Cooper, a Stratford mechanic, worked for Harry and cycled out each day to do maintenance and repair work.

Thousands of tonnes of concrete and tarmac were laid for the runways, roads and bases for buildings. The stone under the runways was brought from Stepstones Farm in Newbold. Electric cables and water pipes were laid and over 200 buildings built. Despite the speed and their short-term purpose, many are still functional today.

The site was an impenetrable cloud of dust in dry weather from the hundreds of heavy machines; in wet weather it was a quagmire of mud. The builders got one bulldozer stuck in a pond. They couldn't get it out, so they buried it in concrete. It's still there, somewhere. A lorry brought a load of wheelbarrows towards the end of the work. The men said they'd finished. 'I can't take them back again,' the driver said. So all those brand-new wheelbarrows were buried in concrete as well.

Operational buildings and barracks were spread across the site. The Women's Auxiliary Airforce (WAAF) site or 'WAAFery' was set apart from the men's

RAF Stratford, August 1946. Used by permission of Historic England. Mature trees were often kept to camouflage buildings. Stooks of corn can be seen in the field at the bottom. It is interesting to compare this with the 1945 photos available on Google Earth: the airfield has been entirely removed for security reasons.

RAF Stratford earlier in the war looking south-west. The hangars are not yet built. Note the Wellingtons on the dispersal pans.
Courtesy of Nick Pratley.

areas. Officers, sergeants and aircraftsmen/women were housed separately. Some officers were accommodated in Beecham Farm. An inscribed brass bell was attached to the house, possibly for use in emergencies.

Airforce and WAAF personnel were also lodged at Alscot Park. One pilot named Gale was badly burnt when his aircraft caught fire – the cockpit could reach several thousand degrees within seconds – and became one of the first patients of plastic surgery pioneer Sir Archibald McIndoe. Another, Leonard Crawley, had a huge moustache and reared ducks in the stables. The West family's dogs hated him and when one had pups the mother bit him on the nose.

The site had no mains water or electric. Electricity was supplied by a generator station near Beecham Farm with a back-up generator near the water tower. The latter had plinths for two generators but only one was installed. A substation near the Mechanical Site is still present. The water tower was an 18m scaffolded structure with a tank on top, filled from a bore several miles away. It was the first piped drinking water in the area and supplied water by gravity to the entire site. It is still an iconic landmark today.

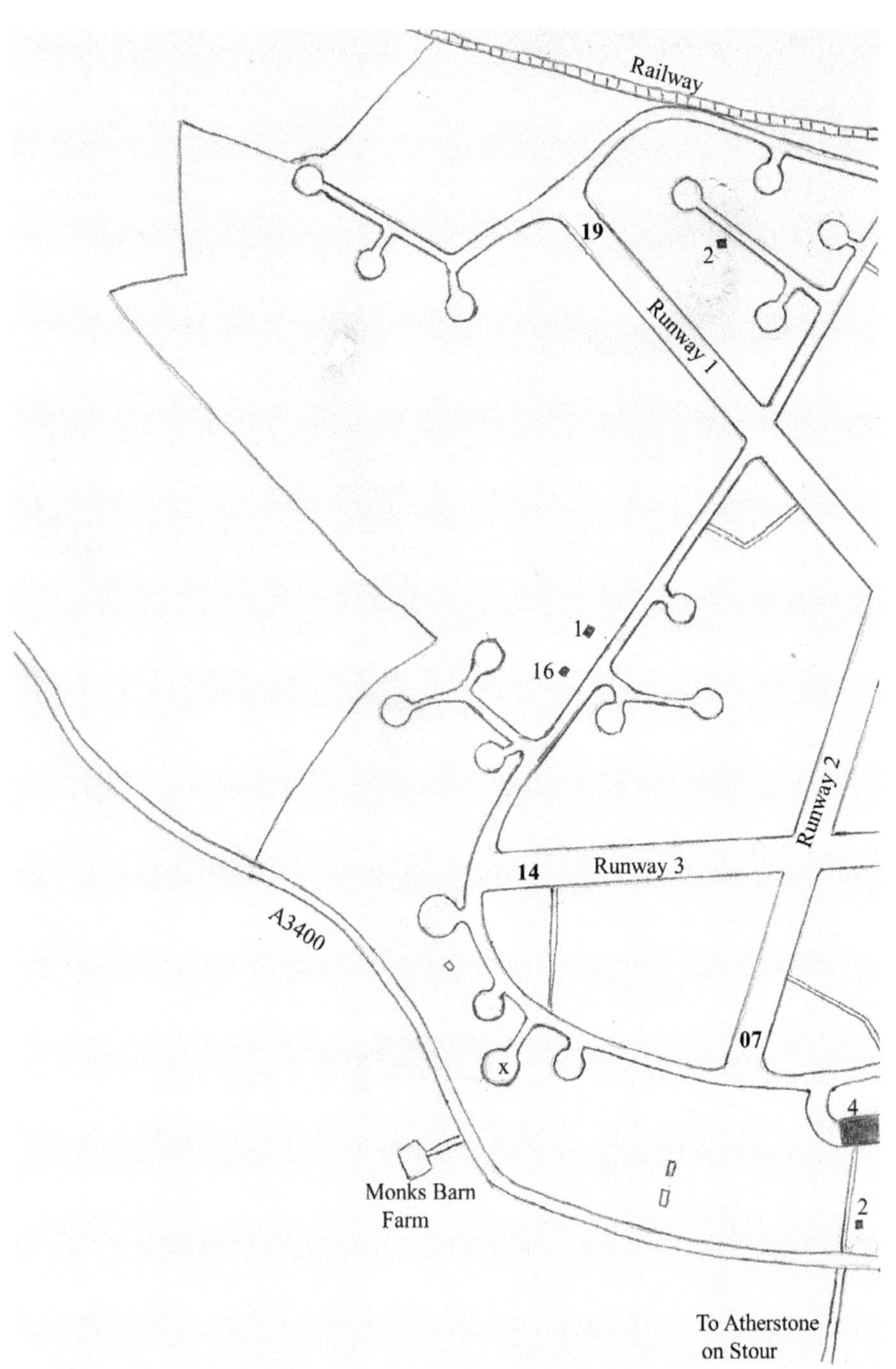
Railway
19
2
Runway 1
1
16
Runway 2
Runway 3
14
A3400
07
x
4
Monks Barn
Farm
2
To Atherstone
on Stour

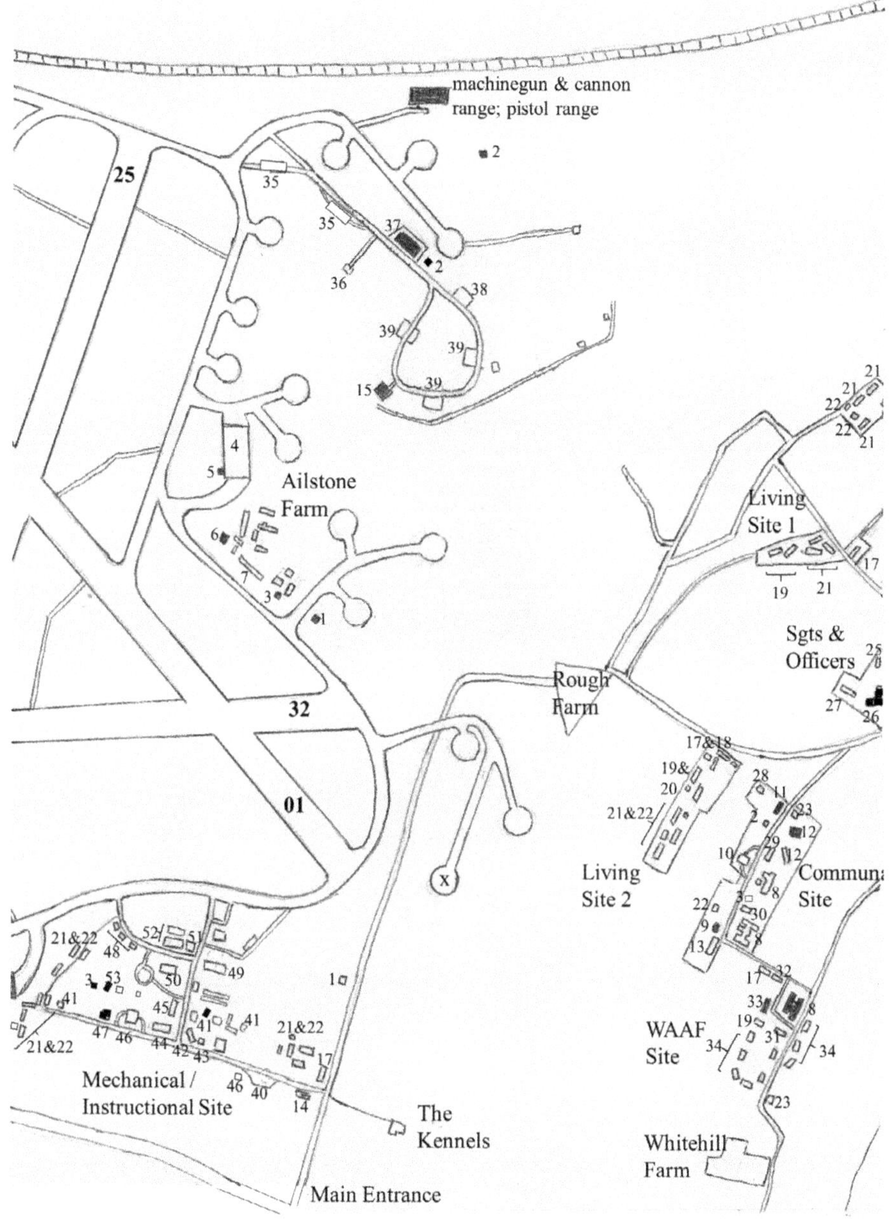
machinegun & cannon range; pistol range
25
32
01
Ailstone Farm
Rough Farm
Living Site 1
Sgts & Officers
Living Site 2
Communal Site
WAAF Site
Whitehill Farm
Mechanical / Instructional Site
The Kennels
Main Entrance

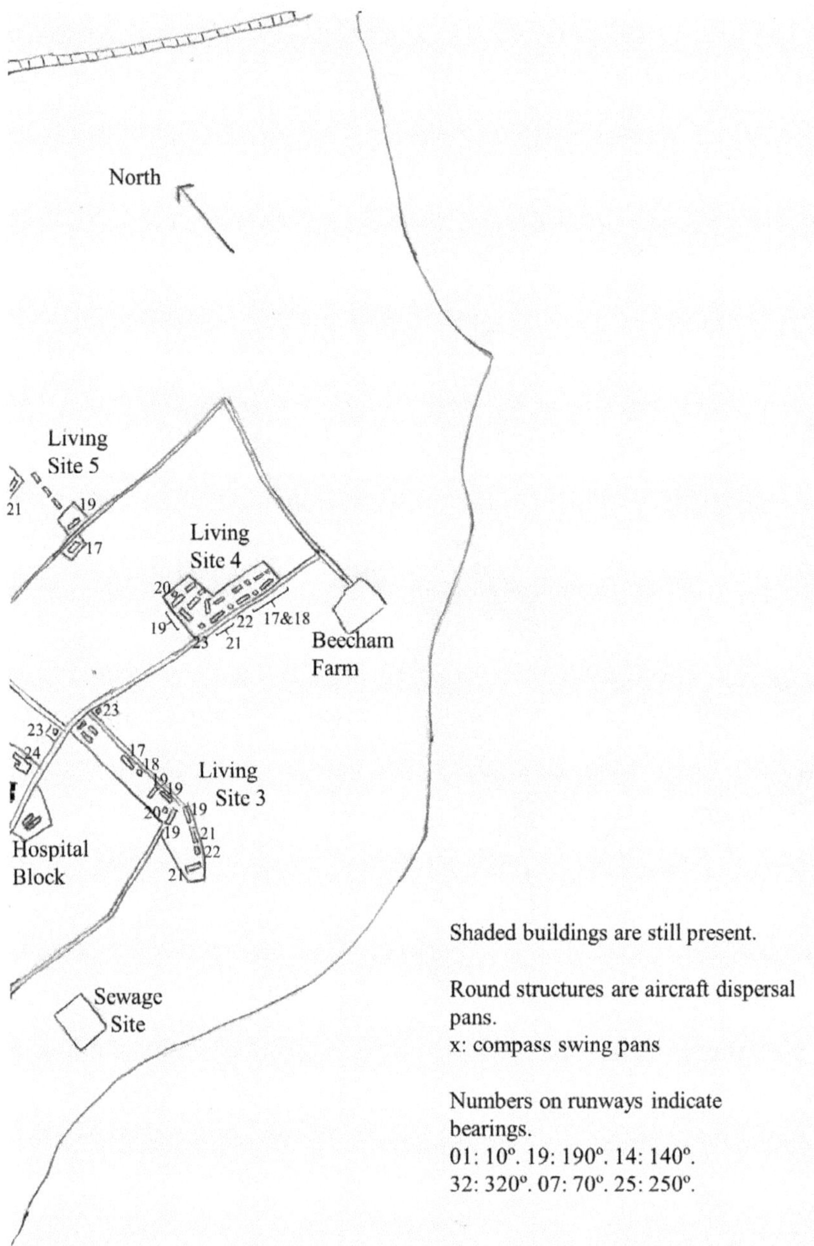

Shaded buildings are still present.

Round structures are aircraft dispersal pans.
x: compass swing pans

Numbers on runways indicate bearings.
01: 10º. 19: 190º. 14: 140º.
32: 320º. 07: 70º. 25: 250º.

Site Plan of RAF Stratford.

1. Pillbox
2. Air raid shelter
3. Blast shelter
4. Hangar
5. Fire station
6. Control tower/ watch office
7. Admin block/ flight offices
8. Dining room/ institute
9. Water tower
10. Coal dump
11. Stand by generator
12. Decontamination chamber
13. Aircraftsmen showers
14. Guard house
15. Component store
16. Battle HQ
17. Officers' quarters
18. Officers' latrines
19. Sergeants' quarters
20. Sergeants' latrines
21. Barrack hut
22. Aircraftsmen latrines
23. Picket post
24. Officers' mess
25. Officers' bath house
26. Sergeants' mess
27. Sergeants' bath house
28. Destructor house
29. Grocery and produce store
30. Ration store
31. Latrine/ablution
32. Sick quarters
33. Bath/decontamination area
34. Aircraftswomen quarters
35. Fusing point shelter
36. Small arms ammunition store
37. Incendiary and pyro store
38. Fused and spare bombs
39. Bomb store
40. Mechanical Transport standing
41. M & E plinth
42. Lubricant & flammable store
43. Oil compound
44. Maintenance and WT unit
45. Armoury
46. Fuel compound
47. Sub station
48. Petrol installation
49. Crew procedure centre
50. Link trainer building
51. Bombing teacher & turret
52. Ground instructional building
53. ?. [See text].

The site had three concrete runways, each over half a mile in length and laid in an 'A' shape so aircraft could always take off and land into the wind. To aid the trainee crews flying at night, sodium flare paths – lights on larch poles in the surrounding fields, some up to two miles away at Whitchurch – aligned on the runways. Electrician Dick Scarret had to climb the poles to change the bulbs when necessary. They were an obvious aid for enemy bombers and were dowsed if aircraft were reported nearby. Lights would then be lit on the decoy airfield at nearby Pillerton Priors. The decoy was bombed on at least one occasion.

Two runways are still visible on Ordnance Survey maps. After the concrete was removed, the much-damaged soil was of little use for agriculture so was planted with conifer trees.

The control tower which coordinated in- and outgoing aircraft stood near the runways, on the south side so the view wasn't impeded by the sun.

The Braithwaite water tower in 2017. The tower with the water tank in 1973.
Courtesy of Richard Parnham.

Generator back-up building in 1998. The wall was knocked down to store farm machinery.
Courtesy of Will Spencer. Rifle range in 1995.
Courtesy of Richard Parnham.

The Mechanical Site substation.
Courtesy of Will Spencer.

Two hangars were built; one is still present. It was designed by Sir Barnes Wallis of bouncing bomb fame, and was the largest possible span using the minimum amount of steel. After a series of bombing raids on airfields, it became more usual to keep aircraft on dispersal pans, frying pan-shaped areas around the periphery of the site, to minimise losses. Some can still be identified: thanks to the soil damage, crops still grow badly where they were. At least two were 'compass swing pans', used to calibrate the aircraft's compass. These were located well away from any metal objects such as buildings or railway tracks.

The control tower, 1940s. Bicycles were the main form of transport around the site. '25' indicates to incoming aircraft the runway to use. The vehicle is the Crossley crash tender.
Courtesy of Nick Pratley.

The control tower in 2017.

The airfield and hangar. Atherstone church is in the foreground.

Courtesy of Pete Summerton.

The stores for bombs, ammunition and incendiaries were built on the periphery of the site for safety reasons, as was the rifle range which comprised a 25yd range for machine guns and cannons, and an 11yd range for pistols.

Several Stanton air raid shelters were built, partly underground and with ribbed concrete panels and soil banks to deflect blasts. Blast shelters – roofless structures to negate horizontal blast effects and shrapnel – were also built around the site.

The hospital block dealt with less serious medical cases: the more serious went to Stratford hospital. It comprised a ward block, with separate wards for officers and airmen, and an examination block including dental surgeries. An ambulance building and mortuary would have been nearby.

The fire station was near the runways, where most needed, and had bays for three fire engines.

The airfield was surrounded by barbed wire fencing and a guard house was built by the main entrance opposite Alscot Park. It had an unusual number of defences, comprising pillboxes, anti-aircraft guns and trenches. This was because of the secret plans to move the government to Stratford in the event of invasion. RAF Stratford would have been converted into a fighter squadron base to defend the town.

The Battle Headquarters or Command Post would coordinate defence and operations in an attack. It consisted of an underground observation post with a 360° view via a narrow, grenade-proof slot, several underground rooms and an emergency escape hatch.

A decontamination building would treat victims of a gas attack, such as mustard gas which would adhere to and burn the skin. Porches over the entrances – one each for men and women – contained bleach-filled footbaths to neutralise the gas. Contaminated clothing was removed and disposed through the hatches. Showers and bleach-based ointment removed the chemical agents, then people moved through an air-locked passage into a clean zone to dress. A tall brick shaft provided air from above the low-lying gas zone. Several pyramid-shaped concrete pits were nearby; their purpose is unclear.

Air raid shelter near the A3400.

Blast shelter near Ailstone Farm.

A Type 24 Pillbox. Interior features are the 'T'-shaped blast/anti-ricochet wall and a swivel bracket for a Vickers machinegun. The impression of planks in the concrete shows its method of construction. Planked walls were simply filled with concrete.

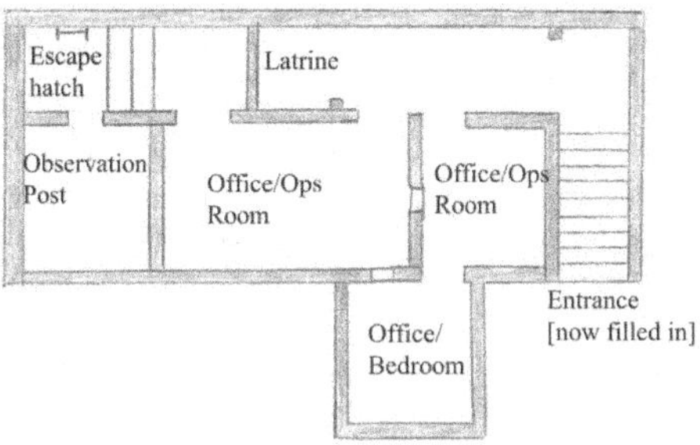

Battle HQ. Exterior shows the concrete roof of the observation post and the escape hatch.

The incendiary store. This comprised three buildings with concrete roofs, separated by brick walls. A surrounding earth bank was for protection and to contain any explosion.

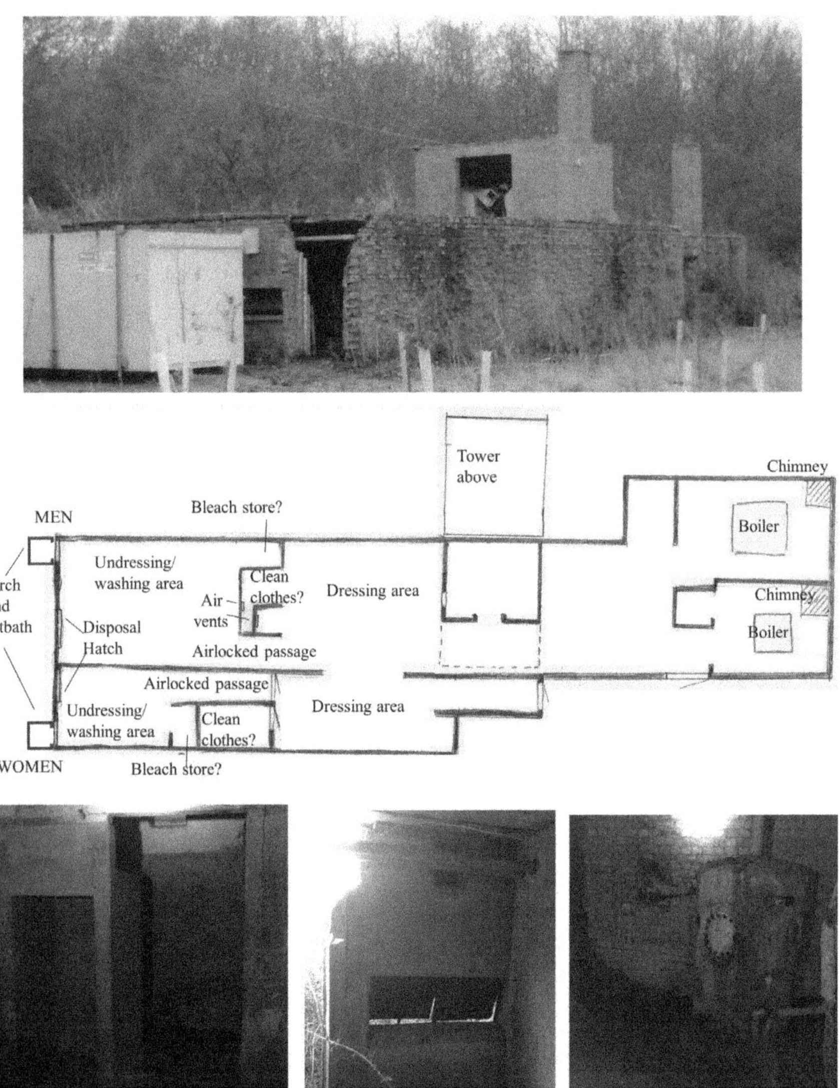

Decontamination building in 1998.
Building layout; view of possible clothing/bleach store; disposal hatch; boiler room.
Courtesy of Will Spencer..

The administration block in 1995. No longer present.

Courtesy of Richard Parnham.

Communal building of the Communal Site, 1973. No longer present. The structures in front are sow feeders. It included a cinema and was painted with murals of Micky Mouse, Donald Duck and Pluto the dog. Note the piers, characteristic of wartime single-brick buildings, which support the roof.

Courtesy of Richard Parnham.

WAAF communal building in 1998.

Courtesy of Will Spencer.

Scenes from Cinderella in the WAAF communal building in 2000.

Courtesy of Will Spencer.

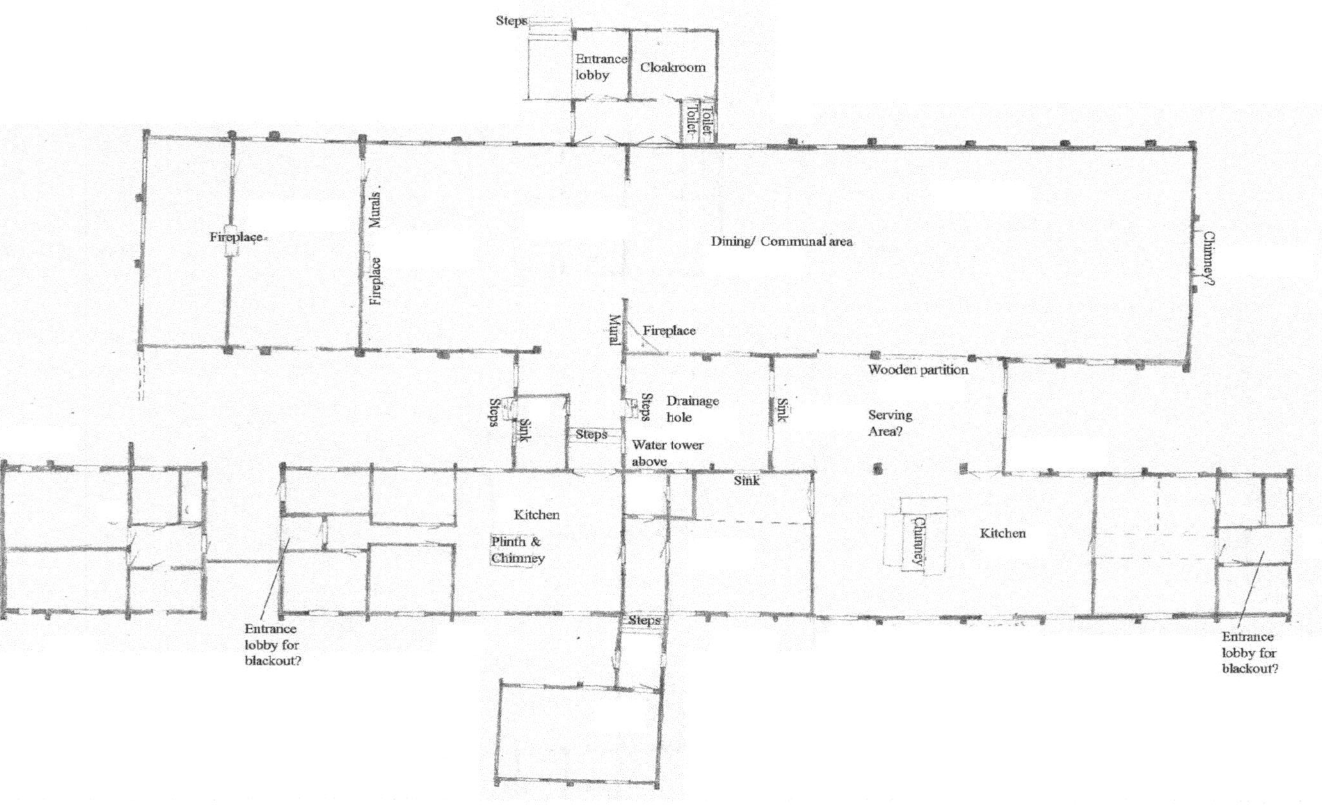

Layout of the communal building. Dashed lines indicate demolished walls; exact layout unclear.

Fittings still present in communal building.

Left: vehicle maintenance plinth on the Mechanical Site. Right: Building 53. Function unclear. The walls are topped with glass; the inside has water supply and a drainage channel.

Courtesy of Will Spencer.

Operational Use

RAF Atherstone on Stour, later renamed RAF Stratford to prevent confusion with RAF Atherstone near Nuneaton, was ready for operational use in July 1941. The aircrews initially lived under canvas as the accommodation wasn't completed until October.

The airfield was initially part of No.22 Operational Training Unit (OTU) and used with RAF Gaydon as satellite airfields for RAF Wellesbourne. They were primarily training sites for Wellington bomber crews. It was occasionally used for overseas bombing missions and was routinely used as an emergency landing ground. Later in the war, American B17 Flying Fortresses used the airfield. It was transferred to No.23 OTU in November 1942 and became a satellite for RAF Pershore, then returned to 22 OTU in March 1944.

The site was intended for 1650 Airforce and WAAF personnel. The majority of aircrews were from the Canadian Airforce, with others from the RAF and the Australian and New Zealand Airforces. Large numbers of ground crew, mechanics, wireless and radar operators, drivers, cooks and many other personnel were needed to keep the site functioning.

Emily Maton from No.5 Preston and her daughter Beryl often did the laundry and ironing. Isolde West from Alscot Park worked in the canteen. George Beauchamp, a farm worker at Rough Farm, worked as a night watchman. Oliver Summerton, a carpenter and First World War veteran from

The first accommodation at Atherstone, 1941. Left: AC1 Pete Rushton; Cpl Keen; ?; AC1 Stan Ursell. Right: members of C Flight.

Courtesy of Nick Pratley.

Atherstone airfield from the control tower, 1940s. A Wellington bomber; a visiting C47 US Airforce Dakota; a Hurricane fighter from 24 OTU.

Courtesy of Nick Pratley.

Alderminster, also worked on the site. One of his regular tasks was mending bullet holes in the roofs. The Canadian airmen had a habit of firing their pistols at the ceilings.

The Training Wing

Aircrews who had completed their requisite operational tour of thirty flying missions became instructors or volunteered for further operational tours. Many did the latter: they grew tired of 'circuit-bashing' and missed the excitement and buzz of the squadrons. Several instructors at Atherstone had received the DFC (Distinguished Flying Cross) for operational missions. Many still had just a few months flying experience.

Joseph Leon Gabriel Taschereau (b1915) volunteered for the RCAF when the war began, completed his initial training in Canada then came to RAF Stratford for bomber training. The first thing the French Canadians had to do was learn fluent English.

On completion of his navigator's training, Gabriel flew 49 bombing sorties over Germany and Italy from bases in Britain and Tunisia, and was awarded the DFC. His aircraft was attacked by an enemy fighter, leaving the wireless operator severely wounded, and he administered life-saving first aid while navigating back to base. He became an instructor at Atherstone and Wellesbourne from April to December 1944, then went to the Warrington

Back: F/Sgt Plemel, W/O Adams, P/O James, F/O J.D. McGillivray, F/O Baker, F/O Solmes, F/O Wood, F/O Turenne, P/O James Noble, F/L MacDonald, P/O Bourgeois, P/O Piquette, P/O Joseph Landry, W/O Racicot.

Middle: P/O Dupont, F/O Peterson, F/O Kennedy, F/O McKenzie, F/O Skinner, F/O Smalley, W/O Noble, W/O Hartley, P/O Cant, F/O Hanson, P/O Seay, F/O Garvey, F/O Hale, P/O Knight,

Front: F/L Freddie Belanger, F/O Willis, F/L Gabriel Taschereau, F/O Spencer-Matthews, F/L Merrifield, S/L J.C. Hebert, W/C Philip Patrick, S/L Robertson, F/L Arthur Diemer, F/L G.A. Fitzgerald, F/O Brochu, F/O Phillip Maries, F/O Kenneth Whittington, F/O Potter.

The Training Wing at Atherstone, mid 1944. Courtesy of Ron Horsley, Wellesbourne Military Museum.
F/Sgt: Flight Sergeant. W/O: Warrant Officer. P/O: Pilot Officer. F/O: Flying Officer. F/L: Flight Lieutenant. S/L: Squadron Leader. W/C: Wing Commander. Double wings denote pilots; single wings other aircrew.

depot in Lancashire and returned to Canada as an instructor. He reached the rank of group captain. In 1989, when he came to England to be appointed an MVO (Member of the Royal Victorian Order), he returned to visit his former airfields.

Joseph Gerard Maurice Landry was a Canadian pilot who became an instructor at Atherstone in August 1944. He had served in 425 Squadron and was awarded the DFC for 'fine fighting spirit, courage, leadership and devotion to duty', after completing a mission to Boulogne through intense anti-aircraft fire which badly damaged his aircraft.

Frederick Belanger was a Canadian WAG (wireless operator/air gunner). He instructed at Atherstone until January 1945 when he was posted to Warrington. His brother Jean was also based at Atherstone and was killed in an accident at the site in June 1944.

Philip King Wilson Patrick was a British pilot and recipient of the DFC. He was deputy chief instructor at Atherstone between August and December 1944.

Arthur Colin Deimer was a pilot from Birmingham. He instructed at Atherstone from August 1943 then transferred to 156 Squadron, a Pathfinder squadron. He was Mentioned in Dispatches and died on active service on 11th March 1945, aged 23.

G.A. Fitzgerald was a Canadian air gunner. He completed his operational tour with 429 Squadron in Yorkshire, then instructed at Atherstone between October 1943 and December 1944. He then went to Warrington depot.

Kenneth Herbert Whittington was a Canadian pilot who completed his operational tour with 102 Squadron and was awarded the DFC. He instructed at Atherstone from May 1944.

Phillip Charles Maries was a British pilot who became an instructor at Atherstone in May 1943. He was promoted to flight lieutenant in September 1945.

J.D. McGillivray was a Canadian air gunner who had been instructing at Atherstone since December 1943.

James Graham Noble was a Canadian navigator and recipient of the DFC who had been at Atherstone since June 1944.

F/O Smalley, a Canadian pilot, had arrived at Atherstone in December 1943.

S/L Hebert was a Canadian pilot who instructed at Atherstone until his transfer to Warrington in December 1944.

Gabriel Taschereau (far right) with his crew at RAF Dishforth, Yorkshire. The wheel chock has been blanked out by the censor.

Courtesy of Pete Summerton.

Airfield Life

The airfield had a great impact on local life. Alfred Bishop farmed at Rough Farm throughout the war and supplied churns of milk to the site kitchens – often the old milk which had sometimes gone sour. The Canadians loved milk and would often come to the farm for a glass. Alfred's daughters Natalie (b1926) and Marion (b1924) both helped on the farm, and Natalie was embarrassed to be seen ploughing with a horse in full view of the airmen who all made pointed comments. On one occasion she was leading a cow and calf through the camp when a WAAF girl came out of a building with a terrier. The cow tossed the dog and then Natalie, leaving her with a nasty gash to her stomach. She wouldn't let the young and handsome camp medic treat her as she was embarrassed at what she was wearing under her coat.

In 1944 Natalie was employed at the site as a secretary to the Air Ministry Clerk of Works, Mr Ellis, an undertaker from Chipping Campden. She cycled to the guard room early each morning to clock in the men working on the camp, cycled back home for breakfast, then returned to a day's work of phone calls, letter-writing and other tasks.

The Bishop sisters had a great deal of fun with the airmen and were considered camp mascots. They made a lot of friends and their mother Jessie would write to the families of those who had been killed, telling them of their friendships.

The airmen had an ethos of work hard, play hard, and soon became an integral part of the local social scene. They were regular visitors at Lower Farm in Preston, where they shared the family life they were missing. The lads were often barely twenty years old and away from home for the first time. The site cinema was very popular and Alfred Bishop kept himself up-to-date with the latest films.

Dances were held every Saturday evening at Whitchurch village hall, the highlight of the locals' week and hugely popular with the airmen. Their dancing skills left the local lads in the sidelines; Eric James from Whitchurch Farm (1926-2016) always remembered the endless energy with which they threw themselves around the hall. They were, of course, much more appealing to the local girls, with the added bonus of smart uniforms, and there were more than a few stolen sweethearts. This wasn't the only thing lost. Bob Spencer of Park Farm in Preston (1917-1997) recalled that nobody could cycle to the dances as their bicycles wouldn't be there when they wanted to go home. But at least they knew where to retrieve them the following day.

Natalie, Marion and Audrey Bishop cycled to regular dances at Ilmington. The RAF band provided music. The dances got going around 10pm when the pubs chucked everyone out, and ended promptly at midnight. The girls usually had an escort home and would occasionally ask lads in for a nightcap. Their father Alfred always left his false teeth on the sideboard before going to bed, and one of the girls would go ahead to hide them before the others arrived.

Pilot Johnny Dawson, an instructor on the site, kept a Jaguar car in the cartshed at Rough Farm and often spent time there working on it. He got the camp commander to issue an order to stop the men using bad language when passing through the farm, thinking it inappropriate in earshot of the girls. He was 'a bit naughty', Natalie remembers, and he once stopped her when she was ploughing and asked if she wanted to fly with him in a Lysander aircraft. She told him she couldn't just leave the horse and plough standing in the field, but he later gave her a tour of a Blenheim bomber, and a kiss as well. He was killed on a mission to Essen in September 1942.

Lyle Wilmot Hicks, an air bomber from Illinois who trained at Atherstone, became Natalie's serious boyfriend. He was posted to 426 Squadron in Yorkshire,

Left: Natalie Bishop with Lyle Hicks at Rough Farm. Right: Natalie with Giles Hall in Newquay, c.1946.

Courtesy of Natalie Hall.

The Canadian Airforce Band. Bob Peer; ?; George Chapel; Steve Sanders; Don MacCuaig; Ted Robbins.

Courtesy of Natalie Hall.

and on 15th February 1944 went on a mission to Berlin. His aircraft crashed into the sea near The Netherlands with the loss of all crew. Lyle's body was one of four bodies washed ashore, and he was buried in Harderwijk Cemetery in The Netherlands. He was 23 years old.

Natalie met George Hall at the end of the war. He had attended Manchester University then joined the RAF in 1941. He spent the war building radar stations all around Britain, then spent a couple of months at Atherstone. He was very taken with both Natalie and her sister Marion, but chose Natalie and bought a Lea Francis car to take her out in. He was posted to Cornwall for two years, but they became engaged and were married at Preston in March 1947.

In June 1943, Stanley Donovan, an airman and First World War veteran, was drinking at The Bell in Alderminster. At 10.15pm, PC Turner of Alderminster found him in the middle of the road using indecent language. Turner, who wasn't in uniform, told Donovan he was a police officer and asked him to desist.

Sergeant James Edward Dayton, a 20-year-old Canadian air-gunner, then approached. Donovan was now on the ground; accounts disagreed as to whether Turner had knocked him down. Dayton later stated he told Donovan to go home else he'd put him under arrest. Turner claimed Dayton said; 'take no notice of this policeman, he's not in uniform', before taking a swing at him. Donovan then punched PC Turner in the face, dazing him for a few seconds, then Turner knocked Donovan to the ground. A struggle followed. Turner denied in court he was excessively violent with Donovan and Dayton claimed he'd remonstrated with Turner for beating up an older man.

PC Turner issued both men with a summons the following morning. He allegedly told Dayton if he contested the case he'd call twenty witnesses to support him, at Dayton's expense. Both men accepted the charges. Dayton was fined 10 shillings. Donovan was fined £4.

Three months later, James Dayton was posted to 419 Squadron in Yorkshire, and went on his first bombing mission, to Mannheim in Germany, on 23rd September. His Halifax bomber was lost, along with all crew members. James was a week short of his 21st birthday, and was buried in Reichswald War Cemetery in Germany.

The Air Crews

The Wellington crews typically consisted five men: a pilot; an air observer; a wireless operator/air gunner (WAG); a bomb aimer; and a navigator. Their gruelling training course lasted around three months and consisted of flying manoeuvres – 'circuits and bumps' – followed by training in bomb-aiming, air gunnery and navigational and cross-country exercises, mainly at night. Bombing

Training Course 29 at RAF Stratford, September 1942. Within twelve months, over half of these men were dead.

Courtesy of Nick Pratley.

ranges, where bomb aimers practiced with paint-filled bombs, were located at Honington and Tysoe. The former was a circular target; the latter shaped like a battleship. The noise could be a problem for the locals, but people and animals got used to it and it was considered part and parcel of the war.

The site was expected to produce six fully-trained crews a fortnight: 44% of bomber crews were lost on active service. 9000 airmen were trained at 22 OTU, and 315 lost their lives while based at the unit. Many more lost their lives when they commenced operational flying through the gauntlet of Luftwaffe fighters, flak, anti-aircraft guns and barrage balloons.

Trainee casualties were also high. The Wellingtons were generally old and prone to mechanical failures: the better ones were needed for operational missions. As soon as an aircraft landed, it was refuelled and sent up with another crew onboard. They were continually mishandled by the trainee crews, and when loaded with fuel and bombs, readily caught fire or exploded on crash-landing. The crews were young; many could not even drive a car. Thirty one airmen are known to have lost their lives in accidents at Atherstone alone. Thanks to the haste in which the site was built, aircraft taking off from Wellesbourne Mountford passed directly over the Atherstone runways, another major safety issue, but one which never caused a problem.

Flight Sergeant Alexander Woodhouse. A Canadian air gunner who joined 419 Squadron and was reported missing in action on a mission to Berlin on 1st March 1943. He was 21. He is commemorated on the Runnymede Memorial.

Two men called Taylor are pictured. It is unclear which is which.

Flight Sergeant James Taylor. A Canadian air gunner who joined 405 Squadron and was killed on a mission to Kiel on 5th April 1943. He is buried in Kiel War Cemetery in Germany.

Sergeant J. Taylor. A British WAG. He became non-effective through sickness in February 1943. Nothing else is known of his future.

Sergeant Rapin. Nothing is known of his background or service history.

Flight Sergeant Earl Rheaume. A Canadian air gunner who joined 431 Squadron. He was an accomplished pianist and played for unit church services and dances. His bomber was attacked by a German night fighter over the Netherlands while on a mission to Dusseldorf on 12th June 1943, and was last seen plummeting in flames. Earl's body was the only one recovered from the wreckage. He was 29 and was buried in Bergen-op-Zoom War Cemetery in the Netherlands.

Sergeant Reed. Nothing is known of his background or service history.

Pilot Officer Robert Graham. A Canadian pilot who joined 420 Squadron and was killed on a mission to Essen on 5th March 1943 aged 29. He was buried in Reichswald Forest War Cemetery.

Pilot Officer George Acton. A Canadian air gunner who joined 408 Squadron. He was on the same aircraft as Bryce Domigan which crash landed after a mission to Berlin in March 1943. He was killed on a mission to Gelsenkirchen on 26th June 1943, aged 31. He was buried in Reichswald Forest War Cemetery.

Sergeant Gray. Nothing is known of his background or service history.

Warrant Officer H.G. Bees. A Canadian who joined 419 Squadron and was taken POW during a bombing mission to Duisberg on 13th May 1943, perhaps on the same aircraft as Walter Alison and Harry Enever. He was promoted to warrant officer on 26th June 1943 while in Stalag Luft 6, in present-day Lithuania. He was moved to Stalag 357 in Germany sometime after September 1944. His future from this point is unclear.

Sergeant Walter Alison. A WAG from Middlesex who joined 419 Squadron. He was injured while on a mission to Duisberg and died in hospital on 13th May 1943, aged 28. He was buried in Hotton War Cemetery in Luxemburg.

Sergeant James Bell. A wireless operator from York who joined 431 Squadron and was on the same aircraft as Earl Rheaume, shot down on 12th June 1943. His body wasn't identified and he is commemorated on a collective grave in Bergen-op-Zoom War Cemetery. He was 22.

Sergeant Alfred Wiles. A WAG from Sussex who joined 424 Squadron in Yorkshire. His aircraft crash-landed after completing a mission to Wilhelmshaven on 25th February 1943. Alfred was one of three crew members killed. He was 28. He was buried in Streatham Park Cemetery in Sussex.

Flying Officer James MacDonald. A Canadian air observer who joined 420 Squadron and was on the same aircraft as Robert Graham which was lost on 5th March 1943. He was 23. He was buried in Reichswald Forest War Cemetery.

Sergeant Melvin. Nothing is known of his background or service history.

Sergeant D.F. Heybourne. He completed an operational tour with 420 Squadron. Nothing else is known of his history.

Flight Sergeant Arthur Ross. A British wireless operator who joined 405 Squadron. His aircraft was hit by flak while on a mission to Stuttgart in March 1943 but made it home safely. He was transferred to 408 Squadron and was shot down by a night fighter off the Dutch coast while on a mission to Bochum on 13th May 1943. Three crew members were killed; three others, including Arthur, were made POW. He received his promotion to flight sergeant that September while in Stalag Luft 6, the same camp as H. Bees. His future from this point is unclear.

Flight Sergeant Wilfred Francis. A Canadian who joined 419 Squadron and was reported missing while on a mission to Berlin on 2nd March 1943. He may have been on the same aircraft as Alexander Woodhouse. He was 23. He is commemorated on the Runnymede Memorial.

Flying Officer Ralph Wright. A Canadian who joined 405 Squadron and was killed on the same mission as James Taylor on 5th April 1943, perhaps serving on the same aircraft. He is buried in Kiel War Cemetery.

Flying Officer Colin McDougall. A Canadian navigator who joined 431 Squadron, serving on the same aircraft as Earl Rheaume and James Bell, shot down on 12th June 1943. His body wasn't identified and he is commemorated on a collective grave in Bergen-op-Zoom War Cemetery. He was 24.

Pilot Officer James Denholm. A Scottish navigator who joined 408 Squadron. He was on the same aircraft as Bryce Domigan which crash-landed after a mission to Berlin in March 1943. His aircraft was hit by flak while on a mission to Le Creusot on 20th June 1943 and crashed near Caen. James was one of three crew members killed. He was 21. He was buried in Bretteville-sur-Laize Canadian War Cemetery in France.

Flying Officer Frank Lewis. A Canadian who joined 7 Squadron. His aircraft was shot down by a night fighter over France on 21st December 1942 while on a mission to Munchen. Three crew were killed; one was taken POW; three evaded capture and made it back to Britain. Frank was one of the latter. He rejoined his squadron and was awarded the DFC in June 1943. He was on a mission to Berlin on 4th September 1943 and was shot down by anti-aircraft batteries near Berlin. His body was not recovered and he is commemorated on the Runnymede Memorial.

Sergeant J. Harrison. A Canadian navigator who joined 424 Squadron. He was injured in the same crash which killed Alfred Wiles in February 1943. Nothing else is known of his future.

Sergeant A.T.E. McCormick. A Canadian observer. Nothing else is known of his service history.

Pilot Officer Richard Nutter. A Canadian navigator. He was on a cross-country training flight from Northallerton in Yorkshire, perhaps as an instructor, on 29th June 1943. The aircraft suffered engine failure and crash-landed. Richard was one of two crew members killed. He was 29. He was buried in Dishforth Cemetery in Yorkshire.

Flight Sergeant W.J. Klein. A Canadian who joined 419 Squadron. He was taken POW when his aircraft came down while on a mission to Duisberg on 13th May 1943, perhaps the same aircraft as H. Bees, Harry Enever and Walter Alison. He was promoted to flight sergeant in 1945 while in Stalag 357. His subsequent future is unclear.

Sergeant Ronald Stanley Perks. A New Zealand airman who joined 76 Squadron, received the DFC in August 1943 and was commissioned to flight lieutenant that September. He survived the war and returned to New Zealand,

Sergeant E.J. Troy A British pilot who joined 408 Squadron. While on a mission to Berlin on 27th March 1943, his aircraft was attacked by a night fighter but suffered no damage, then was hit by flak. They crash landed at RAF Leeming with no injuries to crew. In November 1943, he transferred to 1659 Heavy Conversion Unit to train with four-engine bombers. Nothing else is known of his future.

Pilot Officer Luke. A pilot. Nothing else is known of his service history.

Pilot Officer Peter Geldart. A British pilot. He was involved in an accident in October 1942 when his aircraft collided with another bomber on landing at Atherstone. All crew were unhurt. He remained in the RAF after the war, later flying Spitfires. He retired in 1961 and died in 2004.

Flying Officer Hector Duro. A British pilot who joined 7 Squadron and served on the same aircraft as Frank Lewis. He was shot down and killed on a mission to Munchen on 21st December 1942. He was 34. He was buried in Seraincourt Churchyard in France.

Pilot Officer Bateman. A pilot. Nothing else is known of his service history.

Sergeant Charles Milton. A Canadian air gunner. His aircraft took off from RAF Gaydon on 8th November 1942, suffered engine failure and crashed near Harbury, killing both crew members. Charles was 19 and was buried in Stratford Cemetery.

Flight Sergeant William Foley. A Canadian pilot who joined 405 Squadron. He was killed on a mission to Kiel, perhaps on the same aircraft as James Taylor and Ralph Wright, on 5th April 1943. He was buried in Kiel War Cemetery.

Sergeant A.H. Whitted. He was injured in October 1942 when his aircraft crashed at Salford Priors. Nothing else is known of his service history.

Sergeant Harry Sargent. A Canadian navigator who joined 405 Squadron. He was killed on a mission to Kiel, perhaps on the same aircraft as James Taylor, William Foley and Ralph Wright, on 5th April 1943. He was buried in Kiel War Cemetery.

Pilot Officer Robert Worley. A Canadian who joined 424 Squadron, the same crew as Alfred Wiles. His aircraft crashed-landed after a mission to Wilhelmshaven on 25th February 1943. Robert was one of three crew members killed. He was 25. He was buried in Dishforth Cemetery in Yorkshire.

Sergeant Bryce Domigan. A British bomb aimer who joined 408 Squadron. He was on the same aircraft as Sergeant Troy which crash-landed after a mission to Berlin in March 1943. While on a mission to Aachen in Germany on 13th July 1943, his aircraft was shot down over Holland by a night fighter. Bryce managed to evade capture for two months before being captured in St Jean de Luz in south-west France, 1200km from Aachen. He spent time at Stalag Luft 3 in present-day Poland, was moved to Stalag Luft 6 on 28th February 1944 then to Stalag 357 by 1945. His subsequent fate is unclear.

Pilot Officer Harry Enever. A twenty-year-old bomb aimer from Nottingham. He joined 419 Squadron, along with W. Klein, H. Bees and Walter Alison, and was shot down while on a mission to Duisburg on 13th May 1943. Harry believed they had crashed over Holland, and asked the approaching soldiers if they were Dutch. '*Ja, Deutsch,*' they replied. His capture was straightforward.

He spent time as a POW in Stalag Luft 3, location of the Great Escape. He played a key role in plotting and implementing the construction of the three escape tunnels, and worked as a 'stooge', keeping track of guards' movements during the work. On the night of 25th March 1944, he was next in line to enter the tunnels when the Germans realised what was going on and the escape attempt was over. He was then moved to Marlag und Milag Nord, a POW camp in north Germany. After the armistice he returned to England, married his fiancée and settled in Dorset. He died in 2011, one of the last survivors of the Great Escape conspirators.

Sergeant Harry Lindsay McBeath. A Canadian who joined 7 Squadron, on the same crew as Hector Duro and Frank Lewis. He was shot down on a mission to Munchen on 21st December 1942 and managed to evade capture, eventually returning to England. He was awarded the Distinguished Flying Medal in July 1943. His subsequent future is unclear.

Flight Sergeant Albert Bateman. A Canadian who joined 419 Squadron. He was reported missing on an operation to Berlin on 1st March 1943. He is commemorated on the Runnymede Memorial.

Warrant Officer James Breen. A Canadian who joined 431 Squadron. He served on the same aircraft as Earl Rheaume and was killed with the rest of the crew on 12th June 1943. He was buried in a collective grave in Bergen-op-Zoom War Cemetery.

Warrant Officer L.A. McGaughey. A Canadian observer. Nothing else is known of his service history.

Sergeants Haywood and Boyce sunbathing by the railway at Atherstone.

Courtesy of Nick Pratley.

The first fatal accident at RAF Stratford took place on 6th November 1941. A Wellington took off then the port engine failed. It crashed in Alscot Park as the pilot attempted to circle round to land, hit some trees then caught fire.

Elsie Harding, a young woman who lived with her husband George in the Alscot Park lodge gates, witnessed the crash. Nobody else was nearby. She didn't know if it was British or German, then heard screaming in the now flaming wreckage. She ran to help, at the same time fearing she would be shot. She saw movement in the rear turret, realised it was someone trying to get out. The fuselage was now well alight and the oxygen bottles were starting to explode. Elsie smashed the Perspex with a piece of wreckage, freed the man's trapped leg and dragged him out by his feet. 'Get the others,' he said as he passed out, but there was nothing more she could do. She propped him under a tree and fetched an eiderdown from the house to cover him. The rescue crew arrived from the airfield and two more airmen were freed. Two others didn't survive.

James Rich, 30, and Ronald Clamp, 21, both pilots with the RAF Volunteer Reserve, were killed. James was an experienced pilot and flying instructor who had recently completed an operational tour with 142 Squadron over occupied Europe, and was awarded the DFC a fortnight after his death.

Charles Whitworth, an RAF pilot, Canadian airman Donald Mitchell, and Australian air gunner John Sanders all survived their injuries. It was probably Charles Whitworth that Elsie rescued. Elsie was presented with a silver salver by the RAF for her bravery, but the incident would haunt her for the rest of her life. She could still feel the fear, 65 years later, when she recalled the story for the *Stratford Herald* in 2005.

The salver presented to Elsie Harding, courtesy of Ann Hicks. Charles Whitworth.

Courtesy of Nick Pratley.

Charles Whitworth and Donald Mitchell recovered and returned to active service. It seems Charles completed his operational tour then returned to Atherstone as an instructor. He was killed in an accident on the airfield on 25th May 1942 when two aircraft collided on the runway.

Donald Mitchell went on to serve with 148 Squadron. He was reported missing while on a mission from North Africa to Egypt on 28th September 1942. He was 26. He is commemorated on the Alamein Memorial in Egypt.

John 'Sandy' Sanders, who had suffered a broken leg and severe injuries to his face, also returned to operational duties. He was posted to 265 Squadron in Madagascar and patrolled the Indian Ocean. He ended the war as a Squadron Gunnery Leader then returned home to Australia. *[Additional information courtesy of Pete Summerton.]*

Pilot Officer Ken Mould had trained as a civilian pilot and joined the RAF at the start of the war. He spent nine months training at Stratford between September 1941 and June 1942. On 13th February 1942, he was part of a crew of eight which left Stratford on a night cross-country exercise, flying to Andover, Peterborough and Cambridge, then to Priors Hardwick bombing range to drop their practice bombs, then returned to Atherstone, a flight of 4½ hours.

As they came into land their instructor, Pilot Officer William Arthur Smith, who had completed a tour with 419 Squadron before coming to 22 OTU, decided to show them how to perform an overshoot. The pilot failed to clear the railway embankment beyond the runway and the impact sheared off the front turret and nose section, as well as both engines, the bomb bay and the bottom of the fuselage.

Ken was in the cabin behind the pilots' positions and was flung into the door, bursting it off its hinges, and ended up unconscious under the pilot's rudder bar. The aircraft fortunately didn't catch fire and Ken was dug out by his crewmates. A train sped past the wreckage just a few minutes later. All the crew, including Sergeants George Molozzi, Mitchell, Lane, Normington and Murphy, and Flight Sergeant Swain, suffered just minor injuries. The incident was later attributed to failure of the flaps. *[As interviewed by Pete Summerton.]*

Ken Mould flew his first cross-country flight six weeks later. His starboard engine cut out but he safely made an emergency landing at an airfield in Lincolnshire. A month later, he had another near escape when landing, when he nearly collided with another aircraft. This, it later transpired, was a German intruder. He completed his operational flying and survived the war.

George Molozzi, a Canadian navigator, completed his training in March 1942 and joined 419 Squadron. He then returned to 22 OTU as a navigational instructor. Exactly a year after his first accident on 13th February 1943, George, now a warrant officer, was involved in a near identical accident when a flap pin broke on approaching Wellesbourne Airfield. With no height to recover, the aircraft stalled and crashed in a field near Charlecote. All eight crew members – four instructors and four pupils – were killed. George, aged 27, was buried in Stratford Cemetery.

Sgt Noel McHenry Moore was an American pilot who volunteered for the RCAF before the USA entered the war. He had initially served with 19 Squadron as a Spitfire pilot, and overshot the runway on landing at his base in Norfolk on 5th September 1941, crashing into the perimeter hedge. He escaped uninjured but severely damaged the aircraft. It seems this ended his career as a fighter pilot and he moved to Atherstone to fly Wellingtons. He was awarded a parchment for bravery in January 1942 for his ultimately unsuccessful efforts to rescue a woman who had fallen into the river in Stratford. He was then posted to 419 Squadron in Yorkshire, and was killed on a bombing raid on 30th July 1942. He was buried in Gosselies Communal Cemetery in Belgium.

Airmen at Atherstone. Courtesy of Natalie Hall. Airmen outside the men's quarters, October 1942.

Courtesy of Nick Pratley.

There were many fatal accidents on the airfield. At 3am on 29th June 1942, a Wellington returning to Atherstone from night training overshot the runway. It couldn't regain height and crashed into trees a mile from the airfield. Pilot Harold Jones, 22, from Cheshire; James Fedigan, 27, a bomb aimer from Chicago serving with the RCAF; Canadian WAG Charles Archer, 23; and Canadian air observer Michael Fedirchyk, 22, were killed. One of the crew, Sgt Blott, escaped with serious injuries. Michael Fedirchyk had been at Atherstone for two months and had recently written home: '*I had to join Canada's armed forces. If I hadn't, I never would have been able to hold my head up with self-pride and respect again.*' The Canadians were buried in Stratford Cemetery.

At 2.40am on 25th May 1942, a Wellington waiting for clearance to take off was struck by another landing aircraft and destroyed. It was thought a strong crosswind caused the accident, one of the worst on the site. Five fire appliances from the Stratford Auxiliary Fire Service attended the crash.

Five of the seven crew members of the first aircraft were killed. Douglass Callaghan, a New Zealand WAG, 23; John Williams, a New Zealand air observer, 26; Mervyn Wilkinson, a New Zealand WAG, 21; and Vyvyan Pascoe, an Australian airman, 25, were all buried in Stratford Cemetery. James Hough, an RAF air gunner, 28, was buried in his home town of Macclesfield. F/O John Gale and P/O Morris survived with serious injuries.

The pilot of the landing aircraft was Charles Whitworth, who had been rescued from a burning aircraft at Alscot Park six months earlier. He was buried in his home town in Leicestershire. John Gibby, 27, was a WAG instructor who had served before the war in the Auxiliary Airforce. He had flown on operational flights over Germany and Italy and had been involved in dropping propaganda leaflets. His obituary stated he loved flying and was fully prepared to give his life for his country. Robert Cook, 21, a Canadian WAG, and Ronald Herbert, 23, a New Zealand observer, were buried in Stratford Cemetery. The rear gunner, Sgt Noyes, was the only survivor.

John Gale reached the rank of flight lieutenant and was awarded the DFC. He died on active service on 23rd November 1943, aged 27, and was buried in his home town in Yorkshire.

On 1st September 1942, a Wellington overshot and crash landed at Atherstone. Two of the crew, Sgt RA Nickless and Sgt JM Broughton were injured.

On 7th September 1942, an aircraft from Atherstone suffered engine failure on a cross-country flight. It was unable to find an airfield to land and crashed near Bicester in Oxfordshire, where it caught fire. All five crew were killed. The pilot, Pat Templeton, 19, was from Texas and went to Canada to volunteer for the RCAF. Frederick Dowland, 19, a Canadian WAG; Ronald Jackson, 21, a Canadian air gunner; George Robb, 28, a Canadian air observer; and Albert Temple, 27, a Canadian air observer, were buried in Bicester Cemetery.

On 24th September, an aircraft returning from a night cross-country exercise careered into the control tower when landing with only a floodlight. The rear gunner, Canadian Martin Foran, 24, was killed. The pilot, John Dunford, and the rest of the crew were unhurt.

John Dunford was later posted to 433 Squadron and was killed on a mission to Germany on 23rd April 1944. He was 27 and is buried in Reichswald War Cemetery in Germany.

On 13th October 1942, a Wellington crashed two minutes after take-off having lost power in one engine. Three of the four crew members were killed. William Sinclair, 25, was a Canadian pilot two months into his training. Ernest Hunt, 27, was a Canadian WAG. Reginald Elsom, 32, was an RAF pilot instructor who had been awarded the DFM after operational service with 218 Squadron.

Douglas Broughton, a Canadian air gunner, was injured but subsequently returned to duty. He was posted to 429 Squadron at RAF Harwell on 15th March 1943. Two months later, on 13th May, he was on a bombing raid to Duisburg. His aircraft was shot down by a night fighter over Holland and he was killed. He was 21 years old and was buried in Jonkerbos War Cemetery in Nijmegan.

The Thousand Bomber Raids

The thousand-bomber raids began in 1942, aimed to mount a shattering blow on German targets, and every airfield which could put aircraft in the air did so. Instructors and the more advanced pupils from the training airfields flew on these raids. The first raid was to Cologne on 30-31st May 1942, in which eleven aircraft from Atherstone took part. Thirteen took part in a raid on Essen on 1-2nd June.

Instructor William Arthur Smith, who had suffered minor injuries in a crash in February 1942, flew on the operations to Cologne on 30th May, Essen on 1-2nd June, and Dusseldorf on 10-11th September.

Clifford Sullivan; Edward McCasky; Charles Pollard.
Courtesy of www.aircrewremembered.com

On the latter raid, two Wellingtons from RAF Stratford were shot down with the loss of all crew. One was crewed by five RCAF airmen in the final week or so of their training. Pilot Daniel Pablo, 22; observer Charles Pollard, 20; WAG Wallace Johnson, 22; WAG Edward McCasky, 20; and air observer Clifford Sullivan, 19, were shot down near Osterwick in Germany just after midnight. All were buried in Reichswald War Cemetery.

Cliff Sullivan had enlisted the previous year and arrived in Britain in May 1942. His commanding officer stated he was extremely popular and his keenness and enthusiasm were most marked. The day before the mission he had been chatting to Natalie Bishop at Rough Farm, and arranged to take her to the Friday dance two days later. He didn't live long enough to make his date.

William Smith was promoted to squadron leader and left Atherstone for operational duties with 7 Squadron, a Pathfinder squadron. He was awarded the DFC and was killed on a bombing mission on 2nd February 1943. He was buried in Rotterdam General Cemetery. He was now 23 years old.

Canadian bomb aimer James O'Connor was part of a trainee crew to take part in the operation to Cologne in May 1942. He returned safely and was posted to 419 Squadron. He took part in a raid to Bremen in August 1942 and wrote home that he got direct hits with his 4000lbs bombs, then on the way home over Holland came face to face with a German fighter. James was also front gunner and fired a long burst after which the fighter went into a dive. Their pilot then dived to avoid other fighters, dropping to just 15ft above the ground, skimming searchlight stations and flak operators which couldn't get a fix on them. They reached home safely. On 28th April 1943 he was minelaying off Skaggerak in Norway and his aircraft didn't return. He is commemorated on the Runnymede Memorial.

Trainee air gunner Thomas Owens also took part in the operation to Cologne. He returned safely and was shortly posted to 405 Squadron. On 24th July 1942 he went on a mission to Duisburg and one engine cut out on return. The aircraft crashed into a house with the loss of all eight crew. Thomas, aged 21, was buried in Barmby on the Moor Churchyard in Yorkshire.

On 14th September, two more Stratford crews went missing while on a mission to Bremen. One aircraft had been shot down by a night fighter over Ramspol in Holland; the other was presumed lost over the North Sea. Donald King, a Canadian air observer, Donald Murray, 20, a Canadian air gunner, and George Bickerton, 24, a Canadian pilot, were buried in Amersfoort General Cemetery in Utrecht, the Netherlands. The identities of the other crew are unclear.

The last bombing operation for the trainee crews was scheduled for Essen on the 16th September. One Wellington took off from Atherstone for an air test that afternoon. It reached 800ft then lost power and went into a dive. The force tore off one wing and the tail section, and the aircraft crashed six miles away at Pebworth. All crew members were killed. Harry Casimiri, a Canadian WAG who had been instructing at Atherstone for two months; David Halstead, 21, a Canadian WAG; Albert 'Jack' Fawcett, 22, a Canadian pilot instructor; John O'Brien, 21, a Canadian air observer and instructor; Frank Macauley, 22, a WAG from the Bahamas; and RAF ground fitters Leslie Holloway, 20, and

Left: Jack Fawcett. Right: Harry Casimiri.

Courtesy of Nick Pratley.

Daniel McMillan, 36. Jack Fawcett and John O'Brien had flown thirty bombing missions together, including the Cologne raid on 30th May. Their final mission was to Rhineland where they came home peppered with flak to complete their operational tour. They then went through the ordeal of meeting the king and queen, and came to Atherstone as instructors.

One of the six Wellingtons from Atherstone failed to return from Essen. It had been shot down by anti-aircraft fire near Ahaus in Germany with the loss of all crew. Pilot John Dawson, 32, was an instructor who had been awarded the DFC on operational service. Canadian air observer Philip Brichta, 31, was also an instructor and recipient of the DFC. The other crew were Canadian air observer George Goold, 30, Canadian WAG Lorne Lemoine, 22, and Scottish WAG William Hughes, 24. All were buried in a collective grave in Reichswald Forest War Cemetery in Germany.

Hugh Stiles enlisted in the RAF in 1939, aged 19. After completing his operational tour he came to Atherstone as an instructor in August 1941. After recovering from a serious accident in September, he took part in the thousand-bomber raid to Cologne in May 1942 then returned to operational duties. He was involved in clandestine work delivering SOE operatives into Nazi-occupied Europe, then took part in undercover operations in France himself. He was awarded the DFC and Bar and left the RAF ranked a squadron leader.

Flight mechanic AC1 Hutton with Wellington DV653.

Courtesy of Nick Pratley.

Operations from 1943

On 29th January 1943, five Wellingtons left Stratford on a long cross-country exercise. Two aircraft collided in heavy cloud near RAF Honington in Suffolk and crashed, killing all ten airmen. James Wilson, 20, a Canadian pilot; Ronald Oswald, 34, an air bomber from New Jersey serving with the RCAF; Kenneth Mount, 29, a Canadian air bomber; Michael Kelly, 20, a Canadian navigator; William Harron, 24, a Canadian pilot; William Argo, 20, a Canadian air gunner; Ross Archer, 19, a Canadian navigator; and Robert Alderson, 22, a Canadian air gunner, were buried in Honington Churchyard. The identities of the other two men are unclear.

On 13th March 1943, a bomber returning from a night cross-country flight overshot the runway and crashed. One of the crew, RAF sergeant JT Kidd, suffered cuts to his head. The other crew members, Sergeants CW Jackson and HB Kihorn of the RCAF, were uninjured.

On 24th April 1943, a bomber returning from a navigational exercise landed heavily, the right wing hitting the ground, then spun 180 degrees. One engine then caught fire. Five of the eight crew members were injured: Robert Henderson, J Doyle, EJ Weston, Alan Olsson and CH Balfort. JA Williams, Jack Koivu and KM Pulham escaped uninjured.

Pilot Robert Henderson later went to 70 Squadron, based in Djedeida near Tunis which mounted operations to Italy. Robert, aged 31, was killed on 25th November 1943 while on a bombing raid to Turin, one of seventeen aircraft lost that night. He is buried in Catania War Cemetery in Sicily.

Pilot Alan Olsson and navigator Jack Koivu were sent to 426 Squadron in Yorkshire, and served on the same bomber crew. The squadron mounted regular raids on Germany and on 26th March 1944 they were among 700 bombers which mounted a raid on Essen. Their Lancaster was hit by flak near Essen and exploded at 18,000 feet. All seven crew bailed out, but none survived. All were buried in Reichswald Forest War Cemetery.

On 29th May 1943, three Wellingtons took off from Atherstone for a Wings for Victory fly-past at Pershore. Local air cadet Harry Badger was among those watching when a wing broke off one aircraft. It crashed behind a hotel and burst into flames. All crew were killed but luckily nobody on the ground was hurt. The pilot was Graham Hynam, 22, who had travelled from Ohio to join the RCAF and had been awarded the DFC. Peter Zoeller was a wireless operator from Surrey. Three ground crew, Harry Allan, 22, George Band, 22, and William Gravell, 21, had been taken on the flight for a treat.

The cause was metal fatigue. The pilot had heard a cracking from the wing on its previous flight and had the ground crew investigate, but as the damage was inside and therefore invisible, the aircraft had been pronounced safe to fly.

On 2nd July 1943, a bomber took off for a check flight and a tyre burst. It then crashed out of control. The two crew members, JH Emmerson and JG White, were uninjured.

On 2nd October 1943, the propeller in a Wellington engine jammed a few minutes after take-off. While the pilot attempted to land, the engine stopped and the aeroplane crashed four miles from the airfield. The Canadian pilot, Frederick Partridge, was killed; Canadian WAG John de Macedo, 24, lost a leg and died the following day in hospital. Both are buried in Pershore cemetery. The third crew member, JW Dufton, was injured.

Later that same day, a bomber took off carrying five 500lb practice bombs filled with sand. The engine cut out. The bombs were jettisoned and the plane attempted to land but the undercarriage collapsed on landing. WR Stewart, the only named person on board, escaped uninjured.

On 26th November 1943, a plane took off from Stratford on night flying practice. After two hours the starboard engine failed and the plane came down out of control near Pershore. All four Canadian crew members, pilot Joseph Dubord, 25, navigator Raymond Morand, 19, air bomber Joseph Vennes, 21, and WAG Joseph Chevalier, 25, were killed. All are buried in Pershore cemetery.

On 8th January 1944, a plane was practicing single-engine flying when the engine cut out. Before recovery action could be done, the plane hit a high voltage pylon and crashed into rising ground near Talton Farm. The pilot, Canadian Francis Dolter, suffered cuts to his head and the crash was blamed on his carelessness. The other four crew members were uninjured. Pete Mumford, then five years old and living at Ettington Park, went with his dad on his bicycle to find the crash. When they reached Crimscote the crew were out of the aircraft and asking for a telephone to contact their base. Unusually, there was a telephone in the village. The aircraft remained for some time before it was removed, and local boys including seven-year-old David Lockwood of Crimscote collected souvenirs including strings of machine gun bullets.

Francis Dolter was reported missing while on a mission to Aachen with 424 Squadron on 25th May 1944. He is commemorated on the Runnymede Memorial.

In April 1944, a Wellington piloted by Canadian trainee Joseph Savard lost power in one engine when returning from a bombing practice to Priors Hardwick. Joseph attempted a single-engine landing, overshot the runway and crashed. All crew escaped unhurt.

Joseph then joined 433 Squadron and was shot down by a night-fighter on 17th August while mine-laying in the Baltic Sea. His aircraft crashed into the sea with no survivors. Joseph's body was washed ashore at Magleby in Denmark three weeks later, and he was buried in the local churchyard. He was nineteen years old.

On 11th June 1944, one engine of a bomber piloted by Canadian trainee C Bouchard cut out. The crew were forced to crash land, being unable to pump down the undercarriage. The aircraft caught fire but none of the crew were injured.

On 29th July 1944, a plane set out on exercise around 10pm then was approaching to land at 3.40am the next morning. It crashed into a wood near Coombe Farm, three miles from the airfield. It was later found that the fuel tanks had not been switched over, so both engines stopped simultaneously. Five of the six crew were killed. Canadian pilot Jean Belanger, 20, navigator Ross Cuzner, 19, air bomber Joseph Moreau, 24, WAG Joseph Dauplaise, 21, and air gunner Joseph Martin, 20, were buried in Stratford Cemetery.

Joseph Dion was injured but subsequently recovered. He died on active service three months later on 15th November 1944, aged 24, and is buried in Brookwood Military Cemetery in Surrey.

On 20th November 1944, an aircraft took off from Stratford on a cross-country exercise, piloted by Canadian JW Nezan. After four hours one engine began playing up and it was diverted to Wellesbourne Mountford where it crash-landed. The aircraft was written off but none of the crew were injured.

The same day, another Wellington on a cross-country exercise encountered severe weather over Wales. Ice formed on the aircraft and caused engine problems, and the pilot descended to a lower altitude to try and counter the problem. The

The crew of Wellington MF509. Charles Hamel; Joseph Groulx; Joseph Burke; William Allison; Joseph DuSablon; Gaston Caron (not on board during the crash).

Courtesy of Nick Pratley.

Left: Navigators Bill Allison and Jules Villeneuve at Atherstone, 1944. Right: Joseph Groulx, Joseph Burke and Joseph DuSablon at Atherstone, November 1944.

Courtesy of Nick Pratley.

aircraft then crashed into Carreg Goch in the Black Mountains with the loss of all six Canadian crew. Pilot Charles Hamel, 21, air gunners Joseph Groulx, 22, and Joseph DuSablon, 20, WAG Joseph Burke, 20, air bomber William Allison, 28, and navigator Jules Villeneuve, 22, were on their penultimate flight before their transfer to 425 Squadron. They were buried in Chester Cemetery. The aircraft wreckage can still be seen at the site today.

The last accident at Atherstone was on 8th December 1944, when a Wellington from another site was forced to make an emergency landing at the airfield. The aircraft landed on the runway then careered on until it came to a stop overhanging the railway line. The crew escaped unharmed and the aircraft was barely damaged, until the station master from Stratford sent a train with men to help. It crashed into the aircraft and destroyed it.

The accidents were often witnessed by the local people. Alan Noyce of The Kennels (b1937) remembers going to look at a downed aircraft on the airfield, but the Military Police wouldn't let him near it. When an aircraft crashed into the Ridgeway Field near Preston Pastures Farm, locals including Harry Smith of Lower Farm could see men jumping out with their clothing ablaze, but there was nothing they could do to help. The aircraft was fully armed with bombs and could explode at any second. Ruth Vanderzalm, nee Smith (b1931) of Lower Farm lay in bed counting the aircraft flying over their house as they set off, and prayed the same number would return the following morning.

An accident happened on the airfield one night, when farm worker George Beauchamp of Rough Farm worked on the airfield as night watchman. He was asked about the incident the next morning, and knew nothing about it. It turned out he'd been asleep most of the night.

The End of the War

Operational training ceased on 15th December 1944. The Wellingtons left and the airfield was used as a relief landing ground. In August 1945, it was taken over by the Signals Flying Unit (SFU) which trained crew in radar use. One of the personnel trained was Arthur C Clarke, who became an acclaimed science-fiction author. The SFU left the site in September 1946 and this was the end of Atherstone's use as an operational airbase. The Air Ministry had no further use for the site and it was put to various uses – official and unofficial – over the coming decades.

Residential Use

The accommodation buildings were gradually occupied by families with nowhere else to live. These 'squatters' had no permission to live there and a meeting of Stratford District Council in October 1946 declared that no further actions could be taken against the squatters. The Air Ministry still had jurisdiction for the site and it was for them to say whether the civilians should be evicted. 'Many people are living in the huts,' a council spokesman said, 'which need a good deal to be done to them, but the council is not in a position to do anything.' The council eventually gained control of the site and made the hutments more habitable.

At least forty families lived there over the next decade, many with young children. They included public service driver Alfred Childs and his wife Mary; tool setter Robert Wimperis and his wife Muriel; crane driver Andrew Slavin; gardener Alfred Swan; agricultural worker Gerd Lothain Schindler and his wife Nesta; and factory worker Alfred Wuerth and his wife Emmi. Some may have been Italian POWs or German refugees who remained in the area. The 'aerodrome kids', as they were known, attended Preston School and were given hot cocoa on cold mornings after the long walk down.

Bert and Doreen Hathaway lived with Doreen's parents in Alderminster until Bert was discharged from the army in 1946. They then moved to the aerodrome with their two young children. They lived in a wooden hut in the sergeants and officers accommodation which comprised two bedrooms and a living room, with a washing/toilet block a short distance away. Several other families were living there, including a Polish couple named Busek who worked for Stratford Blue buses.

The water tower still supplied the site with water, although in the cold winter of 1947 the men had to climb up the scaffolding to light a fire to melt the water. Electricity was still supplied from the site generator. The Hathaway family left in late 1947 for a new council house in Alderminster, priority for these being given to ex-servicemen.

In February 1951, a large quantity of goods stored on the site were found to be missing, and eight camp tenants were summoned to the magistrate's court. John Fitzgerald was charged with stealing eight wooden window frames worth £8 and £1-worth of linoleum. He had used them for firewood, claiming his wife and baby were shivering with cold at the time. He had several previous convictions and was fined £5. He and his wife Henriette were also charged with stealing two more frames, again for firewood. They were fined a further £7 for this.

Henriette Fitzgerald was then charged with the theft of a ration book from

Sylvia Bennett, a resident of Site 3. Sylvia left her handbag in Henriette's hut and when she returned for it, the book was missing. Henriette admitted she'd taken it when she was drunk and was fined another £1.

John and Iris Garrett and Marcia Brown of Living Site 2 were charged with stealing three rolls of linoleum and were fined £1 each.

Theresa Saunders was charged with stealing two rolls of linoleum. She pleaded she'd stolen it because her hut was flooded. Her child was a cripple and she thought the linoleum would save the child's feet. The magistrate was unmoved; Theresa was fined £1.

James and Cynthia Turner of Living Site 2 were charged with stealing two rolls of linoleum. They claimed they had only borrowed it, but the court was not convinced. They were fined £4.

Motor mechanic Thomas Parry, 31, lived at Site 4 and was involved in motorcycle collision on the Shipston Road in May 1951. He died soon afterwards and was buried in Preston cemetery.

The last residents left in 1958, moved to council houses with modern amenities in Stratford. A New Zealand pilot who had been based at Atherstone returned every few years to camp on the site. For some, the bonds of the past were unrelenting.

Agriculture

The Warwickshire Agricultural Executive Committee (WAEC) used the land to train farmworkers in the use of modern machinery. By 1948, 200 acres of the former aerodrome had been ploughed up and the land hummed with the roar of tractors as they had resounded to the engines of aircraft a few years earlier. In 1949, the WAEC held a demonstration of modern row-crop and market garden machinery, including the latest tractors, motor hoes and cultivating tools. In 1951, a national demonstration of potato harvesting equipment and sugar beet machines was held. The site was also used to trial progressive techniques in livestock management.

Seed corn was stored in the aircraft hangar. In November 1948, the WAEC bailiff found two bags of wheat missing. PC Turner of Alderminster was summoned, and he accosted WAEC employee Victor Bayliss who admitted the wheat was in his bathroom at home. He said he was going to feed it to his pigs and fowls, but would now return it. Another employee, Joseph Warner, denied any part in the theft, saying he'd simply aided Bayliss load the bags onto his bicycle. Bayliss was fined £4; Warner £1.

In 1952, Ailstone Farm was taken by Gordon Hawkins from Stepstones Farm in Newbold. Whitehill Farm was now farmed by Joseph Spencer and Beecham Farm by Andrew Bishop. Both families adapted the aerodrome buildings for agricultural purposes. The communal building became a potato shed; the WAAF communal building was converted to a turkey shed. Andrew Bishop used the hospital block to house poultry. Other buildings, including the sergeants' mess, were used to house pigs, which would look out of the windows at passers-by.

Other Uses

The hangars were adapted for large scale storage. The Ministry for Food stored sugar in one for several years. The piled sacks weighed several hundred tonnes and syrup formed from the damp was forced out across the floor. The Ministry installed boilers and employed women with mops to collect it and render it back to sugar. In February 1954, Edward Clarke, a 29-year-old labourer, was carrying a 2cwt [150kg] sack of sugar at the site. He slipped and fell and was crushed by the sack. He sustained severe injuries and died in hospital a few days later.

In 1962, the firm Storage and Haulage Ltd took over the hangar and used it for everything from shovels, fire extinguishers and paper to car engines and artificial fertiliser, which farmers would collect from the site. The second hangar, demolished in the 1960s, was used by the car manufacturer Jaguar. A Stratford timber merchant used the site and the Nuffield Tractor Division had a workshop and classroom there.

The runways were used by light aircraft piloted by hobbyists and a go-kart club held races on the runways. Hendon Police College used the site to train drivers, and many locals learnt to drive there.

The site was a handy source of wood, scrap metal, petrol and many other things for the locals. Pete Shadbolt of Storage and Haulage Ltd built himself a greenhouse from wood salvaged from a building on site. Former airman Keith Knight, once stationed on the site, stole four drums of petrol in September 1946. A spark set the petrol on fire and Knight was badly burned. He recovered from his injuries and was fined £10.

In the 1960s it was proposed to keep the site as an airfield to serve Stratford, but the plans came to nothing. Captain James West of Alscot Park applied to park 2000 new motor cars on the site, which was also turned down by Stratford District Council.

The electric cables were removed from the runways and perimeter tracks, as were the remaining lights and transformers. In April 1966, the runways themselves were demolished. 60,000 tonnes of hardcore was smashed and removed and used to provide sub-base for Warwick bypass. The much-damaged soil under the runways was now of little use for agriculture, and much is planted with conifer trees.

In 1979, a grain store and drying plant was built, designed to process 200 tonnes of grain an hour. The plant is still in operation today.

Several of the original aerodrome structures remain, adapted to vastly different purposes, and act as a reminder of those air crews who, seventy five years ago, lived, trained, and lost their lives on this now peaceful farmland.

One hundred and twenty Airforce personnel were buried in Stratford Cemetery during the Second World War. Eighteen are known to have lost their lives in accidents at RAF Stratford.

And Finally…

Thirty years after VE Day, the long hand of the war again touched the people of Preston on the shoulder. In August 1975, the following headline appeared in the *Stratford Herald.*

FARM WORKER HARVESTS TWO LIVE MORTAR BOMBS.

Roy Mainwaring, 21, was helping with the harvest in the Top Park in Preston when he felt the Massey combine harvester he was driving hit something hard. He thought it was a lump of wood, and jumped down to throw it out of the way. He cleared the straw away and realised it was a bomb, caught in the machine's mechanical fingers. He made a very quick exit from the field.

Roy then remembered his boss would soon be coming to check on his progress, so he tied a note to the gate. '*Bomb on Massey. Gone home.*'

The next day the police, fire brigade and an army bomb disposal squad were called to the scene, and they found a second mortar bomb nearby. Roy was, according to Fire Officer Eric Tallis, a very lucky man. An elderly Preston resident recalled some bombs being dropped by a German aircraft during the war, and it was supposed they had lain undiscovered since then.

Will Spencer from Park Farm, 21, ignored the warnings and went out to take a photo of the bomb. They were detonated by the bomb disposal team, causing no damage.

The mortar bomb.

Conclusion

War affects everyone. The troops on the front line, their families, their communities. This was more so than ever during the 20th century. The story of the Alscot villages is a reflection of communities across Britain, and across the world.

When the Armistice was signed in 1918, people's thoughts turned to how the sacrifice of individuals and communities could be remembered. The memorials and cemeteries created in the aftermath of two world wars are their everlasting testimony.

As Major General Burstal, commander of the Canadian division, wrote to the 21st Canadians, in which Will Porter was killed just before the Armistice:

> *'We have many glorious deeds to recall and while we think of them our thoughts turn naturally to those loyal comrades who fought and endured with us and who have paid the full price of devotion to their country. They have died but their names will live. Their graves will be perpetual memorials of our achievements long after we have passed away.*
>
> *The division will now cease to exist but its spirit will live forever. This is to me the grandest thing of all. The gallant actions and achievements, the cheerfully endured suffering and hardships of the past four years, will inspire the future generations of our country in all time to come.'*

As we mark the centenary of the war to end all wars, remembering the stories of those who fought and fell, and the lessons their lives and deaths taught us, is more important than ever. This book is a small part of a worldwide effort to keep the candle of memory alight. As Will Porter's grave in France reads:

Death divides, but memory ever clings.

Gazetteer of Military Personnel

Service No	Rank	Forenames	Surname	Born/Died	Military Unit	Service Dates	Overseas Service
?	Private	William	Allcock	b1843	Royal Marines	1866-1878	At Sea
-	Lieutenant	Algernon Claude Phillip	Alston-Roberts-West	1878-1933	23rd London Regt	1914-(1917)	?
-	Captain	Harry Charles John	Alston-Roberts-West	1872-1931	Royal Navy	1886-1919	At Sea
33582	General	Michael Montgomerie	Alston-Roberts-West	1905-1978	Oxford Bucks Light Infantry; South Lancs Regt	1925-1965	Madagascar, Burma, Korea
-	Lieutenant	James	Alston-Roberts-West	1845-1918	Royal Naval Reserve	1875-(1891)	?
-	Commander	Philip Douglas	Alston-Roberts-West	1876-1937	Royal Navy	1891-1921	At Sea
-	Commander	Reginald Montague	Alston-Roberts-West	1875-1944	Royal Navy	1889-1922	At Sea
17833	**Major**	**William Reginald James**	**Alston-Roberts-West**	**1900-1940**	**3rd Grenadier Guards**	**1920-1940**	**France**
-	**Rear Admiral**	**Robert Keith**	**Arbuthnot**	**1864-1916**	**Royal Navy**	**1877-1916**	**At Sea**
W101405	Lance Corporal	Joan Elizabeth	Ashby (Spencer)	1914-2007	Auxiliary Territorial Service	(1941)-1946	None
9577	Chief Petty Officer	Olive Rosa	Ashby (Parnham)	1920-1988	Women's Royal Naval Service	(1941)-1946	None
?	?	Robert Henry	Ashby	b1895	?	1914; 1916-?	?
29816	Shoeing Smith	Robert	Ashby	1878-1946	Imperial Yeomanry	1901-1902	South Africa
145688	Gunner	James Richard	Ashfield	1885-1952	Royal Garrison Artillery	1917-1920	Egypt; Palestine
5329	Private	Ralph	Bailey	b1882	4th Worcestershire Regt	(1899)	None
61065	Private	Franklin	Baker	1900-1920	West Somerset Yeomanry	1917-1919	None
202026	**Private**	**James Richard**	**Baldwin**	**1894-1917**	**Royal Warwickshire Regt**	**1916-1917**	**France/Flanders**
S4/144055; A/204064	Private	Ernest Richard	Beavington	1893-1991	Army Service Corps; 9th King's Royal Rifles	1915-1919	France/Flanders
S/369672	Private	Percy William	Beavington	1899-1984	Army Service Corps	1917-1920	France/Flanders
7819	Private	Frederick	Beesley	b1884	3rd South Staffordshire Regt	1905-1908	None
?	?	Frank	Bennett	b1892	Warwickshire Yeomanry	(1915)	?
5120	Corporal	George	Bennett	b1890	9th Royal Warwickshire Regt	(1915)-(1919)	Gallipoli; Middle East
11956	**Private**	**Stephen**	**Bennett**	**1895-1917**	**Dorset Regt**	**1914-1917**	**France/Flanders**
?	?	Thomas	Bennett	b1888	Army Service Corps	(1915)	Serbia
543	?	William	Best (Jones)	b1851	?	1875-1887	Canada
?	?	Audrey	Bishop	b1919	Auxiliary Territorial Service	(1940s)	?
?	?	John	Bishop	b1917	Military Police	(1940s)	India
890120	Saddler Corporal	Joscelyn	Bloom	1895-1978	Royal Field Artillery	1914-1920	Gallipoli; Egypt
4644	Private	Charles	Bloxham	b1863	Rifle Brigade	1881-1893	India
12180; 32146	Private	Thomas	Bloxham	b1892	11th Hampshire Regt; Devon Regt	1914-1919	France/Flanders
291311	?	Thomas	Bloxham	b1870	RAF	1918-1920	Italy
JX128382; FX76573	Petty Officer	Thomas John	Bloxham	b1910	Royal Navy	1926-1961	At Sea
5247755	Private	Francis John	Bloxham (Stowe)	1909-1933	2nd Worcestershire Regt	?-1933	?
62553	Gunner	John	Boardman	b(1880)	Royal Garrison Artillery	1915-?	France/Flanders
443145	**Corporal**	**William Barton**	**Boardman**	**1882-1917**	**54th Canadian Infantry**	**1915-1917**	**France/Flanders**
26222	Private	George William	Brookes	1897-1980	Royal West Surrey Regt	1917-(1918)	France/Flanders
?	?	Harry	Brown	b(1893)	?	(1917)	Salonika
267626	**Private**	**Jack**	**Brown**	**(1898)-1917**	**11th Royal Warwickshire Regt**	**1916-1917**	**France/Flanders**
12495; 32018	Private	Arthur Thomas	Burrows	1896-1947	11th Hampshire Regt; Devon Regt	1914-1919	France/Flanders
45450	Wren	Kathleen Joan	Canning (Hughes)	1924-2017	Women's Royal Naval Service	1942-1945	Ceylon

-	Lieutenant	Thomas	Canning	1899-1952	Warwickshire Yeomanry	1917-1919	Middle East; France
30506	**Private**	**Frederick**	**Churchill**	**1881-1915**	**1st Welch Regiment**	**?-1915**	**France/Flanders**
?	?	Frederick	Clark	b1890	?	(1918)	?
1594; 164491	Sergeant	John Alec	Clift	1891-1973	Warwickshire Yeomanry; Machine Gun Corps	(1914)-1919	Middle East
WR/252161	Sapper	Albert Percy	Dale	1894-1978	Royal Engineers	(1915)-(1918)	France/Flanders
12178	Lance Sergeant	Robert William	Dale	1892-1940	11th Hampshire Regt	1914-1919	France/Flanders
M2/202979	Private	Edward	Day	b(1876)	Army Service Corps	1916-1919	Serbia
-	**Captain**	**Arthur Brownlow**	**Denham-Cookes**	**1891-1918**	**24th London Regt**	**1914-1918**	**None**
2132	Corporal	John	Dodd	b1864	1st Royal Warwickshire Regt	1887-1899	India
514385	Private	Percy Harold	Dove	1898-1970	14th London Regt	1916-(1918)	France/Flanders
1777	Private	Edwin	Dyer	1868-1935	Manchester Regt	1887-1899	India
67003	Gunner	Frederick	Dyer	1865-1933	Royal Artillery	1888-1900	India
16024; 22180	Private	George Henry	Edgington	1872-1951	Gloucestershire Regt; Machine Gun Corps	1914-1917	France/Flanders
2678	Private	Albert	Fletcher	b1874	Royal Warwickshire Regt	1890-1891	None
203653	Lance Corporal	Walter	Fowler	1879-1957	Worcestershire Regt	1916-1919	France/Flanders
555404	Lieutenant	Leslie	Francis	b1918	Warwickshire Yeomanry; Scots Greys	1939-1945	North Africa
34489	**Gunner**	**John**	**Garrett**	**1885-1917**	**Royal Field Artillery**	**1904-1917**	**France/Flanders**
?	?	Cyril Maurice	George	1913-2006	RAF	(1940s)	Italy?
60587	**Gunner**	**Frederick**	**George**	**1888-1917**	**Royal Field Artillery**	**(1911)-1917**	**India; Middle East**
4101	Private	Moses Jacques	George	1876-1914	Royal Warwickshire Regiment	1893-1905	Egypt
T4/065311	Driver	Thomas Ernest	George	1881-1970	Army Service Corps	1915-1919	France/Flanders
1429	Private	Thomas	Gibbins	1839-1889	24th Regt of Foot	1863-1865	None
5432983	Sergeant	William	Gibbins	1902-1973	1/7th Royal Warwickshire Regt	(1939)-1944	France
663416	Private	Alfred	Gibbs	b1879	Labour Corps	1918-1919	None
T2/14194	Staff Sergeant	William Joseph	Gilks	1888-1967	Army Service Corps	(1915-1919)	France; Salonika
20325	Private	Edward Oliver Walter	Goodall	1882-1953	3rd Royal Warwickshire Regt	1916	None
?	?	Frank	Goodall	1888-1970	?	?	France/Flanders
G21442	Private	Richard John	Green	1898-1918	Royal Fusiliers; Royal Sussex Regt	1916-1918	Middle East; France/Flanders
50670	Private	Thomas	Hadland	1875-1939	Somerset Light Infantry	1918	None
H/43500; 312750	Private	Alfred Thomas	Handy	1899-1961	Tank Corps; Labour Corps	1918-1919	None
203272	**Private**	**Arthur James**	**Handy**	**1885-1918**	**Royal Berkshire Regt**	**d1918**	**France/Flanders**
129519; 2146; 1162	Private	Edwin Ralph	Handy	1891-1958	Lancashire Fusiliers; Royal Engineers	1909-1919	Egypt
T4/065312	**Driver**	**Harry**	**Handy**	**1886-1919**	**Army Service Corps**	**1915-1919**	**None**
1407482; 36910	Lance Bombadier	John	Handy	1890-1970	Royal Garrison Artillery	1912-1924	India; Afghanistan
T/10082	Driver	John	Handy	b1871	Army Service Corps	1891-1893	None
400	Private	Richard	Handy	1841-1862	96th Regt of Foot	1859-1861	None
201804	**Private**	**Percy Gerald**	**Handy**	**1895-1917**	**1/5th Royal Warwickshire Regt**	**1916-1917**	**France/Flanders**
T/291590	Driver	Thomas	Handy	1887-1954	Army Service Corps	1917-1919	None
K23192	Stoker	Walter Owen	Handy	1896-1972	Royal Navy	1914-1919	At Sea
T4/065315	Driver	Wilfred William	Handy	1896-1968	Army Service Corps	1915-1919	France/Flanders
-	Lt Col	Bernard St John Warren	Hastings	*1872-1940*	The King's (Liverpool) Regt	*1892-(1907); (1916)*	?

-	Chaplain	Francis George Burrows	Hastings	1874-1933	Royal Navy	1905-1924	At Sea
-	Captain	Francis Henry	Hastings	1837-1921	Royal Navy	1849-1882	Crimea; At Sea
-	Lt Col	Wilfred Charles Norrington	Hastings	1874-1925	Manchester Regt; West African Frontier Force	(1894)-1922	South Africa; West Africa
826124	Lance Bombadier	Albert Victor	Hathaway	1913-1998	Royal Artillery	1933-1946	Western Europe
JX128384	?	James	Hathaway	b1910	Royal Navy	1926-(1929)	At Sea
G/86322 (90427)	**Private**	**Walter Henry**	**Hathaway**	**1881-1918**	**Royal Fusiliers; Royal Flying Corps**	**?-1918**	**None**
?	?	Walter Henry	Hathaway	b1918	?	(1940s)	North Africa
6021084	Private	William D	Haylock	b1918	Cambridgeshire Regt	1940-1945	Malaya; Singapore
4112	Private	Reginald Francis	Hawkins	b1894	Royal Warwickshire Regt	1914	None
6541	Private	Arnold	Herbert	1868-1939	Royal Artillery	1894-1906	India
SS/1234	Staff Sergeant	Russell	Herd	1891-1958	Army Service Corps	(1914)-(1915)	India; France
H/1/089; SS112486	Petty Officer	Edward	Hibbard	b1892	18th Hussars; Royal Navy	1911-1921	At Sea
2400	Private	Henry	Hicks	b1868	King's Own Light Infantry	1886-1898	None
36556	Sergeant	John Alfred	Hicks	(1897)-1965	Worcestershire Regt	1916-1920	France/Flanders
5350	**Private**	**Reginald Frank**	**Hicks**	**1889-1918**	**20th Australian Infantry**	**1916-1918**	**France/Flanders**
11964	**Corporal**	**Sidney Charles**	**Hicks**	**1893-1918**	**6th Dorsetshire Regt**	**1914-1918**	**France/Flanders**
?	?	William Reginald	Hicks	1912-1996	RAF	(1940s)	?
2676; 177102; 781633	Private	Frank James	Holtom	1895-1973	Royal Warks Regt; Machine Gun Corps; Tank Corps	1914-1930	France/Flanders
4636	Lance Corporal	Henry	Holtom	(b1875)	Royal Warwickshire Regt	1896-1903	East Indies
11962	Private	George William	Hopkins	b1893	6th Dorsetshire Regt	1914-1919	France/Flanders
2569	Private	William Henry	Hopkins	b1897	Royal Marine Light Infantry	1917-1919	France/Flanders
?	?	William (Curly)	Hopkins	1891-1955	?	1914-?	?
2783	**Lance Corporal**	**Sidney Francis**	**Hornsey**	**1898-1917**	**Royal Warwickshire Regt**	**(1915)-1917**	**Gallipoli; France**
2315	**QM Corporal**	**Albert**	**Horseman**	**1879-1918**	**1st Life Guards**	**1900-1918**	**France/Flanders**
?	?	Albert	Horseman	b1920	Warwickshire Yeomanry	?	?
5788; 47541	Bombadier	Ernest Giles	Horseman	1890-1975	3rd Dragoon Guards; Royal Horse Artillery	1906-1919	France/Flanders
10124	**Lance Corporal**	**Ernest Giles**	**Horseman**	**1892-1915**	**7th South Staffordshire Regt**	**?-1915**	**Gallipoli**
299453	**Private**	**Ernest Henry**	**Horseman**	**1892-1918**	**Army Service Corps**	**1917-1918**	**Middle East**
4330	Lance Corporal	Evan	Horseman	1881-1940	1st Life Guards	1916-1920	None
3591	Private	Giles	Horseman	1862-1916	2nd Derbyshire Regt	1881-1887	India
?	?	Francis (Frank)	Horseman	b1922	Warwickshire Yeomanry	?	?
8064	Lance Corporal	Harold	Horseman	1886-1973	2nd Royal Warwickshire Regt	1901-1915	France/Flanders
31762; 57566	Corporal	Harold Jim	Horseman	1899-1974	Dorset Regt; Worcestershire Regt	(1917)	?
1234	Private	Herbert	Horseman	1868-1956	Royal Warwickshire Regt	1885-1897	None
925455	?	Horace Hazelwood	Horseman	b1895	5th Canadian Infantry	1916-(1917)	France/Flanders
106297	Trooper	Hubert	Horseman	b1891	1st Canadian Mounted Rifles	1914-(1917)	France/Flanders
4103	Private	Joseph	Horseman	1861-1895	Royal Horse Artillery	1878-1890	India
M/302849	Private	Percy	Horseman	1899-1977	Army Service Corps	1917-1920	France; Italy
1362	Private	William	Horseman	1823-1895	60th (Royal Rifles) Regt	1839-1859	India
M2/176724	Corporal	John Edwin	Howes	1897-1970	Army Service Corps	1916-1919	Middle East
14472	**?**	**Joseph**	**Hudson**	**1837 -1859**	**97th (Earl of Ulster's) Foot**	**1856-1859**	**India**

	Lt Commander	Alexander Ian	Hughes	1914-1986	Royal Naval Reserve	(1940s)	At Sea
945734	Driver; Chaplain	Montague Laban	Hunt	b1897	Royal Field Artillery; Chaplain Dept	1914-1919; (1940-45)	France; Italy
5449	2nd Lieutenant	William	Hutchings	b1899	RAF	1917-1919	France
14252	**Private**	**Charles Edmund**	**Hyatt**	**1895-1916**	**2nd Coldstream Guards**	**1914-1916**	**France/Flanders**
12176	Private	Harold	Hyatt	1887-1956	11th Hampshire Regt	1914	None
?	?	John Edward	James	1918-1999	RAF	(1940s)	North Africa
16/171	**Private**	**John Milton**	**James**	**1885-1916**	**16th Royal Warwickshire Regt**	**1914-1916**	**France/Flanders**
941154	**Sergeant**	**William Leslie (Sam)**	**James**	**1921-1945**	**RAF**	**(1942)-1945**	**Europe**
DM2/189850	Corporal	William Henry	Jobe	1885-1933	Army Service Corps	1914; 1916-1919	?
?	?	Arthur C	Jones	b1914	Royal Army Service Corps	(1940)	Middle East
2663144	Lance Corporal	Stanley John	Jones	b1905	Coldstream Guards	(1940)-(1944)	?
?	?	Thomas William	Jones	b1903	Royal Armoured Corps	(1940)	Far East
?	?	Hubert H	Jones	b1912	Royal Artillery	(1940)	Middle East
?	?	Peter Sidney Walter	Jones	1908-1959	Royal Warwickshire Regt	(1944)	France
--	2nd Lieutenant	Cecil Vandelaur	Keighly-Peach	1877-1959	Army Service Corps	1917-(1918)	None
--	Captain	Charles Lindsay	Keighly-Peach	1902-1995	RNAS	1915-1953	At Sea
--	Admiral	Charles William	Keighly-Peach	1865-1943	Royal Navy	1879-1918	At Sea
--	Captain	Henry	Keighly-Peach	1834-1905	49th Madras Native Infantry	?	India
--	?	Peter Lindsay	Keighly-Peach	b1926	Royal Navy	1944-(1955)	Korea
109109	Gunner	Walter Henry	Keyte	1894-1967	Royal Garrison Artillery	1916-?	?
18091	**Private**	**Albert Edward**	**King**	**1889-1918**	**4th Coldstream Guards**	**d1918**	**France/Flanders**
?	?	James	King	b1886	?	1914-?	?
6862	**Sergeant**	**Joseph Albert**	**King**	**1884-1914**	**2nd South Staffordshire Regt**	**(1911)-1914**	**France/Flanders**
53065; 487155	**Private**	**Thomas**	**Kingston**	**1881-1918**	**Machine Gun Corps; Labour Corps**	**1915-1918**	**Serbia/Salonika**
19176	Private	Frederick Reuben	Knight	b1897	Royal Warwickshire Regt	1916-1919	France/Flanders
17265; 567828	Private	Harry Wilfred	Knight	b1893	Ox Bucks Light Infantry; Labour Corps	1915-1919	France/Flanders
13257	Private	Herbert Victor	Knight	1899-1969	Irish Rifles	1918-1919	None
S.E.13370	Farrier Sergeant	Percy Richard	Ladbury	1886-1968	Army Veterinary Corps	1915-1919	?
12184	Private	Sydney	Land	?	11th Hampshire Regiment	1914-1919	France/Flanders
9523 or 11382	Rifleman	William	Lawrence	d1914	King's Royal Rifle Corps	?-1914	France/Flanders
?	?	Harry	Lord	(1885)-1942	Royal Navy	?	?
30960; 27673	**Lance Corporal**	**Tom Job**	**Lowe**	**1899-1918**	**Dorset Regt; Wiltshire Regt**	**?-1918**	**France/Flanders**
37302	Able Seaman	Ernest Alexander	Maton	1885-1956	Royal Navy	1903-1919	At Sea
5112004	**Private**	**Reginald Henry**	**Maton**	**1921-1945**	**1st Royal Berkshire Regt**	**(1942)-1945**	**Burma**
2331207	Corporal	Alfred William	Maull	b1918	Royal Corps of Signals	(1941)-(1945)	Greece
20842	Private	Ernest	Morris	(b1886)	Royal Warwickshire Regt	1916	None
?	?	Walter	Morris	b1912	RAF	(1940s)	Italy?
1597259	Bombadier	George Edward	Nason	1916-2002	Royal Artillery	1940-1946	North Africa; Italy
44545	**Corporal**	**Reginald Thomas**	**Neal**	**1888-1917**	**Royal Army Medical Corps**	**(1915)-1917**	**France/Flanders**
2378	Private	Thomas	Neal	b1861	52nd Foot (Light Infantry)	1880-1881	None
32074	**Lt Col**	**Wilfred George**	**Newey**	**1907-1945**	**Royal Artillery**	**1923-1945**	**Egypt**

5177	Private	Albert Frank	Noyce	1882-1934	Durham Light Infantry	1916	None
M/14768	**Cook's Mate**	**Henry George**	**Padbury**	**1896-1917**	**Royal Navy**	**1915-1917**	**At Sea**
?	Petty Officer	Joseph	Parnham	1916-2003	Royal Navy	1934-1946	At Sea
12181	Private	James	Paxford	1886-1941	11th Hampshire Regt	1914	None
14947	**Private**	**Thomas Frank**	**Paxford**	**1880-1916**	**10th Royal Warwickshire Regt**	**1915-1916**	**France/Flanders**
?	?	William Thomas	Paxford	b1917	Royal Warwickshire Regt	(1940s)	France
69902	**Sapper**	**William**	**Paxton**	**1881-1916**	**154th Field Coy Royal Engineers**	**1915-1916**	**France/Flanders**
?	?	William	Paxton	b1914	Royal Army Medical Corps	(1940s)	At Sea
L8770	Ordinary Seaman	Fred	Pitt	b1882	Royal Navy; RAF	1916-1920	?
?	Private	Edwin	Plumb	b1867	187th Canadian Infantry	1916-?	?
J70259	Petty Officer	Albert Edward	Porter	1901-1968	Royal Navy	1917-1945	At Sea
170	?	Aubrey John	Porter	1893-1973	Canadian ASC	1914-?	France/Flanders
633789	**Lance Corporal**	**Francis William**	**Porter**	**1891-1918**	**21st Canadian Infantry**	**1916-1918**	**France/Flanders**
1169	?	Alan George	Rainbow	b1861	Royal Horse Guards	1881-1886	None
?	Flight Lieutenant	George	Randle	1907-1971	RAF	(1940)-1946	Europe; India
3367	Private	John Charles	Reading	b1887	41st Australian Infantry	1917-1919	France/Flanders
30850	**Private**	**Arnold John**	**Reason**	**1888-1916**	**10th Welsh Regt**	**?-1916**	**France/Flanders**
5117263	Private	Eric Jellicoe	Reason	1915-2009	7th Oxford and Bucks Light Infantry	1940-1945	Middle East; Italy
1637658	**Sergeant**	**Leslie**	**Reason**	**1911-1944**	**Royal Artillery**	**?-1944**	?
?	?	Arthur	Ridgard	1913-2000	Pioneer Corps	(1941-1945)	None
2448	Private	William Aquila	Riley	b1872	Grenadier Guards	1890-1902	South Africa
11970	Private	Edward	Rimell	b1895	6th Dorsetshire Regt	1914	None
12022	Private	John	Rimell	b1890	6th Dorsetshire Regt	1914	None
-	Major	James	Roberts-West	1775-1838	3rd Warwickshire Militia	1808-?	None
12536; 159326	Private	Ernest	Robinson	b1896	11th Hampshire Regt; Machine Gun Corps	1914-1919	France/Flanders
S/363551	Corporal	Harry	Samman	1883-1954	Army Service Corps	1916-1919	None
1963	Colour Sergeant	David	Seal	1853-1927	95th Foot	1870-1890	None
579	Sgt Major	Henry	Seal	1840-1918	95th Foot	1858-1881	India
114851	Able Seaman	Henry	Seal	b1864	Royal Navy	1880-1887	At Sea
?	Dom 3rd Class	Henry Elias	Seal	b1884	Royal Navy	(1901)-1905	At Sea
224367	Petty Officer	Herbert William	Seal	b1889	Royal Navy	1903-1922	At Sea
?	Sergeant	Martin	Seal	1858-1899	Royal Marines	(1884)-(1889)	At Sea
12586	Corporal	Martin John Days	Seal	1887-1968	Royal Marines	1902-1945	At Sea
?	Private	Thomas	Seal	b1846	Royal Marines	1864-1871	At Sea
537	Corporal	William	Seal	b1842	95th Foot	1858-1879	East Indies
M/2138683; 26079	**Private**	**William Henry**	**Sharpe**	**1897-1918**	**Army Service Corps; West Riding Regt**	**1915-1918**	**France/Flanders**
11851	**Lance Corporal**	**George Randolph**	**Sheasby**	**1895-1916**	**1st Royal Welch Fusiliers**	**1914-1916**	**France/Flanders**
28734	**Private**	**Frank**	**Silvester**	**1895-1917**	**11th Royal Warwickshire Regt**	**1917**	**France/Flanders**
29968	**Trooper**	**Edward**	**Simms**	**1880-1902**	**Imperial Yeomanry**	**1901-1902**	**South Africa**
?	?	William E	Simms	b1918	?	(1940s)	France; Middle East
48097	Private	Wilfred	Sivyour	1899-1976	East Surrey Regiment	1917-?	?

5189430	Private	Leonard	Skidmore	?	1st Gloucestershire Regt	1940-1946	Burma
?	Corporal	John	Smith	b1920	RAF	(1939-1945)	Europe
--	Lieutenant	Robert Mansell	Smith	1876-1952	RAMC; 5th Norfolk Regt	1915-(1918)	Egypt
2419	?	William	Smith	b1852	?	1874-?	Canada
?	?	Ernest	South	1897-1941	?	(1917)	France/Flanders
266091	**Private**	**Frederick Henry**	**South**	**1894-1917**	**Royal Warwickshire Regt**	**1914-1917**	**France/Flanders**
17984	**Private**	**Ernest Edward**	**Southam**	**1890-1917**	**Royal Warwickshire Regt**	**1916-1917**	**France/Flanders**
1799; 40614	Sergeant	Frank	Southam	1892-1955	Royal Warwickshire Regt; Worcestershire Regt	(1911)-(1916)	France/Flanders
12024	**Private**	**William George**	**Southam**	**1882-1915**	**6th Dorsetshire Regt**	**1914-1915**	**France/Flanders**
?	?	Reginald	Stoppard	b1907	RAF	(1942-1946)	Egypt
2051; 2244; 9988	CQMS	John	Stowe	b1860	39th Bde; Gordon Highlanders; West Yorks Regt	1880-1903; 1914-1919	Egypt; Sudan
37460	Private	Oliver	Summerton	1899-1978	2/7th Royal Warwickshire Regt	1916-1919	France/Flanders
12185; 32123	Lance Corporal	Frank	Taylor	b1894	11th Hampshire Regt; Devon Regt	1914-1919	France/Flanders
10445	Shoeing Smith	Henry	Taylor	b1892	Royal Field Artillery	1914-1919	France/Flanders
614243	Gunner	Joseph	Taylor	b1896	Royal Horse Artillery	1915-1920	France/Flanders
1344	Private	John	Thorn	b1840	16th Regt of Foot	1860-1884	India
5336; D2/30911	Private	Walter Raymond	Tilling	b1894	1st Hants Regt; Corps of Dragoons; Tank Corps	1914-1919	France/Flanders
--	Major	Henry Stuart	Tompson	1837-1914	51st (King's Own) Light Infantry, Staffs Militia	1856-1884	India
--	Major General	William Dalrymple	Tompson	1833-1916	17th Regt of Foot	1852-1884	Crimea; Afghanistan
?	?	Wilfred	Townsend	b1896	?	1914-?	?
6977	Private	John Tom Eric	Truslove	1897-1965	Worcestershire Regt	1916-1919	France/Flanders
126779	Flight Lieutenant	Raoul Alfred Gerald	Tucker	b1916	RAF	(1942)-(1945)	Europe
?	?	Diana Margaret	Walsh (Langley)	1923-2000	Women's Auxiliary Airforce	(1940s)	None
203324	**Private**	**Bernard David**	**Walton**	**1876-1917**	**Norfolk Regt**	**1916-1917**	**Egypt**
505538	?	Henry George	Walton	b1887	Canadian Army	1916-?	?
92051	Private	Leonard	Walton	b1878	Labour Corps	1915-1919	France/Flanders
?	Lance Corporal	William Edgar	Walton	1915-1991	Devonshire Regiment	(1940s)	France; Germany
	?	Albert Leslie	Ward	1913-1974	?	(1940s)	France
	?	Douglas	Ward	1918-1969	?	(1940s)	?
21850	**Private**	**John William**	**Ward**	**1884-1915**	**3rd Grenadier Guards**	**1915**	**France/Flanders**
	?	Stanley Roy	Ward	b1914	?	(1940s)	France
6965; 267952	**Private**	**Charles Benjamin**	**Waters**	**1891-1917**	**11th Royal Warwickshire Regt**	**1914-1917**	**France/Flanders**
R/8308	**Rifleman**	**Ernest Edward**	**Waters**	**1896-1916**	**8th King's Royal Rifle Corps**	**1915-1916**	**France/Flanders**
?	?	James	Wheeler	b1785	7th Regiment of Foot	(1803-1807)	?
	Private	John	Wheeler	b1836	Horse Guards	1860-1870	?
?	Lance Corporal	Percival	Wheeler	b1916	Royal Army Medical Corps	(1941)-(1945)	Burma
760	**Lt Col**	**John**	**Whiteman**	**1876-1917**	**NZ army; Middlesex Regt; Royal Naval Div'n**	**1900-1917**	**South Africa; France**
?	?	?	Wilkes	?	?	?	South Africa
?	Sergeant	Cyril William	Wood	1918-1989	?	(1943-1945)	India/Burma
?	Flight Lieutenant	Robert Elliott Storey	Wyatt	1901-1995	RAF	1941-1945	None
?	Private	Richard	Young	1783-1852	39th Foot; 95th Foot; Grenadier Guards	1806-1823	?
?	Private	Thomas	Young	1778-1861	Royal B'ham Fencibles; Grenadier Guards	1799-1824	?

A new number was issued when a man transferred to a new unit

Dates in brackets indicate extent of known service dates.

Known Fatalities of RAF Stratford Airmen

Service No	Rank	Name	Surname	Trade	Unit	Home	Date of Death	Age	Cemetery/Memorial
J/18289	P/O	George Nelson	Acton	Air Gunner	RCAF	Saskatchewan	26/06/1943	31	Reichswald Forest War Cemetery, Germany
R/115197	Sgt	Robert Carson	Alderson	Air Gunner	RCAF	Ontario	29/01/1943	22	Honington Churchyard, Suffolk
1377990	Sgt	Walter Herbert David	Alison	WAG	RAFVR	Middlesex	13/05/1943	28	Hotton War Cemetery, Luxemburg
1368090	Cpl	Harry	Allan	Ground Crew	RAFVR	Edinburgh	29/05/1943	22	Edinburgh Cemetery
J/20861	Fl Lt	William Joseph	Allison	Air Bomber	RCAF	Montreal	20/11/1944	28	Chester (Blacon) Cemetery
J/9586	P/O	Charles Douglas Haig	Archer	WAG	RCAF	Ontario	29/06/1942	23	Stratford Cemetery
J/2207	P/O	Ross James	Archer	Navigator	RCAF	Ontario	29/01/1943	19	Honington Churchyard, Suffolk
R/106448	Sgt	William	Argo	Air Gunner	RCAF	Manitoba	29/01/1943	20	Honington Churchyard, Suffolk
1417073	AC2	George Rupert	Band	Ground Crew	RAFVR	Herefordshire	29/05/1943	22	Brumfield Cemetery, Herefordshire
R/114520	Fl Sgt	Albert Leroy	Bateman	?	RCAF	?	01/03/1943	?	Runnymede Memorial
J/35867	F/O	Jean Joseph Donnelly	Belanger	Pilot	RCAF	Quebec	30/07/1944	20	Stratford Cemetery
1127149	Sgt	James Richard	Bell	WOp	RAFVR	York	12/06/1943	22	Bergen-op-Zoom War Cemetery, Netherlands
R/84501	Sgt	George Stanley	Bickerton	Pilot	RCAF	New Brunswick	14/09/1942	24	Amersfoort (Oud Leusden) General Cemetery, Utrecht
R/108675	W/O	James Gerald	Breen	?	RCAF	?	12/06/1943	20	Bergen-op-Zoom War Cemetery, Netherlands
R/71563	WO1	Philip Sibbald Ogilvie	Brichta	Air Observer	RCAF	Ontario	16/09/1942	31	Reichswald Forest War Cemetery, Germany
R/110293	Fl Sgt	Douglas Oliver	Broughton	Air Gunner	RCAF	Vancouver	13/05/1942	21	Jonkerbos War Cemetery, Nijmegan
R/206904	Sgt	Joseph Paul Ernest	Burke	WAG	RCAF	New Brunswick	20/11/1944	20	Chester (Blacon) Cemetery
412313	Sgt	Douglass	Callaghan	WAG	RNZAF	Otago, New Zealand	25/05/1942	23	Stratford Cemetery
J/15844	P/O	Harry	Casimiri	WAG	RCAF	Ontario	16/09/1942	?	Evesham Cemetery
R/141536	Fl Sgt	Joseph Bruno Vionney	Chevalier	WAG	RCAF	Quebec	26/11/1943	25	Pershore Cemetery
104485	P/O	Ronald Richards	Clamp	Pilot	RAFVR	Surrey	06/11/1941	21	Mitcham Cemetery, Surrey
R/62860	Fl Sgt	Robert Douglas	Cook	WAG	RCAF	New Brunswick	25/05/1942	21	Stratford Cemetery
J/38340	F/O	Ross Lloyd	Cuzner	Navigator	RCAF	Ontario	30/07/1944	19	Stratford Cemetery
R/184493	Sgt	Joseph Adolphe Maurice	Dauplaise	WAG	RCAF	Quebec	30/07/1944	21	Stratford Cemetery
61008	Fl Lt	John	Dawson	Pilot	RAFVR	Sussex	16/09/1942	32	Reichswald Forest War Cemetery, Germany
R/143327	Fl Sgt	James Edward	Dayton	Air Bomber	RCAF	British Columbia	23/09/1943	20	Reichswald Forest War Cemetery, Germany
J/12158	F/O	John Bernard Joseph	de Macedo	WAG	RCAF	British Columbia	03/10/1943	24	Pershore Cemetery
157440	P/O	James	Denholm	Navigator	RAFVR	West Lothian	20/06/1943	21	Bretteville-sur-Laize War Cemetery
131121	Fl Lt	Arthur Colin	Diemer	Pilot	RAFVR	Birmingham	11/03/1945	23	Newcastle Crematorium
R/146964	Sgt	Joseph Jacques Louis Phillippe	Dion	Flight Engineer	RCAF	Quebec	15/11/1944	24	Brookwood Military Cemetery, Surrey
J/19999	P/O	Francis Wilfred	Dolter	Pilot	RCAF	British Columbia	25/05/1944	?	Runnymede Memorial
R/106416	Sgt	Frederick Henry	Dowland	WAG	RCAF	Manitoba	07/09/1942	19	Bicester Cemetery
R/174038	Sgt	Joseph Lionel Ulderic Gerard	Du Sablon	Air Gunner	RCAF	Montreal	20/11/1944	20	Chester (Blacon) Cemetery
R/159966	Sgt	Joseph Emelien Jean Cyriaque	Dubord	Pilot	RCAF	Montreal	26/11/1943	25	Pershore Cemetery
1575081	Sgt	John William	Dunford	Navigator	RAFVR	Yorkshire	23/09/1943	27	Reichswald Forest War Cemetery, Germany
88416	F/O	Hector	Duro	Pilot	RAFVR	Nottingham	21/12/1942	34	Seraincourt Churchyard, France

133051	P/O	Reginald Staynes	Elsom	Pilot	RAFVR	Loughborough	13/10/1942	32	Loughborough Cemetery
J/15541	P/O	Albert John	Fawcett	Pilot	RCAF	Ontario	16/09/1942	22	Evesham Cemetery
R/67976	Fl Sgt	James Gerald Joseph	Fedigan	Bomb Aimer	RCAF	Chicago	29/06/1942	27	Stratford Cemetery
R/86326	Fl Sgt	Michael William	Fedirchyk	Air Observer	RCAF	Winnipeg	29/06/1942	22	Stratford Cemetery
R/90930	Fl Sgt	William Joseph	Foley	Pilot	RCAF	?	05/04/1943	?	Kiel War Cemetery, Germany
R/117007	Sgt	Martin Raymond	Foran	Air Gunner	RCAF	Ontario	24/09/1942	24	Stratford Cemetery
R/112757	Fl Sgt	Wilfred George	Francis	?	RCAF	Ontario	02/03/1943	23	Runnymede Memorial
45149	F Lt	John James	Gale	?	RAF	Yorkshire	23/11/1943	27	Beverley Cemetery, Yorkshire
812346	Fl Sgt	John Llewellyn	Gibby	WAG	RAF	Tunbridge Wells	25/05/1942	27	Tunbridge Wells Cemetery
J/15745	P/O	George Clarence	Goold	Navigator	RCAF	Ottawa	16/09/1942	30	Reichswald Forest War Cemetery, Germany
J/16414	P/O	Robert	Graham	Pilot	RCAF	British Columbia	05/03/1943	29	Reichswald Forest War Cemetery, Germany
1411885	AC2	William Alyn	Gravell	Ground Crew	RAFVR	Monmouthshire	29/05/1943	21	Nantyglo Cemetery, Monmouthshire
R/111476	Sgt	Joseph Arthur Edmond	Groulx	Air Gunner	RCAF	Quebec	20/11/1944	22	Chester (Blacon) Cemetery
R/58198	Fl Sgt	David Harry	Halstead	WAG	RCAF	British Columbia	16/09/1942	21	Evesham Cemetery
J/92169	P/O	Charles	Hamel	Pilot	RCAF	Montreal	20/11/1944	21	Chester (Blacon) Cemetery
R/115276	Fl Sgt	William Rehfeld	Harron	Pilot	RCAF	Ontario	29/01/1943	24	Honington Churchyard, Suffolk
127040	F/O	Robert Charles	Henderson	Pilot	RAFVR	?	25/11/1943	31	Catania War Cemetery, Sicily
411721	Sgt	Ronald Ernest	Herbert	Observer	RNZAF	Auckland	25/05/1942	23	Stratford Cemetery
R/145342	Fl Sgt	Lyle Wilmot	Hicks	Air Bomber	RCAF	Illinois, USA	16/02/1944	23	Harderwijk General Cemetery, Netherlands
1332872	AC1	Leslie	Holloway	Ground Fitter	RAFVR	London	16/09/1942	20	Evesham Cemetery
994140	Sgt	James Eric	Hough	Air Gunner	RAFVR	Macclesfield	25/05/1942	28	Macclesfield Cemetery
751551	Fl Sgt	William Kilpatrick	Hughes	WAG	RAFVR	Ayrshire	16/09/1942	24	Reichswald Forest War Cemetery, Germany
R/1106511	Sgt	Ernest Page	Hunt	WAG	RCAF	British Columbia	13/10/1942	27	Stratford Cemetery
J/15652	F/O	Graham Stanley	Hynam	Pilot	RAFVR	Ohio, USA	29/05/1943	22	Pershore Cemetery
R/101378	Sgt	Ronald Adey	Jackson	Air Gunner	RCAF	British Columbia	07/09/1942	21	Bicester Cemetery
R/82881	Fl Sgt	Wallace Hayden	Johnson	WAG	RCAF	Toronto	11/09/1942	22	Reichswald Forest War Cemetery, Germany
965121	Sgt	Harold	Jones	Pilot	RAFVR	Cheshire	29/06/1942	22	Bebington Cemetery, Cheshire
R/117367	Sgt	Michael John	Kelly	Navigator	RCAF	Ontario	29/01/1943	20	Honington Churchyard, Suffolk
J/10413	P/O	Donald Chesley	King	Air Observer	RCAF	?	14/09/1942	?	Amersfoort (Oud Leusden) General Cemetery, Utrecht
J/19263	P/O	Jack Olavi	Koivu	Navigator	RCAF	Quebec	26/03/1944	?	Reichswald Forest War Cemetery, Germany
R/7735	WO1	Lorne James	Lemoine	WAG	RCAF	?	16/09/1942	22	Reichswald Forest War Cemetery, Germany
J/10317	F/O	Frank Edward	Lewis	?	RCAF	?	04/09/1943	?	Runnymede Memorial
R/65534	Fl Sgt	Frank Alfred	Macauley	WAG	RCAF	Nassau, Bahamas	16/09/1942	22	Bexhill Cemetery
J/13076	F/O	James Kenneth	MacDonald	Air Observer	RCAF	Alberta	05/03/1943	23	Reichswald Forest War Cemetery, Germany
R/200158	Sgt	Joseph Marcisse Orval	Martin	Air Gunner	RCAF	Ontario	30/07/1944	20	Stratford Cemetery
R/110750	Sgt	Edward Stanley Joseph	McCasky	WAG	RCAF	Manitoba	11/09/1942	20	Reichswald Forest War Cemetery, Germany
J/22548	F/O	Colin Angus	McDougall	Navigator	RCAF	Nova Scotia	12/06/1943	24	Bergen-op-Zoom War Cemetery, Netherlands
1558953	AC2	Daniel	McMillan	Ground Fitter	RAFVR	Coatbridge, Lanarkshire	16/09/1942	36	Airdrie Cemetery, Lanarkshire

R/113992	Sgt	Charles William	Milton	Air Gunner	RCAF	New Brunswick	08/11/1942	19	Stratford Cemetery
R/61680	Fl Sgt	Donald Alex	Mitchell	?	RCAF	?	28/09/1942	26	Alamein Memorial, Egypt
R/83527	W/O	George Andrew	Molozzi	Air Observer	RCAF	Ontario	13/02/1943	27	Stratford Cemetery
R/74456	WO1	Noel McHenry	Moore	Pilot	RCAF	Georgia, USA	30/07/1942	33	Gosselies Communal Cemetery, Belgium
R/136820	Fl Sgt	Raymond Florent	Morand	Navigator	RCAF	Quebec	26/11/1943	19	Pershore Cemetery
R/2508	Sgt	Joseph Laurent	Moreau	Air Bomber	RCAF	Quebec	30/07/1944	24	Stratford Cemetery
R/108483	Fl Sgt	Kenneth Herbert	Mount	Air Bomber	RCAF	Montreal	29/01/1943	29	Honington Churchyard, Suffolk
R/95318	Fl Sgt	Donald	Murray	Air Gunner	RCAF	Manitoba	14/09/1942	20	Amersfoort (Oud Leusden) General Cemetery, Utrecht
J/17553	P/O	Richard Eric	Nutter	Navigator	RCAF	Ontario	29/06/1943	29	Dishforth Cemetery, Yorkshire
R/70461	WO1	John William	O'Brien	Air Observer	RCAF	Ontario	16/09/1942	21	Evesham Cemetery
R/68264	WO2	James Michael Barry	O'Connor	Bomb Aimer	RCAF	Ontario	28/04/1943	24	Runnymede Memorial
J/19280	P/O	Alan Ludwig	Olsson	Pilot	RCAF	Quebec	26/03/1944	25	Reichswald Forest War Cemetery, Germany
R/97152	Fl Sgt	Ronald Earl	Oswald	Air Bomber	RCAF	New Jersey	29/01/1943	34	Honington Churchyard, Suffolk
R/97143	Fl Sgt	Thomas Reid	Owens	Air Gunner	RCAF	Quebec	23/07/1942	21	Barmby on the Moor Churchyard, Yorkshire
R/109023	Fl Sgt	Daniel Lawrence	Pablo	Pilot	RCAF	Montana, USA	11/09/1942	22	Reichswald Forest War Cemetery, Germany
R/157795	Sgt	Frederick Herbert	Partridge	Pilot	RCAF	?	02/10/1943	?	Pershore Cemetery
40471	Sgt	Vyvyan Roessler	Pascoe	?	RAAF	Queensland	25/05/1942	25	Stratford Cemetery
R/123260	Sgt	Charles Edward	Pollard	Observer	RCAF	Toronto	11/09/1942	20	Reichswald Forest War Cemetery, Germany
R/111159	Fl Sgt	Earl Stewart	Rheaume	Air Gunner	RCAF	Ontario	12/06/1943	29	Bergen-op-Zoom War Cemetery, Netherlands
741105	W/O	James Augustus	Rich	Pilot	RAFVR	Hutton	06/11/1941	30	Hutton Cemetery
R/107812	Fl Sgt	George Barclay	Robb	Air Observer	RCAF	Saskatchewan	07/09/1942	28	Bicester Cemetery
R/109394	Sgt	Harry Bertram John	Sargent	Navigator	RCAF	?	05/04/1943	?	Kiel War Cemetery, Germany
J/88165	P/O	Joseph Georges Marcel	Savard	Pilot	RCAF	Montreal	17/08/1944	19	Magleby Churchyard, Denmark
R/118215	Fl Sgt	William Robert Campbell	Sinclair	Pilot	RCAF	British Columbia	13/10/1942	25	Stratford Cemetery
63414	Sqn Ldr	William Arthur	Smith	Pilot	RAFVR	Essex	02/02/1943	23	Rotterdam General Cemetery
J/85162	P/O	Clifford Roy	Sullivan	Air Observer	RCAF	Ontario	11/09/1942	19	Reichswald Forest War Cemetery, Germany
R/130695	Fl Sgt	James Alexander Campbell	Taylor	Air Gunner	RCAF	Winnipeg	05/04/1943	?	Kiel War Cemetery, Germany
R/100369	Sgt	Albert John	Temple	Air Observer	RCAF	Manitoba	07/09/1942	27	Bicester Cemetery
R/97834	Fl Sgt	Pat Neff	Templeton	Pilot	RCAF	Texas	07/09/1942	19	Bicester Cemetery
R/136704	Fl Sgt	Joseph Jules Jean Jacques	Vennes	Air Bomber	RCAF	Quebec	26/11/1943	21	Pershore Cemetery
R/199834	Sgt	Jules Robert Rene	Villeneuve	Navigator	RCAF	Quebec	20/11/1944	22	Chester (Blacon) Cemetery
1202832	Sgt	Charles Robert	Whitworth	Pilot	RAFVR	Leicestershire	25/05/1942	?	Shepshed Cemetery, Leicestershire
1209651	Sgt	Alfred Albert	Wiles	WAG	RAFVR	Sussex	25/02/1943	28	Streatham Park Cemetery, Sussex
405532	Sgt	Mervyn	Wilkinson	WAG	RNZAF	Auckland, New Zealand	25/05/1942	21	Stratford Cemetery
404977	Sgt	John Syddall	Williams	Air Observer	RNZAF	Westland, New Zealand	25/05/1942	26	Stratford Cemetery
R/106028	Fl Sgt	James Averd	Wilson	Pilot	RCAF	Manitoba	29/01/1943	20	Honington Churchyard, Suffolk
R/115213	Fl Sgt	Alexander Trevor	Woodhouse	Air Gunner	RCAF	Ontario	01/03/1943	21	Runnymede Memorial
R/95634	P/O	Robert Stephen Borden	Worley	?	RCAF	Ontario	25/02/1943	25	Dishforth Cemetery, Yorkshire
R/103487	F/O	Ralph James	Wright	Navigator	RCAF	?	05/04/1943	?	Kiel War Cemetery, Germany

Sources and Bibliography

Most surviving soldiers' service records from the Victorian era to the First World War have been digitised by The National Archives and available online from www.ancestry.co.uk and www.findmypast.co.uk.

The war diaries of many First World War units are also available to download from www.nationalarchives.gov.uk, and have added much detail about life on the front line.

Other useful websites include www.bac-lac.gc.ca, www.archway.archives.govt.nz and www.awn.gov.au for Canadian, New Zealand and Australian servicemen respectively; the Commonwealth War Graves Commission (www.cwgc.org); www.thegazette.co.uk for medal citations; www.icrc.org for prisoner of war records.

During the First World War, the *Stratford Herald* routinely published information on local servicemen, including their letters, details of bravery awards and injuries and photographs. www.britishnewspaperarchive.co.uk provides access to many more newspapers.

The Imperial War Museum (www.iwm.org.uk) and www.longlongtrail.co.uk provided useful background information.

www.aviationarchaeology.org.uk and www.aircrewremembered.com provided information on RAF Stratford and its aircrews.

Books relating to military history of the local area include:

War Isn't Wonderful, Ursula Bloom, Hutchinson & Co, 1961.

Action Stations 6: Military Airfields of the Cotswolds and Midlands, Michael Bowyer, Patrick Stephens Ltd, 1983.

Twentieth Century Defences in Warwickshire, Steve Carvell, Tempus, 2007.

Stratford: A Town at War, Nicholas Fogg, The History Press, 2008.

How the Girl Guides Won the War, Janie Hampton, HarperPress, 2010.

Wings Over Wellesbourne Volumes 1 & 2, Jack Pratley, Self-published, available from Wellesbourne Military Mueseum.
Dunkirk: Fight to the Last Man, Hugh Sebag-Montefiore, 2015, Penguin.
Warwickshire Airfields in the Second World War, Graham Smith, Countryside Books, 2004.
A Warwickshire Boy, John Stoppard, Self-published, 2017.
Almost All From Memory, Mike Woods, Kerenza J Ltd, 2004.

Index of Surnames

Acton 273, 274
Alderson 287
Allan 288
Allison 290, 291
Allcock 49
Allen 207
Alison 273, 275
Arbuthnot 55, 56, 121
Archer 282, 287
Argo 287
Arthurs 89
Ashby 42, 45, 63, 89, 92, 100, 190, 192, 207, 209, 210, 226, 240, 241, 244
Ashfield 109
Attewell 193

Badger 287
Bailey 13
Baker 152, 170
Baldwin 92, 93, 97, 98
Band 288
Barrett 247
Bateman 273, 277, 278
Beauchamp 265, 291
Beavington 83, 85, 97, 106, 111, 116, 117, 144, 148, 152, 155, 164, 168, 174, 208
Beesley 13
Bees 273, 274
Belanger 267, 268, 289
Bell 273, 275
Bennett 63, 74, 75, 88, 124-127, 136, 139
Best 21
Bickerton 285
Bishop 89, 202, 209, 221, 269, 270, 271, 284, 294
Bloom 48, 88, 91, 108, 109, 176, 192, 200
Bloxham 27, 29, 62, 91, 151, 153, 168, 173, 224, 225, 245
Boardman 109, 135, 136, 138, 144-146
Bouchard 289
Bowie 247
Boyce 278
Brawne 2

Breen 273, 278
Brichta 286
Brookes 159, 166, 176
Broughton 282, 283
Browett 193
Brown 137, 144
Burra 61, 85, 112
Burke 290, 291
Burrows 62, 91, 92, 153, 168, 173

Callaghan 282
Canning 131, 177, 178, 210, 211
Caron 290, 291
Casimiri 285
Chappel 271
Chevalier 288
Churchill 76-79, 179
Clamp 279
Clark; Clarke 83, 291
Clift 124
Coldicott 86, 87
Coleman 193
Cook 282
Coomber 193, 194
Cooper 247
Crawley 249
Cuzner 289

Dale 61, 91, 99, 153, 154, 173, 188, 208
Dauplaise 289
Dawson 270, 286
Day 111, 221
Days 16
Dayton 272
Deimer 267, 268
Denham-Cookes 91
Denholm 273, 275
Dion 289
Dodd 27, 29
Dolter 288, 289
Domigan 273, 277
Donovan 272
Dove 137, 138, 141, 149, 152, 160
Dowland 283
Dubord 288
Dunford 283
Duro 273, 277
DuSablon 290, 291
Dyer 28-30, 86

Edgington 76-79, 105
Ellis 269
Elsom 283
Empson 190
Enever 273, 277, 278

Fawcett 285, 286
Fedigan 282
Fedirchyk 282
Fitzgerald 267, 268, 292, 293
Fletcher 17, 208
Foley 273, 277
Foran 283
Fowler 82
Francis 212, 213, 217, 273, 275

Gale 249, 282
Garfield 2
Garrett 58, 59, 106-108, 179
George 13, 36, 89, 92, 113-115, 127, 128, 174, 234
Geldart 273, 276
Gibbins 17, 152, 184, 185, 196, 237, 238, 242
Gibbs 118

Gibby 282
Gilks 114, 116
Goodall 82, 85
Goodway 143
Goold 286
Graham 273, 274
Gravell 288
Gray 273, 274
Green 130, 131, 159, 168, 169, 193
Groulx 290, 291

Hadland 152
Hall 271, 272
Halstead 285
Hamel 290, 291
Handy 13, 16, 18, 92, 97, 109, 110, 113-115, 120, 128, 144, 145, 152, 155, 156, 170-174, 180, 190
Harding 194, 198, 279
Harrison 273, 276
Harron 287
Hartwell 198, 202
Harwood 190, 198, 199
Hastings 9, 10, 20, 37, 38, 40, 41, 43, 45, 48, 49, 55, 119, 131, 132, 176
Hathaway 111, 151, 183-186, 201, 203, 214, 225, 235, 237, 245, 292
Hawkins 64, 294
Haycock 193
Haylock 221, 222
Haywood 278
Hebert 267, 268
Henderson 287
Herbert 28, 61, 282
Herd 90
Heybourne 273, 275
Hibbard 51, 119
Hicks 14, 15, 62, 74, 75, 82, 83, 92, 94, 97, 142-146, 154-158, 162, 166, 193, 196-198, 234, 244, 270, 271
Holloway 285
Holtom 18, 19, 69, 73, 74, 105
Hopkins 62, 63, 74, 75, 83, 92, 164, 165, 173
Hornsey 124, 125, 136, 139-141, 144
Horseman 11-15, 22, 24, 25, 27, 29-31, 43, 57-60, 67, 71, 82, 84, 90, 92, 93, 107, 112, 124, 125, 133-136, 138, 141, 148, 157, 160-163, 172, 180, 192, 196, 206, 212
Hough 282
Howes 112
Hudson 11, 24, 25
Hughes 210, 211, 286
Hulbert 196, 199
Hunt 218, 245, 283
Hutchings 151
Hutton 286
Hyatt 62, 64, 77, 80
Hynam 287

Izard 207

Jackson 283, 287
James 83-86, 152, 153, 192, 200, 212, 229-232, 245, 270
Jaques 13, 87, 88, 195, 196, 199, 247
Job; Jobe 63, 111, 176, 200
Johnson 284
Jones 21, 188, 208, 236, 244, 282

Keen 265
Keighly-Peach 54, 55, 82, 119, 226, 227, 246
Kelly 287
Keyte 107, 108, 177
Kidd 287
Kihorn 287
King 59, 63, 65, 68, 114, 149, 171, 285
Kingston 104, 118, 171, 180
Klein 273, 276
Koivu 287
Knight 124, 137, 138, 141-149, 152, 158, 166, 174, 175, 196

Ladbury 114
Land 62, 91, 153
Landry 267, 268
Lawrence 66, 67
Lemoine 286
Lewis 273, 276
Lockwood 198, 289
Lord 194, 200, 208
Lowe 168, 193
Luke 273, 276

Macauley 285
MacCuaig 271
MacDonald 273, 275
Macedo 288
Mainwaring 298
Maries 267, 268
Martin 289
Maton 90, 220, 221, 223, 224, 265
Mayo 87
Maull 202
McBeath 273, 278
McCasky 284
McCormick 273, 276
McDougall 273, 275
McGaughey 273, 278
McGillivray 267, 268
McMillan 286
Melvin 273, 275
Milton 273, 277
Mitchell 279, 280
Molozzi 280, 281
Moore 281
Morand 288
Moreau 289
Morris 87, 88, 192, 234
Morse 207
Mould 280
Mount 287
Mumford 193, 288
Murray 285

Nason 182, 191, 212-215, 217, 243, 244
Neal 16, 102, 103, 179
Nezan 289
Newey 191, 213, 215, 217, 239
Nickless 282
Noble 267, 268
Noyce 85, 192-196, 208, 235, 291
Nutter 273, 276

O'Brien 285, 286
O'Connor 284
Olsson 287
Oswald 287
Owens 285

Pablo 284
Padbury 120
Parnham 225-227, 244

Partridge 288
Pascoe 282
Patrick 267, 268
Paxford 61, 64, 92-95, 236, 245
Paxton 100, 101, 179, 202, 228
Peer 271
Perks 273, 276
Perry 197
Pitt 120, 121
Plumb 133
Pollard 284
Porter 121, 134-136, 141, 144, 147, 162, 163, 166, 167, 173, 179, 180, 228

Rainbow 18
Randle 234, 245, 247
Rapin 273, 274
Reading 143, 161, 162, 165, 176
Reason 87, 92, 94, 179, 205, 215-219, 223, 242
Reed 273, 274
Rheaume 273, 274
Rich 279
Ridgard 198, 202, 203
Riley 40, 41, 43, 45
Rimell 63, 64,
Robb 283
Robbins 2, 271
Robinson 62, 91, 99, 105, 153, 173
Ross 273, 275
Rushton 265
Russell 188, 189

Sabin 190
Salmon; Samman 116, 117, 175
Sanders 271, 279, 280
Sargent 273, 277
Savard 289
Scarret 253
Seal 11, 12, 14-16, 26, 29, 49-51
Shadbolt 294
Sharpe 110, 157
Sheasby 69, 72, 77, 78, 92-96
Silvester 144, 147
Simms 42, 44, 45, 184, 186, 214, 215, 245
Simpson 198, 206
Sinclair 283
Sivyour 83, 84, 178, 198, 202
Skidmore 202
Smalley 267, 268
Smith 2, 21, 85-89, 128-131, 153, 159, 178, 192, 198, 201, 204, 208, 232, 233, 244, 283, 284, 291
Southam 58, 62, 67, 70, 71, 74, 75-78, 80, 92-94, 136, 140, 144, 147, 177
Spencer 187-190, 200, 206, 207, 244, 270, 294, 298
Staines 207
Stoppard 195, 232, 233, 245
Stowe 33, 35, 64,
Stredder 188, 194
Styles 286
Sullivan 284
Summerton 149, 150, 156, 177, 188, 265
Sutcliffe 222

Taschereau 266-269
Taylor 62, 76, 91, 108, 109, 168, 170, 173, 223, 273, 274
Temple 283
Templeton 283

Thorn 12, 21, 26, 29
Thorp; Thorpe 63, 193
Tilling 70, 73, 74, 177
Tompson 9, 10, 19, 21, 25, 26, 31-33, 55
Townsend 63
Troy 273, 276
Truslove 152, 153
Tucker 232, 245
Turner 272, 293
Tymbrell 2

Ursell 265

Vennes 288
Villeneuve 290, 291

Walsh 209
Walton 105, 118, 129, 130, 133, 194-196, 237, 238
Ward 76-80, 133, 179, 186
Waters 137, 139, 140, 144, 179
Wells 193
West; Roberts-West; Alston-Roberts-West 6, 13, 51-54, 64, 87, 119, 120, 176, 182-186, 194, 208, 222, 223, 239, 246, 265, 295
Westbury 198, 243, 244
Wheeler 6, 7, 21, 202
Whiteman 40-43, 45, 46, 70-72, 80, 98, 99, 136, 139, 140, 180
Whiting 59
Whitted 273, 277
Whittington 267, 268
Whitworth 279, 280, 282
Wiles 273, 275
Williams 15
Wilkes 43-45
Wilkinson 282
Williams 282
Wilson 287
Wood 221, 223, 245
Woodhouse 273, 274
Worley 273, 277
Wright 273, 275
Wyatt 234, 235, 245

Young 5, 6, 190, 192, 199

Zoeller 288